AA

Explorer
Caribbean

James Hamlyn

 Publishing

Front cover
Top: *Palm trees silhouetted against a Jamaican sunset* (Roy Victor).
Middle (left to right):
(a) *A plateful of lobster and vegetables* (Jon Wyand);
(b) *Pelican* (Peter Baker);
(c) *Cocktails* (Roy Victor);
(d) *Horatio Nelson* (S. & O. Matthews);
(e) *Fruit and vegetable stall in Montego Bay* (Jon Wyand).
Spine
Windsurfer (Peter Baker)
Back cover
Left: *Sightseers in Barbados* (Peter Baker). Right: *Girl wearing snorkel mask* (David Lyons).
Page 3: *Sunset off the coast of Jamaica*
Page 4: *Cruise liner at Ochos Rios, Jamaica*
Page 6: *Banana picking*
Page 7(b): *Local art work from Martinique*
Page 8: *Aerial view of Saint-Martin*
Page 67: *Darkwood Beach, Antigua*
Page 105: *A pelican, Saint-Martin*
Page 239: *Policeman, Jamaica*
Page 269: *Food stall, Jamaica*

Written by James Hamlyn
Updated by Lindsay Bennett

Published by AA Publishing, a trading name of Automobile Association Developments Limited, whose registered office is Fanum House, Basing View, Basingstoke, Hampshire, RG21 4EA. Registered number 1878835.

ISBN-10: 0 7495 4824 X
ISBN-13: 978-0-7495-4824-7

The contents of this publication are believed correct at the time of printing. Nevertheless, AA Publishing accept no responsibility for errors, omissions or changes in the details given, or for the consequences of readers' reliance on this information. This does not affect your statutory rights. Assessments of the attractions, hotels and restaurants are based upon the author's own experience, and contain subjective opinions that may not reflect the publisher's opinion or a reader's experience. We have tried to ensure accuracy, but things do change, so please let us know if you have any comments or corrections.

A CIP catalogue record for this book is available from the British Library

Colour separation by M.R.M. Graphics Ltd. Bucks, UK
Printed and bound in Italy by Printer Trento srl

Find out more about AA Publishing and the wide range of travel publications and services the AA provides by visiting our website at www.theAA.com.

First published 1994.
Revised second edition 1998. Reprinted 1998.
Reprinted with a new cover 1999.
Revised fourth edition 2000.
Revised fifth edition 2002.
Reprinted 2004. Information verified and updated.
Reprinted 2006. Information verified and updated.

Titles in the Explorer Series:
Australia • Boston & New England • Britain • Brittany •California • • Canada • Caribbean • China • Costa Rica • Crete Cuba • Cyprus • • Egypt • Florence & Tuscany • Florida • France Germany • • Greek Islands • Hawaii • India • Ireland • Italy • Japan • London • • Mallorca • Mexico • New York • New Zealand Paris • Portugal • • Provence • Rome • San Francisco • Scotland South Africa • Spain • • Tenerife • Thailand • Tunisia • Turkey Turkish Coast • Venice • • Vietnam

A02698

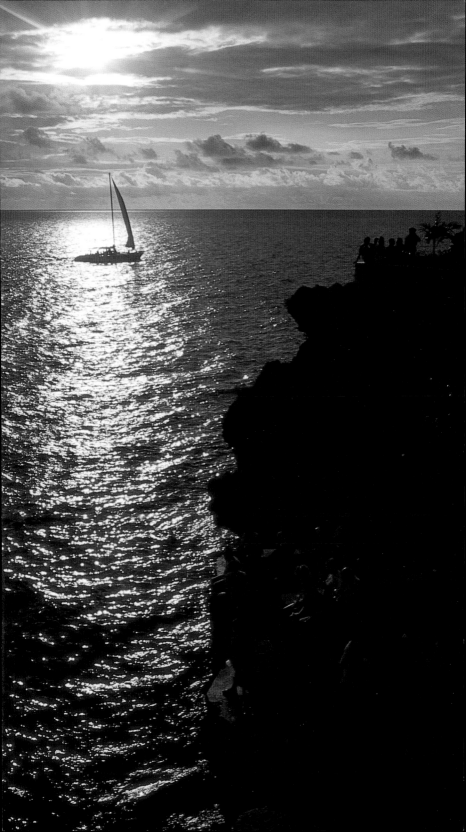

How to use this book

ORGANIZATION

The Caribbean Is,
The Caribbean Was
Discusses aspects of life and culture
in the contemporary Caribbean
and explores significant periods in
its history.

A–Z
Breaks down the islands into regional
chapters, and covers places to visit,
including walks and drives. Within
this section fall the Focus On articles,
which consider a variety of subjects in
greater detail.

Travel Facts
Contains the strictly practical
information vital for a successful trip.

Accommodations and
Restaurants
Lists recommended establishments
throughout the Caribbean, giving a
brief summary of their attractions.

KEY TO ADMISSION CHARGES
Standard admission charges are
categorized in this book as following:

Inexpensive:	under US$5
Moderate:	US$5–US$10
Expensive:	over US$10

ABOUT THE RATINGS
Most places described in this book
have been given a separate rating.
These are as follows:

▶▶▶   **Do not miss**

▶▶   **Highly recommended**

▶   **Worth seeing**

MAPS
Some of the maps in this book use
internationally agreed symbols to
denote nation states:

BS	Bahamas
CO	Colombia
CR	Costa Rica
CU	Cuba
DOM	Dominican Republic
GUY	Guyana
HN	Honduras
NIC	Nicaragua
RH	Haiti
TC	Turks & Caicos Islands
USA	United States of America
YV	Venezuela

Contents

James Hamlyn's childhood was spent on the move around the world—a habit that has stuck, particularly since he discovered the Caribbean islands more than a decade ago. His time now is spent island-hopping, checking out the bars and restaurants, and perfecting his skills with Caribbean dances such as the merengue. He has written several guidebooks to the Caribbean as well as many articles for American and British newspapers and magazines.

My Caribbean

Carnival. A sea of satin costumes shimmers and sparkles in the tropical sun; masqueraders strut and thrust, swaying at the hip, midriffs clamped in a conga line like a massive sequinned snake. The noise is deafening—close at hand the raucous clanging of steel bands, elsewhere the thunder of amplified soca drumbeats. Carnival typifies the exuberance of the Caribbean—the color, the high spirits and the irresistible dancing rhythms. To be part of it is an amazing experience.

After the week's nonstop dancing at Carnival, you will actually need a vacation, but then that's the Caribbean's specialty. Somewhere quiet, perhaps, on a deserted beach, a place to rest and let the ringing in your ears subside with a cocktail and an uninterrupted view over the sea to the sunset. An easygoing life among the charming West Indian people, in a setting of startling tropical beauty and gentle reggae music—this is the other side to the islands.

The Caribbean islands are ideal for a little laziness, but after a while I begin to get the itch for activity. An ideal day would be spent scuba diving or windsurfing in the morning, enjoying lunch in the elegance of an old plantation house, with the afternoon spent walking in the rain forest or exploring a colonial city. As ever, though, the day ends with dancing in the warm tropical night, to rhythms of salsa, merengue and zouk.

Every Caribbean traveler has their favorite island, a charmed isle where they feel they belong. You may fall in love with it the moment your feet touch the sand on coming ashore, or it may grow on you gradually, within the heady mix of tropical smells, music and rum, but you'll know it when you find it.

My favorite island? Well, it's a tough choice and I love them all. There are about 50 islands, ranging from tiny coral outcrops to large and lively industrialized nations, and they each have their own distinct charm and appeal. Read on and you'll find out more...
James Hamlyn

The Caribbean Is

Swimmers off the south coast of Barbados

With its endless beaches, swaying palm trees and a warm turquoise sea, the Caribbean does live up to its idyllic image. But the landscapes extend far beyond the travel agent's clichés— from sheer volcanic mountains and lush rain forests to inhospitable deserts; and Caribbean life has been changed beyond recognition within a relatively short space of time.

10

St. Vincent (top). Shaw Park Gardens, Ocho Rios, Jamaica (above)

THE ARCHIPELAGO Stretching in an arc from the bottom of Florida to the top of South America, the Caribbean archipelago is as varied as it is beautiful. Islands range in size from Cuba (4,124sq miles/10,681sq km) to tiny Saba (3sq miles/7sq km); mountains soar to over 2 miles (3km) in the Dominican Republic and flat sand-spits barely reach sea level. There are extensive rain forests in Puerto Rico and Dominica and barren cactus-filled wildernesses in Haiti and Aruba. The landscape may change around each corner, as mangrove swamp gives way to pasture land and pine forests replace palm trees. Intensive agriculture and tourist development are gradually altering the Caribbean's contours and climate. Blessed with warm weather all the year and cooled by the Trade Winds, the region is also occasionally cursed by violent rainstorms and hurricanes.

Known for its coral reefs and its beaches (every island claims the best), the Caribbean also boasts waterfalls, hot springs and caves. Two bizarre geological attractions are Trinidad's Pitch Lake, a seemingly inexhaustible pool of hot black tar (see page 232), and Jamaica's Cockpit Country, an inhospitable area of limestone hills and hollows, still populated by descendants of runaway slaves (see page 149).

CHANGING NATURE Humans have left an indelible impression on the Caribbean landscape. Many of the islands that were once covered in virgin rain forest are now scarred by deforestation and erosion. In Haiti, part of the island described by Columbus as the most beautiful he had ever seen, tree-felling and over-farming have created virtual deserts in some areas, where drought and famine are constant threats.

Strangely, little of the flora and fauna that make up the typical Caribbean landscape is indigenous to the region. Sugar cane, which still flourishes on many islands, was introduced from the Mediterranean by Spanish colonists. Other crops (bananas, citrus fruits, coffee beans) and animals (cattle, dogs, horses) came from Asia and Europe.

DIFFERENT WORLDS The past has shaped the look of the Caribbean through a variety of influences. Cities, towns and villages bear the unmistakable imprint of former colonial powers. Spanish-built Havana, with its colonnades and plazas, seems a different world from British-built Bridgetown, with its handsome yet pompous Victorian architecture and "tropical Anglican" cathedral.

Differing histories have also molded the countryside itself. In the formerly Spanish colonies of Cuba, Puerto Rico and the Dominican Republic, sugar plantations stretch to the horizon as they have for 500 years. In Haiti, however, where a slave revolution expelled the French at the beginning of the 19th century, precarious smallholdings have replaced the hated plantations.

Despite the proximity of the USA, European influence is still keenly felt. In the French *départements d'outre-mer* of Martinique and Guadeloupe you can buy baguettes, drink *pastis* and see policemen in *képis*. There is no mistaking the Dutch style of Curaçao or Aruba, where gabled pastel warehouses lining the canal and port conjure up a tropical Amsterdam. And Britain has left the paraphernalia of colonial rule in its former possessions: red postboxes, English place names and cricket fields.

> ❏ The Caribbean is one of the last bastions of colonialism. Martinique, Guadeloupe, St. Barts and St. Martin are technically French *régions*; the six islands of the Netherlands Antilles remain allied to Holland; Britain maintains Montserrat, Anguilla, the Cayman Islands and the BVI as crown colonies or dependent territories. Puerto Rico is a "free and associated state" of the USA, but may one day become the 51st state. ❏

11

A dramatic Caribbean sunset over the shores of Tobago

"Out of many one people" is Jamaica's national motto and it applies just as well to the rest of the Caribbean. The region's population is a rich mixture of African, European, American, Asian and East Indian influences, its legacy a fusion of slavery, colonialism and migration. This has created a unique culture, developed from centuries of interaction.

STRANGERS IN PARADISE

The original indigenous population of the Caribbean all but disappeared within half a century of European conquest. Since then, people have come, willingly or not, from every corner of the earth. This process included one of history's biggest forced migrations—the importation of some five million African people into the Caribbean's plantation economy.

ARAWAKS AND CARIBS

Little remains of the people who predated the Caribbean's "discovery" 500 years ago. However, some of their words have entered the vocabulary—barbecue and hammock, for instance—but none of the placid Arawak people survived the cultural devastation of the conquest. Today,

Children in Montego Bay, Jamaica (top)
A flower-seller in Jamaica balances her load with care (right)

only a handful of Carib descendants are still found in areas of Dominica and St. Vincent, scraping a living by selling their handicrafts.

EUROPEANS

Europe conquered, colonized and re-created the Caribbean in its own image. The first Europeans to settle in the Caribbean named cities, villages and rivers after more familiar places at home. But with few exceptions, the physical legacy of European colonization has all but disappeared save in Spanish-speaking areas of Cuba, the Dominican Republic and Puerto Rico, which received influxes of European immigration well into the 20th century. Europeans make up a tiny minority in most Caribbean societies though they tend to be well-connected and play a somewhat paternalistic role outside government circles.

12

The exceptions to the rule are the "poor whites" of Barbados, a community descended from indentured British laborers that has so far refused to intermix at all with any of the other Bajan communities.

AFRICANS The great majority of Caribbean people are at least in part descended from the millions of Africans who crossed the notorious "middle passage." Africa is alive in all dimensions of local life: music, language, religion and cooking. "Jamaica Talk," for instance, the island's patois, is largely based on West African Ashanti dialect, while African speech and customs are commonplace in Haiti and around the eastern tip of Cuba.

INDIANS Around 40 percent of the population of Trinidad is East Indian in origin. The stores and restaurants of Port of Spain, the capital, are filled with the sounds, sights and scents of the Indian subcontinent—from sari shops to street traders. Meanwhile Hindu prayer flags surround many countryside homes. In Guyana, slightly more than half the popu-indentured laborers of the 19th century.

INEQUALITIES This rich diversity of race and color conceals massive inequalities, within and between individual countries. Some Caribbean nations, most notably Haiti and the Dominican Republic, are among the world's poorest, while others, including Puerto Rico, Trinidad and the Virgin Islands, enjoy relative prosperity. Economic hardship has prompted many to leave the Caribbean's poorer countries to live and work in North America and Europe: perhaps one in seven Dominicans lives in the US. In the 1950s, nearly 10 percent of all Jamaicans emigrated to Britain. These exile communities provide Caribbean islanders with a vital financial lifeline.

LANGUAGE A region of many tongues, the language of each island is dictated by its chief colonial influence. Though English is widely spoken, visitors will find a few words of French an advantage in the French Antilles, and Spanish invaluable, even essential, outside tourist areas in the Dominican Republic.

A Trinidad palm-weaver

13

Mangoes, pineapples, papaya, breadfruit, callaloo…the list of Caribbean fruits and vegetables is seemingly unending. Drop a seed in the soil and you'll have a tree inside a week, say local farmers. But despite extraordinary fertility, Caribbean agriculture faces critical problems: what to do with crops that nobody wants and what to put in their place.

14

MARKETS The market is the traditional center of Caribbean social and economic life. By bus or on foot, the market women arrive before dawn to set up their displays of fresh fruit and vegetables. Whether in the town square or simply at a rural crossroads, the market and its mostly female workforce display the vibrancy of the region's tropical agriculture. Vast piles of mysterious tubers (widely known as "ground provisions") sit side by side with bunches of green bananas and plantains, the Caribbean's starchy staples. Red-hot peppers, tangy limes and enormous avocados are some of the other offerings. Beyond the market, most people seem to have a small piece of land, if only enough to grow a few fruit trees. While there is widespread poverty in the Caribbean, few actually go hungry.

The Caribbean is still a largely agricultural region, but important changes are taking place in what crops are grown and where they go. From the earliest colonial days, the region was an exporter of agricultural commodities, most importantly sugar. In its 18th-century heyday, Saint-Domingue (now Haiti) exported more raw sugar and created more wealth than the whole of the British empire. Sugar, the fabled "white gold," made fortunes, caused wars and brought millions of Africans across the Atlantic in slave ships.

❏ In 1975 a pound of sugar fetched 76 cents on the world market; by 2005 it was worth only 12 cents. ❏

The advent of European sugar beet, global overproduction and changing diets have long since undermined the Caribbean sugar industry. Only Cuba is still heavily dependent on sugar exports, while other islands have moved into other agro-industries. The next boom crop to feel the pinch was bananas, especially in Dominica and St. Lucia, where it represented up to 70 percent of export earnings. Bananas grow everywhere in these small volcanic islands: up steep slopes, around houses, by the roadside. They are mostly cultivated on smallholdings by individual farmers, who pack them into boxes and drive them down to the port. After a long period of special access into the British market, Caribbean bananas are now under fire from the big plantation-based producers of Latin America, who grow cheaper, if not better, fruit.

FRAGILE FRUIT Worries about the future of the banana industry reveal the vulnerability of Caribbean agriculture. Worse even than hurricanes are unstable world commodity markets, over which small producers have no control. Every crop—sugar, coffee, cocoa, tobacco—has seen its ups and downs and an uncertain future awaits the new "exotic nontraditionals," which farmers are now trying to export to Europe and the USA. The current generation of export crops includes ginger, mangoes, passionfruit and cut flowers, much of it destined for supermarkets and gourmet food shops in US cities. However, visitors will find no shortage of local delicacies such as soursops and tamarinds.

FISHING Lobster, red snapper and flying fish are found on menus throughout the region. But despite extensive coastlines, most islands have to import fish. The lack of a fishing industry, in part a legacy of slavery and colonialism, has also resulted from inadequate marine nutrients, storage and marketing, as well as a risk of ciguaterra (a neuro-toxin found in tropical reef fish). Consequently, the islands depend on salted and canned fish from Canada and fresh fish flown in from the USA. Attempts to upgrade the fishing industry have been made, but experts warn that the Caribbean Sea cannot withstand intensive fishing.

15

Fish for sale on Aruba

High in the hills of Haiti, animal sacrifices, rhythmic drumbeats and entranced dancers swirling around a crackling bonfire are all part of the island's most famous and mysterious religion: voodoo. It is just one of many faiths in a region that claims more churches per capita than anywhere else in the world.

16

A Baptist worshipper on Tobago. The Caribbean islands accommodate a vast range of religious denominations, imported from all corners of the globe

RELIGION From continuous radio and TV broadcasts to tiny ramshackle churches on every street corner, religion is part and parcel of the Caribbean. There are mosques in Trinidad, Hindu temples in Guyana, and pilgrimage sites in the Dominican Republic. With large communities of Jews, Muslims and Hindus, the region is influenced by most major faiths.

CHRISTIANS Most Caribbean people would describe themselves as Christians. European colonizers brought differing Christian beliefs, a fact reflected in the islands' many churches. Catholicism, officially the main faith of Haiti and the Dominican Republic, is widely practiced in the eastern Caribbean and is now tolerated in Cuba. Anglicanism holds sway in the former British colonies of Jamaica and Barbados. The influence of US Protestant groups is increasingly powerful throughout the Caribbean and these have joined the myriad existing churches. In Barbados, for example, it is estimated that no fewer than 140 different denominations are active, one for every 2,000 Bajans.

AFRICAN RELIGIONS Christianity was the religion of the masters; the slaves had their own faiths, brought with them from Africa. Religious beliefs and practices survived the horrors of slavery, preserving the slaves' identity and memories of their homelands. Over time, these beliefs merged with Christian religion to create new forms of faith and ceremony. These have different names on different islands (*santería* in Cuba, *pocomania* in Jamaica), but the

best known is voodoo in Haiti, where religious activity is evident in all walks of life. Each tiny village has its quota of churches and every church has its faithful congregation. But there are no open signs of Haiti's other religious phenomenon. As an old joke has it, Haitians are 99 percent Christian and 100 percent voodooist. Even so, voodoo remains largely invisible to foreigners, although visitors have ample opportunity to see suitably arranged versions of the authentic ceremonies (see pages 180–181).

RASTAFARIANISM Popularized in the 1970s and 1980s by reggae stars, Rastafarianism has its roots in Jamaica and its followers on many other islands. Rastafarianism expresses many people's longing for an African identity by invoking Ethiopia as the holy land and the late Emperor Haile Selassie as a god and promotes the smoking of marijuana (ganja) as a sacrament (see page 161).

RADICALS IN RELIGION Many priests in the Caribbean have long since left the pulpit to become involved in social and political issues. The churches have traditionally been active in health and education and since "liberation theology" spread from Latin America during the 1970s, they have become increasingly politically outspoken. In Haiti, a radical Roman Catholic priest, Jean-Bertrand Aristide, was elected president in 1991, only to be overthrown by the army nine months later. He was restored to power in 1994 by means of US-led intervention, but was ousted amid mass unrest and violence in 2005.

17

Caribbean politics are anything but dull. Most people love a political argument and insults can often fly thick and fast. Elections are usually a pretext for a party, while parliamentary procedure is guaranteed to be good entertainment. The Caribbean has had—and still has—its share of unrest, but most islands enjoy healthy democracies and lively debate.

POLITICAL SYSTEMS The region's differing regimes are an integral part of its mixed cultural heritage. The British bequeathed the "Westminster model" of parliamentary democracy and all English-speaking islands hold regular elections. The British Queen is still nominally head of state in most Commonwealth countries, represented in each by a Governor General. The Spanish islands, meanwhile, have tended to adopt a presidential system, with a greater tradition of "strong man" leadership.

PARTY GAMES Most independent Caribbean territories have a multi-party electoral system of government. Elections are fiercely contested events and can spill over into violence. On small islands, personalities are often as important as policies, especially when most electors know the candidates personally. Problems have been greatest in Jamaica, where "political tribalism" caused around 800 deaths in the 1980 election campaign. But political violence is not common and most states are proud of their constitutional credentials.

HOT SPOTS Of all the Caribbean territories, only two are generally agreed to have undemocratic governments. Cuba has been dominated by Fidel Castro and the Communist Party since the 1959 revolution and has ever since alienated the USA by refusing to hold free elections. Cuba has become increasingly isolated. Economically strangled by the US embargo, the island suffers intermittent shortages of basic goods, but is now a popular tourist destination for Europeans, Canadians and Latin

Americans, who bring hard currency into the economy.

Haiti has had the most turbulent political history of all the Caribbean nations. Wracked by instability and dictatorship since a slave revolution won independence from France in 1804, the country was ruled by the ruthless Duvaliers until 1986. When "Baby Doc," son of the infamous "Papa Doc," was finally forced to flee the country, a movement for democracy evolved, culminating in the overwhelming election triumph of Jean-Bertrand Aristide, in 1991 (see page 17). Aristide resigned in Febraury 2004 amid mass protest and terrible violence. Dates for new elections were set several times during 2005 but finally held in January 2006 and won by one of Aristide's close allies, Rene Preval. It remains to be seen whether a new government can keep the country stable and improve the economy. A UN security force is in place in the meantime.

BACKYARD POLITICS The US invasion of Grenada in 1983 was an indication of how seriously the White House viewed the rise of radicalism in its "backyard," but with the end of the Cold War, the Caribbean has lost much of its geo-political importance in the eyes of US policy-makers. Since then, support for left-wing movements has dwindled and conservatives hold power on most English-speaking islands.

TRADING PLACES Current political controversy influences the region's position in the world economy. With the coming of the North American Free Trade Agreement between the

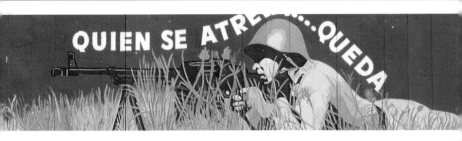

USA, Canada and Mexico, the islanders' fear of marginalization in trade and influence has led to more talk of integration and cooperation in the hope that a united front will help them weather economic storms.

Government House, St. Thomas

They come in the millions every year. Migrating south to the tropics in search of the sun, tourists are the lifeblood of the Caribbean, bringing vital dollars and jobs to the region. Although the locals may laugh at the poolside limbo lessons, they know that, for better or worse, tourism represents their economic survival.

PACKAGE HOLIDAYS With the advent of charter flights and affordable hotels, Caribbean tourism is no longer the preserve of the wealthy. In the 1950s only the rich could afford to go to the Caribbean, normally island-hopping by yacht. Now a few hundred dollars or pounds will buy an all-inclusive package deal to Antigua, Barbados or Jamaica. All the islands are chasing the tourist jackpot; the fastest-growing vacation destination of the Caribbean is Cuba.

20

A modern-day "pirate ship" caters for tourists

Tourism injects billions of dollars into the Caribbean economies and, in many cases, tourist earnings far outweigh exports even in larger and more prosperous islands such as Jamaica and Barbados. Overall, economists believe that it has created hundreds of thousands of direct jobs throughout the region. Add to this the thousands of people who sell agricultural produce to hotels, who make handcrafted goods and who act as "guides," and the figure may be nearer millions.

CRUISING Several times a week, the sleepy port of St. George's, Grenada, springs into frenetic action as the cruise ship arrives. As the tourists gingerly step onto *terra firma*, they are greeted by a horde of taxi-drivers, guides, vendors and scalpers. Few of the hopeful locals will make a fortune. On average, each tourist spends a paltry $45 before returning to the safety of the cruise ship. A cruise tour may cost thousands, but little of that money reaches the islands themselves.

SPENDING Understandably, governments and businesses prefer tourists who stay in hotels, vacation apartments and guesthouses on the islands, and spend time and money in their destinations. The multitude of restaurants, stores and souvenir stands that line the tourist resorts are proof of this single-minded pursuit of foreign currency. But foreign ownership of airlines and hotels often means that bills are paid outside the Caribbean, reducing the hoped-for "trickle-down" effect.

More worrying still is the growing popularity of all-inclusive club vacations, where one price covers every drink or surfboard lesson. This, as the local restaurateurs and taxi drivers will tell you, is not a major incentive for going out and spreading the wealth.

The Golden Lemon Hotel on St. Kitts, in the Leeward Islands

BLESSING OR CURSE? Tourism has brought welcome employment and investment to otherwise stagnant economies. For many young locals, work as a waiter or cleaner is a much better prospect than traditional farming. But tourism's impact is not all positive. Many older people complain that hustling, drugs and petty crime have become a way of life for the young. Others feel that jealousy and resentment are inevitable consequences of the divide between developed and developing countries. More seriously, tourism is a shaky bet for sustainable development, as it is notoriously vulnerable to economic instability in the sender countries. Recession in North America and Europe can send Caribbean tourism revenues plummeting.

BEYOND THE BEACH Ecotourism is the new buzzword in the local industry. Realizing that people can become bored with sand and sea, operators are now offering vacations which appeal to the adventurous and environmentally aware. You can dive among coral reefs in Bonaire, explore rain forests in Dominica, or hike through mountains in Jamaica. Advocates of ecotourism praise it as an intelligent use of natural resources; critics point out that in some instances it can harm the very nature that it sets out to market.

Caribbean food can be as bland or as exciting as you choose it to be. McDonald's, Kentucky Fried Chicken and all the other familiar names are in evidence. But step outside the tourist circuit and there is food to daunt the most adventurous gastronome. Some iguana, perhaps? Or stewed goat? And don't forget the rum—the world's best.

REGIONAL FOOD Real Caribbean food reflects the many diverse influences, historical and cultural, which have shaped the region. The hearty breakfast lives on in Jamaica, but you may be offered mackerel and banana along with your bacon and eggs. In Trinidad, the spicy *roti*, a generous chapati pancake often filled with curry, is an unmistakable taste of India. Meanwhile, the French territories of Martinique and Guadeloupe claim the Caribbean's most sophisticated cuisine. A classic dish is red snapper in white wine, garlic and limes. The hamburger may have made serious inroads into regional tastes, but the imprints of Europe, Africa and India are still very much in evidence. Supermarkets are inevitably stocked with American brands, but don't be surprised to see Camembert in Martinique, Gouda in Curaçao, or Yorkshire pudding mix in Barbados.

VARIETY Most of the Caribbean islands share a few basic dishes. Rice 'n' peas (or red beans) is a staple everywhere and especially good when cooked in coconut water. Root vegetables are a cheap filler, boiled or fried, and go by scores of different names across the region. Bananas and plantains are ubiquitous, as are fruits, such as guava, pineapple and mango. But on top of these staples, each island has developed its own, often idiosyncratic, recipes.

In Jamaica the national favorites are curry goat (often beef), and saltfish and ackees. The latter dish harks back to the era of slavery when salted fish was imported from Canada to feed the island's slave population. The small island of Dominica specializes in "mountain chicken," which is actually a local frog. In the Dominican Republic, *mondongo*, a tripe stew, is considered a miracle cure for a hangover.

RUM There is, of course, ample opportunity to acquire a hangover. Every island produces rum, ranging from mass-market brands to local firewater. Some of the so-called overproof rum (140 proof) is a serious risk to health, especially when mixed in apparently innocuous cocktails. Perhaps the best way to sample the better rums is with ice and lime juice, the basis of the classic Planter's Punch cocktail. Although each island predictably claims to make the best, the better-quality rums are generally those from Cuba, Haiti, Jamaica, Martinique (especially *rhums vieux*) and Barbados.

Colorful Caribbean cocktails can be strong when mixed with overproof rum

22

BEER The Caribbean is not a wine-producing area, but every island, however small, has its own brewery. Some international brands such as Budweiser and Guinness are widely available, but locals swear—often correctly—that their beer is better. Perhaps the best known is Jamaica's Red Stripe, but other superior brews are Barbados' Banks, Trinidad's Carib and St. Vincent's Hairoun. Less known and arguably the best is Presidente from the Dominican Republic, which often comes served in iced glasses.

HUNGER For the tourist, hunger is less of a risk than a gradually expanding waistline. Nor are many people in the main tourist islands likely to go hungry. Hardship is largely restricted to Cuba, where rationing and embargo have drastically reduced dietary intakes for the locals, and Haiti, the hemisphere's poorest nation. Also worrying is the growing dependency of Caribbean countries on importing basic foods in order to feed their own populations. While most countries are now desperate to export their "exotic nontraditionals," they are forced to import basic ingredients such as rice, beans and sugar for local consumption. This means that the Caribbean is increasingly consuming what it does not produce and producing what it does not consume.

One of the Caribbean's distinctive fruits: ackees

Recommended specialties

Antigua Goat water (hot goat stew) and fungi (similar to polenta).

Barbados Flying fish, dolphin (dorado or mahi mahi, not the mammal), pickled breadfruit and blood sausage.

Cuba *Moros y cristianos*—the local name for rice 'n' peas.

Curaçao *Rijsttafel* ("rice table," with up to 40 different meat and vegetable dishes, originally from Indonesia).

Dominica "Mountain chicken" (a large local frog) and agouti (a small rodent, usually stewed or smoked).

Dominican Republic *Mondongo*, *sancocho* (a stew made of six different meats and vegetables), *casabe* (cassava bread).

Grenada *Souse* (pig's feet stew), armadillo, iguana. Also famous for its spices: nutmeg and mace.

Haiti *Griot* (deep-fried pork) and most French-influenced sauces.

Jamaica Saltfish and ackees, curry goat and jerk pork, barbecued and sold from roadside stalls. Also known for producing Blue Mountain coffee.

Martinique and Guadaloupe *Ti-boudin* (spicy sausage), *poulet au coco* (chicken with coconut).

Puerto Rico *Pastillas* (pork, chickpeas and raisins stuffed in dough, wrapped in plantain leaves and steamed), the paella-like *asopao*. (Puerto Rico also has fast food and drive-in services.)

Trinidad *Roti*, *pelau* (rice and curry).

Cooling drinks are a treat and often a necessity in the Caribbean heat

The Caribbean Was

Long before Columbus "discovered" the Caribbean islands, Native Americans had started clearing the ground to build villages and plant their crops. Tribes of Arawaks and Caribs had been living on the Caribbean shores of South America since about 5000BC, but by 1000BC the Arawaks were fleeing their aggressive neighbors and driving out Jamaica's earliest settlers, the Ciboneys.

FIRST SETTLERS Three groups of Arawak settlers established villages on the islands: the Tainos, on Jamaica, Cuba and Hispaniola; the Lucayans, in the Bahamas; and the Borequinos, on Puerto Rico. For a few hundred years they led a peaceful life, left alone by Carib warriors. But the Caribs finally caught up and by the late 15th century, when Columbus arrived, their canoe raids and violent attacks were a constant threat.

NATIVE AMERICAN LIFE While the Arawaks practiced skills such as basket-weaving and traded their crops—cassava, maize, sweet potatoes, cotton and pepper—from island to island, the Caribs sent raiding parties to loot villages for slaves and supplies. Their expertise in making and using weapons was formidable; Caribs were fast and accurate bowmen, shooting fire- or poison-tipped arrows, and they used a variety of clubs and spears with gruesome added extras. Nevertheless, they did develop some talents other than maiming and killing. Caribs were fine potters; each settlement had its own "trademark," often in the form of an animal, which was carved on its pots and, as an essentially belligerent, nomadic tribe, the Caribs excelled at canoe building.

Arawak communities were based on the family, with a *cacique* (clan chief) ruling each group of villages, helped by a committee of elders or *nitayanos*. They were also religious leaders, in touch with the ancestral and natural spirits and sometimes acting as their mouthpiece, inhaling tobacco fumes to induce a trance and

Native Americans gathering seeds

conveying advice or predictions from the spirit world. *Zemis*, wood, stone or bone figures representing the gods of nature, were housed in special huts, set apart from the ordinary round, thatched homes of the villagers. Religious worship involved dancing, games and tobacco-smoking; the powdered leaf was lit inside a forked tube (*tabaco*), which was wedged up the nostrils. Caves were used as burial sites by some clans (bones, canoe paddles and *zemis* have been excavated); carvings of symbols and mask-like faces can still be seen covering cave walls and rocks on several Caribbean islands.

Fighters and killers were the most respected members of Carib society. Chief warriors were elected on the basis of their performance in battle and religious activities revolved

□ Gold was a commodity traded by Arawaks, but it was prized only as an ornament. Carib warriors decorated their bodies with paint, petals, coral bracelets and anklets, and shells or bones were worn in pierced ears, lips and noses. Arawaks used dyed clay and grease to cover their bodies and bound their babies' heads to give them long, tough skulls. □

around appeasing a vengeful god. When European settlers arrived in the Caribbean they painted a grim picture of the Caribs as vicious cannibals who were liable to make a meal out of anyone straying onto their territory. In fact, any cannibalism that did take place is likely to have been

ceremonial; fat from the body of a brave enemy would be rubbed over Carib boys to give them courage. Even so, Carib society was undeniably brutal and prisoners were starved and tortured, as a test of their endurance, before eventually being killed and served up.

Both tribes relied to a great extent on the Caribbean's abundant marine life for much of their food, but any edible creature was regarded as fair game. Lizards, snails and turtle eggs were all snapped up; birds were caught in nets strung between branches, and fish were hooked, speared or even stunned by poison bark thrown into the water. Each day's catch would be added to a pepperpot, a seasoned stew left to simmer for weeks. Pepperpots (now with different ingredients) can still be sampled on Grenada (see page 52).

27

Symbols from a vanished world: Arawak rock carvings in Puerto Rico

After five weeks of sailing the uncharted Atlantic, Christopher Columbus and his crew were within hours of giving up their voyage when land was sighted on the 12th of October 1492. The sailors, who believed they had found Japan, were actually heading for the Bahamas and about to begin an unprecedented era of wealth, war and oppression.

THE GREAT EXPLORER Columbus was born in Genoa in the late 1440s, becaming an avid sea-voyager and a collector of maps and charts. By the 1480s, convinced that Japan and the riches of the East Indies could be reached by sailing west, he set about searching for the finances to back an expedition. Portugal and Britain turned him down—they had their own ideas for finding new trade routes. The Spanish monarchs, Ferdinand and Isabella, made Columbus wait five years while they drove the Moors from the country; then they agreed to his plan, eager to spread the influence of Spain and of the Catholic church and to break the long-established Arab monopoly of trading routes to the Indies.

Columbus set out with his fleet of three ships—the *Niña*, the *Pinta*, and his flagship, the *Santa Maria*—on the 3rd of August 1492. By the time land was sighted he was having trouble preventing mutiny; the worried crew was threatening to throw Columbus overboard and head back home. After naming his first "discovery" San Salvador, the explorer persuaded some of its Arawak inhabitants— who welcomed the newcomers as protection against the Caribs—to come aboard and direct him toward Hispaniola. Here, the *Santa Maria* ran aground, leaving 40 Spaniards to build the first European fort in the Caribbean. Columbus was disappointed at the scarcity of gold and spices on the islands, but returned to

28

Columbus is greeted by Arawak islanders on San Salvador

Spain with a few "Indians," plants and tobacco leaves as promise of wonders yet to emerge.

Explorer and treasure-seeker: a 16th-century Spanish portrayal of Christopher Columbus

THE NEW COLONIES

A second voyage followed in 1493, with a much larger fleet bringing builders and farmers to create new settlements and priests to convert the natives. Many of the settlers were convicted criminals, pardoned on condition that they join the fleet. Before long the colonists—who had no prospect of returning home—started to abuse the Arawaks, demanding food and taxes of gold and cotton, stealing the women and forcing the men into slavery. War broke out and within three years, most of the 200,000 Native Americans were dead, overwhelmed by Spanish guns and swords or by the smallpox that the settlers had brought with them. The Europeans established a capital in Santo Domingo and a row of forts to protect their new colony.

Columbus himself returned to Spain after charting a course to Jamaica and Cuba; five years later he was back again, determined to find the mainland—which he did, after visiting Trinidad and quelling a rebellion among the Hispaniola colonists. The ambitious admiral was intensely disliked, however, and a commissioner sent by Queen Isabella to investigate complaints promptly had him arrested and shipped back to Spain. A fourth voyage also ended in disaster; after sailing along the Central American coast, Columbus's ships were wrecked off the shores of Jamaica and the explorer and his stranded sailors had to wait for a year before a ship could be sent to rescue them.

Columbus died in 1506, having failed to supply the unlimited riches that had been promised. But a new world was now opened to Spain, with gold reserves to be mined, crops to be farmed, and souls to be saved—at the expense of many hundreds of thousands of lives.

❏ Columbus was eager to exploit the Native Americans as free labor, and many were set to work mining for gold. The Spanish monarchy, however, disapproved of enslaving potential converts to Christianity and would only sanction slavery for criminals or captured warriors. European accounts of Native American atrocities and cannibalism were often invented to justify the taking of slaves. ❏

29

Anxious to reap the benefits of Columbus's voyages, Ferdinand and Isabella persuaded Pope Alexander VI to give them legal possession of the Americas. Under the Treaty of Tordesillas (1494), a boundary was drawn up dividing the "New World" between Spain and Portugal and excluding the rest of Europe from claims to these territories.

LAYING DOWN THE LAW The Caribbean was to be a stepping stone for further exploration and Spain was to have a strict monopoly over trade with the new colonies; but naturally developments did not go according to plan. In the years after Columbus's

Pirates attack a Spanish ship

last voyage, thousands of settlers arrived from Spain, eager to find gold, to own land and to be given power over a workforce of native Americans under the royal grants known as *encomiendas*. Their vicious treatment of the Arawaks was bitterly condemned by Antonio de Montesinos, a Dominican friar, and by an ex-*encomendero*, Bartolomé de las Casas. Eventually their outspoken attacks led to two sets of laws, passed by two successive kings. In 1512 Ferdinand assented to the Laws of Burgos, dictating limited working hours and the provision of food rations for Arawak laborers; and in 1542 Charles V put an end to new grants of *encomiendas* under the New Laws. But Spain had little control over the actions of its Caribbean colonists, and by the 1520s so many Native Americans had been killed off, especially by "European" diseases to which they had no immunity, that the settlers were already beginning to ship in African slaves to take their place.

CONQUISTADORES In the meantime, the search continued for richer lands and groups of armed *conquistadores* set out to stake new claims. Juan Ponce de Léon led a party of men to conquer Puerto Rico, massacring the Borequino inhabitants and clearing the land for plantations and ranches. Diego Velázquez took three years to wipe out the Native Americans on Cuba, and by 1520 the *conquistadores* had reached Mexico and the rich prizes of the Aztec Empire. When word got out that the Spanish had struck gold on the mainland, hordes of settlers made for wider, wealthier territories. At the same time, sailors from other European countries saw an opportunity for easy money. Spanish claims to exclusive rights over the spoils of their settlements were ignored, as pirates attacked their ships and ports.

PIRATES Spanish cargoes were also looted by privateers, sea captains who were authorized by their governments to plunder enemy ships in time of war—and the European powers were in an almost constant state of warfare during the 17th and 18th centuries. Spain's monopoly on trade with the colonies could not be maintained. Aside from pirate attacks, the system was unwieldy and inefficient.

A buccaneer pictured in 1905

Caribbean settlers would be kept waiting for months on end while fleets of Spanish ships loaded up with goods underwent rigorous checks at the Customs Office in Seville. Impatient with restrictions imposed by a distant state, colonists were soon doing a brisk illegal trade with ships from Britain, France and the Netherlands, and there was little that Spain could do to stop them. Unofficial trade has continued to be part of Caribbean life ever since.

31

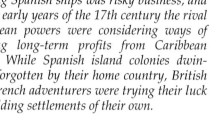

Looting Spanish ships was risky business, and by the early years of the 17th century the rival European powers were considering ways of earning long-term profits from Caribbean lands. While Spanish island colonies dwindled, forgotten by their home country, British and French adventurers were trying their luck at building settlements of their own.

TOBACCO Early experiments in tobacco-growing on the Guyana coast had been dismal failures; the small groups of British and French planters were soon defeated by fever and Carib attacks. In 1622 one of the Guyana colonists, Thomas Warner, decided to try the fresher climate and fertile soil of the Lesser Antilles and

to take up their own plots of land. In the meantime, France was turning its attention to the Caribbean, and in 1635 Cardinal Richelieu formed a company to colonize Guadeloupe, Martinique, St. Lucia and Grenada. For the following 10 years or so, settlers made the best living they could, fending off Carib or Spanish

Slaves being shipped from Africa were forced to dance to keep "fit"

set up a plantation on St. Christopher (St. Kitts). Britain, at war with Spain, was quick to see the advantages of a foothold in the "New World" and within three years the Earl of Carlisle was charged with colonizing St. Kitts, Nevis, Barbados and Montserrat. To cultivate the land, indentured laborers were shipped from Britain and bonded to work for five years, after which they were free

attacks, and sending home their harvests of tobacco and cotton.

TENSION Relations between the colonies and their mother countries were uneasy: British settlers resented the imposition of rents and taxes; the French state neglected its Caribbean territories when their profits failed to live up to expectations. Colonists relied heavily on Dutch ships for their supplies and, in turn, the Dutch took every opportunity to extend their own empire, colonizing Aruba,

Curaçao and Bonaire, which lay near Spanish mainland ports, and Saba, Sint Eustatius and Sint Maarten, conveniently placed on their trade routes with Spain's island colonies.

SUGAR AND SLAVERY In the course of war against Spain and Portugal, the Dutch had captured several sugar plantations in Brazil and their ships brought news of the vast profits to be made from the crop. They also seized Portugal's West African slavery centers and established a monopoly of slave provision for the labor-intensive plantations. African men, women and children, kidnapped from their villages during midnight raids or captured and sold by rival chiefs, were shackled to each other by their necks and marched to coastal slave markets, where dealers picked the healthiest and branded them with irons. Eager for the biggest possible profit margins, captains would fill every available space on their ships, forcing the chained captives to lie shoulder to shoulder beneath the decks for their eight-week voyage. When the ships docked, the surviving slaves were auctioned off to planters, having been oiled and rubbed to cover the effects of their terrible journey.

CONFLICT In an attempt to break the Dutch hold on the slave trade, Britain attacked Dutch strongholds, triggering one of many conflicts between the colonial empires. France, Holland, Britain and Spain were all anxious to strengthen their economies and expand their influence so colonized islands switched hands several times, being stormed by one

I would not have a Slave to till my ground
To carry me, to fan me while I sleep,
And tremble when I wake, for all the wealth
That sinews bought and sold, have ever earn'd.
We have no Slaves at home—why then abroad?

COWPER.

An 1827 condemnation of slavery

navy after another. British Lord Protector Oliver Cromwell sent a small army to Jamaica in the 1650s; in 1664 the French Minister of Finance, Jean-Baptiste Colbert, bought back Martinique, Guadeloupe and other colonies from the private companies that had taken them over 20 years earlier. By 1678 Holland was forced to use ships registered in neutral Denmark to break through trade barriers, encouraging Danish settlement on the Virgin Islands of St. John and St. Thomas. By the end of the 17th century most of the Caribbean islands were divided between the French and British empires, which proceeded to exploit the newfound wealth of their sugar industry and the thousands of slaves who produced it.

During the early years of conquest and settlement, Europeans had hoped to find unlimited supplies of gold in the West Indies. In the 18th century their dreams of immense wealth were realized as the demand for "white gold" soared and the sugar islands became the Caribbean's richest exporters, supplying more than 160,000 tons during the late 1760s.

34

Slaves working on a treadmill in Jamaica, 1830

RIGHTS OF SLAVES The rewards of this trade were restricted to a very few plantation owners—many of whom lived in Europe and left the management of their estates to agents. Even those who lived in the Caribbean tended to build their great houses at a considerable distance from the plantation fields, partly for comfort but also for security: By the 1770s slaves outnumbered whites by about ten to one on the main sugar islands and their harsh conditions had already prompted several revolts. Strict laws controlled the movements and rights of slaves: They were forbidden from gathering in large groups, from owning land, and from giving evidence in court; slaves from the same areas of Africa or with similar cultures were parted to destroy feelings of solidarity and close relationships. Nevertheless,

African culture did survive in the traditions of story-telling (see page 61), dance and music (see pages 80–81), and spirit-worship (see pages 178–179, 180–181). Many slaves risked imprisonment and whipping by running away, and over the years runaways established strong communities in more inaccessible parts of several islands.

For most slaves, however, life was a grind for 16 to 18 hours every day, digging the fields, gathering the sugar cane, feeding it into the crushing mills, or pouring boiling sugar extract into coppers. Freedom was a rare reward, granted to long-serving slaves or to the offspring of white men and slave women. Even freemen had to carry passes guaranteeing their status for seven years and were often forbidden from owning property above a certain value.

BOOM AND DECLINE For 100 years the white minority managed to suppress slave rebellions while they kept up a steady flow of raw sugar (trade laws allowed the refining industry to operate only in the home countries). Wars continued to break out at regular intervals between the European powers, each one ending in an inevitable shuffling around of territories. By 1763, when the Seven Years War between the British and French ended, Britain owned five of the 10 most profitable sugar islands (Jamaica alone produced over 30,000 tons a year) and their planters had become some of the empire's most prosperous and influential men.

The rot soon set in. Plantations were expensive to run and by the late 18th century many had been overused. At the same time the French planters, who paid lower export duties, were selling cheaper sugar to more European markets and Saint-Domingue, the French-owned part of Hispaniola, claimed to be the Caribbean's biggest sugar producer.

When the colonies in North America rebelled against "taxation without representation," sparking off the Revolutionary War, Britain forbade Caribbean planters from trading with the mainland, cutting off a valuable source of income. The Americans turned to French and Spanish sugar islands and British islands were forced to find ways to cut costs and provide their own supplies. New crops were planted, such as mangoes and breadfruit trees (brought by Captain Bligh of *Bounty* fame in 1793), and botanical gardens were opened to cultivate new species: Coffee, cotton and spices were grown to supplement the sugar crop. But, by the end of the 18th century, most of the sugar islands were in decline and the West Indies were on the verge of radical social and economic change.

A Caribbean sugar mill, 1816

Anti-slavery movements were gathering force in late 18th-century Europe. In France the issue was brought to a head with the Revolution in 1789. The National Assembly resisted the demands of abolitionists such as the Paris-based Société des Amis des Noirs, and in Saint-Domingue the free "coloreds," angered by government failure to grant them full legal rights, armed their own slaves.

SLAVES' REVOLT Thousands of whites were killed in the ensuing uprising and 300 plantations were set alight. A French army sent to restore order promised emancipation; the new Jacobin Assembly fulfilled this promise and freed slaves on Guadeloupe in 1794. British and Spanish troops, sent to support Saint-Domingue's planters, were driven out by ex-slave Toussaint l'Ouverture and his army. In 1802 Napoleon had l'Ouverture imprisoned and restored slavery on Guadeloupe; in response, 55,000 blacks took up arms and declared Saint-Domingue the independent state of Haiti.

In Britain, the "West India interest" was losing ground with the decline of sugar profits and slavery was abolished in 1834. Ex-slaves were obliged to serve four years of unpaid "apprenticeship," but many fled from the cane fields and set up their own plots of land; on Jamaica sugar production slumped by 50 percent. To make up the labor shortage planters took on immigrants as indentured laborers; by 1917 about 280,000 indentured workers from the Indian subcontinent had moved to Jamaica and Trinidad. On islands with little spare land, ex-slaves lacked the option of cultivating their own plots and Barbados, Antigua and St. Kitts continued to prosper as sugar islands for many years.

Emancipation alarmed the old plantocracy, who feared the loss of political dominance. In 1865, after an episode of violent racial conflict in Morant Bay, Jamaica's assembly asked to be replaced with direct rule, and by 1898 Britain had imposed the status of Crown Colony on almost all of its Caribbean Islands.

The French finally abolished slavery on its remaining islands in 1848. As on

Emancipation portrayed by François Auguste Biard, 1848

Edmund Burke speaks out against slavery in the British Parliament

the British islands, sugar production plummeted and the planters encouraged thousands of Indian laborers to take up indentures. France pursued a policy of integrating its colonies, allowing each island to send three representatives to the National Assembly and granting the vote to all adult men in 1871.

CUBA Prosperity was late coming to the Spanish islands of Puerto Rico and Cuba, and only when trade restrictions had been lifted in the late 18th century did Cuba's sugar industry flourish. As a result, slavery was not abolished until 1886. Resentment against Spanish rule and taxes led to

fierce civil war in the 1860s and 1870s and again in the 1890s, by which time a separatist movement had won strong US support. In 1898 US warships destroyed two Spanish fleets off Cuba, and under the Treaty of Paris in that year the island gained independence, while Puerto Rico was ceded to America. By 1917, when Denmark sold its Virgin Islands to the Americans, the USA was the Caribbean's main political and economic power, funding successful sugar, banana and coffee industries. To defend this commerce, the USA intervened in the political life of Cuba, Haiti and the Dominican Republic (western Hispaniola) during the 20th century.

The Caribbean suffered badly during the 1930s Depression. Corrupt and repressive governments exacerbated the harsh conditions on Haiti and on Cuba, where Fidel Castro's revolutionary forces took control in 1959. On the British islands economic hardship gave rise to powerful labor movements, riots and strikes. An attempt to form a federation of British Caribbean islands in the late 1950s failed, and in the 1960s Jamaica and Trinidad were the first to gain independence, followed by nearly all the other British islands.

The new millennium has been a time of re-evaluation in the Caribbean. Some islands have found new roles as luxury tourist destinations; many are struggling with severe economic problems and with political instability. This region is still coming to terms with its complex historical legacy of conflict and conquest.

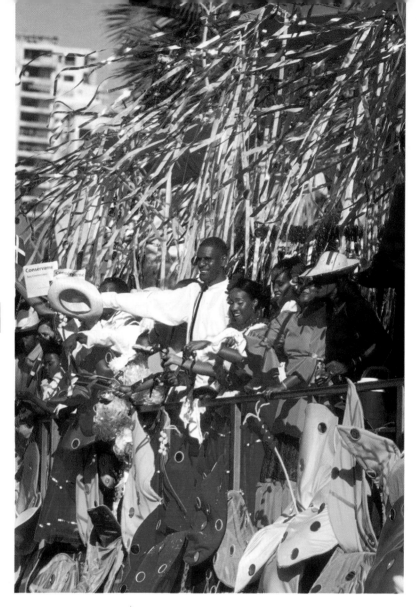

Carnival in Santa Domingo

WINDWARD TRAVEL
The quickest way to travel between the islands is on one of the island-hopping planes that run up and down the island chain at least twice a day. Alternatively you can try traveling by boat. This takes time; you may have to wait several days.

THE WINDWARD ISLANDS Crowned by sheer volcanic peaks and fringed with beautiful beaches, the islands of Grenada, St. Lucia, Dominica and St. Vincent are among the loveliest in the Caribbean region. The advent of eco-tourism has added another, adventurous dimension to the more traditional appeal of beaches, river swimming and yachting. With the necklace of the Grenadine Islands strung between Grenada and St. Vincent offering some of the Caribbean's best sailing, each of the Windwards has its enthusiasts, and each has a range of guesthouses and hotels to suit all tastes and budgets.

The four Windward Islands lie facing the Trade Winds head on, in a line of jagged, volcanic protrusions, some still active and liable to erupt about once every 100 years.

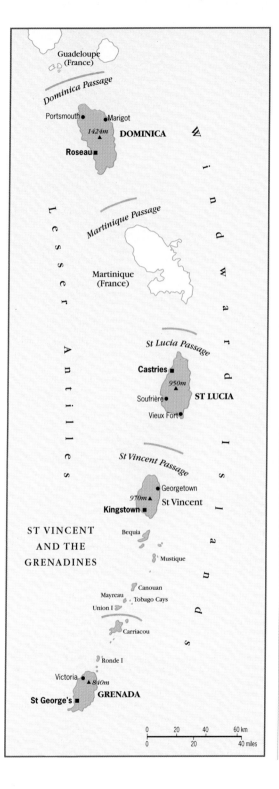

The Windward Islands

The Windward Islands

*Calabash Hotel, L'Anse
aux Epines Bay, Grenada*

Regularly spaced on the tectonic fault line between the Atlantic and Caribbean oceans, these protrusions are similar to each other in appearance and are all very small (not more than 29 miles by 16 miles/46 by 25km), but they are nonetheless physically dramatic, with clouds hanging over the mountain peaks, and thick rain forest and bamboo covering the fertile land.

The islands no longer grow sugar, but their fertility is still the source of some wealth; fruit and vegetables are shipped as far as Trinidad and Anguilla, and the banana is an important export to Europe.

HISTORY Peaceful Arawak islanders were decimated by invading Caribs in about AD1000; five centuries later the Caribs were defending themselves against European colonists. As late as 1748, Dominica was left to the Caribs in the Treaty of Aix-la-Chapelle. After passing between the European powers several times in the 18th century, the Windward Islands finally came into British hands and became a Crown Colony in 1874, administered from Grenada. The islands all gained their independence from Britain in the 1970s, although they remain within the Commonwealth and still use the British judicial system.

ISLAND LIFE At one time during the to-and-fro of colonial control, all the Windwards were owned by France and the French heritage is still strong. Names such as Beausejour Bay and Snug Corner can be seen side by side in Grenada, and French patois is spoken by the country people in Dominica, St. Lucia and Grenada. The strongest influence, however, is African; most islanders are the descendants of African slaves, freed in 1834 and able to survive by working their own plots of land.

These are relaxed yet lively islands, both as tourist destinations—with all the sun, sea, sand, dancing and rum punches that implies—and in the local life.

The Windwards have a remarkable breadth of tourism, from secluded mountain retreats to busy yachting marinas, and from fun-packed, all-inclusive hotels to the most sophisticated elegance. St. Lucia is the most developed island and is becoming increasingly crowded with tourists attracted to its good restaurants and hotels; Grenada is also developing a reputation for stylish hotels and diving. St. Vincent is still practically untouched, but the Grenadines offer easy island life and island-hopping by yacht (or mail-boat). Dominica, which joined in 1939, is not so developed, but has nature tourism and scuba diving.

JEAN RHYS
The novelist Jean Rhys was born on Dominica in 1894 and lived there until 1907, when she left to continue her education in the UK. After traveling to Paris in the 1920s, Rhys began her long writing career and set her most famous work, *Wide Sargasso Sea* (1966), in the Caribbean. This book describes the degenerate and stultifying atmosphere of colonial Caribbean life, as seen through the eyes of a Créole heiress, destined to become Rochester's mad wife in *Jane Eyre*.

Castle Bruce Bay, on the rough Atlantic coast of Dominica

Dominica

Dominica claims to have a river for every day of the year and it's probably true. A lush, green, volcanic island, it is full of spectacular scenery and pretty coastal villages. Not an obvious choice for beach-lovers, this is a must for naturalists and those who want to experience the simple, small-island rural life.

At 29 miles by 16 miles (46 by 25km), Dominica is the largest of the Windwards—but it is also the poorest and least developed. Many islanders scrape a living on the land or by fishing, and access to much of the country is difficult, despite a number of new roads. For hundreds of years this was a Carib stronghold; the descendants of those who survived French invasion in the 18th century still live here. Developed as a free port, Dominica made its money from coffee, sugar and slaves—many of whom escaped into the jungle to live as maroons, occasionally taking up arms against the authorities. British and French colonies were established here in turn; positioned between the French islands Martinique and Guadeloupe, Dominica had strategic value for France and it has retained a strong French heritage. Many of the 71,000 Dominicans are Roman Catholics and Créole-speakers.

LIME JUICE

Dominica was at one time the biggest producer of limes in the world. One of the major buyers was Rose's, the company that supplied the British Navy with fruit juice. British sailors took a daily ration of lime in order to prevent scurvy—hence their nickname "Limeys."

MORNE TROIS PITONS NATIONAL PARK

UNESCO has declared Dominica's Morne Trois Pitons National Park a World Heritage Site, thereby both celebrating and preserving its natural beauty. Guides are recommended for several of the more difficult hikes such as the Boiling Lake and the Valley of Desolation. (For information on this and the island's other magnificent parks, tel: 448 4733. *Admission: inexpensive.*)

The Catholic cathedral at Roseau, completed in 1848

Dominica's capital, **Roseau▶▶**, lies in the southwest of the island; it's a small, working town of about 20,000 people, with a mixture of modern buildings and pretty stone and wooden Victorian townhouses. In the oldest part is Dawbiney Market Square, now the site of a craft market, tourist information center and the Dominica Museum (tel: 448 8923. *Open* Mon–Fri 9–4, Sat 9–noon. *Admission: inexpensive*), which has informative descriptions of island life from colonial times to the present in pictures and exhibits, and includes volcanic geology. The new market is at the other end of the Bay Front. The Catholic cathedral, north of the old market site, was built under cover of darkness, after the government refused to support its construction. Not far from here is Fort Young, now a hotel.

The real beauty of Dominica becomes apparent on the outskirts of town. Beneath the huge white crucifix on Morne Bruce are the **Botanical Gardens▶▶**, now more like a park since the devastation from hurricanes, but still good for a walk to see the 150 species of plants and the endemic Dominica parrots (tel: 448 4733. *Open* daily. *Admission free*). The best place to see plants is directly inland in the Roseau Valley, a fantastically fertile gorge with tiny Dominican houses clinging to the slopes. At its head are the **Papillote Wilderness Retreat▶▶▶** and three waterfalls called the **Trafalgar Falls▶▶** (see panel on page 44). The Rainforest Tram Ride (tel: Miami 001 707/704-3350; www.rainforest-tram.com. *Open* daily 9–5. *Admission: expensive*) offers views of the eco-system.

Reached along another fork in the road, the village of Laudat is an entry point to the scenic **Morne Trois Pitons National Park▶▶▶** (see panel), which takes its name from a mountain peak. The park has the best view of Dominica's forests and walks to the Freshwater Lake (sadly the site of hydroelectric work) and the Boeri Lake. The adventurous might consider walking to the Valley of Desolation, an area of bubbling pools and mudponds and the Boiling Lake, a crater of steaming water that can boil an egg in three minutes.

South of the capital, the road passes a small strip of hotels in Castle Comfort, crossing lime country (see panel) to reach Soufrière, named for the nearby sulfur spring. The best sites for scuba diving are here. Near the pinnacles, caves and drop-offs, a freshwater spring fizzes at truly scalding temperatures.

Some of the last survivors of the Carib race, which gave its name to the Caribbean, live on the east coast of Dominica. Once these proud and warlike people held sway over the Eastern Caribbean, but by the late 18th century, after a war of attrition with the expansionist Europeans, the few hundred remaining had been forced to the remotest part of Dominica and were forgotten. Only in 1903 were they officially granted their own territory.

The Caribs first appeared on the Caribbean islands around AD1000. They came from South America (where there are still distantly related tribes) and island-hopped their way north along the chain, supplanting the peaceful Arawak tribe. Although they grew a few crops, the Caribs were mainly hunters and fishermen, who would stun parrots (for their feathers) by burning pepper beneath them and fire arrows with speed and accuracy.

Caribs were said to be cannibals, but this may well have been a lie circulated by Europeans to justify their acts of genocide. One early traveler tells of being presented with a pickled human arm, but there is little archeological evidence of systematic cannibalism.

On the beach at Castle Bruce you can watch canoes being made by traditional Carib methods (see panel). Just over 6 miles (10km) north of Castle Bruce lies the Carib Territory, established in 1903. There are no "pure" Caribs left and their language has died out, but their descendants still have characteristic silky blue-black hair. As well as canoe-building, they have kept their woodcarving and basket-weaving skills. Carib wares are displayed and can be purchased in little thatched huts along the road. Of interest on the reservation is the Roman Catholic church, whose altar was once a canoe. Also worth seeing is the "L'Escalier Tête Chien" (or the snake staircase), a hardened lava flow that juts down to the ocean like a giant serpant. It is named after the local "Tête Chien" boa constrictor, whose head resembles a dog.

CANOES
Caribs still build their canoes in the traditional way, hollowing them out from gommier trees. In the past, a large Carib canoe could carry over 100 people. Builders would select a suitable tree and fell it, then hollow it out with tools made from conch shells. Rocks and fire were used to widen the sides, which were then built up with planks before the canoe was finally launched. A war canoe could be paddled at the same speed as a European warship in full sail.

43

Spaniards get a hostile reception from Caribs in 1525

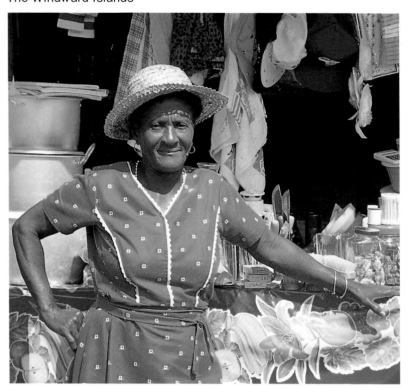

Try your hand at bargaining with the ladies of the Roseau market

WILDERNESS AND WATERFALLS

At the head of the Roseau Valley, a half-hour's journey from the capital, are the Papillote Wilderness Retreat and the Trafalgar Falls (tel: 448 2401. *Admission: inexpensive*). It is possible to climb into the waterfalls, which are harnessed for hydro power as they crash onto sulfur-dyed black and orange rocks. The Papillote Wilderness Retreat (tel: 448 2287) is a small hotel set in a 12-acre (5ha) garden fed by a small stream from a 100ft (30m) waterfall. Paths wind among begonias, bromeliads, orchids and bamboo trees, and visitors can bathe in warm springs.

The road inland from Canefield climbs into the rain forest and mountains, touching the northern limits of the National Park and giving access to **Middleham Falls**▶▶ and the **Emerald Pool**▶ and waterfall (pleasant but tame). From here the road descends to Castle Bruce on the coast and turns north to **Carib Territory** ▶▶ (see page 43).

Back on the calmer Caribbean coast, the Layou River Gorge has good spots for swimming; beyond it, the road passes beneath Morne Diablotin (the island's tallest peak) in the Northern Forest Reserve. Here you can arrange to walk through the rain forest to a hideout, where there is a chance you might see one of Dominica's two indigenous parrots, the Sisserou and the Jacquot.

Portsmouth, set on a huge bay in the northwest, is the island's second town and is even quieter than Roseau. Canoe trips arranged here take passengers through the Indian River mangroves; the area's malarial swamps drove British settlers to Roseau, ruining Portsmouth's chances of becoming the capital. The excellently restored **Cabrits National Park**▶▶ (tel: 448 4733. *Open* daily. *Admission: inexpensive*) is an old military garrison set on the nearby promontory (cruise ships dock on the peninsula itself). Many of the barrack buildings have been repaired and there is a museum in Fort Shirley. The Park also includes a marine section, with scuba diving sites. Portsmouth's black sand beaches are passable, but Dominica's best beaches are to the east, in the hidden north coast coves; try Hampstead or Calibishie—swimmers should beware the fierce Atlantic swells.

Caribbean islands are best known for their picture-postcard beaches, where silken sands are lapped by gentle waves. But there are other treats for waterlovers; the mountainous interiors of many islands are laced with rivers, where cool freshwater cascades crash and tumble through thick forests, and waterfalls pour into clear rockpools, making ideal spots for secluded and refreshing dips after hiking through the rain forest.

Rivers were once gathering places on the Caribbean islands. Before piped water was introduced, the population would go there to collect water and do the Monday washing, and washerwomen (*blanchisseuses* in the French Caribbean) can still occasionally be seen sudsing the clothes up at the riverside and laying them out on the rocks to dry. Another long-standing practice was (and remains) taking a bath in the river. Although West Indians never go nude on their beaches, they do often take off their clothes in order to wash in fresh water.

Rivers play an important part in Caribbean folklore and legend; many islands share the legend of a beautiful girl sitting by a rockpool, combing her hair with a golden comb and perhaps granting a wish. The story goes that anyone who manages to steal her comb and take it down to the sea can keep it. The rockpools of Trinidad are said to be the home of the unpleasant Mama Dlo, the spirit of the water, half woman and half anaconda.

The Windward Islands are so well watered that they sell water to some of the drier islands. The best islands for river bathing are the Eastern Caribbean islands from Guadeloupe down to Trinidad. There are also large rivers in the Greater Antilles. Many of the rockpools and rivers are off the beaten track and so bathers should be careful of their personal security. Rivers of slow-moving water might best be avoided—cases of bilharzia (caused by a parasitic flat-worm that enters the blood and bladder), though rare, have been known to occur.

RIVER HUNTS
On Dominica, hunting parties search the rivers by night for frogs and crabs. Hunters once used flaming torches (they are more likely to be electric flashlights nowadays) to attract the animals, which are so startled by the light that they do not even attempt to hide and can be simply picked up.

RIVERS IN RELIGION
In Haiti waterfalls have religious significance. On saints' days the Catholic and voodoo faithful gather at the riverside for ceremonies that include baptism in the waters of the cascades.

Swimmers can enjoy the pools at Dunn's River Falls in Ocho Rios, Jamaica

FÉDON'S CAMP

High up in Grenada's rain forest, Fédon's Camp takes its name from French Créole planter Julien Fédon, leader of a rebellion against British authorities in 1795. Supplied by French revolutionaries in Guadeloupe, he led a brutal insurrection and set himself up in his estate at Belvidere with 50 prisoners, all of whom were killed. The British eventually regained the island, but Fédon is thought to have escaped to Trinidad or Cuba.

Grenada

Long recovered from the political traumas of the 1980s, Grenada has relaxed into a sleepy island with the Caribbean's most picturesque port, St. George's. A warm, friendly place of small villages and mountain walks, it is ideal for either an active or a completely lazy break.

It was on Grenada that the Caribbean rum punch was perfected. In his book, *Touch the Happy Isles*, Quentin Crewe retells the story of a planter who sprinkled a mystery ingredient into his guests' glasses at a party in 1813. The addition was nutmeg and it was such a success that West Indians have used it in their recipes for rum punch ever since. The nutmeg fruit, which now appears on the Grenadian flag, was for a while one of the country's largest exports; nutmeg trees still grow all over the island. This and the many other spices grown in the hills—cinnamon, cocoa, cloves, pimento and bay leaves to name a few—have given Grenada its title of the Caribbean's Spice Island.

Grenada is the most southerly in the chain of the Windward Islands and is not as mountainous as the others. Of the Grenadines, its string of offshore islets surrounded by coral reefs, only two are inhabited: Carriacou and Petit Martinique. Grenada itself is developing slowly but steadily; package tourism is confined to the southwestern corner of the island, around Grand Anse and L'Anse aux Epines, where the best hotels, restaurants, and bars can be found. Elsewhere on the island you will see Grenadians living a pastoral, country life, often fishing or farming for a living.

Nowadays Grenada's atmosphere is calm and relaxed, but the island has a history of conflict and violence, aggravated by its strenghthening ties to Communist Cuba. In the past, the 1983 "intervention" by the USA and its Caribbean allies provoked strong reactions, of both outrage and approval. The troops moved in after Maurice Bishop, leader of the increasingly repressive People's Revolutionary Government, had been killed by a rival faction, along with nine of his colleagues. A return to the 1974 constitution, established when Grenada gained independence from Britain, paved the way for parliamentary elections and the island returned to a state of comparative stability. Some Grenadians still remember Maurice Bishop favorably—he had taken power in a bloodless coup, replacing the corrupt administration of Premier Eric Gairy in 1979—but only the occasional piece of graffiti remains as a reminder of turbulent times.

ST. GEORGE'S Grenada's capital, **St. George's ▶ ▶ ▶**, is a very pretty town on a natural harbor. Its Georgian stone houses and more recent concrete homes are neatly ranged in curved lines on the crumbled slopes of a long-inactive volcanic crater, their red tiled and tin roofs offset by the tropical greens of the surrounding forest. On the heights above stands a protective ring of churches and fortresses.

BEFORE THE REVOLUTION
When Eric Gairy was elected Grenada's first leader after Independence, he had already built up a large following as a member of the colonial administration, promoting the cause of the workers. However, Gairy's government grew increasingly corrupt and repressive, its policies enforced by the secret Mongoose Gang, and soon an underground anti-government movement gathered strength. The New Jewel Movement united Gairy's socialist opponents; in March 1979 it took advantage of the leader's absence from Grenada to stage a coup, and, with Cuban support, Maurice Bishop's new administration began to implement its socialist policies.

47

"Mango, banana and tangerine," *as sung in the film* Dr. No. *St. George's Market has them all*

A century ago, the cocoa estates of Grenada would ring to the sound of fiddlers, who played for the workers as they "danced" the cocoa beans. The beans were laid out on boucans, *or drying trays, and the workers would shuffle through them, turning them so that they dried evenly. Spices grow throughout the Caribbean, but Grenada's mild climate and fertile soil have earned it the title of "Spice Isle."*

COCOA WALKS
Cocoa trees need to be shaded from the tropical sun if they are to flourish, so planters imported the tall and bushy *bois immortelle* or *madre de cacao* trees for that purpose. Shaded by their leaves, the "cocoa walks" are cool even in the middle of the day. In January and February the *bois immortelle* flowers bright orange and whole hillsides in Grenada, Trinidad and Tobago are patched with flaming orange blooms.

Spice Isle produce

Nutmeg and mace The nutmeg tree (*Myristica fragrans*) actually yields two spices: nutmeg and mace. This bushy tree grows to 65ft (20m) and produces a yellow fruit like an apricot, which splits open when ripe. Its flesh, used to make preserves, protects the nut itself, which is covered with a scarlet waxy netting. This is stripped off and sold as mace, for use as a food flavoring and in cosmetics. The kernel of the nutmeg is used to flavor foods (and to treat rheumatism).

Cocoa The Aztecs used cocoa beans for barter and made their national drink, *chocolada*, with them. The cocoa tree (*theobroma*, "food of the gods") grows to about 50ft (15m) and sprouts yellow, brown and purple oval-shaped pods, in which the beans lie. These must be fermented, to strip the pulp, and then dried in the sun for several days.

Allspice "Jamaica pepper" and "pimento," as allspice is also known, is native to the Caribbean and tastes like a combination of clove, cinnamon and nutmeg. Used as a flavoring for foods, it is an essential ingredient in jerk seasoning.

Other herbs and spices Oil extracted from the leaves and twigs of the bayberry tree (not to be confused with the Mediterranean bay) is used in perfumes and is distilled to make aromatic and medicinal bay rum. Ginger was brought to the Americas from the Far East by the Spaniards. Oil of ginger is used as a pain reliever in the Windward Islands. The sweet-smelling bark of the cinnamon tree is used in confectionery and in cooking.

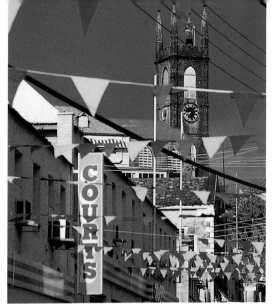

Flags hang in the streets of St. George's in preparation for Carnival in August

THE *BIANCA C*
On the shore of the Carenage, in St. George's harbor, a statue of Christ of the Deep and a plaque commemorate those who died when a cruise ship, the *Bianca C*, caught fire in 1961. Its remains were towed out of the harbor to the southwest and sunk, and it is now the largest upright underwater wreck in the world and a popular dive site. The stern section alone measures about 115ft (35m).

The heart of town is the **Carenage**▶▶▶, the inner harbor, where the traditional island sloops and visiting cruise ships tie up. Waterfront warehouses now house restaurants and bars, and water-taxis pick up passengers for the bay crossing or the return to Grand Anse.

On Young Street, the **Grenada National Museum**▶ (tel: 440 3725. *Open* Mon–Fri 9–4.30, Sat 10–1. *Admission: inexpensive*) is set in a French stone barrack building and shows memorabilia including Josephine Bonaparte's childhood bathtub from Martinique, Arawak rock carvings and artifacts of the plantation era. Dominating the harbor is Fort George, also the island police headquarters, where Maurice Bishop and his supporters were killed.

Over the hill (or through the Sendall Tunnel) the other half of St. George's, the Esplanade, is on the Caribbean seafront. Once the site of the public executions, the **Market Square**▶▶▶ was not easy to reach before the tunnel was built between the town's two halves in the late 19th century. Today it also serves as the bus station for the west coast, and Saturday mornings are renowned for particular chaos, as vendors and busmen exchange shouts and jokes. Vendors hardly ever use the market buildings; they prefer to lay out their wares on tables under golfing umbrellas on the square. Nearby is the Minor Spices Society, where Grenada's home-grown spices are on sale; and the **Yellow Poui Art Gallery**▶▶ (tel: 440 3001) on Cross Street exhibits work by Caribbean artists.

St. George's botanical gardens, on the Lagoon, are somewhat run down; the Bay Gardens on Richmond Hill are a better bet, showing a range of flora from forest walkways.

GRAND ANSE Not far along the coast to the south of St. George's is **Grand Anse**▶▶, Grenada's best beach. There are several hotels on the beach itself (others are ranged behind it) and beach bars on the sand. Grand Anse is also the best area for watersports. Other good, secluded beaches, including **Morne Rouge Bay**▶▶, nestle in the coves toward the southwestern tip of the island.

The daily market is one of the liveliest and most accessible features of Caribbean life. Whether it be the overwhelming press of a large city market or a series of small stalls under a tree, the market is a vital focus of community and business. An amazing variety of goods is sold, from tropical fruit and vegetables to pots and pans, from candy and soap to human hair for braiding—all to the accompaniment of the shouts and patter of the marketeers.

THE FLOATING MARKET
Curaçao's floating market is made up of 15 or so moored boats. Vendors store their goods on board overnight and lay them out on the quayside stalls during market hours, shading them with flysheets (which are attached to the masts and rise and fall with the movement of the boats). The vendors are resupplied every few days with produce from Venezuela.

Caribbean markets have always been more than just a place for buying and selling. In the days before emancipation in the 19th century, slaves would be allowed to make a little money by selling the fruit and vegetables they had grown. After slavery had been abolished, markets became gathering places where people would meet and swap stories. Colonial market buildings are usually made of red corrugated tin (the finest and the busiest is the Marché de Fer in Port-au-Prince in Haiti, which covers about one acre/0.4ha), but vendors often spread their goods out on blankets on the ground outside, rather than on the tables provided. Most stallholders are women, who sit on low boxes or benches with their skirts rolled up over their knees, shaded by two-tone golfing umbrellas. They arrive from the country in the early morning, often leaving by mid-afternoon, when the goods are sold.

Tropical vegetables are an essential feature of most markets and include cassava (see panel); sweet potato, which can be oval or pointed with white, purple, or orange flesh; eddoe, also called dasheen, whose spherical tubers have slender stems and heart-shaped leaves; and yam, which is long, thin and hairy.

Crowds at St. George's market

CASSAVA
Cassava is a familiar item on most Caribbean vegetable stalls. Most of its 160 species contain a poisonous, cyanide-like juice that must be extracted before the vegetable can be consumed. Carib methods included grating the tuber on a sea fan coral and then squeezing the pulp in a woven bag that tightened as it was stretched. Dried cassava can be used like flour to make cassava bread and cakes (called "bammy" in Jamaica).

Ribbons and hair braids for the children of Grand Anse Roman Catholic School

On Grenada's south coast, L'Anse aux Epines has a number of hotels and bars, as well as a sailing marina, and farther east, beyond the offshore island of Calivigny (where Grenadians often go for picnics), there is a charming dark sand beach with a hotel-restaurant at La Sagesse Bay. The **La Sagesse Nature Centre**►► (tel: 444 6458; www.lasegasse.com) is set in a 100-acre (40ha) plantation, where guided trails offer glimpses of plant and birdlife.

A visit to the **Grand Etang National Park and Forest Reserve**►► (tel: 440 6160) is worth the tortuous drive into the mountains. The rain forest can be fully appreciated from the trails, which afford good views of ferns spreading in the upper branches of the taller trees. The Grand Etang Visitor's Centre (*Open* Mon–Sat 10–4 but extended hours when cruise ships dock. *Admission: inexpensive*) contains a museum, and an easy trail circles the Grand Etang crater lake (about 1.5 hours). Longer, more strenuous trails lead to Mount Qua Qua, Concord Falls and beyond.

From here the road descends into Grenada's most fertile valleys. In Grenville, which is not much more than a fishing village, one of Grenada's two large **nutmeg processing stations**►► is based. The **River Antoine Rum Distillery**►► (tel: 442 7109. *Open* Mon–Fri 8–5, Sat 10–4. *Admission: inexpensive*) shows a water-driven cane-crusher in action as well as the process of boiling and distilling in order to make rum; visitors can taste the extremely strong result. The cane-crusher is one of the last of its kind operating in the Caribbean region.

The road north from St. George's follows the switchbacks of the western coastline to Molinière Point, where there is good snorkeling. At the **Dougaldston Estate**►► (tel: 444 8213. *Open* Mon–Sat 10–4 and Sun when cruise ships dock. *Admission free*), just south of Gouyave, Grenadian spices are prepared for sale. In Gouyave itself there is a **nutmeg cooperative**►► where nutmeg and mace are prepared and visitors are welcome (nominal tip required).

NUTMEG PROCESSING PLANTS
It is well worth visiting either of Grenada's two main nutmeg co-operatives; one is in Gouyave, north of St. George's, and the other in Grenville on the Atlantic coast. Each factory is filled with groaning hessian sacks waiting for export and the pungent aroma of the spice itself. Once the mace has been stripped and graded (according to color), the nut of the nutmeg is put through a crusher and the kernel is extracted from the shells. It is then put through a water test: The finest nutmegs sink and are used in food flavoring; those that float are used by the pharmaceutical industry.

MR. CANUTE CALISTE

Artist Mr. Canute Caliste was without doubt Carriacou's most famous son. Born in 1914 his unique naïve style of art brought him notoriety in the US and Europe in the 1980s; he continued to paint well into his 80s at a shack/studio in the back garden of his humble island home at L'Esterre. He died in November 2005 leaving 22 children and more than 100 grandchildren.

The village of Sauteurs, on the northern coast, serves as a reminder of the last Carib people in Grenada, who jumped to their deaths off a cliff here (Caribs' Leap) rather than be taken prisoner by French colonists in 1651. Inland, to the southwest of Sauteurs in the hills, is the delightful **Morne Fendue**▶▶▶ (tel: 442 9330. *Open* daily for lunch), a modest plantation house, where rum punch is served on the veranda and the famous lunch consists of pepperpot, a dish that can last for 60 years if replenished and boiled daily. The last pepperpot had to be abandoned during the revolution, when there was a curfew; the current pot is approaching its twentieth anniversary. Beaches in the northern area include Bathway, where there is a protective reef against the Atlantic waves.

Carriacou and Petit Martinique Carriacou▶▶▶ is the biggest of the two inhabited islands politically attached to Grenada. Attractive, welcoming and extremely laid-back, it measures only 5 miles by 8 miles (8 by 13km) and has 7,000 inhabitants, who earn their living by selling vegetables and livestock in Grenada and pursuing "unofficial" trade with other islands. Boat-building is a major island tradition and the colorful sloops constructed by hand in Windward, on the eastern coast, and Tyrrel Bay are launched with great pomp and circumstance. The festive Carriacou Regatta is held every August. Ferries to Carriacou sail from the Carenage, St. George's, daily and take 30 minutes to 4 hours (they also come from Union Island, farther north), and flights land at Lauriston airport. The island is graced with some magnificent beaches and its southern shore has a view stretching 25 miles (40km) to Grenada and taking some uninhabited islands and cays. Beaches well worth visiting include the one at Anse la Roche, Windward Beach and Paradise Beach. Tyrrel Bay is a superb place to watch the sunset. **Petite Martinique**▶ is situated 3 miles (5km) to the east of Carriacou and has a population of around 900. As there is only one place to stay, this figure does not often increase: It is untouched by tourism.

52

Maurice Bishop, leader of Grenada's People's Revolutionary Government in the 1980s

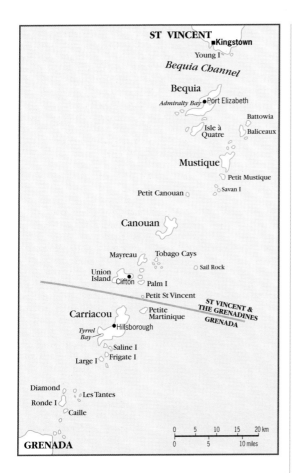

FAIR EXCHANGE
Young Island is said to have been swapped for a horse. Governor Young had brought a black charger with him to St. Vincent from Britain and it was greatly admired by the local Carib chief, so he presented the creature to him as a gift. Some time later the two men were together on the veranda of St. Vincent's Government House, looking out toward the idyllic, forested islet just offshore. When Governor Young admired the island, the Carib chief returned the favor and made him a present of the land.

The Grenadines

Administered by St. Vincent (see page 64), the Grenadines appeal to adventurous singles and couples who prefer sailing, seclusion and sports to glitz, gambling or designer shopping. Hotels are small, the food is simple and the residents' hospitality provides a peaceful, laid-back atmosphere. The 32 islands and cays that make up the lush and mountainous Grenadines offer numerous unspoiled white sand bays and coves, and superb snorkeling, hiking, sailing and swimming.

Just off St. Vincent, **Young Island►** (tel: 458 4826; www.youngisland.com) is a private resort with only about 20 cottages. **Bequia►►►** lies 8.5 miles (13.5km) south of St. Vincent. This is an island of fishermen, seafarers, boat-builders and whalers, where tourists rub shoulders with the locals in an excellent string of waterfront bars in Port Elizabeth, the main settlement and ferry harbor. The best places to stay include Frangipani and the Friendship Bay Hotel on the south coast. You can reach the excellent beaches of Princess Margaret Beach and Lower Bay by water taxi, or walk over to the secluded sand at Industry Bay in the east.

Admiralty Bay, used by the British Navy and then abandoned for lack of water, is now a favorite anchorage for yachts

The graceful profiles of locally built boats are a familiar sight in the Grenadines. Brightly painted sloops still ply their trade from island to island as they have for centuries. Life in the Caribbean has always been dependent on shipping and even now the smaller islands only really seem to come alive when crowds gather to greet the weekly mail boat.

Before island-hopping planes, Caribbean communities were linked by frequent boat services. Unfortunately, the use of small boats has died off on the larger islands, but part of the fun of visiting the Grenadines, the Virgin Islands and the French islands off Guadeloupe is to hop from one island to the next by mailboat, ferry or traditional schooner.

There is a long history of boat-building and seafaring around the Caribbean islands. Caymanians and Sabans were particularly renowned as sailors and they crewed and captained vessels all over the world for the big shipping lines. Closer to home, inter-island trading was established as a necessary way of life— Anguillans would sail west to Jamaica and south to Trinidad to sell their products. Captains would fund the boat-building by traveling abroad to earn money first for the hull, then for the planking and the deck, then finally for the mast and fittings. Nowadays Grenadine sloops travel regularly to Trinidad, taking fruit and vegetables for sale and returning with goods such as crisps and canned food. They also go as far north as Sint Maarten in the Leeward Islands, to buy supplies including export alcohol and goods from Europe.

Today's master boat-builders are the Bequians and Carriacouans; although their trade is now dying, it is still possible to see hulls taking shape on the beach and being painted bright red and orange—essential for clear visibility against a turquoise sea.

Smuggling has always been part of Caribbean life. Although drugs do pass through the islands *en route* elsewhere, inter-island smuggling is usually confined to alcohol, cigarettes and large appliances, primarily for the avoidance of island duty. Buyers are told in advance when a boat will be putting in at a particular cove— usually in the dead of night.

54

Making sure everything is shipshape

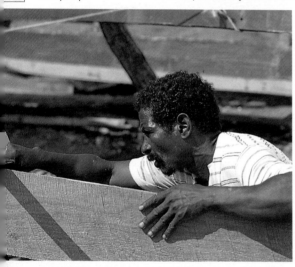

BOAT LAUNCHING
A boat launch is an excuse for a big party. The boat is christened and blessed by a priest with holy water (and sometimes with goat's blood). It is even given godparents, whose duty it is to raise it if it sinks. As the boat is launched, as many people clamber on board as possible, all dressed in their Sunday best, before returning to shore to eat and drink.

A scrubby outcrop 40 years ago, **Mustique▶▶** now has 85 of the Caribbean's most luxurious villas, 58 of which are for rent, for a price (gardener, maids, cooks and motorcycle or donkey thrown in). Just 1.5 miles by 3 miles (2.5 by 5km), Mustique has one hotels; the Cotton House is set in the restored plantation house. Celebrities such as Mick Jagger have been known to emerge from the seclusion of their villas on Wednesdays, jump-up night at Basil's beach bar on stilts (tel: 488 8350; www.basilsmustique. com). The Caribbean seems as incidental to Mustique as it is essential to the island of Bequia (see page 53).

On **Canouan▶▶**, around 1,000 people eke out a quiet living. This small island (3 miles by 1 mile/5 by 0.5km) of gentle green peaks is rimmed with white sand. Offshore reefs protect the windward bays, and Grand Bay, on the leeward side, is a favorite yacht anchorage.

Mayreau▶▶, smaller and quieter, does not even have a jetty. Loading and unloading passengers can be a precarious business when the occasional cruise ships do put in. There are only 150 inhabitants and a couple of cars, but the beaches are wonderful and there are excellent views from Dennis' Hideaway.

Although its towering mountains make **Union Island▶** the most beautiful of the Grenadines, this is a working island; its marina and airstrip are used by a stream of people traveling to quieter islands nearby. Most of the 2,000 islanders work in the resorts or fish and trade by sea.

The five **Tobago Cays▶▶▶**, Petit Rameau, Petit Bateau, Barabal, Jamesby and Petit Tobac, rise gently from the water, protected by a reef 1,000 yards (915m) offshore. They are uninhabited and maintained as a marine park and have excellent sailing and snorkeling.

Close by are two tiny cays, each entirely devoted to a single luxurious hotel. **Palm Island▶▶** (tel: 458 8824; www.palmislandresorts.com) has 24 villas set on the beach or scattered among hundreds of palms. **Petit St. Vincent▶▶▶** (tel: US 1 954/963-7401), known as PSV, specializes in low-key super-luxury, where residents communicate with room service by raising a yellow flag.

BEACHES

Beaches with bright white sand can be found throughout the Grenadines, many of them sheltered in coves formed by the irregularly shaped, mountainous islands. On the northern shore of Admiralty Bay on Bequia are the golden sands of Princess Margaret Beach and Lower Bay; Endeavour Bay is the best beach on Mustique, although the whole island is rimmed with ankle-deep, soft sand. Canouan has a number of pretty beaches and isolated coves, including Maho, Corbay and Rameau Bay. On Mayreau the best beaches are Salt Whistle Bay and Saline Bay. One of the finest beaches in the West Indies is on Carriacou, at Anse la Roche. None of the beaches has formal facilities, but if there is a restaurant, the staff will normally let you change there.

55

Named after a governor in the 1700s, Young Island lies about 200 yards (180m) off St. Vincent's southern shore

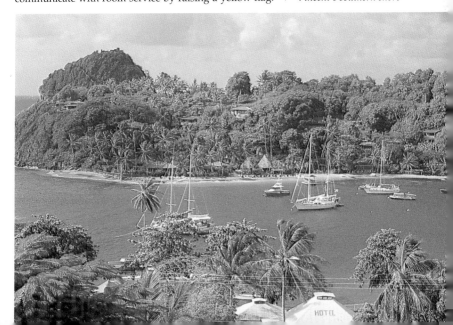

St Lucia Passage

Pointe du Cap
Pointe Hardy
Pigeon Island National Park ■ **Cap Estate Golf Course**
Rodney Bay Gros Islet
Anse Lavoutte
Reduit Beach
Espérance Harbour
Labrellotte Point
Monchy
Cape Marquis
Marisule Estate
Choc Bay Grande Rivière
Rat I *Marquis*
Vigie Peninsula
Vigie Airport Petite Anse
La Toc Bay **Castries**
Babonneau Grande Anse
Morne Fortune ■
Ciceron Girard Fond Assor
Castries Waterworks Forest Reserve
Tortue Point
Anse Massacré
Forestière
Louvet Point
Marigot Bay La Croix Marigot
Piton Flore 571m ▲
Anse Louvet
Roseau Bexon
Dernière Rivière
Anse Povert
Pointe la Ville
Anse la Raye Vanard
La Caye
Anse Cochon
Ravine Poisson
Grand Rivière
Durandeau
Errard Plantation
Fond d'Or Bay
Jambette Point
Grand Bois Forest
Dennery
Canaries Millet
Dennery Waterworks Forest Reserve
Canaries
678m ▲ Mt Tabac
950m ▲ Mt Gimie
Praslin
Praslin Bay
Bouton **Morne Coubaril Estate**
Grand Caille Point
Soufrière Bay Soufrière
St Lucia National Rain Forest
Fond
Mon Repos
Patience
Diamond Botanical Gardens and Mineral Baths
743m ▲
Petit Piton
Fond St Jacques
Troumassée
Micoud
Anse des Pitons
616m ▲ Mt Grand Magazin
798m ▲
Gros Piton Point *Gros Piton*
Vierge Point
Troumassée Bay
Anse l'Ivrogne
Roblot
Ti Rocher
Desruisseaux
Dorée
Belle Vue
Anse Ger
Anse Ger
Choiseul Bay
La Fargue
Vieux Fort
Canelles
Pointe des Canelles
Choiseul
Pierrot
Augier
Piaye
St Urbain
Laborie
Savannes Bay
Piaye
Laborie Bay
Hewanorra International Airport
Black Bay
Vieux Fort
Vieux Fort Bay
Maria Is
Anse de Sables
Cape Moule à Chique

0   2   4   6   8   10 km
0   2   4   6 miles

St Vincent Passage

St. Lucia

On Friday nights crowds gather at Gros Islet, a village on St. Lucia's Rodney Bay, in the north. This Caribbean jump-up transforms the settlement of wooden houses into one big street party: The thumping pulse of local soca, Martiniquan zouk and Jamaican reggae can be heard from afar and dancers spill onto the road, winding and grinding beneath the banks of flashing lights and the stacks of speakers, while vendors sell grilled fish and chilled beer. The mix of people at Gros Islet is typical of St. Lucia, where tourists and locals rub shoulders easily in the towns and on the beach. Lying between the French island of Martinique and St. Vincent to the south, this is one of the most welcoming of the Caribbean islands and has become an increasingly popular tourist destination in recent years. The rapid development of a tourist industry, with beach hotels and restaurants sprouting all over the island, threatens to swamp the quiet agricultural life that has characterized St. Lucia for many years, but as yet tourism is concentrated in the northwest, between the capital, Castries, and the northern tip of the island, where the best beaches are to be found. Venture into the city and beyond and there is still a beautiful island to explore, boasting inland rain forests harboring indigenous parrots, and secluded coves accessible only by boat.

ISLAND LIFE Most St. Lucians are chatty and forthcoming, as will soon become apparent to anyone taking a walk on the streets of Castries or in the country villages. Most speak patois, a Créole language derived mainly from French, but English is the official language.

This was a British colony for one-and-a-half centuries, until Independence on the 22nd of December 1979, but before that the island had a history of struggle and conquest. St. Lucia's strategic importance sparked off several battles for its possession between the British and French until Britain finally took control in 1814. However, the French legacy remains, in the names of many towns, the predominant religion (Catholicism) and the Créole food, which includes such delights as *soupe germou* (pumpkin soup with garlic) and *pouile dudon* (a chicken dish that is cooked in coconut and sugar).

St. Lucia is the most populous (there are around 156,000 islanders) and the most developed of the Windward Islands. Besides tourism, there is some light manufacturing and an extensive agricultural sector that, until recently, depended mainly on bananas grown for export to Britain under special trade arrangements, but is now coming under threat from cheaper producers in Central America (see page 58).

CASTRIES St. Lucia's capital, **Castries**▶▶, was named for a French Minister of the Marine, the Maréchal de Castries, and laid out beside a natural harbor in the 1760s. It soon crept over the heights that surround the bay. Now a sprawling town of 62,000, Castries has burned down many times (most recently in 1948) and only a few colonial buildings remain. However, traditional Caribbean architecture survives on the hills around town, on Vigie Point and Morne Fortune.

The main square in the center of town has been renamed for one of St. Lucia's Nobel Prize winners, Derek Walcott. It is dominated by a huge saman tree and the brick Cathedral of the Immaculate Conception, built in 1897. On the south side are a number of old Créole timber-frame houses.

PRIZE WINNERS
The island of St. Lucia can claim two Nobel Prize winners: In 1979 Sir Arthur Lewis won a Nobel Prize for Economic Sciences, and in 1992 Derek Walcott was awarded a Nobel Prize for Literature. Walcott, born in St. Lucia in 1930, was educated at the University of the West Indies and has taught in a number of American universities. He is best known for his poetry collections, including *The Fortunate Traveller* (1982), *Midsummer* (1984) and *Omeros* (1990). The last, arguably his masterwork, is an ambitious retelling of *The Odyssey* set in the islands Walcott knows so well.

Opposite: harbor view from Castries

57

The edible banana's botanical name is **Musa sapientum,** *or "muse of the wise man." It is said that Southeast Asian sages would sit in the shade of banana trees, enjoy the fruit and have wise thoughts. Since the banana made its way to the Caribbean, this pastime has been readily adopted by islanders.*

THE "BANANA BOAT SONG"

Harry Belafonte's "Banana Boat Song" was originally a Jamaican working song, sung by female banana packers as they raced up and down the gangplanks, loading bunches of bananas onto the United Fruit Company ships. After working through the night, they would sing "Day-oh, day-oh" as day was dawning; the "tallyman" referred to in the song would give the workers tokens each time they came past with a load of bananas, tallying up the tokens at the end of the night and paying the women accordingly.

CLAIMS TO FAME

Bananas are highly valued by sportsmen and women, particularly tennis players and marathon runners, because they have a wide and complex range of sugars. These are digested at different rates, thereby releasing energy over a longer period than other sugary foods, such as chocolate. The fruit has a rather less creditable reputation in Sri Lanka, where the story of Adam and Eve has the serpent tempting Eve not with an apple but with a banana.

Banana plants grow singly and in groves all over the Caribbean, their leaves exploding in graceful, green curves to heights of up to 20ft (6m). Each plant gives fruit only once before it dies, then another plant sprouts from the same root system. As they grow, they throw off drooping stems, on which the 150 or so individual bananas sprout, coming to maturity over nine months. The plants are protected from insects by blue plastic bags, often tied in a cat's cradle of string to prevent them from falling over. Bananas grow in clusters, or "hands,"; a group of ten hands on a single stem is known as a "bunch." Names and species vary. The yellow cavendish is the type of banana seen most in Europe and America, because it travels well, but Caribbean markets sell smaller, fatter, sweeter canary bananas and green vegetable-bananas called plantains. In the Windward Islands bananas range from big yellow *gros michels* to small "rock figs," and plantains called "green fig," "bluggo" and "buggoman."

Since the 1950s the export of bananas has improved life dramatically for many small farmers in Jamaica, the French Caribbean and the Windward Islands. Instead of seasonal work in the cane fields, they now have a year-round income.

In the late 1990s, bananas accounted for three-quarters of the Windward Islands' export earnings. But free market agreements such as GATT and NAFTA have brought Caribbean bananas under threat, especially from "dollar bananas," grown more cheaply in Central America. The loss of traditional markets is hitting the Caribbean growers hard and farmers will have to diversify.

A West Indian woman carrying her cargo on her head

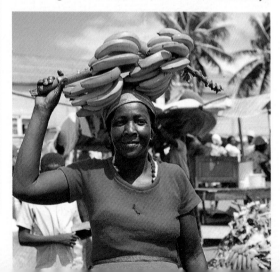

A short walk away, Castries life is at its most ebullient in the market all along the waterfront in the tin-roofed vegetable market and in the craft market.

Cruise ships dock on the north side of Castries harbor and passengers head straight into the shopping complex at Pointe Seraphine, where the St. Lucia Tourist Board provides information on accommodations and events.

OUTSIDE CASTRIES Many of the island's accommodations are set in coves north of the capital, an easy taxi or bus ride from Castries. The most popular area is **Rodney Bay▶▶**, with a marina, restaurants, accommodations and the island's liveliest beach. Reduit Beach is a long strip of white coral sand with watersports facilities. Across the lagoon entrance is Gros Islet, the place to be on Friday nights.

Rodney Bay has long been a center for sailing craft and beach bars, popular with locals at weekends. Before the gin joints came Carib canoes, Spanish galleons, pirate sloops and naval ships. Two centuries ago Admiral Rodney himself fortified **Pigeon Island National Park▶** (tel: 450 5005. *Open* daily 9–5. *Admission: inexpensive*), across the bay from Reduit Beach. It was designated a National Park in 1979 and its walkways pass barrack rooms and gun pits, with a museum and restaurant at the

ROADSIDE REFRESHMENT
In the hot weather it is essential to have a ready supply of liquid, and among Windward islanders there is a tradition of selling soft drinks at the roadside. A cup of crushed ice, topped with water, sweet fruit concentrate and a straw, is a great way to keep cool. Sometimes the vendor offers a topping of condensed milk or crushed nuts. Street snacks include locally grown peanuts, plantain chips or coconut chips cut from the dried copra in the center of the coconut.

59

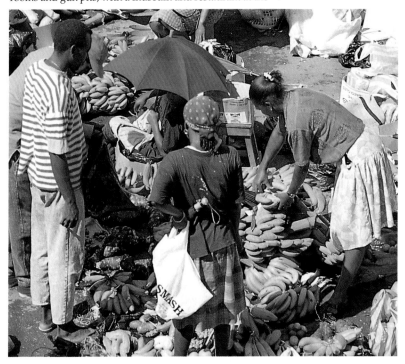

end of the trail. There is one 18-hole golf course among the chic villas of the Cap Estate (tel: 450 8522) farther north; and a nine-hole course at La Toc, south of Castries (www.sandals.com).

South of Castries, over Morne Fortune (pronounced "Fortunay"), there is a less feverish, less developed St. Lucia

Different kinds of bananas and plantains are on sale in Castries market

The Windwards

The two Pitons, volcanic plugs covered by rain forest, rise dramatically from the sea in the south-west of St. Lucia

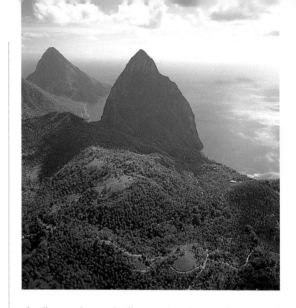

SPA FIT FOR SOLDIERS
King Louis XVI of France provided the funds to build the Diamond Baths in the 1780s after hearing of the volcanic water's healing powers, as described by the governor, Baron de Laborie. According to reports at the time, the water was believed to cure rheumatism, among other ailments, and Louis was eager for his troops to feel the benefit. Water flows from the volcano at temperatures of about 105°F (40.5°C).

HOT WATER
The volcanic Windward Islands are active beneath the surface of the water as well as above it, and in the sea off the Pitons you will find patches of warm water let out by the Soufrière. In Dominica, for instance, the bubbles released make scuba diving feel like swimming in champagne.

of valleys and coastal villages, where banana farmers and fishermen are unaffected by tourism. Beyond Cul de Sac on the west coast is **Marigot Bay▶▶▶**, a steep-sided inlet lined with palm trees, which was once a hideout for pirates and navvies. There are a couple of cafés on the road down to the bay, and bars on the beach. At Canaries the coast road turns inland and climbs into rain forest beneath Morne Gimie (3,117ft/950m), the highest peak on the island. The descent into the town of Soufrière affords fine views of the **Pitons▶▶▶**, two pyramid-shaped volcanic mountains that soar from the sea to 2,439ft (744m) and 2,620ft (799m).

Soufrière, the first settlement to be built on the island but rejected in favor of Castries and its better harbor, is a town of clapboard houses with overhanging balconies. Its name comes from the nearby **Soufrière▶**, the world's only drive-in volcano, a simmering cauldron of mud that can be tracked down by its foul smell. This is a solfatara—a volcanic vent that steams steadily rather than blowing cataclysmically. Inland from Soufrière, at the **Diamond Botanical Gardens and Mineral Baths▶** (tel: 459 7565. *Open Mon–Sat 10–5, Sun 10–3. Admission: inexpensive*) it is possible to bathe in the naturally heated pools. Botanical gardens nearby give a good introduction to tropical flora. At the **Morne Coubaril Estate▶▶** you can see cocoa-making and go hiking and horseback-riding (tel: 459 7340). The **St Lucia National Rain Forest▶▶** is a protected area with walking trails and is also home to St. Lucia's own species of parrot, now nearly extinct. Contact the St Lucia Ministry of Agriculture and Fisheries (tel: 450 3321, ext 316; www.slunaffe.org) before using the trails; guides are also available.

The road from Castries down the east coast is an easier run, as it is used to meet flights into Hewanorra international airport, near the southern tip. After passing over the rainforested Barre de l'Isle mountain range, it descends into banana plantations at Dennery before reaching the more remote villages strung out along the coast. You can visit working cocoa, coconut and coffee plantations at the **Marquis Estate** at Errard Plantation near Dennery.

> *Before the age of television, whole villages would gather under a tree to enjoy an evening of storytelling. Many of the tales, often with song, centered around Anancy the Rogue and a cast of other characters—Dog, Goat, Jackass, Kisander the Cat and Tiger—all of whom had human characteristics. All over the Caribbean, Islanders still tell stories about them.*

Anancy is the best-loved character in Caribbean folklore. Sometimes a man, sometimes a spider, he is a sweet-talking trickster who, as a man, is considered rather laughable because he speaks with a lisp, but who can turn into a spider and hide when the need arises. Anancy is lazy and greedy and far happier tricking a slow neighbor out of his meal than working honestly. But he is also fully capable of outwitting his opponents—particularly Tiger, his traditional enemy. Even in his greed, Anancy wins the listener's sympathy and is often used to deliver home truths—though storytellers may dissociate themselves from his actions by ending their tales with the words: "Jack Mantora me no choose any."

Above all, Anancy is good entertainment. When he wants a meal of crabs he dresses up as a priest and persuades them to be baptized (promptly throwing them into boiling water); having taken a bet that he cannot catch Snake, he taunts him into bragging about his length and while measuring him against a log, ties Snake to it and captures him.

The island of Trinidad has a strong tradition of folklore, illustrated in Port of Spain's National Museum. Papa Bois, the guardian of the forest, warns animals of the hunter's presence (see panel).

La Diablesse, the devil woman, appears as an old crone whose petticoats clank with chains or as an attractive girl who can drive men mad with desire, and the *soucouyant* is an old woman who turns into a ball of fire at night and goes around sucking human blood.

Mama Dlo, the mother of the water, is half woman, half anaconda and sometimes sings at the water's edge, but vanishes immediately if she is disturbed.

PAPA BOIS
Papa Bois will usually let hunters keep their kills from the forest, but if any become too greedy he will appear as a deer and lure them deep into the forest before turning back into an old man and issuing a stern warning, sometimes sentencing the offending hunter to be married to Mama Dlo.

61

DUENNES
Never shout the name of your child in the Trinidadian forest; he or she will be stolen by the Duennes. These infant tricksters, who reputedly roam among the trees, are the ghosts of children who died before they were christened and if they hear a child's name, they will call and lead the child away into mischief.

The soucouyant *(top) Mama Dlo (below) and Papa Bois (left)*

The Caribbean climate is virtually ideal. Surrounded by sea, the islands enjoy an almost constantly warm temperature, even at night, and during the day the sun is tempered by the Trade Winds, cooling breezes that rise on the Atlantic. But at times, the benevolent ocean will deliver disaster in the form of a hurricane. These whirlwinds, accompanied by torrential rain, are immensely destructive. Land movement can cause chaos in the Eastern Caribbean, an area of tectonic activity where volcanoes occasionally blow and earthquakes strike.

HURRICANE SEASON
A traditional rhyme serves as a reminder of when hurricanes are most likely to strike: "June, too soon; July, stand by; September, remember; October, all over." Most hurricanes do, in fact, occur in the middle of September.

TRADE BY NAME
Although they were useful to merchant ships and used by sailors from the very first days of transatlantic travel, the Trade Winds are not named for their commercial value. The term was coined in the 16th century as "tread winds"—meaning directional winds.

The calm after the storm, but a wrecked boat sits offshore after a hurricane

Trade Winds These equatorial winds flow from a high pressure area in the mid-Atlantic to low pressure regions nearer the equator. They hit the Caribbean islands from the northeast, at an angle that varies through the year because of the earth's tilting. The Trade Winds reduce humidity, while bringing plenty of rain to the more mountainous islands. Known as *Les Alizes* on the French islands, the *Passaatwinden* on Dutch land, and *Brisas Aliseas* in the Spanish territories, the so-called "Christmas winds" blow most strongly in the winter months, bringing with them the balmiest temperatures.

Hurricanes Terrible damage can be inflicted by hurricanes, whose name is derived from the Carib language. They rise in the Atlantic, at the meeting point of the Trade Winds from both hemispheres (north of the equator in the summer). In a phenomenon known as the "coriolis effect," the warm, moist air rises and then condenses, releasing heat, falls and then rises again, strengthening the updraft until it begins to spiral. Immature hurricanes set off west-northwest, moving at around 12mph (19kph) and steadily building up size and power. The winds spiral inward around a vortex known as the "eye" (about 12 miles/19km across) and can reach sustained speeds of up to 105mph (170kph), with bursts of around 185mph (300kph). Extending up to 500 miles

(800km) across, hurricanes are immensely powerful; their effect is measured in atom bombs per second. They are identified by alternately male and female names.

All the Caribbean islands from Grenada northward lie in the hurricane zone and in recent years some have been very badly hit. Hurricane Gilbert swept through Jamaica and the Cayman Islands in 1988, and in 1989 Hurricane Hugo laid waste to Guadeloupe, St. Croix and Montserrat. 1995 brought Marilyn on the heels of Luis, both causing terrible destruction in St. Maarten, Anguilla and St. Thomas in the USVI. 1998's Georges wreaked havoc in the Dominican Republic and tore up Nevis, St. Kitts, Antigua, Puerto Rico and Haiti. Grenada and other islands were battered when Hurricanes Ivan and Jeanne swept through the region in 2005, and 2005 was the busiest hurricane season since records began.

Volcanoes The Eastern Caribbean is also an area of active volcanoes. This line of islands stretches in a curve from Saba to Grenada in the south, on the meeting point of the Atlantic and Caribbean tectonic plates. As the plates move slowly against each other, hot molten rock beneath them occasionally escapes in volcanic eruptions.

Volcanoes in the Eastern Caribbean all go by the name Soufrière, taken from the French word for sulfur because of the foul smell that they give out. The most active volcanoes are on St. Vincent, Guadeloupe and Martinique; these erupt about once every 100 years with lava flows and plumes of smoke 20,000ft (6,000m) high.

St. Lucia and Dominica experience less devastating "fumaroles," where the pressure is let off constantly and more steadily—though the heat and pressure in Dominica is enough to make a lake boil. There is also an active volcano in the Grenadines: Kick 'em Jenny is underwater at the moment, but is expected to reach the surface in the future. Galway's Soufrière in Montserrat became active in 1995, showering the south of the island with ash and lava and rendering large areas uninhabitable.

Earthquakes Another effect of living on the bridge of two tectonic plates are earthquakes, which may accompany major volcanic eruptions and cause land slippages.

The Soufrière "drive-in" volcano, St. Lucia

HOME SAFE HOME
Traditional Caribbean architecture was designed to cope with rare but severe climatic problems. Stone foundations gave a solid base during earthquakes, while a wooden upper story could wobble but survive in the windblasts of a hurricane. St. John's Cathedral in Antigua has been lined with wood to preserve it from the effects of hurricanes and earthquakes.

CAPTAIN BLIGH
The 18th-century mutiny on the *Bounty* has become a popular subject for films and books, but less well known is the reason for Captain Bligh's eventful voyage. He had been commissioned by the Society of West Indian Merchants to bring breadfruit plants to the West Indies from the South Pacific. Bligh's second attempt to transport the plants, in 1793 in the ship *Providence*, was more successful and he delivered the plants to botanical gardens around the Caribbean. Trees grown from cuttings of the original plants can still be seen in the St. Vincent Botanic Gardens. The ackee tree—*Blighia sapida*—is named for the captain, who brought it to the region from West Africa.

St. Vincent

St. Vincent is a fertile and beautiful island, from its cultivated valleys to the rain-forested slopes of its active volcano, Soufrière. Linked to Grenada by the 60-mile (100km) string of the Grenadines, it is usually considered as a starting point for yachting trips; however, its rugged east coast and fascinating Arawak settlement are worth seeing. There is also first-rate diving and snorkeling and hiking on trails as verdant as any in Hawaii.

The 110,000 Vincentians are mainly of African origin, the descendants of plantation slaves, but this was not always a plantation island. Like Dominica, St. Vincent was one of the last strongholds of the Carib people. Here, the local tribe, known as the Yellow Caribs, and escaped African slaves produced a race of Black Caribs, who held out against the colonists. In 1797 they were eventually defeated and their survivors were deported to Roatan, an island off Honduras. The British took over St. Vincent and built up a trade of sugar, cotton and arrowroot. Independence was gained in 1979, though St. Vincent remains within the British Commonwealth.

Agriculture still provides much of the island's living; exports include arrowroot starch, bananas and coconuts. St. Vincent is relatively undeveloped, with a small area of hotels in the southeast and a few other isolated spots.

The capital of St. Vincent and the Grenadines is **Kingstown**▶▶, a few streets of Georgian townhouses with cobbled, arched walkways set on a wide south-western bay. The town is fairly quiet, except around the Grenadines pier when ships come in and at the market on Halifax Street, the center of island gossip. Nearby are the Law Courts, where the St. Vincent Parliament sits, and the unusual neo-Gothic and Romanesque Roman Catholic church, which was built in 1823.

Away from the waterfront, the ground rises through outlying suburbs to the range of hills surrounding the town. In the northwest are the 20 acres (8ha) of the **St. Vincent Botanic Gardens**▶▶▶ (tel: 457 1003 *Open* daily), dating back to 1763. Here, species include the seal-ing wax palm, red hot cat tail and roucou, used as body-paint by the Carib tribes. On the heights to the southwest lies Fort Charlotte where, on a clear day, the view extends south to Grenada. Also here, within the botanical gardens, is the National Museum, with its collections of Amerindian relics.

Past the airport in the southeast nestles Villa Point, where restaurants and bars are set among the pretty tin-roofed villas on the waterfront, looking across a small stretch of water to Young Island. Inland are the fertile valleys where St. Vincent's market produce is grown and at Yambou, off the road to the town of Mesopotamia, Arawak **rock carvings**▶▶ date from before AD1000.

A journey up the west coast on the Leeward Highway reveals the West Indies at its most natural: small and simple villages filled with hordes of shouting school-children. There are rain forest trails in the **Buccament Valley**▶▶ and the hike up the Soufrière (3,865ft/1,178m) is a day's trip, best started from the Rabacca Dry River, north of Georgetown, or Richmond, north of Chateau-belair. Boats sail from Kingstown to the Falls of Baleine, a 60ft (18m) cascade into a rockpool at the island's northern tip, past the villages of the leeward shore.

The port at Kingstown is a picturesque place

UNDER SHELTER
It rains so regularly in the Windward Islands that the old streets were built with colonnades so that the market vendors could sell their wares under cover and people would be sheltered as they walked around the town. Where other islands had wooden houses (now often burned down), Kingstown has some particularly attractive stone arches and cobbles. Most modern buildings are made of concrete and topped with tin roofs.

FORT DUVERNETTE
Young Island is the nearest of the Grenadines to St. Vincent's shore and, beyond it, perched on its 200ft (60m) overgrown rock, is the defensive bastion that once protected the larger island's southern waters. Cannons dating from the 18th century are still at the ready, but these days only tourists are likely to invade the fort (via steps in the rockface), to enjoy the impressive views.

The Leeward Islands

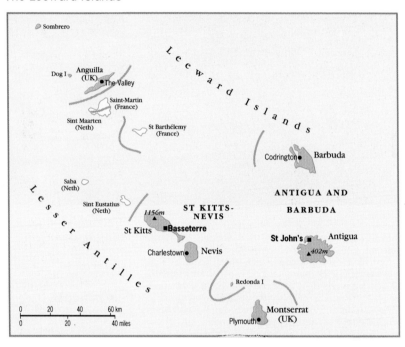

One of the Leeward islanders: a resident of Antigua

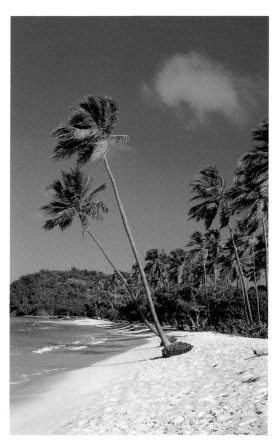

THE LEEWARD ISLANDS The English-speaking Leewards have maintained much of their small-island charm in the face of growing tourism. With a vast choice of beaches, friendly small towns and varied local customs, they stand in refreshing contrast to the bigger tourist destinations. Antigua is the most developed vacation island; Anguilla has developed quite quickly over the past few years and St. Kitts and Nevis have followed a policy of sustainable development. Poor Montserrat, which was developing its tourism slowly, has been stopped in its tracks by the eruption of its volcano. Two centuries ago the islands were isolated outposts and fast communications were essential. Now their remoteness is a selling point, and many visitors pay a lot of money to enjoy it, particularly on Anguilla and St. Kitts.

The six Leeward Islands (they were to the lee side of ships arriving from Europe) lie in two lines. To the west, Montserrat, Nevis and St. Kitts are the rain-forested peaks of a relatively young volcano chain (about 15 million years old). To their east are the protrusions of a much older range: Antigua, Barbuda and—beyond the French islands of St. Barts and Saint-Martin—Anguilla, the most northerly of the Lesser Antilles. Capped with coral limestone, the Lesser Antilles have some of the finest sand in the Caribbean.

The Leeward Islands

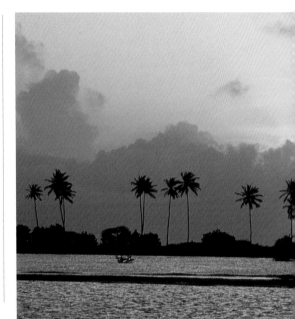

HISTORY The islands are connected by a common history, having been British colonies for many years, but most have now gone their own way. The islands of Antigua and Barbuda negotiated their full independence in the early 1980s and were soon followed by St. Kitts and Nevis, but they remain in the British Commonwealth. Montserrat and Anguilla are still British Overseas Territories.

British settlers first arrived at St. Kitts in 1623, but continual disputes over the island's possession took place between Britain and France right up until 1783. Using an army of slave laborers, the colonizers planted sugar cane frantically and became immensely wealthy. But when slavery was abolished in the British Empire in 1834, the Leeward Islands quickly went into decline. The freed slaves took to the land, dividing it into small individual plots and scraping a poor living from subsistence farming. Today you will still see subsistence farmers living on the Leeward Islands; their lifestyle is only gradually changing now after 150 years.

ISLAND LIFE Unfortunately, the Leeward Islands' economies are precarious and, despite the success of a few small industries, all depend to some extent on tourism. This has developed steadily over the past 20 years and in places it seems to have swamped local Caribbean life and traditions, which have all but disappeared in some parts. The more developed islands, Antigua and Anguilla, tend to have better restaurants, but a stroll around Nevis, or a visit to one of its rum stores, is more likely to give a taste of local life. Each island has its special points, whether it is rum-soaked rumbustiousness during Sailing Week (usually the last week of April) on Antigua, a glimpse of the planters' leisurely way of life amid historic surroundings on St. Kitts and Nevis, the marine reserve and wildlife of Barbuda or the deserted beaches of Anguilla. There are also good opportunities for hopping by boat and plane to other islands nearby.

The islanders are English-speakers (as they are on the nearby Dutch Windward Islands), but accents vary from island to island, as do the characteristics of their people. Distinct traces of Irish can be heard in the inflections and pronunciations of Anguillan and Montserratian islanders, which are not present in the accents of St. Kitts, Nevis and Antigua. While there is a certain reserve and politeness on Montserrat and Nevis, the people of Anguilla and Barbuda have a reputation for a proud and independent outlook. Nevertheless, all Leeward Islanders are known for their easy-going attitude, which is well expressed in the favorite Caribbean expression "no problem."

Coconut palm silhouettes in the calm of an Antiguan sunset

REMISSIONS
The economies of the Leeward Islands have traditionally depended on "remissions" from abroad. Since the sugar industry foundered, people have either cultivated small plots of land or traveled in search of work, sending some of their earnings home to their families. Many islanders worked on the digging of the "Ditch"— the Panama Canal—and in the Dominican Republic's cane fields at the turn of the century. Later there was a rush to the oil refineries of Aruba and Curaçao and in the 1950s and 1960s there was widespread emigration to Britain. Most emigration is now to the USA or Canada.

Anguilla

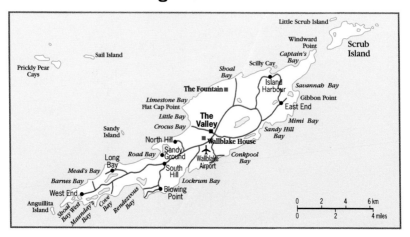

REBEL MARINE
You will soon come to know the sleek contours of boats made by Rebel Marine, an Anguillan boatyard. The gull-winged ferries that make the run from Blowing Point to Saint-Martin are made by them (as is the North Sound Express boat in the British Virgin Islands), and many others lie at anchor in Sandy Ground and around the island. The designs take traditional Anguillan lines (from a long tradition of boat-building) and adapt them to modern materials.

Only 20 minutes by ferry from Saint-Martin/Sint Maarten, Anguilla has deliberately turned its back on the duty-free shopping and cruise market and offers laid-back relaxation, plus some of the best restaurants and beaches in the Caribbean. There are about 30 tiny, secluded coves, snorkeling beaches and walking strands, all with fine sand washed by a clean turquoise sea. Anguilla has a string of luxurious accommodations, though it is possible to find cheaper options: The tourist office, The Valley (tel: 497 2759) can offer useful advice. There are no buses on the island, but taxis can be picked up at the airport, from the Blowing Point ferry dock, or from hotels. Just 16 miles (26km) long, the island is made up of coral limestone. Its flat land is covered in thick scrub, which is steadily being cleared for building. Anguilla is developing rapidly, but it is still a quiet place with little visual history and comparatively few "sights." Its chic and expensive hotels are a second home to film stars and executives seeking a retreat from the humdrum. (Those who are wanting nightlife and shopping can always sneak over to Sint Maarten.)

It may come as something of a surprise to learn that this peaceful island once had a revolution (albeit bloodless).

Lobsters: a specialty on the island

In the 1960s Anguilla became part of the Associated State of St. Kitts-Nevis-Anguilla, but its inhabitants objected to St. Kitts' prominent role (see panel). Anguilla was separated from the three-island state in 1971 and regained its status as a UK-dependent territory.

In the middle of the island, close to the airport, is the small capital, The Valley, where the administrative offices, banks, stores and the only hospital are all based. The other main settlements are Sandy Ground, the main port, and Island Harbour, a fishing village in the northeast. Near by is the Fountain, a cave used by the indigenous Arawak Indians, where carved faces are arranged to be lit by the sun in turn.

Beaches ring the island and most hotels have watersports facilities. On the north coast, near the western tip, **Barnes Bay▶▶** is a strip of sand backed with rocks and broad-leaved sea grape trees. Heading east, **Mead's Bay▶**, a curve of deep sand, has a lovely sunset view from the Malliouhana end. Calm and protected **Road Bay▶▶** harbors local boats and some larger ships and has a string of restaurants and bars. Just beyond Crocus Bay is **Little Bay▶▶▶**, access to which is by boat or by climbing down the cliff, and **Limestone Bay▶▶**. **Shoal Bay▶▶▶** has fine sand, a modest string of beach bars, watersports concessions and snorkeling offshore. On the north coast lies **Captain's Bay▶▶**, a half-moon of secluded sand (ask for directions and follow the coastline). On the south coast, past Blowing Point, is **Rendezvous Bay▶▶**, a mangrove and dune-backed walking strand with a clear view of Saint-Martin and an excellent bar like a shipwrecked galleon, The Dune. The moorish domes of the Cap Juluca Hotel (tel: 497 6666; www.capjaluca.com) dominate crescent-shaped **Maunday's Bay▶▶**; beyond here, **Shoal Bay West▶▶▶** is overlooked by the tall, white curves of the Cove Castles hotel villas (tel: 497 6801; www.covecastles.com). Sandy Island and Prickly Pear Cays have fine beaches and are good for a day's sailing trip: One departs from Island Harbour for the spit of land called Scilly Cay, famed for its grilled lobster and beach party atmosphere.

THE REVOLUTION
As Britain divested itself of Caribbean colonies in the 1960s, Anguilla was faced with independence and a marriage of convenience to St. Kitts and Nevis. The Anguillans rebelled. A few shots were fired and St. Kitts policemen were expelled from the island. As tension grew, the British sent a detachment of paratroopers in 1969—an "invasion" (welcomed by the Anguillans) that was later dubbed the "Bay of Piglets." Anguilla's rebels got their way and the link with St. Kitts was cut forever, but a satisfactory political solution was found only in 1982, when the island was eventually granted its own constitution, headed by a Council of Ministers and a House of Assembly.

Boon Point
Soldiers Bay   Beggars
                      Point
Dickenson Bay   •Cedar Grove   Long Island
Runaway   New
Bay   Winthorpes
         St John's Harbour •Barnes Hill   Maiden Island Great Bird Island
Fort   Cedar Valley   North Sound
Barrington   Golf Club
Hawksbill   VC Bird   Guiana Island
Bay   St John's   Parham
      Five   Int Harbour
      Islands   St Johnstone Airport
Fullerton   Crump Island
Point   Five Islands   •Potters   •Parham   Pelican Island
        Harbour   Indian Town Point
Pearns Point Jennings Golden   Seatons Willikies Devil's
                        Grove Antiguan Pares   Bridge
         172m▲   Pottery   Glanvilles Nonsuch
Lignumvitae Green   Freemans • Betty's Collins Dam Bay Green Island
Bay   Castle Hill Suckleys   Hope
      Bolans   All   Harmony Great Deep
Ffryés Point   Sweets Saints Potsworks Newfield Hall Bay
         402m▲   Dam   Freetown York Island
Dark Wood Boggy Peak   Liberta Bethesda St Philips
Beach Crab Shekerley Mts Rain 368m Monks Hill Fort Half Moon Bay
Hill   Urlings Forest Signal Hill Falmouth Willoughby Soldier Point
Johnson's Point   Bay
      Cades Bay   Old Road Falmouth English Harbour Town
                     Harbour Clarence House
              Carlisle Old Road Rendezvous Nelson's Dockyard
              Bay   Bluff   Bay   English Shirley Heights
                          Harbour Nanton
                                   Point

0   2   4   6 km
0 1   2   3   4 miles

Antigua and Barbuda

Contentment on an island cruise

The territory of Antigua and Barbuda actually consists of three islands: Antigua, the main island at 108sq miles (280sq km) with excellent beaches and most of the 66,000 population; Barbuda, a smaller, wooded island to the north with a population of 1,100 and excellent, undeveloped beaches; and Redonda, a small, uninhabited rocky islet lying 25 miles (40km) southwest of Antigua.

73

Pirate ships were once feared and avoided in the Caribbean's waters; now "pirate cruises" are popular tourist attractions

PLANTATION ESTATE
At Betty's Hope (tel: 462 1469. *Open* Tue–Sat 10–4. *Admission: donation*) you can see the layout of a typical Caribbean plantation estate. The windmill was placed high up not only to catch the wind, but also so that the cane juice could run downhill in a sluice to the boiling house. The estate house had the best position—for the view and so that the owners could watch the activity on the estate. There is a huge cistern because, on a dry island like Antigua, water collection was vital.

ANTIGUA The largest, the most popular and the most developed of the Leewards, Antigua has a mostly dry and flat landscape. Its foremost attractions are the superb beaches, the restored English Harbour historic area of Nelson's Dockyard, and Falmouth Harbour and its sailing facilities. English Harbour is also a hive of sailing activity during Race Week at the end of April every year.

Antigua is made of limestone coral, covered in grassy flatlands that rise steadily to the southwest. Two centuries ago the island was blanketed with sugar cane and ruins of the windmills in which the cane was crushed dot the countryside. The two main centers are the capital, St. John's, in the northwest, and English Harbour.

St. John's is a busy harbor town, particularly when a cruise ship is in dock. Founded in the early 18th century, it has attractive 19th-century buildings, with wooden gingerbread balconies. Some of the finest are in **Redcliffe Quay**▶ ▶, where restored warehouses and townhouses are now occupied by stores and cafés. The Old Court House of the island now houses the **Antigua and Barbuda Museum**▶ ▶ (tel: 462 1469; www.antiguamuseums.org. *Open* Mon–Thu 8.30–4, Fri 8.30–4, Sat 10–2. *Admission: donation*) with displays on Amerindian Antigua and the colonial past. **St. John's Cathedral**▶ ▶ is a towering building from 1848, close to the Recreation Ground, where international cricket matches have been hosted here since Antigua and Barbuda became independent on the 1st of November 1981. **St. John's Public Market**▶, south of town, is liveliest on Saturday mornings.

Antigua's main tourist areas are to the west of the capital on the beaches of Five Islands Peninsula and to the north on **Runaway** and **Dickenson Bays**▶ ▶. From here, the road follows the coastline north through chic residential areas and past secluded coves to VC Bird International Airport and the Cedar Valley Golf Club. In the eastern area of the island the coastline and sea are spectacular (but not suitable for bathing except in well-protected bays) and at Indian Town you can see the Devil's Bridge, an archway of rock carved out by the waves. The 200-year-old plantation estate of **Betty's Hope**▶ (see panel), to the west, has been restored, with a visitor center and a renovated windmill. In another windmill on the southeast coast is the **Harmony Hall**▶ ▶ gallery (tel: 460 4120; www.haramonyhall.com), selling good-quality Caribbean arts and crafts.

VIV RICHARDS
Antigua's greatest hero was captain of perhaps the strongest West Indies cricket team ever. Considered to be the world's finest batsman, he regularly destroyed the bowling of English, Australian, Indian and Pakistani teams. Born in 1952, Richards played for Antigua and Leeward Islands teams. He moved to Britain in 1974 to play for Somerset and in the same year played for the West Indies for the first time, becoming captain in 1984. Richards retired from international cricket in 1991 and was knighted by the Antiguan government in 1999.

An extraordinarily fertile and colorful marine life exists beneath the Caribbean waves. Corals grow like forests on the reefs and slopes, and hiding among them are weird and wonderful shellfish and crabs, while schools of tropical fish with exotic names and colors cruise by.

Corals, sponges and shellfish Corals are animals that grow in salt water shallow enough to be within the range of the sunlight. Of the 75 or so species in the Caribbean Sea, about ten account for nine-tenths of the growth. Perhaps the most familiar is the white brain coral, with a surface that resembles a human brain; other hard corals include staghorn, which grows like crusty deer antlers; elkhorn, with huge sloping branches; starlet coral, with polyps like teeth; and orange clump coral, which has a mass of tentacles. Gorgonians consist of sea fans, which face the tidal flow to sift nutrients, and sea whips, which blow like feathers in the tide.

Sponges and anemones add their own color and variety to the

marine world. Tube sponges can grow to 7ft (2m), in shades of orange, purple, pink and yellow, and the white cryptic sponge hides in crevices. Anemones look like intricate flowers, with many only open at night; those that emerge during the day will often snap back into the rock if the water around them is disturbed. Shrimps (visible in daylight) often live in conjunction with anemones—the banded coral shrimp has a striking red-and-white striped body.

Night-diving reveals another, self-contained, submarine society. Crabs and spiny lobsters come out for food, while starfish, some of which look like underwater plants, open up to feed in the dark. An octopus, squid or a tiny seahorse might be spotted—though their camouflage is excellent; the sea cucumber, by contrast, is easy

AQUARIUMS
For non-divers several aquariums in the Caribbean provide alternatives to viewing from glass-bottom boats. The Guadeloupe Aquarium is between Bas du Fort and Gosier and has well-marked displays of tropical fish from the Caribbean and elsewhere. On Curaçao the Sea Aquarium is in the Underwater Park, east of Willemstad. A spiral-shaped aquarium operates in the Parque Lenin, south of Havana, in Cuba. All aquariums charge an entry fee; prices vary, but they can be expensive.

to make out, resembling a mobile underwater hot dog. The biggest and best known of the molluscs (shell animals), which are also best seen at night, is the conch, known as the *lambi* in the French-speaking Caribbean. Lobsters migrate in their hundreds, like a herd of galloping horses.

There are a number of species to avoid when underwater: A touch from the fire coral can give a nasty sting, as can some jellyfish. Avoid the spiny black sea urchin at all costs—its spines cause agonizing wounds if they break off in your flesh.

Fish Around a thousand species of fish live in the Caribbean, many of them on the reefs, where there is plenty of food. Schools of angelfish and butterfly fish can be seen waving in the current; the four-eye butterfly fish has an imitation pair of eyes on its tail to confuse predators. Other species are dazzlingly beautiful—such as the queen angelfish, which is a luxurious shade of velvet-like blue and gold; and the yellow and black rock beauty. Many fish have names that describe their forms and habits. Damsel fish hide and lay their eggs in the reefs, grazing on algae, and striped sergeant majors defend their eggs aggressively. Grunts are named for the noise they make when alarmed, and surgeon fish have scalpel-sharp fins in their tails.

Wrasses are scavengers that school in a harem, with a single male. If the male is eaten, the biggest female simply switches sex and takes over his job. Parrotfish eat off the reef, biting the polyps and their rocky coral base and spitting out crunched-up coral.

Predatory fish include groupers (who have been known to use scuba divers as a smokescreen in the hope of a meal—other fish are also attracted by them and come out of their crevices) as well as snappers, one of the most numerous species. They school facing into the current, all moving in time and snapping at any food that passes by. Barracuda patrol in small groups or singly, often around a chosen rock. Larger fish such as blue marlin tend to live in deep water drop-offs, where they are pursued by big-game fishing boats (see page 202).

Orange clown fish (top)

EATING HABITS
The dentist or cleaner shrimp cleans the teeth of other, larger fish, thereby getting food for itself. The sponge crab takes small lumps of sponge to use as camouflage and when it fails to find food, it takes the sponge off its back and eats it. The remora, or sucker fish, is a long, thin fish that attaches itself to a larger fish, such as a shark, and feeds off the remains of its meal.

75

CORAL CLAIMS
In 1726 the French naturalist Jean André Peyssonnel declared to the Paris Academy of Sciences that coral reefs were made up of living animals, not marine shrubs, as was generally thought. He was ridiculed and had to live out his life as a scientist in exile in Guadeloupe—and though he was proved right during his lifetime, Peyssonnel received no credit.

The angelfish (above left) is one of the prettiest in the Caribbean waters

Barbuda

THE FRIGATEBIRD COLONY

The crooked wingspan and forked tail of the huge, black frigatebird is easy to recognize. Its most surprising feature is the male's gullet, a bright red balloon blown to the size of a basketball during display. Although it can be seen on Barbuda, it also flies to the other islands to feed, traveling at up to 90mph (145kph). It even attacks other birds on the wing for food, swooping in from above, grabbing a tail or leg, and shaking the victim until it drops its meal. Barbuda's frigatebird sanctuary is well worth a visit; the birds soar high above it, returning to the mangroves to nest in large colonies. Located on the north end of the Codrington Lagoon, the sanctuary is only accessible by boat and so can only be visited during daylight hours; you'll have to hire a local person to take you there.

The hilly southwest of Antigua has excellent beaches, fine views from Green Castle Hill and a ring of stones thought by some to be ancient megaliths. Beneath Boggy Peak (at 1,319ft/347m the highest point of the island), Old Road, now a small village, was the site of Antigua's first European settlement in 1632. Nearby Fig Tree Hill is a lush valley covered with large, shiny "elephant ear" leaves and bananas, an example of vegetation more usual on the larger Windward Islands to the south.

In the southeast are the fortifications erected by British colonists when Antigua was at the height of its strategic and economic importance. Opposite Falmouth Harbour towers Monks Hill Fort, a refuge for women, children and animals in case of attack. Beyond it are English Harbour and **Nelson's Dockyard**►►► (see opposite), which faces Clarence House, built in 1787 for the future King William IV, who was posted to Antigua by the Royal Navy. The dockyard is the centerpiece of the Nelson's Dockyard National Park (tel: 460 1379; www.antiguamuseums.org. *Open* daily 8–6. *Admission: moderate*), extending above the harbor to **Shirley Heights**►►, a series of Georgian barrack buildings and gun emplacements built in the 1780s against the French. Here the **Dow's Hill Interpretation Centre**►► (tel: 460 2777. *Open* Mon–Sat 9–5, Sun 8.30–4.30. *Admission: moderate*) has a multimedia show of Antiguan history, from Indian settlement through Columbus and the colonial era, to the present day.

BARBUDA Lying 30 miles (48km) to the north of Antigua, Barbuda is one of the few undeveloped Caribbean islands. Like Antigua, with which it was politically merged in 1860, it is all coral limestone and has glorious beaches. Otherwise, its 60sq miles (154sq km) are covered in scrub, where goats, donkeys and wild boar roam. The only town is Codrington, named for the family who owned the island and used it as a private ranch for 200 years before its incorporation into Antiguan territory. (When Antigua began negotiations for independence from Britain, it was the proud Barbudans who objected, calling for more governing powers of their own.) Sights include the **frigatebird sanctuary**►►► (see panel; tel: 460 0081. *Open* Mon–Sat 8–5. *Admission: inexpensive*), caves in the northeast, with Indian rock carvings, and River Fort, which is a Martello tower on the south coast.

Inventive headgear on one of the streets in Codrington, Barbuda's only town

Nelson's Dockyard is as active today as it was 200 years ago, when English Harbour was the most important naval base in the area. But in place of whistles and cannon blasts, there is now a peaceful atmosphere. Preparations may occasionally be as feverish as they were during the 18th-century wars, but today's sailors are more likely to be doing battle in yacht races.

The pillars of the old Boat House and Sail Loft, where the sails were laid out for repair.

77

Nelson's Dockyard is the best-preserved colonial ship-yard in the Caribbean, restored and rejuvenated into one of its top sailing destinations. Covered in bougainvillaea and hibiscus, the beautiful old stone warehouses contain accommodations, bars, galleries and a museum; but life still centers on the harbor, where boats line the wharves.

Tucked into the recesses of a deep and sinuous bay, the dockyard was first developed in 1725 as a victualing and repair station. Ships sheltered here during hurricanes and could be careened (beached on their sides) to be cleaned. Eventually the dockyard became one of the most important stations in the British Caribbean and the massive fortifications of Shirley Heights were built in order to defend it.

The dockyard's first building is the old Pitch and Tar Store (pitch was used to waterproof ships' hulls), now housing the Admiral's Inn, a small hotel whose restaurant and bar is *the* spot for the yachting set. Next door are the pillars of the old Boat House and Sail Loft (the building has lost its upper story), where ships' sails were laid out for repair. A museum in the Naval Officer's House (*Open* daily), across the way, has been restored and has excellent hands-on exhibits, maps and model ships from the dockyard's heyday. Next door is the Old Copper and Lumber Store, where sheet metal and wood were kept and able seamen slept in upstairs dormitories; today the old store houses a comfortable hotel. In September 1998, Hurricane Georges seriously damaged the Dockyard seawall and the old officers' quarters building. A multi-million dollar restoration of the seawall around the complex includes a new yacht basin.

NELSON
It is unlikely that Horatio Nelson would ever have consented to give his name to the dockyard. The famous British admiral served here between 1784 and 1787 while he was captain of HMS *Boreas*—and he hated it, considering the dockyard itself a "vile spot." He was lonely and had the unpleasant job of putting a stop to unofficial trading between the Leeward Islanders and ships from the young American nation. At one point Nelson was confined to ship for eight weeks, knowing that if he set foot ashore he would be arrested by the resentful planters. He returned to the Caribbean only once, for 24 hours in 1805, when he was searching for the French Admiral Villeneuve in the chase that culminated in the Battle of Trafalgar.

Hibiscus in bloom

North West Bluff
Little Redonda
Hell's Gate
403m
Rendezvous Bay
Silver Hill
Little Bay
Yellow Hole
Carr's Bay
Marguerita Bay
Davy Hill
Collins
Old Norwood
Cudjoehead
St John's
St Peter's
Judy Piece
Soldier Ghaut
Bottomless Ghaut
Lime Kiln Bay
740m
Trant's Bay
Katy Hill
Trant's
Blackburne Airport
Centre Hills
Salem
Farm
Spanish Pt
Frith
Belham
Windy Hill
Bethel
Old Road Bay
Iles Bay
Molyneux
Bramble
Montserrat Volcano Observatory
Dyer's
Harris
Tuitt's
Streatham
Brandsby Point
St George's Hill
Lee's
Long Ground
Fort Ghaut
Soufrière Hills
915m
Plymouth
Chances Peak
Sugar Bay
Aymer's Ghaut
Galway's
Roche's Bluff
Gingoes Ghaut
Soufrière
Trials
White
Dry Ghaut
St Patrick's
Germans Bay
Morris
Old Fort Point

0 1 2 km
0 1 mile

Approx area covered by ash

The Montserratian smile

Montserrat

The Caribbean's very own self-styled Emerald Isle, Montserrat's lush green hills and fertile valleys, volcanic sand beaches and tranquil bays once offered discerning visitors one of the most charming retreats in the region until the Soufrière Hills volcano rumbled into action in 1995. Since then, volcanic eruptions and lava flows have transformed about two-thirds of the 40sq mile (100sq km) island into an uninhabitable danger zone. However, this activity has quietened down considerably, and the Montserratians are now trying to rebuild their low-key tourist industry by attracting day trippers from Antigua and visitors who fancy a close-up look at a live volcano.

Sighted in 1493 by Christopher Columbus and named by him after an abbey in the mountains of Spain, Montserrat is the most southerly of the Leeward Islands. It was originally settled, in the 17th century, by the descendants of Irish catholics, refugees from Protestant persecution of St. Kitts. Although Montserrat remains a British Overseas Territory, the Irish gave it its nickname and also contributed elements of Irish style: St. Patrick's Day is celebrated and the island's stamps feature an Irish harp.

Tragically, much of Montserrat's emerald green has been replaced by ash gray. In the summer of 1995, after over 350 years of dormancy, Soufrière Hills began erupting on the southern half of the island. A major fall of ash landed on the capital town of Plymouth, on the southwest coast, in August of that year and the town was evacuated. By October 1995, a dome of flowing lava could be seen protruding from the crater. There was erratic volcanic activity until June 1997, when the dome collapsed, causing a high-speed pyroclastic flow that leveled seven villages, destroying over 200 homes and killing 19 people. This lava flow also forced the closure of the airport runway and emitted so much ash that people were forced to wear ash masks. Two months later, a shower of red-hot rocks landed on Plymouth, now an ash-covered ruin.

As well as destroying Plymouth and many other smaller towns and villages, the volcano has ruined or rendered inaccessible several of the island's main tourist attractions, including the Great Alps Waterfall and Galway's Soufrière. However, it has created a new attraction in the form of the **Montserrat Volcano Observatory**▶▶ (tel: 491 5647; www,mvo.ms. *Open* Mon–Fri 8.30–4.30, tours Tue and Thu 3.15. *Admission: inexpensive*), which houses scientists monitoring the island's volcanic activity. Visitors can tour the observatory with a guide and watch videos of volcanic action. Other activities include boat rides with views of Plymouth and other ruined settlements; sport fishing; and even hiking and birdwatching in the Silver and Centre Hills with the Montserrat Forest Rangers (see panel).

At present Montserrat's entire population (dramatically reduced from 11,000 prior to the 1995 eruptions down to 4,000) is confined to the northern portion of the island and this is where visitors will find the handful of hotels, restaurants and other businesses ready and willing to serve them. (Two rather optimistic hotels even have conference facilities.) Although Montserrat is in no position to offer the classic sun and sand Caribbean vacation experience, it is by no means inaccessible and it might even be argued that those still living there deserve as many visitors—and dollars—as they can handle.

HELICOPTER FLIGHTS
There are regular helicopter flights from Antigua departing Mon–Tue, Thu–Fri 8am, 10am, 5pm; Sat 8am and 5pm; flights depart from Montserrat 30 minutes later. The journey takes about 20 minutes. A ferry service also operates between the two islands. The trip takes about an hour, departing Antigua at 6.30am and 4pm daily except Sun. Return trips are scheduled for about 90 minutes after arrival on Montserrat.

For more information, contact Montserrat Aviation Services (tel: 491 2362/2533, fax: 491 2362); in Antigua, contact Carib World Travel (tel: 480 2999, fax: 480 2995) or Carib Aviation at VC Bird International Airport (tel: 462 2522). For updates on volcanic activity and listing of available accommodations, the Montserrat Tourist Board can be reached on 491 2230/8730.

Lush vegetation typical of Montserrat

Music is played everywhere in the Caribbean: on buses, on vast personal stereos, in bars and clubs, and at Carnival, when whole islands stop work to dance in the streets. West Indians will tune almost anything to make music: wheel hubs, bamboo poles and even cheese graters, but the most famous instrument of all is the steel drum, or "pan," invented in Trinidad about 60 years ago.

80

Almost every Caribbean island has its own unique musical style; all of them have a strong rhythm that irresistibly inspires dancing. Particular styles vary from island to island, but the movement always centers around the hips and pelvis.

Caribbean music also incorporates a tradition of social comment. The Calypsonians of Trinidad are the most famous satirists and many other styles have carried messages of protest: Ska was a shout from the poor ghettos of Kingston in Jamaica in the 1950s, and even in Cuba, where dissent is not traditionally tolerated, *trova* songs have been known to question the integrity of party members and government officials.

Reggae and soca The British Caribbean has two main rhythms: The best known is, of course, reggae from Jamaica. This has developed full circle since Bob Marley popularized it in the 1970s, becoming dancehall in the 1980s to culture reggae in the 1990s and influenced by rap in the last few years. Soca, which originated in Trinidad, is played in the southeastern Caribbean. Soca (a contraction of "soul-calypso") consists of a fast and hard rhythm with a double beat.

Salsa and merengue Salsa comes from Puerto Rico and Cuba (other Cuban rhythms include the rumba and the cha-cha-cha). This is a bustling, Latin rhythm; dancing partners face one another as if

FESTIVALS
A biennial World Steel Band Music Festival takes place in Trinidad in October and the biannual Pan Jazz, a mix of steel band music and jazz, is held in November in even years. Other music festivals include Cuba's December Jazz Festival, St. Lucia's Jazz Festival in May, Jamaica's Reggae Sunsplash in February and, in July, the Merengue Festival in Santo Domingo, in the Dominican Republic. The Barbados Jazz Festival takes place in January.

Transforming a steel drum into a musical instrument

they were waltzing, while their legs move in a subtly sensual movement. Merengue is another hip-swinging Latin rhythm from the Dominican Republic.

Zouk and compas The French islands of Martinique and Guadeloupe have produced their own rhythm with a double beat and a very quick tempo, zouk, whose songs have French Créole lyrics. In Haiti, compas is another French-inspired, raw rhythm.

Steel pans The steel band, whose sound has come to represent the whole Caribbean, was invented in Trinidad during World War II. It started in the back streets of Port of Spain, where the discarded oil drums of Trinidad's oil industry were beaten, tuned and turned into musical instruments. Initially pan was regarded suspiciously by the authorities, partly because the yards where the music developed were the hangouts of ghetto gangs. But its popularity grew and soon pan replaced "tamboo bamboo" (musical bamboo poles) as the music of Carnival.

Steel pan lids are bashed out in a bowl and given a number of flat surfaces to produce different notes. There are five different ranges in the pan orchestra. Bass pan players have nine full-size drums. Cello pan players have three pans which are cut down to three-quarter size, each having seven notes. Guitar pans and double second pans both come in pairs, playing notes in the middle range (the guitar pan plays chords, while the double second takes the melody). Tenor pans, or "ping pongs," are the lead instruments in the orchestra and the highest in the range. They have 30 notes, covering a two-and-a-half octave range.

A steel band has as many as 120 players. Not only is the noise impressive (a symphony of pings, clangs and bongs that combine into a coherent sound) but the energetic drummers are also a form of sheer entertainment in themselves.

Pan yards play all year round, though the best time to see them at work is during the run-up to Carnival at the beginning of the year. Steel bands with colorful names—"Desperadoes," "Renegades" and "Invaders" —have nowadays been superseded by soca as the main music of Carnival, but they still play at Jouvert, the parade which takes place on the Monday of Carnival week.

A musician from the Dominican Republic

INDEPENDENCE

Ever since St. Kitts and Nevis joined forces to achieve independence from Britain, the Nevisians have in turn contemplated independence from St. Kitts. In 1998, a referendum narrowly failed to return the two-thirds majority required to sever the twin-island nations' individual parts. However, many Nevisians still believe they should go it alone, though it is unlikely St. Kitts will want them to do so.

ALEXANDER HAMILTON

Nevis's most famous son is Alexander Hamilton, who is commemorated in the museum set in his former home in Charlestown. Born in 1755, he lived here for the first five years of his life, until his mother moved to St. Croix (now one of the US Virgin Islands). Impressed by the wealth of merchants on St. Thomas, he described them as "wheeling their gold through the streets in wheelbarrows." Hamilton moved to North America, where he fought in the Revolutionary War as George Washington's aide and was instrumental in establishing the American Constitution, becoming the first Secretary of the Treasury. Known as the Little Lion, because he was a short man with a fierce temper, Hamilton died in a duel in 1804.

Nevis

The small volcanic island of Nevis lies between St. Kitts, across a strait called the Narrows, and Montserrat. It is almost circular—just 5.5 miles by 8 miles (9 by 13km)—and rises to a central peak of 3,232ft (985m). A semi-permanent wreath of clouds on the summit reminded early travelers of snow and inspired the name Nuestra Señora de la Nieves—Our Lady of the Snows. Nowadays, life for the 10,000 Nevisians is pretty gentle and the grandeur of the island's past—when it was known as the "Queen of the Caribbees"—has pretty well disappeared; but the island is proud of its beautifully restored plantation houses, which is where many visitors stay. The atmosphere of the island has changed with the arrival of a large beach hotel, but it still has a certain regal calm and an evening stroll along its lit walkways, while the air rings to the singing of tree frogs and flashes with fireflies, is an unforgettable experience.

Nevis is politically attached to St. Kitts (see panel) but its personality is very different. Visitors to Nevis enjoy the peace and quiet, the hammocks for snoozing and lobsterbakes on palm-fringed beaches. The island's capital is **Charlestown▶▶**, a small collection of stone and timberframe houses laid out irregularly on the leeward coast. Except on market days (Monday and Saturday morning) and when the ferry arrives from St. Kitts, the town is pretty quiet. Inland from the waterfront is Memorial Square, a triangular park overlooked by banks and stores. Nearby are the Court House and Library and a small tourist office. At the northern end of the town is the **Museum of Nevis History▶▶** (tel: 469 5786; www.nevis-nhcs.org. *Open* Mon–Fri 9–4, Sat 9–12. *Admission: inexpensive*), set in a townhouse (see panel), in which the Nevis Assembly conducts its business four times a year.

North of Charlestown, **Pinney's Beach▶▶▶** is the island's best beach: a 3-mile (5km) strip of golden sand backed with tall palms, with views across the Narrows to St. Kitts. The island's first settlement of 80 planters, who

Beach bar with palm-thatched parasols

arrived from St. Kitts in 1628, was situated here, until it was tipped into the sea by an earthquake. It is now the site of the Four Seasons Hotel, with its 18-hole golf course. The circular island road passes other good beaches en route to Nevis's airport (Oualie Beach is lovely, as is Lover's Lane Beach) and the only other town, Newcastle.

To the south of Charlestown are the ruins of **Fort Charles▶**, the island's primary defense in colonial times; nearby is the **Bath Estate▶** with a plantation house built in 1778. This was once a high-class hotel but is now surrounded by 15 acres (6ha) of land designated as a nature area (www.nevis-nhcs.org).

A little farther down the road, the **Nelson Museum▶** (tel: 469 0408; www.nevis-nhcs.org. *Open* Mon–Fri 9–4, Sat 9–12. *Admission: inexpensive*), displays mementoes and artifacts from the Admiral's life, including letters and pictures. At **Fig Tree Church▶**, on the road east of Charlestown, you can see a copy of the official register of Horatio Nelson's marriage to Nevisian Fanny Nisbet on March 11, 1787, during a moment off from his lonely duties around the Leeward Islands. Look for the right turn to the Montpelier Estate, where Nelson and Fanny were married. Down the lane, the **Botanical Garden of Nevis▶▶** (tel: 469 3509; www.botanicalgardensnevis.org. *Open* Mon–Sat 8.30–4.30. *Admission: moderate*) covers seven beautifully landscaped acres (3ha). From here you pass into the less populous eastern parts, where abandoned plantations are now moldering ruins. However, several gracious plantation house hotels survive, such as the Montpelier Plantation Inn (tel: 469 3462) and the Hermitage Plantation (tel: 469 3477), both serving lunch and dinner to non-residents. The tourist office in Charlestown and the tourist boards can supply details of other plantation houses (see **Travel Facts**).

A deserted windmill stands as a reminder of colonial wealth

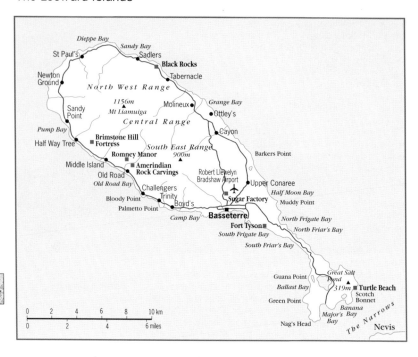

Dieppe Bay
Sandy Bay
St Paul's
Sadlers
Black Rocks
Newton
Ground
Tabernacle
North West Range
1156m
Molineux
Grange Bay
Sandy
Point
Mt Liamuiga
Ottley's
Central Range
Pump Bay
Cayon
Half Way Tree
Brimstone Hill
Fortress
South East Range
Romney Manor
900m
Barkers Point
Middle Island
Amerindian
Rock Carvings
Robert Llewelyn
Bradshaw Airport
Old Road
Old Road Bay
Challengers
Upper Conaree
Half Moon Bay
Bloody Point
Trinity
Boyd's
Sugar Factory
Muddy Point
Palmetto Point
Camp Bay
Basseterre
North Frigate Bay
Fort Tyson
North Friar's Bay
South Frigate Bay
South Friar's Bay
Guana Point
Great Salt
Pond
Ballast Bay
319m
Turtle Beach
Scotch
Green Point
Bonnet
Banana
Major's Bay
Bay
The Narrows
Nag's Head
Nevis

0 2 4 6 8 10 km
0 2 4 6 miles

84

St. Kitts (St. Christopher)

Looking towards Nevis from Timothy Hill, St. Kitts

Two centuries ago, most of the West Indies looked like St. Kitts, with vast tracts of bright green sugar cane swaying in the breeze and estate houses standing aloof in colonial elegance. Many of these houses have been preserved, along with an atmosphere so English that it seems natural to play croquet and take afternoon tea. But the modern age has caught up with St. Kitts, in the form of beach tourism. The island's southeastern peninsula, which has the best golden sand beaches, has been set aside for development and the tourist race is on—although it remains relatively low-key for the time being.

St. Kitts is larger and livelier than its sister Nevis, appealing to a more active crowd. Nevis is just a few miles to the south and the Dutch island of St. Eustatius 5 miles (8km) to the north. Measuring around 68sq miles (176sq km), St. Kitts is shaped vaguely like a paddle, with forest-clad mountains and an old volcanic crater occupying its blade. In the northwest the highest peak, the impressive 3,793ft (1,156m) Mount Liamuiga, is believed to take its name from the indigenous Indian name for the island.

St. Kitts is an informal version of the island's original European name, St. Christopher, given by Columbus on his second voyage in 1493. Historically, this was the "Mother Colony" of the West Indies—the first island in the Eastern Caribbean to be settled successfully by Europeans, in 1623. British and French colonists helped each other to establish a foothold in hostile Indian and Spanish territory, before sending colonizers to other islands. Using indentured workers and slaves, they turned St. Kitts into a rich plantation island. They also began to fight over it, as they were to do for centuries afterward. For proof of the bitterness of their battle, you need only visit Brimstone Hill, one of the biggest forts in the Caribbean (see page 87). An early French Governor of the island was de Poincy, whose name is remembered in the poinciana, a tree that grows all over the Caribbean islands. Together with Nevis, St. Kitts became independent in September 1983. There are 35,000 Kittitians, many working in agriculture or tourism.

Basseterre▶▶, the island's capital, was built on the protected Caribbean coast. Its name is one of the few remaining vestiges of the island's French heritage—unfortunately its French buildings were all destroyed in fires. However, there are attractive British colonial timber-frame and stone buildings around the center, some of which are cafés and restaurants. The Port Zante waterfront complex has been developed with stores, a marina and a new cruise ship terminal. Just behind here is the original town center, the Circus▶▶, an open traffic circle (roundabout) overlooked by stone buildings with elegant balconies, a colonial clocktower, the Berkeley Memorial is at its center. Independence Square▶▶, nearby is an open park with a fountain and palm trees.

The square is surrounded by elegant townhouses, one of which contains the splendid Spencer Cameron Art Gallery▶▶ (10 Independence Square, tel: 465 1617; www.stkittsart.com) displaying local and expatriate Caribbean works of art, and the Catholic Cathedral of the Immaculate Conception, with its twin spires and a magnificent rose window. On Cayon Street stands the Anglican St. George's Church, built of brown stone in traditional English parish church style. The St. Kitts Tourist Board has its office in Pelican Mall, just down from the new waterfront buildings.

85

Rawlins Plantation is one of a number of hotels in St. Kitts that are set in former sugar estate houses

The Black Rocks make an ideal spot for fishing

The main tourist area on St. Kitts is southeast of Basseterre. There are accommodations, a golf course and a popular beach in **Frigate Bay▶▶**, while **Friar's Bay▶▶▶**, over the next hill, has a marvelous beach of soft golden sand, which gets busy as soon as cruise ships arrive. The rollercoaster peninsular road leads up and down hill and past the salt ponds, which used to form common ground in the days of joint English and French occupation, to the southern beaches, where there is a beach bar and superb views across the narrows to Nevis.

Northwest of the capital, the road emerges into sugar cane country, which is planted on the coastal flats beneath the central mountain range. A circular road follows the coast, touching all the small Kittitian villages; it can be driven comfortably in a day. A walk into the rain forest on the mountain can be arranged by tour operators.

Old Road Bay▶ marks the site of the first British settlement and was the capital until 1727. Amerindian **rock carvings▶▶** can be seen on the Wingfield Estate, nearby. Romney Manor, a 17th-century great house set in tropical gardens, is the home of **Caribelle Batik▶▶**, a store selling silk-screened prints and clothes, where you can watch local women practicing the art of batik. At Middle Island is the **grave of Thomas Warner▶**, who led the successful settlement in 1623. From here the road soon passes under the huge defenses of **Brimstone Hill▶▶▶** (tel: 465 2609; www.brimstonehillfortress.org. *Open* daily 9.30–5.30. *Admission: moderate.* See opposite).

Around the northern tip of the island the **Black Rocks▶▶** are a curious formation of volcanic lava; from here the road leads south along the wild Atlantic coast, passing through quiet villages and returning to Basseterre via the airport and the **sugar cane factory▶▶**, which is open to visitors between January and June.

Huge forts still tower over many Caribbean settlements as monuments to an era when imperial fleets and armies were sent to defend their valuable territories. Two centuries ago the Caribbean was a hardship posting, beset by disease, and these massive bastions recall a time of violence and instability, when loud drum rolls and frantic whistle blasts would herald urgent preparations for war.

Building and maintaining a fort the size of Brimstone Hill, on St. Kitts, which could hold over 1,000 troops, involved a complex operation. Every stone had to be dragged up to the summit to create the huge structure's bastions and ramparts, inner stronghold, parade ground, barracks, cookhouses and hospital.

Brimstone Hill (named for the satanic whiffs of sulfur from a nearby volcanic vent) took 100 years to build and was occupied by both British and French during the long 18th-century wars. In 1782 it faced its severest test when it was attacked by 8,000 French troops. The defenders, who held out for a month, were bombarded so heavily that only two rooms in the fort were left undamaged. When they eventually surrendered, the soldiers were allowed to march out with colors flying as a tribute to their bravery. A museum in Fort George, the central bastion, has exhibits explaining the history of St. Kitts and the fortress, and the store has a video presentation.

Other forts On Antigua, the hills around English Harbour, an important link in the chain of British defenses, are cluttered with ramparts and barracks, described at the Dow's Hill Interpretation Centre.

Puerto Rico's two bastions overlook the approaches to San Juan, itself surrounded by walls 33ft (10m) thick. On the point stands San Felipe del Morro, with its 100ft (30m) ramparts and a maze of tunnels; at the other end of Old San Juan is the imposing 17th century Fuerte San Cristobal, built so each of the outer bastions had to be captured before the citadel could be taken.

The most impressive Caribbean fort is Haiti's Citadelle. Its walls are over 100ft (30m) high and 30ft (9m) thick. However, thousands died building it.

CANNONS
Cannons litter the Caribbean islands, some abandoned in the forts, others put to good use, buried upright in the ground at the corners of buildings to protect them from passing truck wheels. On the British islands many cannons are printed with the cypher of King George III, a crown superimposed over the letters GR (George Rex). A small arrow can often be seen, stamped into the metal—the symbol used by naval stores.

87

A cannon at Brimstone Hill fortress covers the northern approaches from St. Eustatius

The Virgin Islands

Tranquil touring among the Virgin Islands by yacht

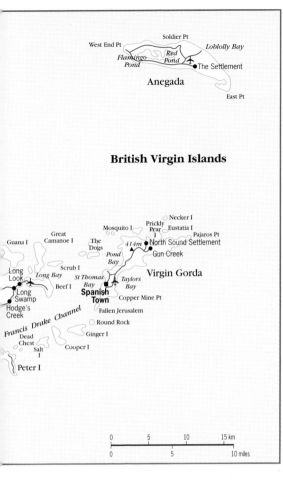

West End Pt | Soldier Pt | Loblolly Bay
Flamingo Pond | Red Pond | The Settlement
Anegada
East Pt

British Virgin Islands

Guana I | Great Camanoe I | The Dogs | Mosquito I | Prickly Pear I | Necker I | Eustatia I | Pajaros Pt
Long Look | Long Bay | Scrub I | St Thomas Bay | Pond Bay | 414m | North Sound Settlement | Gun Creek
Long Swamp | Beef I | **Spanish Town** | Taylors Bay | **Virgin Gorda**
Hodge's Creek | *Francis Drake Channel* | Copper Mine Pt
Dead Chest I | Fallen Jerusalem
Salt I | Round Rock
Cooper I | Ginger I
Peter I

0   5   10   15 km
0   5   10 miles

THE VIRGIN ISLANDS In mood and style, the US and British Virgin Islands (BVI) are worlds apart. The British islands are quieter and less developed, with secluded and isolated bays, and beaches and scattered cays ideal for sailing—islanders have an old-world reserve and courtesy. The US islands of St. Thomas and St. Croix have more in the way of attractions and entertainment. With sailing and watersports almost a way of life, these prosperous and sophisticated islands are ideal for those who don't intend to stray too far from the beach. For something more laid back, visitors gravitate to St. John or the BVI, where Tortola is less crowded and largely caters to yachts.

Scattered over an expanse of incomparably blue sea, the Virgin Islands are, with the exception of Anegada, steep and green, being the peaks of a submerged chain of volcanoes. Just under half the 90 or so islands are a British Overseas Territory; the rest are "an unincorporated territory of the USA." In the west are the three main United States Virgin Islands (USVI): St. Thomas and St. John with St. Croix lying 40 miles (64.5km) to the south. Sprinkled to the east, the British Virgin Islands are smaller and more numerous: The largest are Tortola and Virgin Gorda.

The Virgin Islands

A deserted sugar mill

THE DANISH IN THE CARIBBEAN

The Danes settled St. Thomas in 1665, encouraging its use as a trading base by declaring it a free port. They moved on to St. John in 1717 and St. Croix in 1733 and planted them entirely with sugar cane, bringing in slaves to work the fields. The Danes were the first to ban the slave trade, in 1792, but slavery itself continued on the islands until 1848, when the governor went against his king's orders and declared emancipation.

In the USVI, where people work at resorts on land once owned by their forebears, there is great disparity between rich and poor, and some resentment toward American immigrants and tourists. In the BVI people tend to own the land. There is virtually no shopping or nightlife here; on Tortola and Virgin Gorda no hotels are taller than a palm tree and most are owned by locals or expatriates. The USVI are for visitors who want a bustling environment; the BVI are for sailors and those who want to escape the crowds.

HISTORY The Virgin Islands were given their name by Columbus when he sailed among them on his second voyage of exploration. He compared the islands to the 11,000 beautiful followers of St. Ursula, who according to legend were killed by Huns on a pilgrimage to Cologne. For many years, pirates roamed the islands' shores, waiting for ships to plunder and refitting their vessels in hidden coves. Charlotte Amalie, on St. Thomas, became a busy marketplace for the pirates' captured goods.

The USVI were owned for centuries by Denmark, but not much remains of Danish influence except in street and town names such as Charlotte Amalie, Christiansted and Dronningens Gade (Charlotte Amalie's main street); the Dutch influence can be seen in the islands' many red-roofed buildings. The islands were bought by the US in 1917 for $25 million.

Meanwhile the BVI remained barren backwaters, planted while the going was good, but soon falling back into obscurity. At one point the British Government considered selling these islands to America as well. It never happened, but the pull to the US is still strong. The BVI have adopted the US dollar as their currency and many islanders move to find work on St. Thomas.

ISLAND LIFE Today, the USVI offer all the expected American comforts and conveniences, but with a tropical setting and lilting Caribbean accent. The banks are American, as are the fast food joints, the currency, the supermarkets and the baseball. St. Thomas and St. John are geographically close, but in character they could not be further apart. St. Thomas is overdeveloped and crowded (particularly when cruise ships dock), but has great shopping in Charlotte Amalie, as well as good bars and restaurants. St. John, just a 20-minute ferry ride away, is quiet and undeveloped. About two-thirds of it is undisturbed jungle, protected by its National Park status. There are, nevertheless, a number of places to stay in Cruz Bay and at Coral Bay in the East End. The third island, and the largest of the Virgin Islands, is St. Croix, which has a good variety of beach hotels, restaurants and interesting town buildings in Christiansted and Frederiksted. St. Croix's first casino opened late in 1998, and there are a couple of good golf courses.

By comparison, the pace of life on the British islands is slow and peaceful. For every 15 people who travel to the USVI on vacation, the BVI get one. Of the BVI's 150,000 or so visitors a year, three-quarters come from the US—and most come to sail, without even booking into a hotel. The BVI are not about discos, high-rise hotels, fast food and casinos. They are about superb beaches, many only accessible from the sea, and excellent bars. While the USVI have gone for numbers, the BVI target bank rolls, so the islands are expensive. Tortola is the hub of BVI yachting and from here there is access by ferry to many other islands, including tranquil Jost van Dyke or Virgin Gorda, with its top-rank accommodations, secluded beaches and offshore cays. Like the pirates of yore, you can sail among the Virgins by day and anchor in a cove for the night; but nowadays you can order dinner over the radio and have a barbecue waiting when you arrive.

A British touch on Virgin Gorda

91

Bomba's Surf Side Shack is famous for its full-moon parties

New marina developments are springing up in Tortola; this one is at Frenchman's Cay near West End

GUANA ISLAND

Guana Island is a wildlife sanctuary off the north-eastern tip of Tortola. Its 847 acres (343ha) are said to harbor the richest fauna seen on any island of its size in the world— from flamingos to hawks, from bats to cats, and from wild donkeys to sea turtles.

A bar sign at Frenchman's Cay, western Tortola

Tortola

A century ago, when even St. Thomas was a backwater, Tortola was written off as "forsaken." Today the island is enjoying something of a boom, which has led to growing development, as the 16,000 islanders and expatriates build on the island's towering hillsides. A dock for cruise ships has been constructed and the island is developing steadily, but there are still plenty of charming, isolated spots to be found.

Tortola is only 12 miles by 3 miles (19km by 5km) and has a scrubby and meandering spine of steep mountains, rising to 1,709ft (521m) at Mount Sage. The main settlement is Road Town, a modern, sprawling capital made up of a few streets collected around a deep bay in the southern coastline. Features include yachting marinas, a small museum, a botanical garden, bars and restaurants, and a number of stores. Tortolans themselves live in small settlements on the coast; transportation around the island is customarily by taxi or rented car.

The best bays and beaches are on the island's north side. At the West End, where most of the hotels are, you will find waterside pubs and stores at the Soper's Hole marina complex and the main ferry terminal; to the north is a perfect, isolated curve of sand called **Smuggler's Cove▶▶▶**. Heading east you come to Long Bay, a superb run of white sand, and Apple Bay, where surfers enjoy the big waves (look for Bomba's Surfside Shack, a beach bar made of driftwood). The long and lovely **Cane Garden Bay▶▶▶** has small places to stay and a string of excellent beach bars; Quito's Gazebo has live music most nights in season. From here, there is an almost impossibly steep climb to the mountain's spine, which eventually descends into Road Town.

East of Road Town, the road follows the coastline to Long Look, where there is a small town. Just offshore is Beef Island, the site of Tortola's airport. There are good beaches here, including Josiah's Bay and **Long Bay▶▶** on Beef Island. The Last Resort is a lively restaurant and bar on an island in Trellis Bay and you can also spend the day on Marina Cay, which has good watersports; there is a free ferry.

Virgin Gorda

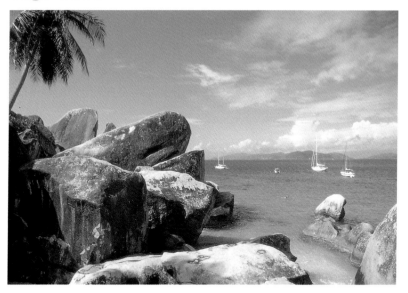

Virgin Gorda is even quieter than Tortola, but it has some chic resorts hidden in its coves and offshore cays. Lying east of Tortola (and reached by ferry), it was patronized, like St. John in the USVI, by Laurance Rockefeller, who built the Little Dix Bay hotel here. Virgin Gorda means "the fat Virgin"—the island supposedly looks like a reclining woman. Its 8sq-mile (20sq km) area is divided into three mounds and covered in scrub and cactus, rising to a 1,358ft (414m) peak in the north. The most distinctive scenery is in the south, where massive granite boulders form The Baths, a maze of water-filled caves.

Boats from Tortola dock at the southern settlement of The Valley, where many of the 3,000 or so islanders live. The town is really little more than its marina, with bars and an easy-going atmosphere. Virgin Gorda's best beaches—including The Baths—are south of The Valley. In the southeast of the island are the ruins of an old copper mine which was active during the last century.

The road to the north of the island passes isolated coves such as Savannah Bay and Pond Bay before reaching Virgin Gorda's second town, Gun Creek. This overlooks the North Sound, a stretch of water surrounded by tall peaks, cays and small islands with fine beaches. Two splendid hotels lie at this end of the island, accessible only by boat from Gun Creek. Biras Creek (tel: 494 3555; www.biras.com) is a place of understated wealth overlooking a calm sound, a bay (with the main beach) and wild Atlantic surf. The Bitter End Yacht Club (tel: 494 2475) newspaper shows the range of watersports on offer. Gathering places on the islands around the sound include The Restaurant (tel: 495 7154) in Leverick Bay; an elegant restaurant, Drake's Anchorage (tel: 494 2254), on Mosquito Island; a beach bar on Prickly Pear Cay; and the tiny Saba Rock, a bar that wakes up in the evenings.

The Baths, where waves wash through tunnels and caverns made from jumbled rocks

93

THE BATHS
The Baths form a series of coves to the south of The Valley. Best approached by sea, the boulders are stacked in jumbled piles and backed by coconut palms. From the land you can reach them through the scrub from the Top of the Baths restaurant. Made of granite, a stone that does not normally appear in the Caribbean, they may have been carried here by glacial movement during the ice ages.

Watersports are an integral part of a Caribbean vacation. The warm seas and constant Trade Winds make its islands excellent places for windsurfers, scuba divers, jet-skiers and para-sailors. But there is nothing to beat the freedom of sailing, and the calmer stretches of sea are flecked with white as yachts of all shapes and sizes ride the ocean breezes, with dolphins dipping and darting alongside their prows.

REGATTAS

The biggest annual sailing event in the Caribbean is Race Week in Antigua in late April, which includes five days of races. A major regatta is held in the British Virgin Islands every April and Martiniquans race the *yoles rondes*, with distinctive square sails and crews of 12 leaning out over the water on booms. In August Anguilla's race week pitches locally built boats against each other; and Carriacou, in the Grenadines, stages its own small regatta. The Caribbean Ocean Triangle Series (CORT) sets sail in March and April and includes the St Croix International Annual Regatta in February and the Puerto Rico International Regatta, in addition to, BVI's Spring Regatta.

With such a variety of islands lying within easy reach of one another, island-hopping is an enjoyable way of seeing the Caribbean. Yachts are readily available for four to eight people or more and can be rented as bareboats (no crew) or crewed (with captain and hands to order the supplies and do the sailing and cooking). All yachts have fridges, kitchenware and bedding, most provide masks and snorkels, and some carry windsurfing and diving equipment. Day sails are available from all the islands and many beachfront hotels have small sailing boats. For a bird's-eye view, have a go at parasailing.

The best sailing destinations are the Virgin Islands and the Grenadines. Both regions are spectacularly beautiful, with convenient sailing distances separating their islands. The Virgins have good marina facilities, but this means crowds during the high season. The Grenadines have a wilder beauty, but restaurants and bars have found their way even to many of the quieter bays.

Reliable year-round winds make windsurfing a popular Caribbean sport. The best windsurfing areas are: the Dominican Republic, particularly around Cabarete on the northern shore, where World Championships are occasionally held; Barbados's southern shore around Maxwell and Silver Sands; and Aruba. The sport is catered to in the French Caribbean around St. François and Le Moule on Guadaloupe and in the southeast of Martinique.

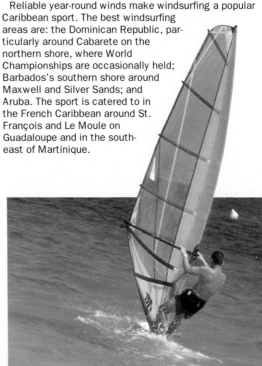

Divers acknowledge the Caribbean as an ideal setting for one of the world's most exotic sports, with its vast areas of colorful coral and its strange and beautiful tropical fish. Snorkelers, too, can enjoy access to offshore reefs from most islands; and glass-bottom boat trips provide views of underwater wonders without even the need to get wet.

Although it does not have the abundance of the Indo-Pacific area, the Caribbean can boast around 75 species of corals, which include brain corals, sea fans and whips, hydra-headed anemones, gorgonians and sponges. More mobile sea creatures include crabs, spiny lobsters, starfish, rays, eels and even turtles or sharks. Diving at night reveals a completely different world, as some corals close and others open, while fish emerge to feed on them, crunching away at the polyps, or sleep tucked away in sleeping bags of mucus so that their scent cannot be picked up by predators.

DIVING SITES
The best diving sites are off the Cayman Islands, particularly Little Cayman, with sheer drops to limit-less depths, and Bonaire, where the coral-clad slopes are gentler. Saba, a steep-sided volcanic cone, has an abundance of corals and the Grenadines' waters are not as crowded.

95

As well as the natural beauties of the sea, shipwrecks are a source of endless fascination and near some islands ships have been sunk deliberately in order to provide artificial reefs for underwater explorers. Off the shores of Anguilla, divers can swim over a 200ft (60m) hulk sitting upright on the seabed.

Scuba diving was invented in the early 1940s and developed rapidly as a sport, popularized by divers such as Jacques Cousteau, one of its inventors. There are several suppliers in the Caribbean and diving can be easily arranged on most islands. Many hotels offer qualifying courses with the affiliated dive organizations (PADI and NAUI); there are also non-qualifying resort courses that enable novices to dive almost immediately. (Remember to arrange personal insurance before leaving home if you intend to go diving.)

MARINE PARKS
Several islands, including the US and British Virgin Islands, Saba and Bonaire, have created marine parks around their shores in order to protect their corals and fish. Divers are forbidden from picking coral or hunting fish with spear-guns within these areas. Never buy coral jewelry on the islands—it is made from live coral that is culled from the reef.

BVI FERRIES
Regular ferries criss-cross the waters of the Virgin Islands. There are frequent services between Road Town on Tortola and The Valley in Virgin Gorda. The sleek North Sound Express runs between Beef Island (the airport at the eastern end of Tortola) and the expensive hotels of the North Sound (the east end of Virgin Gorda), while a daily service links The Valley and Beef Island. Several daily sailings carry passengers to Jost van Dyke from West End on Tortola. Some offshore islands have their own water ferries: Peter Island's ferry, for example, leaves from the CSY Marina just out of Road Town and Marina Cay (from Beef Island).

Smaller British Virgin Islands

Anegada▶ is not a typical Virgin Island. It stands alone, 19 miles (30km) out in the ocean, and whereas the other Virgins are tall and volcanic islands, Anegada is a 7-mile (11km) curve of coral. The island is scrubby and flat (only 30ft/9m at its highest point) and culminates in a submerged tail called Horseshoe Reef, a magnificent living coral expanse, which has claimed more than 300 unwary ships over the centuries. The name Anegada means "inundated"—which it occasionally is, by passing waves. Only 200 people live here, sharing the island with goats and iguanas; their sole collection of houses is called The Settlement. The island is not much visited by tourists, but there are a couple of places to eat and stay, and Loblolly Bay on the north coast is the best of many beaches.

Jost van Dyke▶ ▶ ▶ is almost devoid of tourism, other than visiting yachts. It lies north of Tortola and takes its name from a Dutch pirate. Just a few hilly square miles in area, the island is reached by ferry from West End on Tortola. Great Harbour, the main port, is a port of entry to the Virgin Islands and has a church, a police station and a

Perfect peace in an ideal anchorage: Jost van Dyke

few beach bars (one the owners, Foxy, welcomes visitors with a personalized calypso). There is an excellent beach at White Bay, and yachts put in at Sandy Cay, one of a couple of sheltered off-island cays. The best time to visit is on New Year's Eve, when 2,000 or so revelers sail in for a night's drinking and dancing on the sand.

Necker Island▶ ▶ ▶ (www,virgin.com) is an idyllic green speck rimmed with blinding white sand and translucent blue water. Set off the northeastern tip of Virgin Gorda, it is owned by the founder of Virgin Airlines, Sir Richard Branson, who has built a Balinese house and rents the island to groups, families or companies—at a high cost.

Sir Francis Drake Channel

Sir Francis Drake Channel is the sailing heartland of the Virgin Islands—a magnificent stretch of water off Tortola, where the white triangles of yacht sails beat back and forth over an unbelievably blue sea. On its southern side the channel is bounded by a necklace of small, irregularly shaped islands, which run southeast in a graceful curve from Virgin Gorda to St. John in the USVI. In their isolated coves are some superb, secluded stretches of sand.

Starting in the northeast (most sailing trips sail out of Road Town south toward Peter Island, then northeast toward Gorda and Anegada), **Fallen Jerusalem** and **Round Rock** lie off Virgin Gorda. Designated a National Park, Fallen Jerusalem has rocky terrain that gives it the appearance of an ancient city in decay. **Ginger Island** is uninhabited, but the next in line, **Cooper Island▶▶**, has about 10 inhabitants—the staff of the Cooper Island Beach Club on Manchioneel Bay, which often attracts a lively crowd of "yachties" at lunchtime and in the evenings. Scuba-diving facilities are available and there is a very beautiful beach.

Salt Island▶▶ takes its name from a salt pond that is still farmed. Rent, payable to the Queen of England, is set at a sack of salt a year, but apparently it has not been collected recently. This is one of the Virgin Island's most popular dive sites, with the wreck of the RMS *Rhone*, which sank in the 19th century, lying offshore. Part of the wreck is shallow enough to snorkel in and you will find yourself bathing in the exhaled bubbles of divers below you. Next in line is **Peter Island▶▶**, where there is just one chic island resort with rooms scattered along Deadman's Bay (a charming place, despite its name; tel: 495 2000). Offshore is a small outcrop called Dead Chest, where Bluebeard, aka Long John Silver, put his mutinous crew ashore with one bottle of rum. **Norman Island▶**, the last island in the chain before St. John, is also uninhabited, but is worth visiting for the eerie, waterbound caves at Treasure Point, offer exceptional snorkeling and kayaking.

97

Sailing—the only way to travel between the many beautiful Virgin Islands

St. Croix

St. Croix (pronounced "St. Croy") is the largest of the Virgin Islands and lies alone, 31 miles (50km) to the south of the main USVI group. This was the senior island in Danish colonial days because of its successful plantation economy, but whereas St. Thomas has been overtaken by the hustle of modern America, St. Croix has retained a quieter, historic feel, with two attractive harbor towns, one at either end of the island. Roughly twice the size of St. Thomas, it is a sparsely populated island, with varied scenery: mountains, rain forest, beaches and dairy and cattle-breeding farmlands.

St. Croix's main town is Christiansted▶▶▶, on the waterfront in the east. The Danish influence can still be seen in the town's architecture, with its terraces, patios and arched yellow colonnades. Fort Christiansvaern was the town's old defense. The commercial center is around the Old Customs House and the Scale House near the wharf. The Steeple Building is a museum of Native American artifacts, and on King Street Government House still houses government offices. The whole downtown area has been designated a National Historic Site, preserving several blocks for future generations. The dry east has most of the island's hotels, and there are golf courses at Buccaneer and Teague Bay and Carambola. One of the best beaches is on Buck Island, a national park known for its snorkeling.

Centerline Road heads west toward Frederiksted through agricultural land that made St. Croix wealthy during the 19th century. The St. George Village Botanical Garden▶ (tel: 692 2874; www.sgvbg.org. *Open* daily 9–5. *Admission: expensive*) is a peaceful retreat on an old plantation estate, growing Amerindian and other Cruzian plants. Also off the main road is the Cruzan Rum Factory▶, (tel: 692 2280. *Open* Mon–Fri 9–11.30, 1–4.15. *Admission: inexpensive*) offering guided tours, tastings and sales. Farther on is the moated Whim Great House▶▶ (tel: 772 0598. *Open* Tue–Sat 10–4. *Admission: moderate*), an unusual rounded estate building restored with colonial-style antiques; in the kitchen, old utensils and sugar machinery are displayed. There are more colonnaded trading buildings in Frederiksted▶▶, including restored Fort Frederik and its museum. Mahogany Road leads northward through rain forest.

FACT OR FICTION?
Herman Wouk's *Don't Stop the Carnival*, one of the finest books to have come out of the West Indies, was inspired by life on the Virgin Islands. His Gull Reef Club is supposed to have been modeled on a hotel on Hassel Island, in Charlotte Amalie harbor, and on the hotel on the Cay off Christiansted in St. Croix. The book tells of the succession of disasters that befall a hotelier, and rumor has it that Wouk didn't dare return to the island because the story was so painfully accurate and because so many of the hoteliers thought they recognized themselves in the main character, Norman Paperman.

For the finest sunset, a Frederiksted beach bar on the west coast is what is required

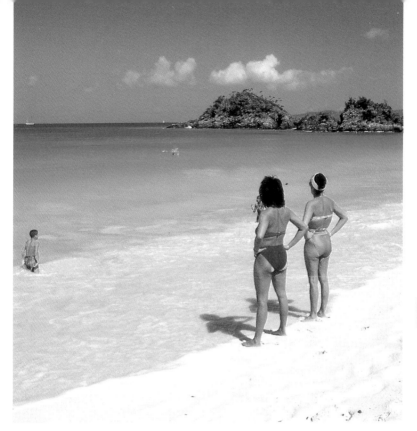

St. John

One of the most beautiful islands in the Caribbean, St. John is the smallest and least developed of the USVI. It is a few miles east of St. Thomas, which is a short ferry ride across the Pillsbury Sound, but is so tranquil that it seems a world away. Approximately two-thirds of the island are given over to the Virgin Islands National Park, so most of its steep, volcanic hills are left to grow as natural jungle.

There are numerous trails through the park (on foot, on horseback and underwater through the corals of Trunk Bay), with hikes and activities led by well-informed rangers. Get schedules from the National Park Visitor Center in Cruz Bay (tel: 776 6201; www.nps.gov. *Open* daily 8–4.30). On the north coast you can see the ruins of the **Annaberg Plantation▶▶**, a relic of Danish days, when the island was covered with sugar cane. Camping can accommodate travelers with or without tents.

Around the fringes of the National Park, St. John's coastline has been developed. **Cruz Bay▶▶**, at the western tip of the island, is the main town and here you will find many good bars and restaurants, as well as the **Elaine Ione Sprauve Library and Museum▶** (tel: 776 6359. *Open* Mon–Fri 9–5), with marine life displays and artifacts dating from a slave revolt against Danish planters in 1733; after nearly a year, the rebels were defeated by imported French troops and many committed suicide rather than return to slavery.

The sand is crystalline and the surf gentle at Trunk Bay, on St. John's north shore

TRAVEL BETWEEN THE ISLANDS
Most of the Virgin Islands are linked by ferry: Regular links connect St. Thomas (Charlotte Amalie and Red Hook), St. John (Cruz Bay) and Tortola (West End and then Road Town). Sometimes the link continues to Virgin Gorda (The Valley). A hydrofoil service now connects Charlotte Amalie and Christiansted on St. Croix. The oft-choppy trip takes about 90 minutes each way. St. Croix is best reached by air—a novel way to make the link is by sea plane (Seaborne Airlines, www. seaborneairlines.com)

Three centuries ago the Caribbean waters were infested with pirates. Bands of seaborne outlaws would lie in wait in hidden coves before taking to the high seas in their fast ships and attacking passing trade. Piracy was a dangerous lifestyle—capture usually meant death— but the rewards were great; a good haul could provide life on Easy Street for months on end.

Sir Henry Morgan

100

Piracy started in the Caribbean soon after the word spread that the Spaniards were taking gold from the Aztecs. The stakes were high from the start—intrusion into Spanish waters was punishable by death—but adventurous interlopers like François le Clerc and Pie de Palo ("Pegleg") were willing to take the risks. British adventurers arrived in the late 16th century, including Sir John Hawkins and Francis Drake, who made their fortunes on slave-trading expeditions and later by ransacking cities on the Spanish Main.

Known variously as freebooters, buccaneers and sea rovers, pirates often started out as privateers, permitted by local governors to attack enemy shipping in times of war—but the rewards were so good that the practice was extended to include any ships that might bring in a prize and was continued in peacetime. A single capture could bring vast riches (usually a cargo of goods—silks, arms, animals and grog). Once these had been sold the pirates would spend their loot on alcohol and women until the money eventually ran out and they had to go in search of more.

On board ship, however, there was a strict regime. Generally pirates were accomplished sailors who operated small, fast ships. The crew would sign "articles" stipulating their obedience to the captain and their duties: Keeping their weapons clean, dispatching themselves bravely in battle, and refraining from playing cards and bringing women aboard (which carried a death penalty). Punishments included lashes of the whip and "marooning" (being left ashore on an island with water, a pistol, gunpowder and shot). Each man had a share in any prizes captured on the venture, and injured men were compensated from the loot. There was usually a musician on board, who was expected to play six nights a week but rested on Sundays.

When faced with a pirate attack, a captain knew that he would be killed if he put up a fight. There are some particularly gruesome stories of pirates' cruelty: The Frenchman Montbars was said to cut out men's guts and make the victims dance till they died; and his compatriot l'Ollonios removed the heart of one man and fed it to another.

Gallery of rogues For a century until 1700, no ship was safe in the Caribbean, and pirates were feared and reviled. They operated from hideaways on Tortuga and, after 1691, the Bahamas. But, there is no disputing

WOMEN AT SEA

Two women joined the macho world of piracy in the 18th century. Anne Bonney was the fiery daughter of an Irish lawyer and Mary Read was brought up as a boy and served as a soldier and sailor before setting off to the Caribbean. Both women fell in with Jack Rackham and joined his pirate crew. They were all caught off the shores of Jamaica and sentenced to death; both women "pleaded their bellies" (pregnancy) and Bonney escaped execution, but Read died in prison.

that there were colorful characters among their ranks. Perhaps the best-known Caribbean pirate was Blackbeard (Edward Teach). This huge man cultivated a diabolic image, tying ribbons in his long pigtails and beard and putting slow-burning fuses under his hat so that he appeared to be on fire. A reward of £100 was offered for his capture, and he was eventually caught after a chase at sea. Blackbeard died fighting rather than suffer the ignominies of surrendering, and his head was hung from the bowsprit of his ship. Defiant to the last, it is said Teach's body swam several laps around the ship before it sank.

Bartholomew Roberts is thought to have captured 400 ships in two years. A dandy, he went into battle in fine dress, drank only tea and always kept the Sabbath; he was killed in a skirmish with a British ship.

Known as the "gentleman pirate," Stede Bonnet was a Justice of the Peace and a landowner from Barbados, who decided to buy a ship and become a pirate. All their stories are told by Exquemeling in his *History of the Pirates*.

HENRY MORGAN

Henry Morgan was an indentured laborer who became the leader of the Port Royal buccaneers in the 1660s, directing expeditions against Spanish cities and netting 750,000 pieces of eight in an attack on Panama City, which he destroyed in the process. Having made his fortune, Morgan switched sides, becoming the lieutenant governor of Jamaica, a position that entailed stamping out piracy.

Treasure from the New World is loaded onto a 16th-century ship

PUTTING ON THE STYLE

As dandies and natty dressers, some pirates wore tricorn hats, coats and cordoba boots—but looting was hot work in the Caribbean and most wore baggy shirts and trousers with no shoes. Hats included Jacobin caps and turbans, and hair was often braided and then stiffened with water and flour. Earrings were believed to improve the eyesight—and the pirate who sighted a prize gained an extra share.

St. Thomas

Cruise ships and yachts anchor side by side in St. Thomas's harbor

HURRICANES LUIS AND MARILYN
The last decade or so has been pretty cruel to the USVI. In 1989, Hurricane Hugo caused terrible destruction in St. Croix. Then it was the turn of St. John and particularly St. Thomas, which was dealt a double blow in September 1995. First Hurricane Luis swept through, causing some destruction, and then a week later Hurricane Marilyn tore through the islands, causing maximum damage because it brought very heavy rains. The island was declared a disaster area. Many long-term residents left for good. It took over a year to rebuild because many people were uninsured (rates were so high that they could not afford insurance).

St. Thomas is the USVI capital island and the most developed of all the Virgins. It is a mountainous 12 miles by 3 miles (19km by 5km) and has a population of over 50,000, so is hardly a secluded tropical retreat; on the other hand, it does have excellent bars, clubs and restaurants, many of which are concentrated around **Charlotte Amalie▶▶**.

Charlotte Amalie owes its birth and its still-thriving life to a fine harbor, sheltered by hills and protected by islands. Pirate ships and ocean traders once brought business here; now it arrives on cruise ships and yachts. A major trading center for centuries, the waterfront is still a magnet for shoppers looking for gold, French perfume, Colombian emeralds and fashions. The town has another side, however: The arched facades of its stone trading buildings and the hillside mansions recall centuries past.

The cooler slopes above Charlotte Amalie are dotted with grand mansions, linked by stepped alleyways and sinuous roads. **Government House▶** (1867), once the seat of the Danish council and now the Governor's official residence, stands above the town center. Just above it is Blackbeard's Tower (where the pirate was supposed to have lived), reached by the 99 Steps (there are actually 102 of them). Even beyond Charlotte Amalie the hillsides are covered with houses. On the spine of the hills above the town is Drake's Seat with magnificent views, where the sailor supposedly watched for Spanish ships There are botanical gardens at **Estate St. Peter Greathouse▶▶** (tel: 774 4999; www. greathouse-mountaintop.com. *Open daily 9–5. Admission: moderate*), high above the north coast. In the east of the island beyond Red Hook, the ferry point for St. John, you will find **Coral World▶▶** (tel: 775 1555; www.coralworldvi.com. *Open daily 9–5. Admission: expensive*) with an underwater observation tower, 50,000-gallon (190,000L) Predator Tank, and living coral reef display, plus all sorts of aquariums, touch tanks and a tropical nature trail.

Most of the beaches on St. Thomas are heavily developed (except Magens Bay, on the National Geographic's Top 10 Beaches list), so it is easy to find watersports.

CHARLOTTE AMALIE

0 250 m
0 250 yards

NYE GADE
Blackbeard's Tower
Synagogue
Crown House
Lavalette House
99 Steps
Government House
CRYSTAL GADE
GARDEN STREET
KONGEN'S GADE
Park
Frederick Lutheran Church
BACK STREET (VIMMELSKRAFT GADE)
SAVAN GADE
Pissarro Building
DRONNINGEN'S GADE
NORRE GADE
Market
MAIN STREET
TROMPETER GADE
DRAKE'S PASSAGE
RAADET'S GADE
HIBISCUS ALLEY
POST OFFICE ALLEY
Post Office
Grand Hotel
GUTTET'S GADE
STORETVAER GADE
PALM PASSAGE
ROYAL DANE MALL
Emancipation Park
FORT STRADE
STRAND GADE
KOLBODI GADE
VENDORS PLAZA
Fort Christian
Havensight Mall →
WATERFRONT HIGHWAY (KYST VEJEN)
King's Wharf
Legislature

St Thomas Harbour

103

Walk

Charlotte Amalie

Ferries arrive at this downtown waterfront, but many disembark at the cruise ship dock across the harbor and head straight for Havensight Mall, the first of the island's shopping centers, which has been converted from a series of warehouses. Safari buses and taxis provide transportation for passengers from here into town. Opposite the entrance to Havensight, the **St. Thomas Skyride**▶▶ (tel: 774 9809; www.paradisepointtramway.com. *Open* daily 9–5. *Admission: expensive*) provides visitors with a 7-minute, 700ft (213m) lift to a spectacular viewpoint overlooking the town and bay. On a clear day St. Croix may be visible.

Charlotte Amalie's old trading streets are laid out in a gridiron pattern with a series of narrow alleys with stores and restaurants running down to the waterfront. As you arrive, you will pass the light green **Virgin Islands Legislature Building**▶, which was built by the Danes as a police barracks in 1874

and is now the USVI Senate. Across the road is the dark red and gold **Fort Christian**▶▶, which dates from the Danes' arrival in the 1660s. It now contains the Virgin Islands Museum, tracing early and colonial life on St. Thomas.

Beyond the old Grand Hotel and the neoclassical Post Office, at the head of Main Street, is the main shopping area. Here, the old brick and stone warehouse buildings bear well-known names alongside local stores such as A. H. Riise (selling perfumes, jewelry, crystal and watches).

Wander through the passages and alleys between Main Street and the waterfront, where there are yet more stores and pleasant cafés. A plaque on Main Street, between A. H. Riise and the town's market, marks the birthplace of the Impressionist painter Camille Pissarro.

The 19th-century Virgin Islands Legislature Building, on the waterfront, is the headquarters of the USVI Senate

The French Antilles

Anguilla (UK)

Marigot • Saint-Martin
(France)

Sint Maarten
(Neth)
Gustavia • Saint-Barthélemy
(France)

Barbuda

Saba
(Neth)

Sint Eustatius
(Neth)

ANTIGUA AND
BARBUDA

ST KITTS
AND NEVIS

St Kitts

Antigua

Leeward Islands

Nevis

Redonda

Montserrat
(UK)

Guadeloupe Passage

La Désirade

Lesser Antilles

Guadeloupe
(France)

Pointe-à-Pitre

1467m ▲

Basse-Terre •

Marie-Galante

Les Saintes

Dominica Passage

DOMINICA

Martinique Passage

1397m ▲

Saint-Pierre •

Le François

Fort-de-France •

Martinique
(France)

Saint Lucia Passage

ST LUCIA

| 0 | 50 | 100 km |
| 0 | 50 miles | |

104

FÊTES PATRONALES
Fêtes patronales take
place on the French- and
Spanish-speaking islands
to celebrate the saint's
day of each town's patron
saint. Check for dates
with each island's tourist
board.

*Above right: Chutes du
Carbet, Guadaloupe*

THE FRENCH ANTILLES Unmistakably French in their
food, culture and general outlook, the "overseas depart-
ments" of Martinique and Guadeloupe combine tropical
scenery with a European-influenced lifestyle. Visitors can
explore Guadeloupe's bustling capital Pointe-à-Pitre, its
sandy beaches and rain forests; Martinique's historic
towns and villages, the restaurants of Saint Martin and
the chic beach resorts of Saint-Barthélemy; while the tiny
isles of Les Saintes, La Désirade and Marie-Galante offer
white sand beaches and quiet island life. Variety and
beauty are the hallmarks of the French West Indies, made
up of the single island of Martinique and the six
islands which comprise the *région* of Guadeloupe.

The main island, Guadeloupe, is actually two islets of contrasting landscapes, linked by a small land bridge. The administrative *région* of Guadeloupe is an archipelago, consisting of the islands of Les Saintes, La Désirade, Marie-Galante and Saint-Barthélemy, as well as the half-French, half-Dutch island of Saint-Martin/Sint Maarten. As the French islands are in the northern and center sector of the Antilles, they enjoy similar climates and vegetation. Only one of the islands (Martinique) is in the region that is defined by the Windward group.

Lying between the Caribbean Sea and the Atlantic Ocean, the French Antilles spread across 350 miles (565km) of sea and include two of the region's three

French stores under the tropical sun in Guadeloupe

volcanically active islands. Apart from the inner, Caribbean side of Guadeloupe and central/northern Martinique (which are covered in tropical mountain forest), the islands are green and humid, with excellent beaches and deep coves and bays. The eastern section of Guadeloupe remains part of an arc of limestone isles, and the western parts are a continuation of the volcanic link. Also in this chain, Martinique, the largest volcanic connection of the Windward islands, has three major peaks. At 4,813ft (1,467m) Guadeloupe's volcano, Soufrière, is the highest peak to be found in the Eastern Caribbean.

The names given to the main islands in the Carib language—*Karukera* ("Island of Beautiful Waters") for Guadeloupe and *Madinia* or *Madinina* ("Island of Flowers") for Martinique—illustrate the mystical appeal of these islands. Even the French half of Saint-Martin has relatively fertile, scrub-clad, hilly terrain. The smaller islands off Guadeloupe and the most northerly island of the French Antilles, Saint-Barthélemy, are arid and rocky, with sparse, drought-loving vegetation; Guadeloupe's limestone islands and the volcanic Les Saintes feature coral reefs and beautiful, sandy beaches. The karst landscapes on Marie-Galante and Saint-Barthélemy (and on parts of Guadeloupe), together with poor soil, generally restrict arable cultivation, unlike the rich, watered lands of most of Guadeloupe, Martinique and Saint-Martin.

Although situated in and among staunchly British or Dutch islands, the French Antilles have maintained their unmistakable French air. Rather than negotiating a political break with her colonies, France has taken the view that they should be a full part of the republic, and since 1974 Guadeloupe and Martinique have had the right to elect their own representatives to the National Assembly. A small independence movement has emerged in Guadeloupe, and there are still occasional protests. In Martinique, the statue of Josephine Bonaparte, who was born on the island, was beheaded as a protest against French colonial dominance (her head was never found).

HISTORY French settlers first colonized Guadeloupe and Martinique in 1635, and African slaves were shipped in to work the new sugar plantations. By 1669, Martinique was such a successful colony that the French moved their administrative base there from St. Kitts. In the wake of the French Revolution, Guadeloupe's slaves were freed, their colonial masters were killed and their plantations wiped out. Martinique reacted differently, calling on the British to maintain the status quo. Slavery was re-introduced in

1802 and the British occupied Guadeloupe, but France confirmed her hold on the island in 1815—which was unfortunate for the slaves, for although slavery was abolished in the British colonies in the 1830s, emancipation did not come to the French territories until 1848. To fill the labor gap, the French Antilles encouraged the immigration of thousands of East Indians, who moved in as indentured laborers.

In the 1930s, Martinique became a center for the black consciousness movement known as *Négritude,* led by Aimé Césaire and Etienne Lero. Guadeloupe and Martinique were granted departmental status in 1946, giving them equal rights with every other *département* in mainland France.

ISLAND LIFE The French Antilles have capitalized on their greatest assets: the vivacious mingling of races from many lands, and the enchanting surroundings. Tourism has brought an unprecedented influx of revenue and has transformed the lot of the islands without undermining their natural beauty or affecting the local way of life. The people of Martinique and Guadeloupe are known for their physical beauty and Gallic style. Although French is the official language and French influence permeates island life, from the food and buildings to the designer stores and the *boules* games, there is also a distinctively Caribbean side to the culture. The air pulses to zouk, a classic Caribbean beat; the countryside is laden with rain forests, sugar cane and tropical fruit; and the people speak a form of Créole, heard everywhere—although its exclusion from official life has made it something of a poor relation.

With the mingled attributes of a robust culture, fertile soil and abundant seas, a climate combining aridity with high rainfall and all the requisites of the voracious tourist trade, the French Antilles seem to have arrived at a fairly happy balance of nature and development. Certainly they are among the most attractive and peaceful islands to be found in the entire Caribbean region.

CRÉOLE CUISINE
The French Caribbean has a strong tradition of Créole cooking, turning the techniques of French cuisine to Caribbean ingredients, including seafood and tropical fruits. Many restaurants serve classic and *nouvelle* French cuisine and some also offer the Caribbean equivalent, *nouvelle cuisine créole.* *Blaff* is a traditional manner of frying fish in spices; for *court bouillon,* fish is poached in a special mixture of lime, wine, onion and tomatoes. *Touffé is* a casserole and *colombo* is a sort of Caribbean curry. You may come across *z'habitants,* a local dish of crayfish. *Accras* are batter balls, usually made with fish, and *souskaï* is a savory way of marinating fruit.

107

Hobie cats on a Saint-Martin beach

Hobie Cat

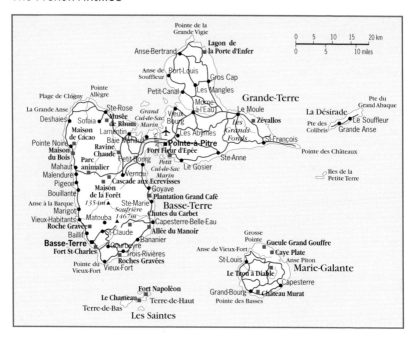

The map shows the French Antilles islands including:

Grande-Terre: Pointe de la Grande Vigie, Lagon de la Porte d'Enfer, Anse-Bertrand, Anse de Souffleur, Port-Louis, Gros Cap, Les Mangles, Petit-Canal, Morne-à-l'Eau, Le Moule, Zévallos, Vieux Bourg, Les Grands Fonds, Les Abymes, St-François, Pointe-à-Pitre, Fort Fleur d'Epée, Petit-Bourg, Le Gosier, Ste-Anne, Pointe des Châteaux, La Désirade, Pte du Grand Abaque, Le Souffleur, Grande Anse, Pte des Colibris, Iles de la Petite Terre

Basse-Terre: Plage de Clugny, Pointe Allègre, Ste-Rose, Grand Cul-de-Sac Marin, La Grande Anse, Musée de Rhum, Deshaies, Sofaïa, Maison de Cacao, Pointe Noire, Maison du Bois, Ravine Chaude, Parc animalier, Mahaut, Malendure, Pigeon, Bouillante, Maison de la Forêt, Anse à la Barque, 135 m, Marigot, Ste-Marie, Soufrière 1467 m, Vieux-Habitants, Matouba, Roche Gravée, Baillif, St-Claude, Baie Mahault, Petit Cul-de-Sac Marin, Vernou, Cascade aux Ecrevisses, Goyave, Plantation Grand Café, Chutes du Carbet, Capesterre-Belle-Eau, Allée du Manoir, Bananier, Basse-Terre, Fort St-Charles, Gourbeyre, Trois-Rivières, Pointe du Vieux-Fort, Roches Gravées, Vieux-Fort

Marie-Galante: Grosse Pointe, Gueule Grand Gouffre, Anse de Vieux-Fort, Caye Plate, St-Louis, Anse Piton, Le Trou à Diable, Capesterre, Grand-Bourg, Château Murat, Pointe des Basses

Les Saintes: Fort Napoléon, Le Chameau, Terre-de-Haut, Terre-de-Bas, Pointe des Basses

Scale: 0 5 10 15 20 km / 0 5 10 miles

Guadeloupe

Guadeloupe has two distinct halves, like the wings of a butterfly. In the west is Basse-Terre, a rain-forested volcanic monster which is similar in appearance to Dominica, farther south. The eastern wing, across the narrow Rivière-Salée (Salt River), is Grande-Terre, a relatively flat, coral-based outcrop from a much older range of volcanoes.

Many of Guadeloupe's hotels sit along the southern shore of Grande-Terre, which offers watersports and good waterfront restaurants and bistros. This "wing" of Guadeloupe is composed of a shattered limestone outcrop with karst hills, known as *montagnes russes*. Low plains (*fonds*) reach out to the white, sandy beaches and spectacular rocky cliffs along its coastline. The terrain on Basse-Terre is for the most part mountainous, rain

FRENCH FESTIVALS

In keeping with their love of food, the French Antilleans stage a Chefs' Festival each year (in April on Martinique and in August on Guadeloupe). Each island's leading cooks are invited to bring along their finest creations for judging, and there follows a general feast. Carnival in the French Caribbean features the main processions on Mardi Gras (Shrove Tuesday) and Mercredi des Cendres (Ash Wednesday). On the Wednesday the color scheme is black and white, and the day culminates in the burning of the carnival figure, Momo.

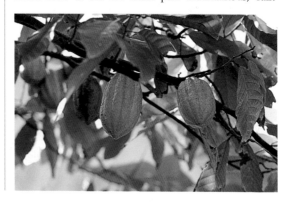

A cocoa tree growing on Guadeloupe

forested, and nourished by cascading waterfalls and mountain streams such as the Grande Rivière Goyaves, the island's longest river at nearly 20 miles (32km). Inlets of black, volcanic-sanded beaches lie on the south and southeast coast of the island, but there are excellent golden sand beaches in the northwest.

Guadeloupe's climate is tempered by the cooling northeast Trade Winds, generally no more than breezes—Les Alizes. Hurricanes occurred in 1979 and 1989, but the islands usually enjoy idyllic weather.

ISLAND LIFE About 448,713 people live in the archipelago of Guadeloupe, almost 50 percent of whom are under 20 years of age. Most are of African descent; some are descendants of early settlers—*Békés*—or of East Indian

indentured workers. Tourism and administration provide work for nearly half the population; agriculture and industry are the other economic mainstays.

Officially, the language in Guadeloupe is French. Créole, however, is the language of the people.

Waterfront market and ferry departure point, Place de la Victoire

POINTE-À-PITRE This large city, sprawling along the coastline in the crook of Guadeloupe's two large islands, has a population of about 170,000. Its heart is the **Place de la Victoire**▶▶, a large square set with royal palms, mango trees, statues of famous Guadeloupeans and lined with cafés, overlooking the busy harbor, La Darse, where ferries depart for the offshore islands. The tourist information office can be found near La Darse (tel: 0590 90 70 02; www.sivap.gp) and the cathedral, built mainly of metal in order to withstand the occasional fierce Caribbean hurricanes.

From here the crowded streets stretch in all directions, overlooked by houses with intricate balconies and shutters. On the rue Frébault, in the main shopping district, a **covered market**▶▶ provides Caribbean mayhem and

Boats on Ste-Anne

GETTING AROUND GUADELOUPE

As one half of the island is flat, with plantations and beaches, and the other is mountainous (with a 75,000-acre/30,350ha national park), Guadeloupe is no easy place to view on one excursion. Grande-Terre is criss-crossed with roads that do not give straight-forward access to all its attractions, and should be divided into at least two journeys.

every imaginable kind of produce. The **Musée Schoelcher**►► (tel: 0590 82 08 04; *Open* Mon–Fri 9–5. *Admission: inexpensive)*, set in a stone and stucco house at 24 rue Peynier, displays memorabilia associated with Victor Schoelcher, the 19th-century anti-slavery campaigner; and the **Musée St-John Perse**► (tel: 0590 90 01 92. *Open* Mon–Fri 9–5, Sat 8.30–12.30. *Admission: inexpensive)*, on rue Nozière, traces the life of Alexis Saint-Léger, the Nobel Prize-winning Guadeloupean poet. East of the town, the **Aquarium de la Guadeloupe**►►► (tel: 0590 90 92 38. *Open* daily 9–7. *Admission: expensive)* in Bas du Fort displays tropical fish, and the **Fort Fleur d'Epée**► (tel: 0590 23 57 57) an 18th-century defensive bastion built of coral rock, has been partly restored.

OUTSIDE POINTE-À-PITRE Tourism centers around the towns along Grande-Terre's south coast—Le Gosier, Ste-Anne and St-François—where beaches and waterfront restaurants are packed. Farther east, the beaches are emptier, and at the Pointe des Châteaux there are superb strips of sand where nudism is permitted.

North of this coastal strip the country opens out and cane fields rustle in the breeze; here, the towns are quieter and isolated from the tourist clamor. In Morne-à-l'Eau, the cemetery is full of the distinctive local checked gravestones, covered with black and white tiles.

To the west of Pointe-à-Pitre, across the Rivière-Salée, the scenery suddenly changes and Basse-Terre's mountains tower ahead. The quickest road to the capital town, also called Basse-Terre, runs south along the island's eastern shore. At the **Plantation Grand Café**► (tel: 0590 86 33 06. *Open* May–Oct Mon–Fri 9–4.30, Sat 9–12. *Admission: expensive)*, you can see a working banana plantation. Past Ste-Marie the route runs through the **Allée du Manoir**►►, an avenue of 100ft (30m) royal palm trees. Inland, the Etang Zombi and the Grand Etang lakes, and three waterfalls known as the **Chutes du Carbet**►►, grace the slopes of the Soufrière. Near the coast, there are Arawak carvings at the **Parc Archéologique des Roches Gravées**►► (tel: 0590 92 91 88. *Open* daily 9–5. *Admission: inexpensive)*, dating from around AD1000.

One of Guadeloupes's historic trails is the "Trace des Contrabandiers" (The Smugglers' Trail). It follows the spine of Basse-Terre's mountain range and carves its way through the magnificent rain forest. Two centuries ago, this was a long and possibly dangerous hike, but if no ship was available travelers simply had to walk. Such routes are now opening again as beautiful hiking trails.

Waterfalls and luxuriant ferns in Guadeloupe's rain forest

PERPETUAL RAIN
Rain forests create their own rain. Atlantic winds are laden with water, and when they hit the island slopes they are forced upward, condensing into huge white clouds above the mountain peaks. These clouds drop their loads onto the forest, and when the sun comes out it causes evaporation, putting water from the forest back into the sky, where it joins a never-ending cycle.

Maison de la Forêt, Guadeloupe

The Caribbean's mountainous islands are criss-crossed with paths. Most were cut by armies, but used by rebel maroons, who hid out in the hills, and by runaway slaves. In the 19th century, traders would carry up to 100 lb (45kg) of goods for sale on trays placed on their heads. These *porteuses* were immensely fit, capable of walking up to 25 miles (40km) a day across the mountains.

Tropical rain forests grow on all the tall, well-watered islands of the Eastern Caribbean and in the Greater Antilles. At lower elevations, gommiers and other hardwood trees such as mahogany tower over fern-covered floors, with canopies at about 80ft (24m). Above 3,200ft (975m) are the montane or cloud forests, where ferns and orchids form curves from the upper branches of the trees. Higher still, above 5,000ft (1,500m), are the elfin forests of stunted trees covered with mosses and lichens.

Most of the Eastern Caribbean islands have national parks to protect their precious rain forest areas and the flora and fauna they support. Forest trails have been created in Dominica, St. Lucia, Martinique and Guadeloupe among others. Jamaica has excellent walking in the Blue Mountains and Puerto Rico has a number of national parks. Virgin Islands National Park on St. John (USVI) also has many hiking trails.

Guided tours are the safest; even on small islands it is easy to get lost. Guides also know the local flora and the uses of plants in traditional medicine. Trainers or light ankle-height boots are normally adequate; a sweater is needed for higher climbs and a waterproof jacket is useful for protection against downpours.

Morne-à-l'Eau cemetery

INTRODUCING THE PINEAPPLE
Columbus was "astonished and delighted" with the pineapple when he was presented with it on his arrival in Guadeloupe, during his second voyage to the Caribbean. After its introduction to Europe, it was regarded as a luxury and became a symbol of hospitality; pineapples can still be seen crafted in stone on the entrance gates to many country houses in Europe.

Spread over the hillside, the namesake capital of Basse-Terre has a number of attractive stone and wooden town buildings. The 1650 former **Fort St-Charles**▶▶ (tel: 0590 81 37 48. *Open* daily 9–4.30), overlooking the harbor, is a huge defensive bulwark with a small museum. It was renamed Fort Delgrés in 1990 after a noted abolitionist, Louis Delgrés. Inland from Basse-Terre, on the slopes of the Soufrière volcano, is the town of Matouba, where a 200-year-old trail, Trace Victor Hugues, leads to hot baths fed by volcanic springs (an 18-mile /29km haul). Near the Bains Jaunes hot springs, the narrow road heads up to Savane à Mulets and stops 1,000ft (300m) short of the crater itself, which still spews out dust and even lava.

The north of Basse-Terre makes a day-trip tour in itself. Heading north up the east coast, through traditional cane-growing flats, a working sugar factory complete with steam-driven crusher operates at the **Domaine de Sévérin**▶▶ (tel: 0590 23 50 66) at Ste-Rose, and the story of sugar production is told at the **Musée de Rhum**▶▶ (tel: 0590 28 70 04. *Open* Mon–Sat 9–5. *Admission: inexpensive*). On the northwestern corner of the island are some of Guadeloupe's best beaches, particularly the Plage de Cluny and la Grande Anse, a 2-mile (3km) sweep of golden sand and palms. Near the 17th-century town of Pointe-Noire is the **Maison du Bois**▶ (*Open* Tue–Sun 9.30–7. *Admission: moderate*) which shows local building techniques. Also look for the **Maison du Cacao**▶▶ (tel: 0590 98 21 23. *Open* Mon–Sat 9–5. *Admission: inexpensive*), to see a pictorial history of cocoa and chocolate.

La Traversée crosses through the middle of Basse-Terre, passing the **Cascade aux Ecrivisses**▶▶ and the **Maison de la Forêt**▶▶ (tel: 0590 80 86 00. *Open* daily 9–5. *Admission free*), which traces the development of the island's natural life. Past a small zoo, the road descends to the sea and rejoins the coast road, turning south toward Basse-Terre. The Jacques Cousteau Marine Reserve is located off the popular black sand beach at Malendure.

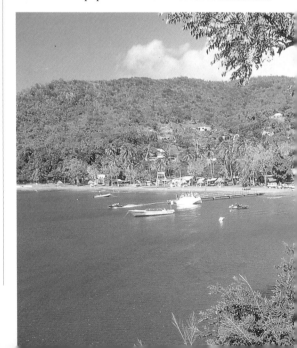

Malendure has a string of beach bars; the Ile de Pigeon is an excellent site for scuba diving

LA DÉSIRADE Virtually unspoiled by tourism, La Désirade offers a quiet getaway and white beaches. The "Desired One" was often the first island spotted by 16th-century sailors longing for land after a tedious Atlantic crossing. Their desire was frustrated, however, as ships would sail past this barren, windy island.

Only 7 miles by about 1 mile (11 by 1.5km), La Désirade is a table mountain lying 5 miles (8km) east of Grande-Terre. Its population of under 2,000 is spread along the southern shore between the town of Grande Anse and the village of Le Souffleur.

La Darse, Pointe-à-Pitre

113

MARIE-GALANTE The beach at Petit Anse is the draw of Marie-Galante, the largest of Guadeloupe's offshore islands. Almost circular, it measures nearly 60sq miles (155sq km) and has a population of 12,400, half of whom live in the main town of Grand-Bourg. Named by Columbus in 1493 after his flagship, *Santa Maria de Galante*, it was a longtime Carib stronghold but was eventually captured by Europeans and turned into a sugar island. The main island museum, Musée Associatif sur les Traditions et la Découverte de Marie-Galante (tel: 0590 97 59 67. *Open* Tue–Sat 8–1, 3–5, Sun 8–11am. *Admission: inexpensive*) offers more historical details. Beyond Grand-Bourg, ruined windmills are reminders of the sugar trade's peak. The **Château Murat▶** (tel: 0590 97 94 41. *Open* Mon–Fri 8–1, 2.30–5.30, Sat–Sun 9–noon, 2–4. *Admission free*), a restored 18th-century plantation house east of Grand-Bourg, contains a museum. There are also excellent walking paths around the island.

LES SAINTES The lures of Les Saintes include a nudist beach, scuba diving and a beautiful bay that's been called a mini Rio. These volcanic peaks lie to the south of Basse-Terre. Only two are inhabited: Terre-de-Bas and Terre-de-Haut. The population of the former is descended from plantation slaves. **Terre-de-Haut▶▶**, which was never planted, centers around tourism, with hotels on the waterfront of Bourg, its only town. White fishermen—descended from French colonials—wear *salako* hats which are made in Terre-de-Bas. There are good beaches on Terre-de-Haut, and sights include Fort Napoléon, with a museum andexotic garden (tel: 0590 61 01 51. *Open* daily 9–noon, 2–4. *Admission: inexpensive*), on the highest point.

THE BATTLE OF THE SAINTS
The Battle of the Saints, so-called because it took place just off Les Saintes in 1782, was a turning point in the fight for European imperial supremacy over the Caribbean islands. It was also a first in naval terms; the British Admiral Rodney saw a gap between the French ships and managed to "break the line," splitting the French fleet into two parts so that the flagship could not communicate with most of its fleet. The battle ended in victory for the British, who held sway over Caribbean waters for the next two decades.

PETIT PUNCH

This popular French Caribbean drink is taken before lunch. A heap of brown sugar crystals is dashed with local white rum and stirred. A quarter of lime is squeezed in and the mix is downed in one gulp. Ice water is then swilled around to collect the last of the sugar and downed as a chaser.

Martinique pâtisserie

Martinique

Martinique—which is far more tourist-oriented than Guadeloupe—has always been the heart of the French Caribbean. St-Pierre, once its most important town, was known as the Paris of the Lesser Antilles, and its booming sugar trade was vitally important to the French, who were even prepared to give up their claims to territories in India and Canada in return for keeping the island in the 18th century. As its Amerindian name, *Madinina* ("Land of Flowers") implies, this is a fertile island, and since the French arrived in 1635 (they have owned it almost continuously ever since) it has been successfully farmed. Agriculture and fishing are still important, and there are vast acres of bananas, pineapples and sugar cane. Martinique lies midway down the chain of the Lesser Antilles, between the independent islands of Dominica and St. Lucia. Shaped something like a boxing glove, it measures 50 miles by 20 miles (80km by 32km) at its widest point. In the mountainous north, the highest peak, the active volcano

Montagne Pelée, stands 4,583ft (1,397m) high; rain forests cover the Pitons du Carbet and, to the south, the land descends to fertile plains and *mornes* (or foothills).

The island's relatively large tourist industry is not immediately visible, as there is a strong local community. The population is made up of a diverse mix of French, African, East Indian, Chinese and Arab races; French is the official language and the French influence can be seen in everyday life, from the croissants to the Peugeot cars. But there is also a lively Créole culture and good Caribbean restaurants, stores and bars.

FORT-DE-FRANCE Martinique's capital is a modern town set in a bay on the calm Caribbean shore. It has grown enormously since the eruption of Montagne Pelée devastated St-Pierre in 1902, and over 100,000 inhabitants now live in the center and in the suburbs that have clambered all over the surrounding hills. Overlooking the waterfront on the Baie des Flammands, the center of the town is **La Savanne**▶▶, an open park studded with 100ft (30m) royal palm trees. There is a headless statue of Josephine Bonaparte, the French empress, who was born across the bay at Trois-Ilets. You can visit **Fort St. Louis**▶ (tel: 0596 59 86 06 for opening hours. *Admission: inexpensive*), the fortress that protected the town in the days of the empire. The **Musée Départemental d'archéologie précolombienne**▶ (tel: 0596 71 57 05. *Open* Mon 1–5, Tue–Fri 8–5, Sat 9–noon. *Admission: inexpensive*) has a display of Amerindian pottery. Nearby, **Bibliothèque Schoelcher**▶▶(tel: 0596 70 26 69. Open Mon 1–5.30, Tue–Fri 8.30–5.30, Sat 8.30–noon), a domed structure of brightly colored metal and glass, was built for the 1889 Paris Exhibition and transported here to house a library commemorating Victor Schoelcher's anti-slavery campaign.

Driving in Fort-de-France is not a good idea. The streets are crowded and several are given over to markets—such as the fish market on the Rivière Madame, near the geological displays of the Parc Floral. Beyond the suburbs, the scenery turns into mountainous rain forest to the north and sugar cane flats to the south and east. Here, life is simpler: Catholic churches overlook town squares and orange and green fishing boats are moored in the bays.

THE HEAD CODE
There is a certain elegance and coquettish air about some French Antilleans that mirrors their metropolitan counterparts. A century ago there was even a flirtatious message in the way island women wore their madras headdresses. Tied with checkered silk material, the headdress indicated a code in the number of points protruding. One corner meant that the woman had no lover; two points meant that her heart was taken. Three points meant that officially her heart was taken, but that a man might try his luck.

Jardin de Balata

Ian Fleming, the creator of James Bond, lived on the north coast of Jamaica and took the name for his famous spy from a real ornithologist, the author of The Birds of the West Indies. *The Caribbean is on migratory routes north and south, and many birds from farther north like to winter in the Caribbean. With so many habitats (shoreline, mangrove swamp, forests) within a relatively small area, human visitors can expect to see a striking variety of different species.*

116

Scarlet ibis (top)
Jamaican mountain goats (right)

ZOOS
The Caribbean islands have a small number of zoos. In Santo Domingo, the capital of the Dominican Republic, the Parque Zoologico Nacional keeps elephants as well as tropical animals, and in Port of Spain, Trinidad, the Emperor Valley Zoo has tropical animals seen in Trinidad, including the tree porcupine, the crab-eating racoon and monkeys such as the weeping capuchin and the red howler. Animals are free to roam in the Barbados Wildlife Reserve, in the north of the island, and on Guadeloupe the Parc Zoologique et Botanique, on the Route de la Traversée (D23) in Basse-Terre, has walkways through the rain forest. There are also small zoos in Sint Maarten and in Mayaguez, Puerto Rico.

Mangrove swamps and coastal lagoons are good places to look out for herons, ducks and more exotic creatures such as gallinules and jacanas, whose long toes enable them to walk over lilies. Colonies of flamingoes nest on the island of Bonaire, and kingfishers can often be spotted flitting along rivers.

Pelicans are a familiar sight on many islands, flying in formation around the shoreline or diving into the sea for food. Tropicbirds occasionally soar near the coast, and the magnificent frigatebird cruises high in the air, waiting for passing meals. Gulls, terns, gannets and boobies skim along the surface of the sea before rising and plunging to catch fish, while small crowds of oystercatchers and sandpipers walk along the beaches as they feed, dodging the breaking waves.

On open ground, the white cattle egret can be seen wherever there are grazing cows, and thrushes, finches and larger birds, such as crows (called John Crows), are common. Slightly harder to spot are mockingbirds and flycatchers, which snatch up insects on the wing, and tanagers, which feed on fruit.

In contrast, some of the most familiar birds are self-assured enough to try stealing the sugar from breakfast tables: The carib grackle, which is also called a blackbird in some areas, has a V-shaped tail and displays by puffing out its feathers. The cocky bananaquit has distinctive yellow and black plumage.

It takes a lot of luck to see the Caribbean's more exotic birds. Shimmering hummingbirds flit around the flowers on a permanent search for nectar; the purple-throated and green-throated hummingbirds and the Antillean crested hummingbird live in most islands of the Eastern Caribbean. High in the forests there are still Caribbean parrots, though these are now an endangered species, particularly in the Eastern Caribbean, where there are parrots unique to St. Vincent, St. Lucia and Dominica (the imperial and red-necked parrots).

The island of Trinidad is an exception in the Caribbean, both in its animal and its bird life, because it has considerable spill-over from the South American continent. Over 400 bird species make this the best island for bird-watching, but the most spectacular sight is the scarlet ibis, with its vivid red plumage and downward-curving bill. It might just be possible to see a bright blue mot-mot or maybe a mannikin; the male mannikin, with its white breast and black cap and wings, spends about 70 percent of its time displaying, strutting with its competitors around the female, making noises like a little firecracker, and even turning somersaults.

Caribbean animals Most animals on the Caribbean islands—goats, chickens, donkeys, cattle and even monkeys and mongeese—were imported by settlers. Indigenous survivors, most of which are endangered, include the coney, which is something like a guinea pig and lives in the Jamaican John Crow mountains and on Hispaniola; the agouti, a tail-less rodent the size of a rabbit, living in the Eastern Caribbean; the American racoon; and the tatou, an armadillo that survives in Grenada. Reptiles are more widespread. Tiny geckos and lizards crawl over walls and tree frogs peep noisily in gardens. Iguanas, which can grow to nearly 4ft (120cm), are found on a number of islands, and the few snakes include small constrictors and the notorious fer de lance, with eyes that glow orange at night.

Perhaps the most curious of a wide range of insects are Hercules beetles, which can measure 6in (15cm) long and have claws protruding from their heads, and Cuban tarantulas, which can grow to the size of a man's hand.

ANIMAL SETTLERS
In the early days of European settlement, sailors would leave animals ashore and plant fruit-bearing trees on remote islands so that there would be a supply of food for anyone who might be shipwrecked. Père Labat, an early French traveler, recounts a sailors' tale that a shipwrecked crew with a pig on board should throw it into the sea and row after it, as it would know innately the direction of the nearest land.

SANDFLIES
Apart from mosquitoes, the most annoying insects that frequent beaches are sandflies. So small that they are virtually invisible, sandflies are known on some islands as "no-see-ums," and their bite causes an infuriating itch.

117

Iguanas live on many Caribbean islands

DIAMOND ROCK

The sheer-sided Diamond Rock stands just off the south coast of Martinique and is rarely visited, but for 18 months in 1805 it was occupied by 100 British sailors, who built a fort there in order to deny the channel to French ships. All the supplies, building materials and food had to be winched up from ships below. Eventually the French made a serious effort to take it back and bombarded the Rock for three days before the commander surrendered.

118

*St.-Pierre, once a
bustling city*

OUTSIDE FORT-DE-FRANCE Martinique is a large island and although the roads are good, a leisurely circuit can take a couple of days. Buses run from the waterfront at Fort-de-France, and shared taxis follow regular routes. Car rental companies operate in Fort-de-France and the main tourist areas, and at the airport.

The closest tourist resort to Fort-de-France is Pointe du Bout and its beach, Anse Mitan, south across the bay (take a ferry from the waterfront). This is a lively area with good restaurants and cafés, though the beaches are not the best. To the south, beyond Trois-Ilets, is the **Musée de la Pagerie►►** (tel: 0596 68 38 34. *Open* Tue–Fri 9–5.30, Sat–Sun 9–1, 2.30–5.30. *Admission: inexpensive*), dedicated to Josephine Bonaparte and set in the farm where she was born. There is a golf course and a museum of sugar, the **Maison de la Canne►►** (tel: 0596 68 32 04. *Open* Tue–Thu 8.30–5.30, Fri–Sat 8.30–5, Sun 9–5. *Admission: inexpensive*).

West along the coast, there are three attractive coves at **Les Anses-d'Arlets►►**, isolated on the southwestern shore, and worth a detour. As the coast road winds its way to Le Diamant, it passes the solitary Diamond Rock, a few miles offshore (see panel). For an excellent potted history of the island (in French), and Amerindian and colonial artifacts, visit the **Écomusée de la Martinique►**, Anse Figuier (tel: 0596 62 79 14. *Open* Tue–Thu 8.30–5.30, Fri 8.30–5, Sat 8.30–1, 2–5, Sun 9–1, 2–5. *Admission: inexpensive*). Le Martin, which has a large marina, and Ste-Anne are the two main tourist towns in the southeast. The best beaches in Martinique are at the island's southern: **Grande Anse des Salines►►►**, a 2-mile (3km) sweep of palm-backed sand, and nearby Anse Trabaud.

The east coast of Martinique is mainly agricultural and the sea can be rough, though there are beaches tucked into the folds of the coastline. Near Le François, **Habitation Clément►►** (tel: 0596 54 62 07. *Open* Oct–Aug daily 9–6. *Admission: expensive*) is one of the most attractive plantation houses in the Caribbean. The **Rhum St. James rum distillery►►** (tel: 0596 69 30 02. *Open* daily 9–5. *Admission free*) at Ste-Marie and the **Maison de la Banane►►** (tel: 0596 69 45 52. *Open* daily 9–5. *Admission: moderate*), which is farther inland, are open to visitors.

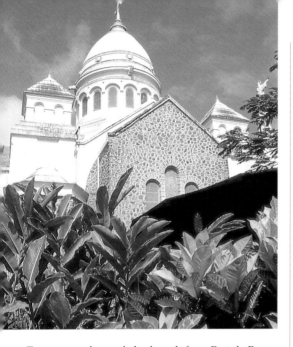

Balata's version of the Sacré-Coeur rises out of the tropical greenery above Fort-de-France

ST-PIERRE'S SURVIVOR
At one time, St-Pierre was the most chic and stylish town in the Eastern Caribbean. It boasted a theater and a cathedral, and "Pierrotins" followed Paris fashion to the letter. Although the town was almost totally destroyed by the volcanic eruption of 1902, one man was saved because he had been put in a police cell overnight after a drinking spree. The walls of the cell protected him from the heat and gases of the explosion. He later joined a circus, exhibiting himself in a reproduction of his cell.

119

Two spectacular roads lead north from Fort-de-France to the town of St-Pierre, one climbing into the rain-forested mountains and the other following the coast. The Route de la Trace, an old forest road cut by the Jesuits three centuries ago, climbs up through the suburb of Didier and passes through Balata, where a replica of the Sacré-Coeur in Paris was built in 1923 as a World War I memorial. The road continues to the **Jardin de Balata**▶▶▶ (tel: 0596 64 48 73. *Open* daily 9–5, reduced hours in Sep. *Admission: inexpensive*), where walkways lead past hundreds of tropical plants. From here, La Trace forges into the peaks of the Pitons du Carbet.

The coast road passes through fishing villages such as Case-Pilote, and Le Carbet, where Paul Gauguin lived for two years in the 19th century; the **Musée Gauguin**▶ (tel: 0596 78 22 66. *Open* daily 9–5.30. *Admission: inexpensive*) exhibits reproductions of his works.

Though it was never the official capital, St-Pierre was the business and social center of Martinique—until the 8th of May, 1902, when the whole town was engulfed by a volcanic ash and nearly all the 26,000 residents were killed. The town is still inhabited and many of its old buildings, including the theater and some water-front warehouses, still exist, though as ruins. There are a couple of museums on the rue Victor Hugo—the **Musée Historique**▶ (tel: 0596 78 15 16. *Open* Mon–Sat 9.30–5. *Admission: inexpensive*), with displays about town life before 1902, and the **Musée Volcanologique**▶▶ (tel: 0596 78 15 16. *Open* daily 9–5. *Admission: inexpensive*), which has grim exhibits from the day of its destruction. Montagne Pelée itself looms quietly over the remains of the town.

St-Pierre souvenir

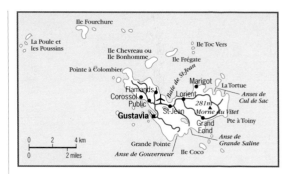

BRETON HERITAGE
St. Barts was first colo-
nized by Bretons
and Normans and there
is still a community of
white Barthéleminois,
whose language has
retained some remnants
of 17th-century Breton.
Another curious hangover
of their ancient heritage,
still occasionally seen,
is their *calèche* hats,
cotton bonnets fitted with
wooden slats that stick
out above the face like a
visor. Apart from shading
the wearer from the sun,
they keep away other
intrusions, earning them
the nickname
quichenotte—supposedly
a corruption of "kiss-me-
not."

Saint-Barthélemy

Saint-Barthélemy, a tiny speck set in an aquamarine sea,
has seen the full ebb and flow of Caribbean fortune. From
a backwater visited occasionally by pirates it became a
thriving trading post for 50 years before slipping back into
obscurity. Today, the island is one of the Caribbean's most
luxurious and desirable destinations.

St. Barts (or Saint-Barth in French), as this most French of
the French Caribbean islands is affectionately known, has
a rarified and exclusive air. It is the favored retreat of a
chic clientele of stars and the seriously rich, who zip
around the island's boutiques and beaches in Suzuki jeeps
and on *mobylettes* (mopeds). Tropical sophistication is
taken to perfection here—at a very high price.

Although St. Barts is just under 8sq miles (20sq km) in
size, with no hill rising above 920ft/280m (Morne Vitet),
the scrub-covered scenery is rough and dramatic and six
large lagoons are scattered across the landscape. The
island lies 15 miles (24km) to the southeast of Saint-
Martin, on the same coral geological shelf, and this gives it
magnificent white sand beaches. More than 20 tiny islets
and islet groups lie in its waters, of which the largest is Ile
Fourchue; others include the Ile Frégate twin islands, Les

*Offshore islands near
Saint-Barthélemy*

Balines and La Baline ("The Whales" and "The Whale"), and La Poule et Les Poussins ("The Hen and Chickens").

Like Saint-Martin, St. Barts is a *commune* of Guadeloupe, 155 miles (250km) to the south, administered by a *sous-préfet* from Paris, but it has not always been French. After 100 or so years of trading with smugglers and pirates, the 1,000 French settlers learned in 1785 that the island had been leased to the Swedes in return for trading rights in the Baltic. Sweden made St. Barts a free port and for half a century the island prospered. When it was handed back to the French in 1878, its duty-free status was retained.

The capital of St. Barts is **Gustavia▶▶▶**, named for Gustav III, the Swedish king who made the 1785 exchange. It has just a few pretty streets, some with Swedish names, set on three sides of a natural harbor. In its heyday the town was defended by four fortresses, of which two, Fort Gustav and Fort Karl, can be visited. The **Museé de Saint-Barth▶▶** (tel: 0590 29 71 55. *Open* Mon–Thu 8.30–12.30, 2.30–6, Fri 8.30–12.30, 3–6, Sat 9–11am. *Admission: inexpensive*) is set in the restored Wall House on the seaward arm of the bay. Unfortunately, much of the original town was destroyed by fire in the 1850s, but some of the old stone warehouses have been restored and now provide atmospheric settings for bars and restaurants.

St. Barts can easily be explored in a day. A drive around the steep, switchback roads takes in the occasional old church or traditional country house with plastered walls and tin roofs dotted among the modern villas. You might even hear a bit of local dialect or see an islander dressed traditionally in a long white skirt and bonnet or *calèche*. Good beaches include Anse du Gouverneur and **Anse de Grande Saline▶▶▶** on the south coast; also the Baie de St. John and Anse de Grand Cul de Sac on the north.

North of Gustavia, the road runs through Public to Corossol, an old fishing village with a shell collection at the **Inter Oceans Museum▶▶** (tel: 0590 27 62 97. *Open* daily 9.30–noon, 2–5. *Admission: inexpensive)*. The village is also the best place to find St. Barts weaving, made from the latanier palm, which grows all over the island.

To the northeast of the capital, the Plaine de la Tourmente is the site of the island's airstrip and of a graveyard. St. Jean, to the east, is one of the centers of the tourist industry, with boutiques and restaurants. At Lorient, farther east, local fishermen work as they have for centuries; beyond this point, the country opens out, though there are hotels tucked away in the bays. When the winds are up, the windsurfing is excellent in the east.

The hair-raising landing strip at St. Barts only accommodates small planes

121

The Hôtel la Banane— a tourist's-eye view of St. Barts

THE PARTITION

A fanciful story describes the partitioning of Saint-Martin/Sint Maarten between the French and the Dutch. Two men, one from each side, stood back to back and set off around the coastline until they met up again; the line between the departure and meeting points was to be the border. The French ended up with the larger share of the island—so the Frenchman presumably walked faster—but there are tales that the Dutchman was delayed by snoozing after too much French wine, or by a pretty French girl who happened to be passing.

Saint-Martin

The border that divides the island of Saint-Martin between France and Holland (see also pages 140–142) is barely noticeable. The countryside is much the same on both sides. Only an obelisk and a bilingual sign mark the fact that this is the smallest island in the world to be divided between two sovereign states. France, which owns the northern half of the island, looking toward Anguilla, marginally got the better of the division (see panel), with 21 of the total 37 square miles (54 of 95sq km).

This is a rugged island with tall, green and yellow concave slopes (the tallest is Pic du Paradis, at 1,391 feet/424m) and a tortuous coastline indented with coves and superb white sand beaches. The main landmass is pierced with lagoons and salt ponds and one "wing" is almost entirely occupied by a vast lake—one of the largest natural lakes in the Antilles, divided between the Dutch and French territories; the French part is attended by two low islands, Ilet Pinel ("Penal Island") and Caye Verte, to which there are daily ferry trips.

Saint-Martin is a *commune* of Guadeloupe and has a distinctly French air—policemen wear *képis* and French restaurants, cafés, bistros and boutiques abound in the main resorts. But the atmosphere of the island is basically international and modern, having boomed, like the Dutch side, from a lazy backwater 20 years ago to a large tourist destination. The population has likewise exploded to cope with the influx of tourists; this is not the best Caribbean island for getting away from the crowds.

Marigot▶ ▶ is the capital on the French side, a small nexus of streets set between the Baie de Marigot and the Simpson Bay Lagoon. The few old townhouses with wrought-iron balconies and the waterfront warehouses have been restored and now buzz with shoppers and drinkers taking time out from the beach. On the Boulevard de France, overlooking the bay, is the **market square**▶ ▶ and the tourist office. The ruined Fort St. Louis, the town's defense in the days of imperial wars, has a magnificent view over Anguilla and the town's approaches, as well as the lagoon, where the busy **Marina Port la Royale**▶ ▶ yacht basin is packed with pleasure craft and

BIENVENUE EN PARTIE FRANÇAISE
— WELCOME TO THE FRENCH SIDE

123

lined with cafés and restaurants. Heading west out of town you will come to the **Musée de Saint Martin**▶ ▶ (tel: 0590 29 22 84. *Open* Mon–Sat 9–1, 3–6. *Admission: inexpensive*), which traces the island's indigenous and colonial history.

Marigot harbor…

Beyond here, some of the island's best beaches can be found in Baie Rouge and Baie Longue at the western tip of the island. The road south out of Marigot leads past the obelisk, which marks the border, to the main airport.

North of Marigot is a more natural Saint-Martin, although the hills are dotted everywhere with modern villas. There is a lookout near the summit of the Pic du Paradis that gives marvelous views of the nearby islands.

Beyond the local settlement of Colombier and an excellent, often uncrowded beach at Friar's Bay, is the appealing town of **Grand-Case**, set along the sandy waterfront. Known as the gastronomic capital of the island, it has a row of excellent restaurants and bars set above the sea.

Past the airstrip to the east the countryside does become surprisingly sparse, although most bays are now developed with hotels. Of the east coast beaches, the best for windsurfing are Baie de l'Embouchure and **Baie de l'Orient**, partly a nudist beach.

…and café society

The Netherlands Antilles

Aruba
Oranjestad ■ *188m*
Sint Nicolas ▲

Netherlands Antilles

Westpunt ●
▲ *372m*   Curaçao

240m ▲ Bonaire
Rincon ●
Kralendijk ●

Willemstad ■
New Port

YV

0   25   50 km
0   25 miles

Aruba's white-sand beaches

Boca Tabla, on Curaçao's northern shore

THE NETHERLANDS ANTILLES The six Dutch islands of the Caribbean carry the imprint of their colonial history; on Curaçao, even canals and gabled warehouses can be seen. The dry island of Aruba has superb beaches and Bonaire has some of the region's best preserved reefs. Aruba, Bonaire, Curaçao and especially Sint Maarten all have developed tourist infrastructures, while the tiny outcrops of Saba and Sint Eustatius see far fewer visitors. The islands lie in two groups, separated by 500 miles (800km) of sea: the volcanic Dutch Windwards, Sint Maarten, Saba and Sint Eustatius, nicknamed Statia (the SSS islands), near the northern end of the Lesser Antilles; and the Dutch Leewards, Bonaire and Curaçao, off the coast of Venezuela. Aruba was politically part of this group until it separated from the Netherlands Antilles in 1986, but many still refer to these as the ABC islands. The two groups contain some of the more beautiful—as well as the most inhospitable— landscapes found in the West Indies islands.

A Dutch heritage spanning 350 years has formed much of the character of each island. The official currency is the Netherlands Antilles florin or guilder (Aruba has its own Aruban florin), island cuisine includes dishes such as *keshi yena* made with melted Gouda cheese, and souvenir shops are as likely to stock Delft blue chinaware as they are more traditional Caribbean crafts. Red-bricked, pastel-painted and gabled houses recall the heyday of the Dutch Empire, contrasting with the modern buildings erected since the oil boom of the 20th century, all set incongruously among golden beaches and coconut palms. The ABC islands have their own language, Papiamento, a curious-sounding mix of Spanish and Dutch, seeded with Portuguese, English and African.

HISTORY The Dutch West India Company first spotted the strategic and economic significance of the Lesser Antilles in the 1620s; Sint Maarten was a neat stepping stone to Dutch colonies in Brazil; and Aruba, Bonaire and Curaçao (colonized on a small scale by the Spanish in 1511) provided salt for the profitable herring industry at home. As trade increased, Curaçao became a center for the slave trade, attracting the interest of rivals, and during the 18th century the islands were seized by one European power after another. The other great Dutch success story was tiny Sint Eustatius, nicknamed the Golden Rock after the riches its traders piled high in their waterfront warehouses. Its rather bizarre downfall occurred when the island's governer saluted an American brig flying the Stars and Stripes as it sailed into the harbor on the 16 of November 1776. This innocent gesture made Holland the first nation to recognize the newly constituted United States, provoking an outraged Britain to send a naval expedition to sack the island in 1781, a blow from which it never recovered.

In 1816 the Dutch regained their hold, but the era of booming trade was over and the islands fell into decline until the arrival of the oil companies in the early 20th century. Refineries were set up on Aruba and Curaçao, bringing in workers from neighboring islands and new prosperity. In the 1980s the oil industry, faced with falling profits, reduced its Antilles operations, and islanders have become increasingly reliant on the tourist trade.

The Netherlands Antilles

A yacht-borne picnic excursion passes Saba at sunset

126

PATH TO INDEPENDENCE?

The Dutch islands were in step with the rest of the Caribbean in their growing desire for political self-government in the early part of the 20th century. Labor union movements in the oilfields increased the political awareness of the islands, and, in 1936, a *Staten*, or parliament, was formed. During World War II, while Holland was occupied by the Germans, the Dutch islands were left to fend for themselves and gained experience of self-government. There was not the headlong rush for independence after the war that was seen among the British islands, but autonomy was granted in 1954. Holland has stated that it will allow the islands to become fully independent when their economies are reliably stable, but many islanders prefer to remain within the Kingdom of the Netherlands for the foreseeable future.

Red roofs in The Bottom, the capital of Saba

127

Today the Netherlands Antilles are divided into three territories: Curaçao (the administrative capital), Bonaire, and the three Windward islands—Sint Maarten, Sint Eustatius and Saba. Each has its own representative body (the Island Council), elected every four years, which chooses commissioners. Together they form the Executive Council for each island or island group. The Queen of the Netherlands appoints the Lieutenant-General and the island Governor, who serves a term of six years and appoints Antillian ministers. Aruba was deemed a state apart (*Status Aparte*) from the other administrations in 1986 and is now an autonomous part of the Netherlands, but plans for full independence were put on hold in 1996.

"African" carvings at a craft stall in Aruba

Aruba

From the air, Aruba seems small and flat, with a ribbon of blinding white sand running down its western side. In fact, although the island is only 19 miles by 6 miles (30km by 10km), its hills rise to over 490ft (150m) and the combined stretch of Palm Beach and Eagle Beach is one of the Caribbean's finest strips of sand. The island's distinctive beauty lies in its countryside—an almost extraterrestrial landscape of arid rocky deserts, cactus jungles and secluded coves. With its low humidity and average temperature of 82°F (28°C), Aruba has the climate of paradise; rain falls mostly during November. The 78,000 Arubians have Spanish, Portuguese, East Indian and Caribbean origins, as well as Dutch.

The official language is Dutch, and English is widely spoken, but most Arubians speak Papiamento, a dialect drawing from Spanish, French, Portuguese, Dutch, African and English (see panel). Colonization came relatively late to Aruba, which was virtually ignored by European powers until the

Oranjestad: a modern interpretation of traditional Dutch-Caribbean style and colors

20th century, and this has resulted in its people retaining a strong sense of independence.

The capital, **Oranjestad►►**, lies on the protected south-western shore; the town and its outlying suburbs are the center of Aruban life. Named for the Dutch royal house of Orange, this is Aruba's main port. Some of the older buildings around the main street, Nassaustraat, date from the oil boom early in the 20th century, but most are modern imitations with traditional flourishes, containing the banks and shopping complexes of the modern town. A line of fishing boats forms the quayside Schooner Market, selling produce from Venezuela.

Fort Zoutman (1796) is the island's oldest building and contains the **Historical Museum►** (tel: 5826099. *Open* Mon–Fri 9–noon, 1.30–4.40. *Admission: inexpensive*), tracing Aruba's history. The **Archeological Museum►** (tel: 828979. *Open* Mon–Fri 8–noon, 1–4. *Admission free*), at the Instituto di Cultura depicts indigenous life, while the **Numismatic Museum►►** (tel: 9656969. *Open* Mon–Thu 9–4, Fri 9–1, Sat 9–noon. *Admission free*), on Weststraat, has a collection of 30,000 bills and coins.

To the west of Oranjestad, the coastal road runs past the cruise ship dock to Aruba's magnificent beaches: **Eagle Beach►►►** ("low rise strip") and **Palm Beach►►►** ("high rise strip"). There is no shortage of watersports or bars here—nor is there any lack of crowds, especially in June, when Aruba hosts a windsurfing festival.

East of the town, the road passes through suburbs into the scrub. Sprinkled among the new houses are traditional buildings, with talismanic symbols painted on the clay walls and roofs made of cactus wood and grass.

Aruba's highest hill is Jamanota (617ft/188m), but its most distinctive is the **Hooiberg►**, standing over 540ft (165m) high, with a stairway that will help to ease the climb. To its north are the huge, gray and rounded **diorite boulders►►** at Casibari and Ayo, and on the north coast, east of Oranjestad, are the ruins of the Bushiribana gold mines, whose discovery in 1825 led to a brief gold rush. One smelting site produced 2 million pounds (1 million kg) of gold.

Also in this area are the ruins of a 16th-century fortress, and at **Andicouri►►**, the sea has carved the spectacular Natural Bridge from the coral. San Nicolas is Aruba's second town and site of the former refinery.

129

Aruba's Dutch legacy is still apparent…

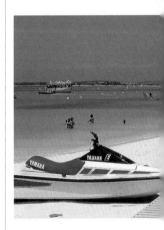

…while tourism is taking over on its inviting beaches

Salt stacks awaiting shipping glare in the tropical sun of Bonaire (above and far right)

130

THE SALT INDUSTRY
As you drive south on Bonaire you will come to the vast white stacks of Bonaire's salt, beneath which several cranes bustle about. Salt production has been revived for industrial purposes; sea water is let into shallow "pans" and the sun and the wind then do their work, evaporating the water. The resulting brine is channeled into other pans to increase the evaporation effect, and eventually a bed of white crystals appears. These are harvested and cleaned before being stacked by a crane on rails in mounds ready for shipping.

Bonaire

Bonaire is a stark desert island, perfect for the rugged individualist who is turned off by the commercialized high life of the other Antillean islands. A magnet for divers, the island has one of the most unspoiled reef systems in the world. The water is so clear that you can lean over the dock and look the fish straight in the eye. This is not the island for connoisseurs of fine cuisine or for shopping addicts, but what lies off its shores will keep divers enthralled. Most visitors to the island come for the scuba diving. The **Bonaire Marine Park**►►► (www. bmp.org)—a model of ecological conservation—almost surrounds Bonaire as well as Klein Bonaire from the high-water tidemark to a depth of nearly 200ft (60m). The corals and fish are some of the finest and least disturbed in the Caribbean, and they make Bonaire well worth visiting for a relaxing vacation with a sporting focus.

Shaped somewhat like a foot, Bonaire is a crooked 23.5 miles (38km) long. In the bight of the protected coast is the football-shaped Klein Bonaire, about to be kicked toward Curaçao. Like its neighbors, Bonaire is dry and windswept, covered in scrubby vegetation and dotted with tall cacti. From the salt flats in the south, the land rises to the 787ft (240m) Mount Brandaris in the northwest. Much of the coastline is limestone coral shelf, but there are breaks in the wall where the sand collects to form decent beaches. Two colonies of flamingoes nest on the island and can be seen feeding in the lagoons during the day. A circuit of the island can be completed in a day; cars can be rented from hotels or car rental companies.

Industries on Bonaire include oil bunkering (storing oil fuel for ships), salt harvesting and radio transmitting stations, but tourism (mainly diving) is the most important economic sector and it has changed the island radically in the last 15 years. From a lazy backwater (which the island had remained from the moment the Dutch arrived in 1636) it has suddenly geared up for large numbers of visitors, but a certain funky sleepiness has survived. Bonaireans speak Papiamento, although Dutch is the official language and English is widely understood.

The capital, **Kralendijk▶▶**, lies in the protected bight of the western shore, on the coral (*kralen*) wall (*dijk*). A few traditional Bonaire houses, painted gold with white stucco, stand among the mostly modern buildings; bars and restaurants line the waterfront and hotels are spread along the shores on either side of the town.

Fort Oranje, the town's old defense, now contains the island museum, displaying indigenous native American and colonial Bonairean artifacts. The whole town comes to life for the Lenten Carnival and for parades and festivals during late June.

Beyond the hotel strip, going north, the road passes the oil storage depot and continues to **Goto Meer▶**, one of the flamingoes' favored nesting spots. The island's northwestern tip is made up of the 13,490-acre (5,460ha) **Washington Slagbaai Park▶▶**, where marked roads give views of Bonaire's semi-arid flora, as well as possible glimpses of iguanas and some of the estimated 130 species of birdlife (including pelicans, bananaquits and sandpipers). Visits can be made by car and by bicycle. Another road heads back to Kralendijk via Rincon, the island's second town, and Indian inscriptions at **Onima▶**.

A circular road runs around the southern toe of the island beyond the airport to **Pink Beach▶▶**, named for the striking color of its sand, and then to the vast white stacks of harvested salt at the **salt works▶▶** (see panel opposite). Another flamingo colony nests here. Colored obelisks stand on the coast, built as shipping guides on an otherwise indistinguishable coastline. Two groups of small huts huddled on the shore were once two-man dormitories for slaves who worked the salt pans in 1850. Lac Baai has two good beaches; nudism is permitted on one.

NATURE AND WILDLIFE
The divi-divi tree, which grows in the Dutch Leewards, has a gnarled but vertical trunk about 6ft (1.8m) high, but the strong Caribbean wind forces its branches to grow at 90 degrees to the trunk. The ABC islands are mainly dry and covered with cactus and scrub. Birds include the orange and black troupial, Curaçao's national bird, and the oriole, which lays its eggs in a nest 3ft (90cm) high.

Kralendijk waterfront at dusk

131

Curaçao

In Willemstad, Curaçao's capital, handsome rows of pastel-colored townhouses look as though they were transplanted from Holland. The island's Dutch architecture makes a cheerful contrast to the cactus-dotted back country scrub known as the *Kunuku*. Curaçao's soft white sandy beaches are small, but watersports attract enthusiasts from all over the world, and some of the best reef diving is here. The shopping is first-rate, too, and the sun smiles, but thanks to the gentle trade winds it never gets too hot. The largest of the Netherlands Antilles, the island lies between Aruba and Bonaire, 34 miles (55km) from the coast of Venezuela. Curaçao is a long and thin island, measuring 37 miles by 9 miles (60km by 15km), created from lava emissions encrusted with coral limestone.

HISTORY Curaçao is the traditional heart of the Dutch Caribbean and has been the administrative capital since the Dutch arrived in 1634. Dubbed the "Land of Giants" by explorer Amerigo Vespucci, who felt dwarfed by the indigenous Caiquetios tribe, Curaçao was left alone by early colonizers, though many of its inhabitants were taken as slaves to the Hispaniola gold mines. By the early 17th century, there was a handful of Spanish settlers, but these were chased out by Dutch merchants. Slave-trading was the island's prime source of wealth and emancipation signaled its decline. In 1915 a new source of prosperity was introduced with the building of an oil refinery, and the population soared as workers moved in. During the 1960s and 1980s the oil industry was dealt two blows: "Automation," which reduced the number of employees,

DUTCH CUISINE

Food in the Dutch Leewards is very different from dishes elsewhere in the Caribbean. A number of restaurants specialize in local cuisine, made even more exotic by its Papiamento names. Dishes include *sopi* (soup) and *stoba* (stews), made with *galina* (chicken), *bestia* (lamb), *carco* (conch) and *kreeft* (lobster) or even *juwana* (iguana). Side dishes include *snijboonchi* (stringbeans), *giambo* (cactus fruit), *funchi* (maize meal) and *toetoe* (cornmeal mixed with beans and bacon, topped with Edam cheese). *Keshi yena* is spicy chicken, covered with Dutch cheese.

and the effects of rising prices. Eventually the business was wound down and there are now plans to expand the tourist industry. Curaçao's hotels are concentrated on the larger beaches to either side of Willemstad, but within easy reach of the capital's stores and restaurants. The island has some excellent restaurants and it is well worth experimenting with local cuisine. Venture off the beaten track and seek out some of the picturesque and secluded craggy coves carved into the rugged north coast.

ISLAND LIFE Curaçao is the most populous of the Netherlands Antilles, and its life as a trading port has given it an extremely varied mix of people. Though Dutch is the official language, Curaçaoans generally speak Papiamento as a first tongue; most also speak English and Spanish. Of all the Dutch Caribbean islands, Curaçao shows the strongest Dutch influence, in its buildings, its food and its faces.

The Penha building: Dutch-influenced architecture on the Handelskade waterfront

WILLEMSTAD Lying on the protected southern shore, Willemstad has developed around the Schottegat, a huge natural harbor, which attracted the first Dutch colonizers. The oldest part of the town is **Punda▶** ("the Point"), of which the main quay, the **Handelskade▶▶**, is one of the most striking sights in the Caribbean; its buildings (such as the 1708 Penha House) combine the curly gables of Amsterdam with the bright colors of the West Indies. Like the streets behind it, the Handelskade still works as a trading area, now serving cruise-ship passengers. At right angles to it is the **Floating Market▶▶▶**, a line of wooden boats docked at the quayside, where you can buy fresh fruit and vegetables shipped in from Venezuela.

The **Mikve Israel Synagogue▶▶** (tel: 461 1633. *Open* Mon–Fri 9–11.45, 2.30–4.45. *Admission: inexpensive*), on Columbusstraat, dates from 1732; the Jewish Historical Museum, in its courtyard, displays among other artifacts a 250-year-old ceremonial bath, and other ritual and Torah objects are still in use today. **Fort Amsterdam▶**, the town's original defense, was built in 1634. It is now the residence of the governor of the Netherlands Antilles and the seat of their Parliament.

133

Willemstad's main quay, Handelskade

A museum in the **Fort Church▶** (tel: 461 1139. *Open Mon–Fri 9–noon, 2–5, also Sun when cruise ships dock. Admission: inexpensive*) displays maps and religious artifacts dating back to 1635. Four other 17th-century forts surround the port; two are now restaurants. A fascinating Maritime Museum (tel: 465 2327. *Open Mon–Sat 9–4. Admission: inexpensive*) showcases the city's seafaring heritage and offers harbour tours. **The Museum Kurá Hulanda▶▶**, Klipstraat 9 (tel: 434 7765. *Open* daily

10–5. *Admission: inexpensive*) features moving exhibits on the history of slavery. The museum is the centrepiece of a new hotel and restaurant complex.

Otrabanda, on the other side of the main harbor channel, is reached by the **Koningin Emmabrug▶▶▶**, a pedestrian pontoon bridge formed by about 15 barges that move constantly on the waves. Occasionally the bridge opens to let ocean-going vessels through; small passenger ferries operate at these times.

In Otrabanda there are more excellent examples of the distinctive Dutch Créole architecture: colonial houses, with their orange tiles and curly gables, many painted with Curaçao gold. **The Curaçao Museum▶▶** (tel: 462 3873. *Open Mon–Fri 9–noon, 2–5, Sun 10–4. Admission: inexpensive*), in an old townhouse once used as the naval hospital, exhibits among other interesting items part of the first airplane to fly here from the Netherlands. The Beth Haim Cemetery has some of the oldest European tombs in the Americas.

Shading under the sails at the floating market at Willemstad (above and above right)

OUTSIDE WILLEMSTAD The suburbs of Willemstad creep around the Schottegat harbor. The autonomy monument, on the eastern side, is a 1954 sculpture of six birds, commemorating the year when the six Netherlands Antilles were granted self-rule. Farther along is the **Curaçao Liqueur Distillery**▶▶ (tel: 461 3526. *Open* Mon–Fri 8–noon, 1–5, also Sun when cruise ships dock. *Admission free*), in the Landhuis Chobolobo, where Curaçao liqueur is produced from the peel of small, green oranges. The oil refinery on the northwest shore was once the largest in the world, best viewed from the hills around Fort Nassau, behind Punda. Near the sports stadium is the restored 18th-century **Landhuis Brievengat**▶▶ (tel: 737 8344. *Open* Mon–Fri 9.15–12.15, 3–6. *Admission: inexpensive*), a cochineal plantation house. Close to the airport are the **Hato Caves**▶, with Indian petroglyph drawings, as well as stalactites and stalagmites.

East of Willemstad is the **Curaçao Sea Aquarium**▶▶ (tel: 461 6666. *Open* daily 8.30–5.30. *Admission: expensive*), with re-created reefs and tropical fish. Glass-bottom boat trips and scuba diving are available in the nearby Curaçao Underwater Park, a restricted marine area, where divers can swim with rays and feed sharks through a mesh.

Westward is the bush countryside, where isolated plantation houses (*landhuisen*) stand among scrub and cacti. Near the island's western tip is **Christoffel National Park**▶▶ (tel: 864 0363. *Open* Mon–Sat 8–5, Sun 6–3. *Admission: expensive*), on the slopes of the Christoffelberg (1,220ft/372m), with marked driving and walking trails and a natural history museum. Curaçao's best beaches are toward the western end, on the south shore.

135

Fishing in Spaanse Water, eastern Curaçao

FLAT POINT AND THE ROAD

Flat Point is, in fact, on a gentle slope, but it is the only area of Saba large enough to have an airstrip (1,300ft/400m long). The Road is a feat of engineering that it was said would be impossible to build. Between Windwardside and The Bottom there is a plaque to Joseph Lambertus Hassell, who followed a correspondence course in engineering and then designed and built The Road, starting at Fort Bay and heading up to The Bottom, on to Windwardside and eventually via 19 hairpin bends down to Flat Point. The Road is still in good condition, after nearly 50 years.

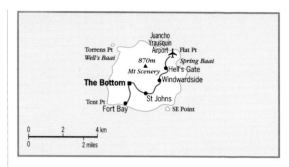

Saba

Not long ago, Saba almost passed a law decreeing that all the roofs on the island be painted red. Draconian, perhaps—but red roofs have long been a tradition on Saba. They go well with the white cottage walls, the picket fences and the striking greens of this fertile island.

Another draconian aspect of Saba is its geography. It is small, extremely rugged and difficult to reach. Mount Scenery, the waterborne peak of an extinct volcano, soars to 2,854ft (870m), on an island only 3 miles by 2 miles (5km by 3km). The 1,349 hardy Sabians have their island neatly tamed; they must, in order to survive here.

Dutch colonists from Sint Eustatius were the first Europeans to settle on the island, in 1640. Twenty-five years later, Saba was taken by a British privateer and all non-English speakers were shipped away. In the 19th century the island was returned to Dutch possession, and Saba survived on the money sent home by its menfolk, who earned a reputation as skilled sailors, and on the lace-making and threadwork of the women. The oil boom on Aruba and Curaçao provided work for islanders in the 20th century, but after its collapse the island turned to its small tourist industry. There are a few places to stay, which are more like friendly mountain guesthouses than Caribbean beach hotels. Saba has no natural beaches, but then visitors to the island mainly come for the excellent scuba diving.

The island's four settlements are all linked by a sinuous artery, respectfully known as The Road

One of Saba's pretty white cottages

(see panel). Its capital is a village by the name of **The Bottom**▶▶, thought to derive from the Dutch *Botte* (bowl), though ironically it's situated 820ft (250m) above sea level. Most of the houses do, indeed, lie at the bottom of a bowl, but new buildings are steadily creeping up the towering, forested peaks that surround it. The Governor's Residence, in the village, is an attractive balconied Caribbean house. A number of bars are run from timber-frame houses, such as Scout's Place, where you can join the Sabans for an afternoon drink.

On the sheltered coast beneath The Bottom are Saba's two harbors: Ladder Bay and Fort Bay. The first is reached by steps; in the days before The Road, Sabans had to carry all their supplies up here on their shoulders. Fort Bay has been the principal port here since 1972, when the jetties were built. It is also the departure point for scuba diving operations. From here there is nowhere to go but back up to the village, from which The Road leads to St. John's, a small collection of houses built on an expanse of relatively flat ground.

Magnificent views of the coast open out 1,200ft (365m) below as The Road reaches **Windwardside**▶▶, Saba's other principal village. The tourist office can be found here, as well as banks and hotels. Windwardside is even neater and prettier than The Bottom, its white houses set behind stone walls, with gardens of bougainvillea and hibiscus. The **Saba Museum**▶ (*Open* Check with tourist office. *Admission: inexpensive*), set in a private home, shows Amerindian artifacts and 19th-century exhibits. Older village women still knit the renowned Saba lace, which can be bought at several craft shops, and brew "Saba Spice," a potent concoction of rum and various herbs and spices.

Beyond Windwardside is the village of Hell's Gate, and from here The Road descends tortuously to the optimistically named Flat Point, site of the island's airstrip (see panel opposite).

Like many of the old trails used by the islanders before The Road was constructed, the steep path to the top of Mount Scenery has carefully laid steps (they start just outside Windwardside) leading through the rain forest and elfin forest; on a clear day the views from this laborious climb are superb.

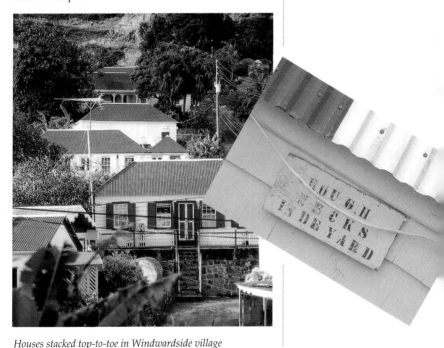

Houses stacked top-to-toe in Windwardside village

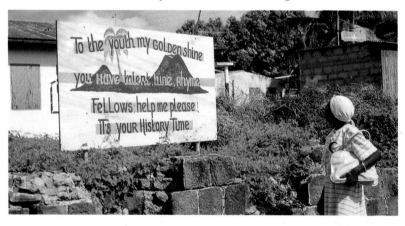

Map showing Sint Eustatius with locations including Boven Bay, Venus Bay, Jenkins Bay, Bergine Bay, 227m Signal Hill, Franklin D Roosevelt Airport, Fort Royal, Fort Oranje, Oranjestad, 155m Round Hill, 594m The Quill, Fort de Windt

SINT EUSTATIUS MUSEUM

For further details on the the Sint Eustatius Historical Foundation Museum. *Open* Mon–Fri 9–5, Sat–Sun 9–noon. *Admission: inexpensive.*

Sint Eustatius

Two hundred years ago, Sint Eustatius was one of the richest and most important islands in the West Indies. As many as a hundred ships would put in to this busy trading port at a time. But the stretch of warehouses that once ran along the Lower Town's shore has gone and only a few walls remain from the island's era as the "Golden Rock."

Almost all of the 18th-century's booming business was breaking the trade laws, as goods which should have been sold to the colonies' governing countries were smuggled to Statia (as the island is usually known) for quick and direct payment. A brisk arms trade developed during the Revolutionary War, and as colonial powers battled over their possessions, the island changed hands over 20 times.

A Statian resident contemplates island philosophy

Statia's golden age ended after the British captured the island and sold off all its goods (see panel opposite).

Today Statia is a quiet backwater with only 2,900 inhabitants, mainly of African descent and English-speaking, although the official language is Dutch. The island is undeveloped—there are only a few hotel rooms and no white-sand Caribbean strands—though with the help of the EU, Statia has renovated its historical buildings and is planning several new museums. Lying 30 miles (48km) south of Sint Maarten (the main access to Statia), between the volcanic peaks of Saba and St. Kitts, the island is just 12sq miles (30sq km) in size. In the south rises a perfectly formed extinct volcanic cone called the Quill; the volcanic sand makes all Statia's beaches dark.

The capital and only town, Oranjestad, sits on a cliff 525 feet (160m) above the island's sheltered Caribbean coast. Its **Upper Town▶▶** has cobbled streets and a few old stone houses with wooden wraparound balconies among the newer buildings, and from its clifftop courtyard of cobbles, date palms and cannon, **Fort Oranje▶** enjoys a superb view of the bay. The **Sint Eustatius Historical Foundation Museum▶▶** is set in the Simon Doncker House built in the 1700s for Doncker, the most prominent Statia merchant of his era. There are rooms devoted to Arawak and Carib Indian culture, colonial years and more recent island history. Some of the Upper Town's historical buildings are no more than shells, but it is worth climbing the tower of the Dutch Reform Church for its fine view. The ruined Honen Dalim synagogue, on Synagoogpad, is one of the oldest in the western hemisphere.

Lower Town▶▶ is where the trading warehouses once stood; as trade expanded, a dyke was built to reclaim more land from the sea. An ancient stone walkway descends from Fort Oranje to the small line of restored buildings re-created with the original bricks. Statia has a growing reputation for scuba diving and boats depart from here, heading out to the reefs offshore. Occasionally divers find blue beads, which were used as a currency on the island two centuries ago.

Beyond the town, Statia's countryside is relatively open, although modern homes are steadily filling the available space. An older Statia is still just visible in the fences of spiky agave and cactus plants and the inevitable goats. It is an easy walk to the lip of the **Quill's crater▶▶**, where lush rain forest grows down in the bowl (it can be a very slippery climb). In the south of the island there is a good view of St. Kitts from the tiny Fort de Windt; in the north, an area of uninhabited hills is the site of Statia's only major industry, an oil bunkerage and a refinery that produces 250 barrels a day.

139

ADMIRAL RODNEY'S REVENGE
A few years after the First Salute, the British had their revenge when Admiral Rodney captured the harbor and kept the flags flying as though the island were open for trade, impounding 150 ships that unwittingly came into harbor. Rodney carried off the merchandise and destroyed the retaining walls. His suspicions were aroused by a sudden rise in the number of deaths on the island: Rodney had several coffins dug up, to find that merchants were hiding their gold in them.

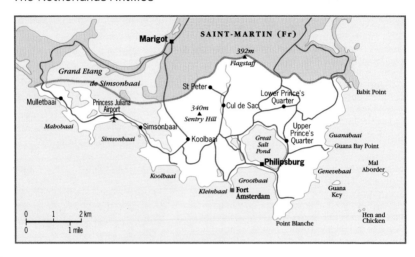

Map of Sint Maarten / Saint-Martin:

SAINT-MARTIN (Fr)
Marigot
392m
Flagstaff
Grand Etang
de Simsonbaai
Mulletbaai
Princess Juliana Airport
Mabobaai
Simsonbaai
Simsonbaai
St Peter
Lower Prince's Quarter
Babit Point
340m
Sentry Hill
Cul de Sac
Koolbaai
Koolbaai
Great Salt Pond
Upper Prince's Quarter
Guanabaai
Guana Bay Point
Philipsburg
Genevebaai
Mal Aborder
Grootbaai
Kleinbaai
Fort Amsterdam
Guana Key
Point Blanche
Hen and Chicken

0   1   2 km
0   1 mile

SHOPPING SPREES
Amid the vast cruise ships that dock at Sint Maarten's capital are smaller, wooden craft, whose captains also come to enjoy some of the Caribbean's best shopping. Sint Maarten is where many West Indians go at Christmas, for wine, electrical goods, tobacco and alcohol. Local yachts make the run from as far down as the Grenadines, where many were built.

Philipsburg's beach

Sint Maarten

Seen from a distance, Sint Maarten (or Saint-Martin) appears serene, rising from the sea in graceful curves to form steep mountain peaks. But this peaceful air belies the hectic activity of Sint Maarten, one of the busiest and most developed territories in the Caribbean.

Despite being just 37sq miles (95sq km) in area, the island is divided between two countries (the smallest island in the world to fly two flags). Since it was first settled in 1648, it has been shared between the Dutch and the French (see pages 122–123 for the French territory, Saint-Martin), and give or take the odd invasion, relations have been pretty amicable. There is even a peak called Mount Concordia as a tribute to their goodwill. The island stands on the same landmass as Anguilla and St. Barts, an ancient volcanic bank, inactive and coral-encrusted, and has superb white beaches. Dutch Sint Maarten occupies 16sq miles (41sq km) in the southern part of the island.

Given its size, Sint Maarten's tourist industry is huge and this has changed the island dramatically over the last 20 years. There has been extensive building and rebuilding after Hurricane Luis in 1995, and the population has boomed. Though Dutch is the official language, a whole range of spoken languages can be heard here, from Haitian Kreyol and Papiamento to English.

The island is crammed to the hilt with hotels, restaurants, bars, clubs, casinos, and heavy traffic. Princess Juliana International Airport is a hive of activity, with flights arriving from the main Caribbean islands as well as from European and US cities. Sint Maarten is also popular as a cruise ship stopover, and its status as a duty-free port brings in streams of high-spending tourists, as well as neighboring islanders keen to take advantage of the bargain prices.

One of the most attractive features of Caribbean architecture is "gingerbread" design, which embellishes houses with an elaborate latticework of wood carved into squiggles, sweeps and twirls. The term is supposedly derived from 16th-century German pastry-makers, who were known for their ornately decorated gingerbread creations.

The flamboyance of gingerbread appealed to plantation owners and estate managers, who had grand houses built to show off their wealth, with elaborate verandas overlooking their estates. Public buildings were also given the gingerbread treatment, the most fanciful of which are in Haiti. Saba, one of the Dutch Windward Islands, has several well-maintained gingerbread houses with green or red window frames, surrounded by pretty tropical blooms (Windwardside and The Bottom). Gingerbread's popularity spread and the style was taken up in the USA during the prosperous 1860s and 1870s, after the Civil War. Good examples can be seen in the beach resort of Cape May, New Jersey.

Traditionally, Caribbean houses were constructed in wood, as there was no need for the warmth provided by stone and brick. Wood was cheaper and buildings could even be dismantled and taken away (in Barbados, farmers' homes were known as "chattel" houses because they could be moved with other goods and chattels). These houses, their walls made from strips of clapboard and their roofs tiled with wooden shingles, are steadily disappearing as the islands develop, but you will see examples of them if you drive through the countryside.

Curaçao, Bonaire and Aruba's houses are made with brick and plaster—wood was scarce and at risk from fire, so its use in building was banned. The walls are painted in gold, light brown, purple and deep green, and the effect is completed with orange "dakpannen," clay roof tiles and white borders. The story goes that Admiral Kikkert, a governor of Curaçao, suffered from headaches brought on by the reflection of the sun bouncing off Willemstad's whitewashed buildings, so he ordered that they be painted any color other than white.

Old San Juan's city hall, Puerto Rico

COUNTRY SHACKS
Traditional Caribbean country shacks were made with "wattle and daub," a latticework of springy twigs covered in mud and dried in the sun. The roof was topped with thatch, providing a cool indoor environment. More recently, concrete has become popular as a hurricane-resistant building material.

A restored colonial house in French Saint-Martin

141

A West Indian market in the mural—tourists shopping in real life at Philipsburg

PETER STUYVESANT
Peter Stuyvesant was an early governor of Curaçao (in 1638) and later of all the Dutch possessions in the Americas, which he governed from Nieuw Amsterdam (New York). An autocratic leader, he lost his right leg in a fight for Sint Maarten in 1644 and wore a silver ornamented false leg as a replacement. Stuyvesant was forced to surrender the North American possessions to the British in 1664, but later returned to live in the Great Bouwery in Manhattan until his death in 1672.

The capital and main town on the Dutch side of Sint Maarten is **Philipsburg►**, set on a narrow spit of land between Great Bay and the Great Salt Pond (the source of the salt which originally attracted the Dutch West India Company to the island). It has just four streets and a sprinkling of traditional houses among an otherwise modern town that has sprouted since the tourist boom. The town faces south, toward Saba and Sint Eustatius, the other two Dutch Windward Islands.

Visitors who stream off the cruise ships arrive at de Ruyterplein, a small square which is the setting for the pretty Old Courthouse Building and a tourist information office. Leading through it is Front Street, Philipsburg's mile-long shopping arcade, where the best of the duty-free bargains can be found—cameras and electronic goods, jewelry, crystal and porcelain—as well as plenty of cafés and bars. In an arcade at the head of Front Street, the **Sint Maarten Museum►** (tel: 542 4917. *Open* Mon–Fri 10–4, Sat 10–2. *Admission: inexpensive*) has exhibits of pre-Columbian and colonial island life. Its displays highlight the contrasting lifestyles with items such as Native American pottery and Delft dinner services.

Philipsburg's outlying areas completely encircle the lagoon and determined shoppers will find yet more arcades around its shores, but generally this is where the islanders themselves live. **Sint Maarten Zoological and Botanical Park►** (tel: 543 2030; www.stmartenpark.com. *Open* summer daily 9–6, winter 9–5. *Admission: inexpensive*) on the Madame Estate keeps animals from both South America and the Caribbean. The island's eastern side is relatively untouched and secluded.

The main route out of Philipsburg is often clogged with traffic; in Koolbaai (Cole Bay), a left turn leads alongside the Simpson Bay Lagoon to the busiest tourist area. Simsonbaai (Simpson Bay) itself has a good beach, and beyond the airport are Mandsaoi (Mano Bay) and Mulletbaai (Mullet Bay), with watersports, stores and a golf course. The road to Marigot crosses the border, which is marked only with an obelisk and a sign saying *Bienvenue à la Partie Française*.

Almost every brochure for a Caribbean vacation includes a picture of a waiter with a tray of sweet and exotic tropical fruit. Not all will be in season at any one time, but a visit to the market is always worthwhile for the displays of this fertile region's appetizing produce.

143

The pineapple, used by Native Americans for food and wine-making, grows on a stem in the center of a low bush of about 30 stiff, spiky, cactus-like leaves and takes about 15 months to mature. Black pineapples are slightly smaller and sweeter.

Pawpaw, or papaya, grows on a tall and slender tree of very light wood. The fruit, which matures to yellow and orange, can grow to 18in (45cm) in length. Papaya is said to be good for high blood pressure, and the seeds are used as a remedy for constipation.

The fruit of the soursop, which is not sour at all, is irregularly shaped, sometimes oval, with small, black hooks protruding from its aromatic, light green skin. Inside, black seeds sit in a white, pulpy flesh that tastes like a combination of mango and pineapple. Its seeds make it difficult to eat fresh—so it is probably best tasted in ice cream.

Related to the soursop, the sweetsop looks like a fleshy green pine cone. It is known locally as the sugar apple or custard apple; its seeds are contained in a sweet, creamy pulp, rather like custard.

Guava fruit is really an outsize berry, which turns from green to yellow when ripening. Inside, its seeds sit in a white or pink pulp. Guava has a bittersweet taste and provides five times as much vitamin C as orange juice.

Mango trees, although not native to the Caribbean, grow throughout the region with their sweet yellow and red fruits. Other exotic fruits include the Otaheite apple, shaped like a pear with a red skin and a crisp white pulp, or the carambola, yellow-skinned with crunchy white flesh and shaped like a five-pointed star in cross-section.

TENDER FRUIT
Papain, from the papaya, is used as a meat tenderizer; West Indians simply wrap their meat in pawpaw leaf and leave it to stand. Pineapple is also a meat tenderizer, with pretty powerful effects: Stranded soldiers on a South Sea island during World War II found that their teeth fell out if they ate too much of the fruit.

Young breadfruit, usually eaten baked or roasted

HYBRID FRUIT
Jamaica has created two hybrids of other citruses. The ortanique is part orange, part tangerine; the size of the former but with a skin that peels like the latter. The lumpy ugli fruit is a cross between a grapefruit, an orange and a tangerine.

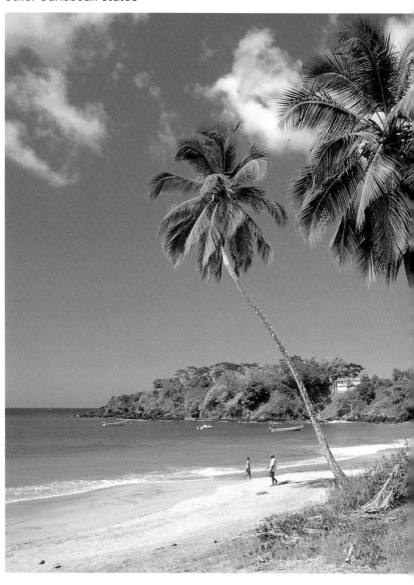

Great Courland Bay, one of a number of deep, palm-fringed coves cut into Tobago's northern shore

OTHER CARIBBEAN STATES The larger, independent nation states of the Caribbean, separated by physical and cultural obstacles (and often suspicious of each other, if not openly hostile), are marked by their diversity. Jamaica's lushness and extensive rain forests are a reminder of what Haiti, 100 miles (160km) east, must have been before generations of impoverished peasants cleared the hillsides in search of charcoal. Jamaica has all the attributes of the travel agency clichés—beaches, rivers, mountains—but it also has social and economic problems, as any visitor to downtown Kingston will see. Cuba is cracking and crumbling behind its wall of isolation. The colonial splendor of old Havana is gradually collapsing

Other Caribbean states

from neglect; yet this was once the most inviting tropical resort in the world. Haiti and the Dominican Republic share an island, but their border is more often closed than open. For all the Dominican Republic's colonial treasures and natural beauty, thousands of poor islanders risk their lives each year to cross the Mona Passage to Puerto Rico, where rural and US-influenced lifestyles exist side by side. The oil-producing nation of Trinidad and Tobago, famous for its Carnival and calypso, faces an uncertain future after years of wealth, while Barbados is perhaps the most developed of all the islands. No two islands are similar. If you want to know more than a little piece of the Caribbean, explore some of these fascinating states.

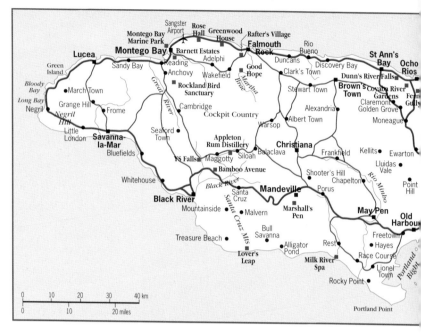

Jamaica

The third-largest island in the Caribbean (after Cuba and Hispaniola), the English-speaking nation of Jamaica enjoys a self-sufficiency based on tourism, agriculture and mining. Its attractions include jungle mountaintops, clear waterfalls and unforgettable beaches, yet the country's greatest resource may very well be the Jamaicans themselves. Although 95 percent of the population trace their bloodlines to Africa, their national origins lie elsewhere: in Europe, the Middle East, India, China, South America and many of the other islands in the Caribbean. The music, art and cuisine of Jamaica are vibrant, with a spirit easy to sense but as hard to describe as the rhythms of reggae or a flourish of streetwise patois.

HISTORY Jamaica was born of strife, as a colonial outpost, first of 16th-century Spanish settlers (who destroyed the Arawak inhabitants) and then of the British, who cut their plantations in the hills. Pirates brawled on the coastline, and the flourishing plantations, worked by slaves, were attacked by runaway maroons (see panel opposite).

Jahbah's health food center in Negril

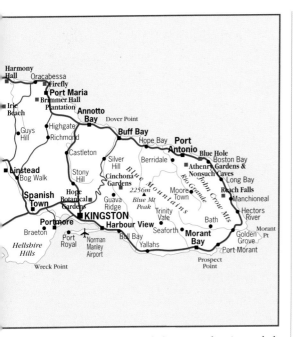

On the map: Harmony Hall, Oracabessa, Firefly, Port Maria, Brimmer Hall, Plantation, Iris Beach, Annotto Bay, Dover Point, Guys Hill, Highgate, Richmond, Buff Bay, Hope Bay, Port Antonio, Castleton, Silver Hill, Berridale, Blue Hole, Boston Bay, Athenry Gardens & Nonsuch Caves, Long Bay, Linstead, Bog Walk, Stony Hill, Cinchona Gardens, 2256m, Blue Mountains, Rio Grande, Reach Falls, Spanish Town, Hope Botanical Gardens, Guava Ridge, Blue Mt Peak, Moore Town, John Crow Mts, Manchioneal, KINGSTON, Trinity Vale, Bath, Hectors River, Portmore, Harbour View, Seaforth, Morant Bay, Morant Pt, Braeton, Port Royal, Norman Manley Airport, Bull Bay, Yallahs, Golden Grove, Port Morant, Hellshire Hills, Wreck Point, Prospect Point

MAROONS

The maroons were a community of runaways who lived high in the inaccessible Jamaican interior, in the John Crow Mountains in the north-east and the Cockpit Country in the northwest. Their name comes from the Spanish word *cimarrón* ("wild"); the earliest maroons were slaves left behind by the Spaniards when they fled from the British in 1655. Maroons were highly successful guerrillas and were never conquered; eventually the colonial authorities were reduced to negotiating with them, agreeing to guarantee their freedom and a considerable measure of self-government (which they still have today), in return for certain conditions, which included returning runaway slaves.

147

Uprisings among the slaves led to several serious rebellions and terrible bloodshed, and even after emancipation in the 19th century the cycle of hardship and violence continued. A number of demonstrations marked the run-up to full enfranchisement in 1944, and preceded complete independence from the UK in 1962.

Over the past 40 years the island has built one of the biggest tourist industries in the Caribbean, providing easy access from Europe and the US and a full range of places to stay: beachfront luxury, all-inclusives (offering all meals and accommodation), guesthouses on the cliffs in Negril, villas and mountain retreats. The resort towns of Montego Bay, Ocho Rios and Negril have good restaurants, lively bars and nightclubs.

ISLAND LIFE Jamaica is a cultural leader in the Caribbean; its boisterous culture of reggae and rastafari is known throughout the world and attracts visitors who are looking for a little more than the traditional Caribbean image of sun, sea and sand. Economically, though, the 2.6 million islanders have not had an easy ride recently; rising prices for imports and a fall in earnings from the main export, bauxite, led to austerity measures in the 1980s, and there is still considerable unemployment and inflation. From time to time there are outbursts—troubles tend to come to a head, particularly in Kingston, during the fiercely contested elections, when traditional political rivalries are at their height.

There is no reason why this should affect visitors to the island, most of whom will be on the north coast anyway. Besides, the majority of Jamaicans are welcoming and friendly. Jamaica remains primarily a place of peace and beauty, with all the character and vibrancy that has come to characterize the Caribbean.

JAMAICAN JERK

Jerking is a special way of cooking meat that was started by the maroons in their hideaways.
Originally it was wild hog, shot in the hills, that was cooked slowly in a barbecue sunk into the ground, but now you can buy jerked chicken, sausages and fish. These days there are "Jerk Centers" all over the island, but the traditional home of jerk pork, a very hot and spicy dish, is Boston Bay, near Port Antonio, where you can choose your meal, as it is cooked at a number of roadside shacks.

A safari cruise on the Black River into the mangroves of the Great Morass

SWIMS
On the road between Black River and Bamboo Avenue you will see vendors holding plastic bags of pink "swims"—local shrimps cooked in pepper sauce. Swims are tasty, but the pepper sauce, made from Scotch bonnet peppers, is very hot. The peppers get their name from their shape, said to look like a Scottish highlander's headdress.

COFFEE FACTORIES
Blue Mountain coffee is renowned as some of the best in the world. At the Mavis Bank and Silver Hill coffee factories, berries are pulped and fermented to reveal the beans, which are then dried and husked before being bagged for export (much of the crop goes to Japan). Take a formal tour at Mavis Bank, or an informal one elsewhere.

▶▶ Black River

Southwest Jamaica, around Black River, is a little-known corner of the island, where a quiet, rural lifestyle still exists, relatively untouched by the development and tourism of the north coast. The fishing town of **Black River▶** is somewhat run down, although there is still some charm in its old wooden buildings, set up when log-wood exports (the source of indigo before synthetic dyes were developed) brought prosperity a century ago. On the **Black River Safari▶▶** (tel: 965 2513), you can cruise along the river itself into Jamaica's largest swamp, where mangroves form a tunnel around you, and you may glimpse herons, egrets and even crocodiles.

There are a few isolated, usually deserted bays scattered along this coastline. From Crane Beach, just outside the town, the scrubby savannah land extends to the southeast, where lone cows graze attended by white cattle egrets. It eventually reaches **Treasure Beach▶▶**, a lost and lazy settlement set on a superb strip of sand. There is a wonderfully relaxed atmosphere, providing a perfect antidote to the more commercial resorts in the north. Another good beach can be found at Bluefields, to the northwest of Black River.

Inland, north of Black River, the main road skirts the swamp and then leads to **Bamboo Avenue▶▶**, a fine sight that is worth a quick detour. For just over 3 miles (5km) the huge bamboo plants form an arch over the road, hanging in graceful bushy curves. Just north of here are the **Y.S. Falls▶▶**, a series of waterfalls and ponds where you can swim. These can sometimes be crowded with tourists, but the falls themselves are stunning.

▶▶▶ Blue Mountains

The heavily forested **Blue Mountains** tower above Kingston, but the pace of life in the small mountain communities there is much slower than the capital. Granted the status of a National Park, these mountains are the second tallest in the Caribbean after the Dominican Republic's Cordillera Central and, in the distance, they do appear a hazy shade of blue. You can walk the Blue Mountains, including the 7,400ft (2,256m) Blue Mountain peak, with guides arranged by Cockpit Country Tours (Albert Town, tel: 610 0818). Another great place to head for is higher up: Strawberry Hill, in Irish Town, is an elegant hotel with traditional architecture (tel: 944 8400). You reach it from Papine; at this point the road passes into gorges and steep-sided valleys where fruit and vegetables are grown.

At Castleton, on the road to Annotto Bay on the north coast, botanical gardens dating from 1862 are laid out beside a river; here, guides will show you exotic flora, birds, butterflies and the ingenious trapdoor spider. There are gardens at Cinchona (reached from Clydesdale, to visit contact Jamaican Ministry of Algriculture, Mr Ramdon, tel: 927 1733), where quinine was once extracted from cinchona trees; other places worth visiting include the World's End Rum Distillery at Guava Ridge and the coffee factories at Mavis Bank, nearby and at Silver Hill (see panel opposite).

► Cockpit Country

Cockpit Country lies in the northwest of Jamaica, to the south of Falmouth. This is one of the most inaccessible and remote areas of the island and for years it provided a hideout for the guerrilla-style runaway maroons. Its romance lies in its appearance—shaggy, pointed mountains of karst limestone—and in its names. During the maroons era, it was known as the Land of Look Behind and had districts such as "Quick Step" and "Me No Sen, You No Come," which were so dangerous before a peace treaty was signed in 1739 that British soldiers would ride back to back on their horses. Even today Cockpit Country is rarely visited and the few roads are hardly used.

In the cane fields among Maggotty, the **Appleton Rum Estate►►** (tel: 963 9215. *Open* for tours Mon–Sat 9–4. *Admission: expensive*) is a working sugar cane factory and rum distillery that is well worth a visit during the cane-cutting season from January to July. Tours show the newly cut cane rolling through crushers to release the juice, which is boiled before being crystallized into sugar using massive centrifuges. There is a restaurant and bar at the distillery.

MANATEES
The endangered manatee is a large marine mammal that occasionally appears on the shores around Milk River and in the river estuary. Also known as the sea cow, it can grow to 13ft (4m) in length and can weigh up to 310 lb (140kg). With its small, rounded tail, front flippers and tiny, underdeveloped eyes, the manatee is believed to have been the source of many sailors' tales of mermaids on distant rocks.

149

TREE OF LIFE
The national flower of Jamaica is the delicate, light blue bloom of the *Lignum vitae* tree. Its name means "wood of life," and it is valued for many things. The wood, which is extremely hard, can be used to make axle shafts, bowling balls and even to replace metal ball-bearings, and the resin is used in the treatment of breathing disorders.

A dance troupe in traditional costume in Kingston

►► Kingston

Kingston, the capital of Jamaica, sits on the southern shore of the island, between a huge natural harbor and the Blue Mountains. It is a far cry from the north coast resort towns; Kingston is very much a Jamaican city, whose character is mostly unaffected by tourism. Downtown it is a mêlée of traffic, people and streetside trade: noisy buses, neatly dressed schoolchildren, stray goats and vendors touting their wares. There are not many formal sights here, nor much of architectural interest, but with a population of over half a million, Kingston is a good place to catch genuine Jamaican life. Unfortunately, this includes a criminal element as in most busy cities, so be careful when walking around and avoid garrison towns and ghetto areas like Trenchtown.

The heart of Kingston pulses around the **Parade►►**, a bus terminal and market area, where vendors sell every conceivable consumer item from the sidewalks and "busmen"—good-humored bus ticket collectors—do their utmost to persuade passengers onto their buses, watched over by the stately Ward Theatre and Kingston Parish Church. Visit the **National Gallery of Art►►** (tel: 922 1561. *Open* Tue–Thu 10–4.30, Fri 10–4. *Admission: inexpensive*), or visit the **National Heroes Park►►** (see panel).

Most visitors to the capital stay uptown in New Kingston, a business and residential area with a more relaxed tempo and good restaurants and bars. **Devon House►►►** (tel: 929 7029; www.devonhousejamaica .com. *Open* Mon–Sat 9.30–5. *Admission: inexpensive*) is a historic oasis in the modern town, and it is worth spending time in its atmospheric grounds. The main house was constructed in 1881 in neoclassical style adapted to the tropics, and is open to visitors. Its courtyards contain stores and restaurants. Farther along Hope Road, you pass Kings House, the governor general's residence, and the **Bob Marley Museum►►** (tel: 927 9152; www.bob-marley-foundation.com. *Open* guided tour only starting at 9.30. *Admission: moderate*) in the Tuff Gong Studio that was also the reggae legend's home from 1975 until his death in 1981. The **Hope Botanical Gardens►►** (tel: 970 3504. *Open* daily 8.30–6.30. *Admission free*) has an orchid house and a small zoo (*Admission: inexpensive*).

THE NATIONAL HEROES
The Jamaican national heroes, whose statues stand in Heroes Park, are Paul Bogle, a preacher, and George William Gordon, who were both blamed and executed for a rebellion in Morant Bay in 1865; Marcus Garvey, the activist and founder of the Universal Negro Improvement Association, which was so influential among black people in the early part of this century; and Independence leaders Alexander Bustamante and Norman Manley. Nanny, a female maroon leader, has also joined the ranks of the national heroes.

SPANISH TOWN
Kingston did not become Jamaica's capital until 1872. Before that the capital was Spanish Town, where you can still see the grand old Georgian colonial administrative buildings and courthouse in the main square. In the cathedral there are tablets in the floors and walls dating back to the late 17th century. It is worth the half-day's trip from Kingston by bus or taxi to see these reminders of the past.

Devon House, New Kingston, built by George Stiebel, Jamaica's first black millionaire

Rich and debauched Port Royal earned the names "Gilded Hades" and "the wickedest city in Christendom" in the 17th century, when pirates would sail into town laden with loot and binge until their next escapade. In 1692 the revelry came to an abrupt halt. At about noon on the 7th of June, a massive earthquake struck and the city disappeared under the waves, killing 2,000 people.

Port Royal lies on the tip of the Palisadoes Peninsula, at the mouth of Kingston Harbour. It was fortified by the British in 1655 and became a gathering place for English buccaneers. Soon, this was the Caribbean's richest town; merchants shipped their wares here for onward sale, and buccaneers, hounded from their base on Tortuga, off Haiti, brought their own loot. Taverns (one for every 10 inhabitants) were crowded with prostitutes and men were killed at the drop of a hat. When the earthquake struck, the townspeople thought it was Judgment Day. Whole streets slipped into the bay and ships were flung into the town's remains on a tidal wave. Of 3,000 houses, only 200 were left standing—but the spirit of Port Royal wasn't immediately extinguished; as the dust settled, some of the survivors simply carried on drinking.

After the earthquake, Port Royal was rebuilt, only to be devastated by a fire in 1703. Its remaining residents then moved to Kingston, leaving their town to the navy.

Port Royal today Nowadays Port Royal is a quiet village, reached by ferry from the Kingston waterfront and known for its fried fish and bammy (a flat Jamaican cake made with cassava). **Port Royal Museum** (tel: 922 0620. *Open* Mon–Thu 9.20–4.30, Sat 9,30–4.30. *Admission: inexpensive*), a lumbering stone fortress whose embrasures are still lined with cannons, survived the earthquake, although it sank a few feet. Inside the fort, in quarters where Nelson stayed in 1779, the **Maritime Museum** has models of ships and maritime memorabilia. The nearby Giddy House is a Victorian armory that ended up at its weird angle and received its name in 1907, after another earthquake.

LUCKY BREAK
In the graveyard of St. Peter's Church (1725), the story of Lewis Galdy is written on his tombstone: he was "swallowed up in the Great Earthquake," but was disgorged into the sea a few minutes later as another shockwave passed, and kept swimming until he was eventually rescued by a boat. Next to him are buried the remains of three children found underneath a collapsed wall by marine archeologists and who were reburied in 1992.

151

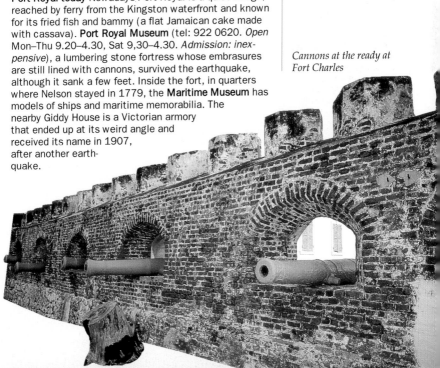

Cannons at the ready at Fort Charles

Jamaica is musically the loudest and the most productive of all Caribbean islands. Folk culture and religious traditions have given birth to a wealth of dance rhythms, and music has a strong element of protest, developed by singers ranging from the "rude boys" of the 1960s to the dancehall singers of today. But this does not restrict the scope of musical life; tune the radio to Irie FM for certain proof that Jamaicans can put just about any song to reggae and make it sound good.

MARCHING BANDS

In the British Caribbean there is still a tradition of marching bands, very much in the British military fashion. Musicians dress in suitably formal and colorful tunics, but when marching, rather than keeping to a formal, disciplined style, they swagger and swing their instruments around.

Until 50 years ago, the popular dance rhythm in Jamaica was mento. With its slow, melodic sound and strong lyrics, this was similar to the old calypsos of Trinidad—and, like them, mento had a satirical edge. Ska dance music emerged in the late 1950s, at a time of political upheaval. As Jamaica moved toward independence "rude boys" were introduced, usually delivering a socially conscious message.

Rocksteady, a slower version of the ska rhythm, incorporating a heavier bass riff and stronger vocals, put in a brief appearance in the mid-1960s, but it was soon superseded by reggae. This immensely popular

Maxi Priest and Shabba Ranks; Shaggy, top

TOASTING

Toasting developed in clubs, as DJs sang their quickfire lyrics over popular tunes when introducing records. This rapid, off-the-cuff patter is difficult for the uninitiated to understand, requiring a lightning mind and a good deal of skill.

music combined elements of ska and rocksteady and its "chaka-chaka" rhythm was given international appeal by bands such as Bob Marley and the Wailers, and Third World.

Reggae has had lasting success, spawning new bands in many other countries, but in Jamaica the music scene has moved on. In the 1980s it adapted rap music to produce "dancehall," a hard and repetitive rhythm overlaid with a heavy rapping voice. The strutting rude boys came to the fore again, headed by DJs such as Shaggy and Yellowman, the king of "slack" (vulgar songs). Other singers have begun to sing softer, more melodic songs and culture reggae.

▶▶ Mandeville

The central town of Mandeville is 2,000ft (6100m) above sea level and enjoys a cooler climate than the coast. In imperial days beaches were considered unhealthy and the British colonials would come here for their summer retreat from Kingston. Nowadays the town has expanded from a traditional rural center to incorporate some industry. It's all a far cry from the beach-hustling and resorts of the north coast. There are just a few places to stay and they have a relaxed and stately (if faded) air.

Mandeville itself was built along the lines of an English country town, with a parish church and a Georgian courthouse facing each other across the grassy common, or green. The colonials would have taken their constitutional walks here, but the green now serves as the bus terminal and is a focus of chaotic Jamaican life.

On the hills around Mandeville is some of Jamaica's most fertile land; the roadsides are lined with stalls selling all the fruits and vegetables in season: mangoes, oranges, bananas, peanuts and cashews. Just south of town is **Marshall's Pen**▶▶ (pre-booked groups of 6 or more, tel: 904 5454. *Admission: moderate*), a classic Jamaican mansion surrounded by gardens on what was once a coffee plantation. Built in the late 18th century, the wooden house is furnished in period style. It is possible to arrange bird-watching trips on the estate. On the coast to the south of Marshall's Pen is Lover's Leap, where there is a spectacular lookout. There are also superb views from Spur Tree Hill, southwest of Mandeville.

The region around Mandeville is Jamaica's bauxite mining country. Used to make aluminum, bauxite is a major export, and open cast mines form orange scars across the landscape before being returfed and returned to grazing land. At Shooter's Hill, to the northeast, you can arrange a tour of the **Pickapeppa Factory** (manufacturing a popular spicy sauce); ask when they are likely to be boiling up—this is the best time to visit (by appointment, tel: 603 3441. *Admission: inexpensive*). Milk River, on the south coast, is an old spa town, popular before beach holidays.

Stately Mandeville, once a colonial retreat

JAMAICAN BIRDS
Of the 250 or so birds that spend time in Jamaica (the island is on a migratory route), there are 25 native species. These include the Jamaican owl, with its eartufts and guttural whirring call; the Jamaican woodpecker, black and white except for its red head; the yellow-bellied cuckoo, which can be seen in the Mandeville area; and the Jamaican becard, which suspends its nest from a tree, entering through a hole in the bottom.

CASHEWS
The cashew nut, cultivated in the Mandeville area, grows in a shell at the end of the cashew apple on an evergreen tree. Inside the shell is an oil that can blister human skin and is poisonous if burnt; it must be dried in the sun and roasted to remove the oil before an inner shell can be broken off to reveal the nut. This laborious process is the reason why cashews are so expensive.

Other Caribbean states

▶▶ Montego Bay

Montego Bay, in the northwest, is the most famous of Jamaica's resorts. Mo Bay, as it is known, is a lively town; there are plenty of bars along Gloucester Avenue and some good restaurants, both international and local, set in the old stone buildings and down on the waterfront. The hotels include some of the Caribbean's snazziest, such as the Tryall Club and Round Hill. These are not in the town itself, but scattered in coves along the coast to the east and west. There are many package hotels around Montego Bay, but independent travelers will also be able to find cheaper accommodations, particularly on Queen's Drive and Sunset Boulevard, and in the suburbs. Activities in the area include river rafting trips and visits to a number of great houses, which can be arranged by tour operators (see **Travel Facts**).

The heart of Montego Bay itself is **Sam Sharpe Square**▶▶, where vendors hawk their colored T-shirts, peanuts and sky-juice (plastic bags of ice crystals with a dash of fruit concentrate) to passersby. In the corner of the square is the Cage, a jail for errant slaves from the days before emancipation, and a statue of Sharpe himself, a slave leader who was executed after an uprising in 1831. Toward the sea from here you will find the **Craft Market**▶, with souvenirs, wooden carvings and straw hats. North along Gloucester Avenue is **Doctor's Cave Beach**▶▶, the most popular beach in the town, and another fine Jamaican institution: the **Pork Pit**▶▶, where you can buy jerked chicken and pork. Tours can be made of the **Montego Bay Marine Park**▶ (tel: 952 5619; www.mbmp.org) in glass-bottomed boats, arranged on the main beaches, or by mini-sub with Mobay Undersea Tours (tel: 940 4465. *Open* daily. *Tours expensive*). For those who want a closer encounter with Caribbean sea life head to the Half Moon resort just east of town to Dolphin Cove (tel: 953 2211. *Open* daily. *Admission: expensive*) where you can swim with these lovable mammals.

As you leave town heading east along the north coast, you pass the Half Moon Club hotel and its golf course and come eventually to **Rose Hall**▶▶▶ (tel: 953 2341. *Open* daily 9–6. *Admission: expensive*), Jamaica's best-known great house. Set in stately gardens overlooking the coast, Rose Hall was built in the 1770s in imitation of British

Doctor's Cave Beach, Montego Bay; Jamaica's first and best-known public beach

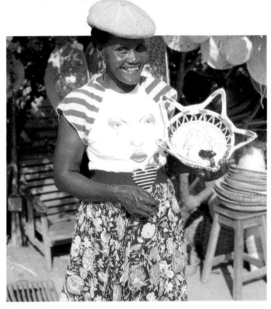

Bargaining at the craft market, downtown Mo Bay

JAMAICAN DOCTOR BIRD
The doctor bird, or the red-billed streamertail, is the Jamaican national bird and one of the prettiest hummingbirds. As its name suggests, it has a red bill; the male's chest is a shimmering fluorescent shade of green. In flight it displays a pair of back tail feathers about three times as long as its body.

SEAFORD TOWN
Seaford Town, south of Montego Bay, looks like a normal Jamaican town but has an unusual history. Lord Seaford granted the land to German settlers, who came here to farm it in 1835, and their blond descendants can still be seen. A similar experiment involved importing Indian laborers to Little London on the south coast, near Savanna-la-Mar; they, too, were absorbed into the local community and culture.

mansions of the period. The grand interior is furnished with antiques, but the guides concentrate on telling you about the house's former mistress, Annie Palmer (see panel). The less pretentious **Greenwood Great House**▶▶ (tel: 953 1077. *Open* daily 9–6. *Admission: expensive*) stands on a hill about 5 miles (8km) beyond Rose Hall. Built during the same period, it was owned by the family of the poet Elizabeth Barrett Browning. But perhaps the most attractive plantation house is **Good Hope**▶▶▶ (tel: US 301/229-4300), which has a wonderful view over the fertile Jamaican lands. It is a hotel, but also offers horse-riding (By appointment. *Admission: expensive*).

Beyond the town of Falmouth is the Martha Brae river. Hour-long rafting trips with **Jamaica Rafting**▶▶ (tel: 952 0889. *Open* daily 8.30–4.30. *Admission: expensive*) start upstream at Rafter's Village. At Rock, a phosphorescent lagoon glitters at night when disturbed.

Heading west from Montego Bay, the road skirts the bay itself and heads for the area of Reading, passing hillsides dotted with expensive villas. Beneath them is Catherine Hall, where the Bob Marley Performing Center hosts the annual reggae gathering, Reggae Sunfest. From here the coast road leads to Negril, passing the mouth of the Great River and the hotels at Round Hill and Tryall, with its golf course.

Turn south at Reading and climb into the hills. Near Anchovy is the delightful **Rockland Feeding Station**▶ (tel: 952 2009. *Open* daily 9–5.30. *Admission: moderate*), a bird sanctuary best visited after 3.30pm. At Catadupa, **Croydon in the Mountains**▶▶ (tel: 979 8267. *Open* Tue and Fri 10–2. *Admission: expensive*) is worth visiting for a view of a working plantation where they grow coffee, pineapple, cocoa and bananas.

Bob Marley shot to international fame in the 1970s, popularizing reggae and rastafari across the world. Although he had the toughest Jamaican roots, Marley was awarded Jamaica's highest public honor, the Order of Merit, and his legacy remains in the hundreds of songs that are still played all over Jamaica.

TUFF GONG

The Tuff Gong Studio was bought by Marley as his home and recording studio in 1975. Set on Hope Road in New Kingston, an uptown area of Kingston, it is a far cry from the shanties of Trenchtown. Tours of the studio show the gold records awarded for Marley's top-selling discs and video recordings of Marley performing his songs.

156

Robert Nesta Marley was born on the 6th of February 1945. Deserted by Norval Marley, her white Jamaican husband, Marley's mother, Cedella, raised Nesta in Nine Miles village, in the parish of St. Ann's, on Jamaica's north coast. When he was a youth they moved to the poorest shanty area of Kingston and he worked as a welder.

Determined to succeed as a musician, Marley formed "The Wailing Wailers" in the early 1960s with Bunny Wailer and Peter Tosh. Together, they typified the "rude boy" image and found popular success with over 30 ska songs; but, having made little money, the band split up and Marley had to turn to welding again to make a living.

The 1970s finally brought financial success and the new Wailers were signed by Island Records. By this time Marley had become a rastafarian, and the band began

MARLEY MAUSOLEUM

Bob Marley's mausoleum, in his home village of Nine Miles, is a site of pilgrimage to many fans. Prepare for a mild onslaught of high-pressure selling, but it is interesting to see the small house and the tomb itself, which is decorated with memorabilia important to the great singer.

playing reggae. The album *Catch a Fire* hit enjoyed international success and was followed by *Natty Dread*, *Exodus*, *Kaya* and *Uprising*.

By now a world-famous celebrity, Marley emigrated from Jamaica after an attempt on his life, but returned in 1978 to stage the One Love Peace Concert, in which he persuaded Prime Minister Edward Seaga and opposition leader Michael Manley to make a gesture of unity against the gangland wars that were then plaguing the island.

Bob Marley died of cancer at the early age of 36 on the 11th of May 1981. His body was laid to rest in a mausoleum at Nine Miles in St. Ann's (see panel).

▶▶▶ Negril

The town of Negril lies at the far western tip of Jamaica and, more than any other place on the island, typifies the Jamaican image of a hedonist's hideaway on an idyllic beach. Sunset-watching has been a hallowed pastime here since the 1960s, when the village was adopted as a home by hippies. Since then, Negril has been discovered by tourists; there are large hotels on the beach and people are bussed in daily to watch the sunset from Rick's Café. But the old laid-back life still exists and it is just possible to escape the crowds. There is not much to see in Negril—but then that is hardly the point of the town. You can expect to be hustled there—but then who could resent a vendor who arrives by canoe bearing a briefcase, or who greets you by massaging your leg with aloe?

Negril divides neatly into two halves: the beach and the cliffs. If there is a town center it is at the rotary (roundabout), from where the road runs inland toward Savanna-la-Mar. To the north, the road reaches Montego Bay, alongside **Long Bay▶▶▶**, one of Jamaica's best beaches—5 miles (8km) of superb sand with hotels and beach bars (try Cosmo's at the top end) scattered along it. Beyond Hedonism II, on the point, is **Bloody Bay▶▶**, which takes its name from the days when whalers used to clean their catch here. Behind the beach is the Great Morass, a mangrove swamp that can be visited by boat.

South of the rotary, the coastal road of Negril's West End winds its way along the clifftops, where there are small hideaway hotels, guesthouses and plenty of bars, or try the more "jet-setty" Xtabi and Rock House. Although not very high, the cliffs traditionally remain a challenge for cliff divers and jumpers. Negril has a number of outdoor music parks where you can hear big Jamaican bands. At the southern end of Negril is the 100-foot (30m) **lighthouse▶** (tel: 640 2227. *Open* daily 10–6. *Admission free*), which has good views of the surrounding area.

157

A sunset cruise off Rick's Café on the cliffs of Negril

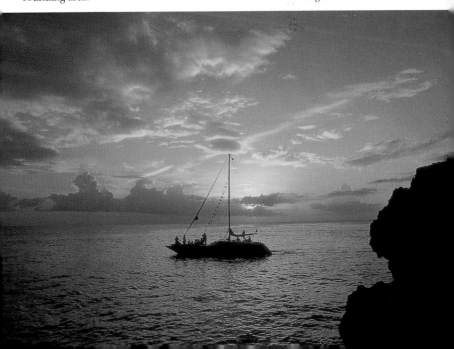

Other Caribbean states

ACKEE AND SALTFISH

Ackee and saltfish was once a hardship food, but has now achieved the status of national dish. Ackee is the fruit of a tree that originates in Africa. Its red pods must ripen and open naturally before the lobes of yellow flesh can be taken out and boiled (otherwise it is poisonous). When cooked, ackee looks and even tastes rather like scrambled egg. Saltfish (salted cod) was the cheapest high-protein food available in the 18th century, imported to feed slaves. It has since become expensive, but this has not lessened its popularity.

COLUMBUS IN TROUBLE

After exploring the coast of Central America on his fourth voyage, Columbus was stranded with his crew when his ships sank in St. Ann's Bay in 1502. The island's inhabitants, the Arawaks, agreed to feed the explorers, but after an altercation withdrew their aid. Columbus managed to change their minds again by calling on God to take away the moon, knowing that a total eclipse of the moon was due. Eventually, as there was no sign of rescue (a ship from the Santo Domingo settlement sailed away, leaving the unpopular Columbus behind), two members of the crew took a canoe and braved the seas between Jamaica and Hispaniola to fetch a ship and collect the stranded sailors.

►► Ocho Rios

Halfway along the north coast, Ocho Rios is Jamaica's second biggest resort town. As in Montego Bay, the resorts are scattered for several miles on either side of the town, which itself stretches along the seafront and has become a much-frequented vacation spot for Kingstonians. Ochie, as it is known, is well provided with beaches, watersports and entertainment; there are expensive resorts and some cheaper hotels, and a clutch of lively bars on James Avenue, near the town center. The main Ocho Rios bay public beach is directly beneath the twin skyscrapers on the seafront; to the west of Ocho Rios there is a good strip of sand at Mammee Bay. Many excursions can be made into the surrounding countryside, making this a popular cruise ship destination.

The town centers around the clock tower, where cars and buses, market vendors and the occasional goat vie for supremacy. There is nothing much to see in Ocho Rios itself, but Jamaica's best-known tourist attraction, **Dunn's River Falls►►** (tel: 974 2857; www.dunnsriverja.com. *Open* daily 8.30–4 (Wed, Thu and Fri 7–4. *Admission: expensive)*, lies to the west of town. The falls are a remarkable sight, as the river cascades over limestone outcrops, dropping steadily nearly 650ft (200m). Most people start at the bottom and climb through the lips and falls, pausing occasionally to swim in the pools (swim suits are essential and trainers are recommended). The falls are popular with tour buses and tend to be crowded.

Farther along the coast road to the west of Dunn's River Falls are a number of small towns and occasional hotels in an isolated bay. **St. Ann's Bay►** is the birthplace of black activist Marcus Garvey. There is not much to detain you here, but spare a moment to think of Christopher Columbus, who was forced to spend over a year here

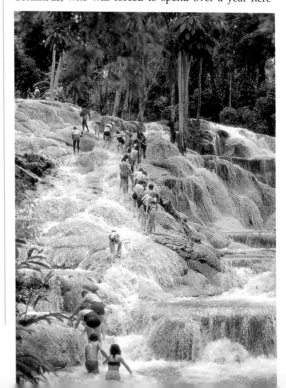

Tourists climb up Dunn's River Falls, Ocho Rios

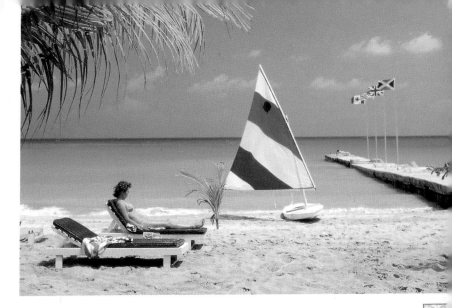

Relaxation at the north-east resort of Ocho Rios

waiting for rescue when his ships sank (see panel). Close by is the site of Jamaica's first Spanish settlement, Seville Nueva, restored as an archeological park.

The road south from Ocho Rios climbs immediately into the hills. **Coyaba River Gardens**▶▶ (tel: 974 6235. *Open* daily 8–5. *Admission: inexpensive*) makes a pleasant stop, as the gardens are festooned with flowering bushes and trees set among streams and ponds. The **Shaw Park Botanical Gardens**▶▶ (tel: 974 2723. *Open* daily 8–5. *Admission: moderate*) also make an interesting tour of tropical plants and lily ponds. The main road to Kingston then passes into **Fern Gully**▶▶, a deep, cool cleft in the hills. Huge ferns flourish on the banks and trees hang over the road, blocking out the light.

Heading east from Ocho Rios, you cross the White River, where there are daytime rafting trips and torchlit night excursions with dinner; these can be arranged at hotels. **Prospect Plantation**▶ (tel: 974 2058. *Open* daily for tours. *Admission: expensive*) is a working plantation where native fruit and vegetables, including soursop, cocoa, tamarind and ackee, are grown, and trees (bearing plaques) were planted by celebrated visitors including Winston Churchill and Charlie Chaplin. It can be toured by tractor-drawn carriage or on horseback. **Harmony Hall**▶▶ (tel: 974 2870. *Open* Oct–Aug Tue–Sun 10–6. *Admission free*) is an art gallery set in a restored house, exhibiting works by Caribbean artists. At **Irie Beach**▶▶—not actually a beach, but a gulley inland where a river cascades over small falls into rockpools—you can swim and sit in the sun.

About 15 miles (24km) farther on is **Firefly**▶▶▶ (tel: 725 0920. *Open* Mon–Thu and Sun 8.30–5. *Admission: expensive*), where Noel Coward lived until his death in 1973. The house itself is simple and has a few furnishings and musical scores still as Coward left them. However, the most spectacular feature is its view, extending along the north coast as far as the Blue Mountains. As you travel to Firefly, you will pass another literary-connected establishment: Goldeneye, the house of James Bond's creator, Ian Fleming. This can be rented as a villa.

MARCUS GARVEY
Marcus Mosiah Garvey was a black activist during the early 20th century. His aim was to help Africans and their descendants improve their situation in a white-dominated, colonial world. Through his Universal Negro Improvement Association he built up a massive following in the Caribbean and the US, keeping in touch with the organization's branches throughout the world by means of its newspaper, *Negro World*. Garvey died in relative obscurity in Britain, but in 1964 his bones were brought back to Jamaica, where he was proclaimed the first Jamaican national hero.

BEACHES

Set against the backdrop of the John Crow Mountains, the beaches around Port Antonio tend to be steep-sided coves, but there are pleasant strips of golden sand in the area. Be careful of currents—the sea can become rough when onshore winds are blowing. There are good beaches at Winifred and at Boston Bay, and Frenchman's Cove is often deserted. Although not a beach, the Blue Lagoon is a favorite spot: a stunningly blue sea pool with edges fringed by palm trees and a waterfall restaurant.

Street scene, Port Antonio: red roofs and telegraph poles

BANANAS GALORE

The banana trade made Port Antonio rich at the turn of the century, reaching its heyday in the 1920s. The fruit was brought down the Rio Grande on bamboo rafts, to be shipped out to the US. When Errol Flynn bought Navy Island in Port Antonio harbor in the late 1940s, he popularized the use of these rafts for pleasure; it has since become a staple of a Jamaican vacation.

▶▶▶ Port Antonio

The northeast is a lesser-known corner of Jamaica, but one of the most rewarding. Although there are hotels here, the area is distinctly less commercial than the big resort towns on the north coast. Small rural communities are dotted along the steep slopes of the John Crow Mountains, which tumble down to the coast. The scenery is fertile and unspoilt; nature quickly reclaims any human invasion, with fences becoming hedges and telephone wires covered with vegetation in no time.

Port Antonio itself is a charming town with an easy, relaxed pace, set between mountains and a magnificent double harbor. The few streets of clapboard houses have become a bit run down since the decline of the town's prosperity, which flowed from the banana industry early in the 20th century and then from its brief reign as Jamaica's most exclusive resort in the 1950s, when the likes of Errol Flynn and Bette Davis were frequent visitors.

There is a fine panorama of the town from the Bonnie View Hotel. Beneath it, behind the harbor, is the oldest part of town, with stone buildings such as the courthouse and parish church; beyond is the Point, with beautiful old wooden townhouses. Just off the Point is Navy Island (guided tours by reservation; tel: 993 2667), once owned by Errol Flynn; his former residence is now a hotel. Not far southeast of town are Athenry Gardens and the Nonsuch Caves, illuminated caverns festooned with stalactites.

East of the town, beyond the Blue Hole (see panel), is **Boston Bay▶▶▶**, the home of jerk, which is freshly cooked at roadside stalls. Also worth a visit are the **Reach Falls▶▶▶**, some of the island's prettiest and normally free of tourist buses.

Inland from Port Antonio, Berridale marks the start of two-hour river-rafting trips on the **Rio Grande** (tel: 993 5778. *Open* daily 8.30–4.30. *Admission: expensive*; transportation is provided from the Rafter's Rest, on the river mouth). You descend gradually through magnificent, fertile scenery punted by a raftsman with a bamboo pole. The road then climbs farther into the John Crow Mountains and leads to **Moore Town▶**, an old maroon settlement; visits can be arranged by the Port Antonio tourist office. Walking tours in the hills above Port Antonio are offered by Valley Hikes (tel: 993 3085. *Open* Mon–Fri 9–4.30, Sat–Sun 9–12. *Admission: expensive*).

The word "rasta" tends to conjure up a picture of musicians dressed in red, gold and green and sporting hydra-heads of dense dreadlocks. But the picture is a misleading one. In Jamaica, most of the rastafarians live quiet, religious, often reclusive lives and rarely set foot in tourist-dominated towns.

Rasta beliefs first emerged during the 1930s in the poor ghettos of west Kingston as the religious crystallization of anti-colonial black consciousness movements. Although it has often been sensationalized and misunderstood, rastafari is still a Judeo-Christian-inspired faith, and many believers carry bibles and go to services.

Rastas have no central church, but there is a system of recognized beliefs common to all followers. According to the rastafarian interpretation of the Bible, Ras (prince) Tafari is a divine incarnation, believed to have taken earthly form as the Emperor Haile Selassie of Ethiopia. To rastas, Africans are God's chosen people and some look ahead to eventual black supremacy. Ethiopia is believed to be Zion, or heaven on earth—a belief linked with the "back to Africa" movement. Other countries, particularly Jamaica (to which blacks were forcibly brought to atone for their ancestors' sins) and white nations, are regarded as Babylon, or hell on earth.

True believers lead simple, austere lives, rejecting the trappings of modern Western life. They eat "ital" (from "vital" or natural), mostly vegetarian foods, and usually prefer herbal remedies to Western medical treatment. Most rastas wear their hair in long, thick "dreadlocks," and regard smoking marijuana, or "ganja" (illegal in Jamaica), as a sacred activity.

Rasta beliefs have been obscured as the following has become internationally known; many of the famous Jamaican reggae stars adopted the faith and to the west it became associated with messages of militancy and ganja-smoking. Unfortunately, the trappings of the movement have been hijacked in the Caribbean by small-time opportunists and hustlers, who don rastas' clothing and are known as "wolves" or "dreads."

LION OF ZION
Haile Selassie was known as the "Lion of Judah"; as a proud, African animal, the lion is often used in rasta art. A full head of dreadlocks is taken to symbolize the lion's mane and followers will consciously emulate the lion's slow, proud bearing.

161

Rasta craft market in Montego Bay

GANJA
Marijuana was introduced into the Caribbean by agricultural workers from India, who arrived as indentured laborers on contracts to work the canefields after the abolition of slavery in the 19th century. Smoked in a "chalice," and believed by rastas to bring wisdom, the leaf has several names in Jamaica, including ganja, cully weed, holy herb and wisdom weed.

Sunrise at Cayman Brac

The Cayman Islands

Thousands of visitors fly down to the Cayman Islands for reliable sun and sand and the finest diving seas close to the mainland US, and the islands are well geared up to receive them. The Caymans' successful tourist industry is supplemented by the offshore finance sector; the islands' status as a tax haven and the presence of numerous millionaires has given the 42,397 Caymanians the highest average per capita income in the Caribbean—although many islanders have menial, low-income jobs.

The Cayman Islands are formed by limestone caps of submerged mountain peaks, rising 25,200ft (7,680m) from the valley floor. These three British-dependent islands have distinctly different atmospheres. They lie to the northwest of Jamaica, separated into two groups. Grand Cayman, the senior island and site of the capital, George Town, is 20 miles by 7.5 miles (32km by 12km) and is busy, commercial and flat. It is also by far the most developed island of the three. About 85 miles (137km) to its northeast are the twin cays of Cayman Brac (population about 1,800) and Little Cayman (population about 115), which have some of the region's best fishing. The gradual development of a tourist industry is distinctly low-key here.

All three islands are generally dry and scrubby, with areas of swamp, and lie very low in the water. But for all their featureless appearance above the waterline, they boast some of the most impressive underwater scenery and marine life in the Caribbean.

There are a number of scuba operations on the islands, diving mainly off the walls—vertical underwater drops clustered with coral—in the north and west of Grand Cayman. If you are not a diver, you can see the corals from the Atlantis Submarine (tel: 800 887 8571), which offers reef trips some 120ft (36m) down near George Town.

Tourism on Grand Cayman has mainly taken hold along Seven Mile Beach, where bars and restaurants stand shoulder to shoulder among the many hotels and from where there is an excellent view of the sunset most days. You can dine extremely well here, in chic restaurants, but there are also a number of fast-food chains and rib joints.

From Mondays to Saturdays, bars and clubs provide plenty of nightlife, and there are shows in the hotels and a couple of places to dance. Cayman Brac and Little Cayman are, on the other hand, very peaceful and quiet, and their inhabitants, like those of Grand Cayman, are generally known as some of the most easy-going people in the Caribbean.

A Cayman Islands totem pole

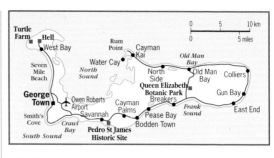

BEACHES

Seven Mile Beach is an archetypal Caribbean beach with perfect golden sand that shelves gently away to the west. The water is calm on this protected side of the island, and there are magnificent sunsets. All kinds of watersports are available here, from water-skiing to parasailing; the only problem is that it is sometimes pretty crowded. Caymanians tend to go to Smith's Cove, an inlet between the coral rocks to the south of George Town. Other beaches that are worth exploring include Cayman Kai and Water Cay, on the north coast.

Swimming with stingrays off the Cayman Islands

GRAND CAYMAN This is the largest and most developed of the Caymans, and it is here that you will find the capital and the only real town, George Town, a small collection of wooden and concrete buildings on the waterfront in the protected southwest of the island. Its quiet streets come alive with the arrival of cruise ships and during the annual festivities, the Batabano Carnival (April) and Pirates' Week (late October), when choreographed hordes of swash-bucklers carouse there. The **Cayman Islands National Museum▶▶** (tel: 949 8368; www. museum.ky. *Open* Mon–Fri 9–5, Sat 10–4. *Admission: inexpensive*), in a traditional Caymanian building, the old Court House, is run by the National Trust and has excellent displays illustrating the islands' history and natural life. It includes an interesting section on seafaring traditions, with artifacts found both on land and in the sea.

Life for most visitors to Grand Cayman is centered on Seven Mile Beach, which is heavily built up with hotels and condominiums along its 5.5 mile (9km) length. Here you will find the liveliest bars and restaurants. In their prosperity, the Cayman Islands have been swamped with satellite dishes, big cars and other trappings of North American culture, but as the tourist development thins out to the north and east, you will occasionally see the neat, wooden buildings of the old-time Caribbean; the white clapboard houses, with their pink or blue shutters and shingle-tiled roofs, are often set in carefully tended gardens blooming with hibiscus and bougainvillea.

In West Bay, north of Seven Mile Beach, **Hell▶** is a pitted and scorched terrain of worn coral limestone. At the **Cayman Turtle Farm▶** (tel: 949 3894. *Open* daily 8.30–5. *Admission: moderate*) you can learn about the life cycle of the turtle. There is a turtle release program, but this is a sad place, as the animals are cooped up quite severely. Off the east coast, **Stingray City▶▶** is the island's most famous (and touristy) dive and snorkel site, which is visited by friendly stingrays.

East of George Town, on the coast, seek out **Pedro St. James Historic Site▶▶** (tel: 947 3329. *Open* daily 9.30–5. *Admission: moderate*), which is a heritage park arranged around a restored 1780s great house. Built with slave labor, it was a fitting backdrop for the announcement of the abolition of slavery in 1835. Farther east and inland, the award-winning **Queen Elizabeth Botanic Park ▶▶** (tel: 9947 3558. *Open* daylight hours. *Admission: moderate*) showcases exotic local flora and fauna.

Local straw craft in the making, Cayman Brac

LITTLE CAYMAN AND CAYMAN BRAC The other two Cayman Islands, both thin and each about 12 miles (19km) long, lie tip to tail some 85 miles (137km) to the northeast of Grand Cayman. The channel in between them may not look dangerous but it is, in fact, a treacherously deep stretch of water. It is possible to arrange day trips by airplane to both Cayman Brac and Little Cayman.

Cayman Brac takes its name from the "brac" or cliff at its eastern end, the highest point in the Caymans (a princely 148ft/45m). There are just 1,800 Brackers and they have a reputation for their friendly hospitality. Cayman Brac has a museum (tel: 948 2222) in Stake Bay and a few stores, but generally it is as sleepy as it has been for the last 100 years. Apart from the people and the opportunity to do nothing in warm surroundings, the best reason to visit is the coral. Superb dive sites and snorkeling grounds can be explored around the island's western tip.

There are a handful of hotels on Little Cayman; these offer diving in the stunning Bloody Bay Wall Marine Park and fishing facilities. The island is also home to hundreds of birds, including the Caribbean's largest population of red-footed boobies, and a rare frigate bird breeding site.

Golfo de México

HAVANA (LA HABANA)

Cojimar Santa Cruz del Norte Varadero

Archipélago de Sabana

Canal Nicolás

Marianao

Matanzas

Cárdenas

Archipélago de los Colorados

Cayo Levisa Bahía Honda

Sagua la Grande

Palma Rubia

Viñales

Artemisa Güines

Golfo de Batabanó

Colón

Santa Clara

Cayo Coco

Caibarién

Sierra de los Organos

Playa Larga

Guamá Rodas

Placetas

Morón

Bahía de Guadiana

Guane

Pinar del Río

Zapata

Archipélago de los Canarreos

Playa Girón Cienfuegos

Sierra Escambray

Cabo San Antonio

La Fé

Nueva Gerona

Bahía de Cochinos

1156m

Sancti Spíritus

Ciego de Ávila

Cabo Corrientes

Canal de los Indios

La Fé

Trinidad

Cayo Largo

Golfo de Ana María

Canal de Yucatán

Isla de la Juventud

Canal de Bréton

Archipélago de los Jardines de la Reina

| 0 | 50 | 100 | 150 | 200 km |

| 0 | 50 | 100 miles |

Cayman Islands (UK)

*A Cuban passion:
1950s cars*

Cuba

An extraordinary, enigmatic country, Cuba is strikingly different from other Caribbean islands—a place of revolution, violence and hardship; but also a beautiful land where ancient and modern exist side by side.

Havana (La Habana), Cuba's capital, is less than 100 miles (60km) from Florida's Key West, but the political gulf between the two countries is huge. Before the 1959 Revolution, 90 percent of visitors to Cuba were from the US. Today, US citizens are forbidden to spend their dollars in Cuba; only excursions for scientific or research purposes are permitted, although many US tourists now travel there from countries such as Canada, Jamaica and Mexico. US citizens wishing to travel in Cuba should contact the Department of Treasury, Office of Foreign Assets Control, Washington, D.C. 20220 (tel: 202/622-2520; www.treas.gov/ofac).

Cuba lies at the gaping mouth of the Gulf of Mexico and is the largest of the Caribbean islands, a snake-like 777 miles (1,250km) long, though never much more than 75 miles (120km) wide. Much of the fertile land is covered in sugar cane. There are three mountain ranges: in the west, the karst formations of the Sierra de los Organos, whose red earth is covered with tobacco plants; the Sierra Escambray, halfway along the island; and the Sierra Maestra, in the island's

CUBAN COCKTAILS
Two of Cuba's best-known cocktails were favorites of Ernest Hemingway and he was supposed to have had a saying: "My mojito in the Bodeguita, my daiquiri in the Floridita" (the Bodeguita del Medio and El Floridita are long-established Havana restaurants). A mojito is made with rum, sugar, fresh mint leaves and Angostura Bitters (from Trinidad). It is then shaken with ice and strained into a glass. A daiquiri is also based on rum, which is blended with cane sugar and fresh fruit, so that it comes out as an ice-cold, crystalline sludge. A Cuba Libre, named soon after the Revolution, consists of rum on ice with the juice of a lime, topped with cola (a version of which the Cubans still produce).

eastern province, which includes the highest peak of Pico Turquino at 6,580ft (2,005m), where revolutionaries hid in the 1950s. The entire island is ringed with around 4,000 miles (6,450km) of sandy beaches, coral cays and large, secluded bays.

Even without official American visitors, Cuba lays great emphasis on tourism. It has to, in order to bring in much-needed hard currency—especially now that financial support from the former USSR has dried up. Europeans and Canadians flock here for inexpensive vacations; Havana and Santiago de Cuba, the second city, are now linked by air to many European capitals, including London.

HISTORY Cuba was Columbus's second landfall in 1492, and for the next four centuries Spanish adventurers arrived here expecting to make their fortunes. They decimated the indigenous population, replacing them with African slaves, who worked the prosperous sugar plantations. Over the years the slaves mingled with Spanish colonists to form today's mixed Cuban race. During the 16th and 17th centuries, "New World" treasure flooded into Spain via Havana, which quickly became the richest city in the Caribbean.

Spanish colonization gave way briefly to British rule; then the US took control of the island until, in 1902, independence was declared. During the early 1940s, Americans began to exploit Cuba and its cheap labor. The island played host to thousands of visitors from the US, and a wide variety of entertainments and diversions became available, ranging from privately organized gaming casinos to explicit shows. Havana's streets were the setting for extortion, illicit alcohol distribution, trade in narcotics and prostitution. The state, under the dictatorship of Fulgencio Batista, exploited tourism at the expense of the Cuban population and the country.

Embittered Cubans, led by Dr. Fidel Castro, rose up against the Batista regime but were incarcerated on the

Main square, Trinidad, Cuba

REVOLUTIONARY ART
There are no billboard advertisements in Cuba, but revolutionary posters are an art in themselves —brightly colored and featuring famous Cuban faces or working scenes. Some rail against the "Yankee Imperialists" of the United States; others show Fidel and other state heroes (such as José Martí, the poet and journalist who was killed soon after taking up arms against the Spanish in 1895) and the Argentinian Che Guevara, encouraging the Cubans to fulfill their social duties.

Isla de Pinos (renamed the Isla de la Juventud after the Revolution) in 1953. On their release, Castro and the revolutionaries undertook military training in Mexico, joined by Argentinian doctor Che Guevara. In 1956 they sailed to Cuba on the *Granma* and hid in the Sierra Maestra, with a band of guerillas that at one stage numbered only 12. Their following grew as soldiers deserted Batista to join the rebels. Batista fled Cuba on the 1st of January 1959, and the revolutionaries took control. Castro defeated a US-sponsored invasion at the Bay of Pigs in 1961, and in 1965 he made the Communist Party of Cuba the island's sole legal political party.

STAYING IN CUBA The number of hotel rooms in Cuba has almost quadrupled in the last decade. However, facilities can vary dramatically. The most popular and largest of Cuba's beach resorts is Varadero beach, in Matanzas Province, east of Havana, but there are quieter resorts around the coast, such as the Isla de la Juventud, an offshore island in the southwest. Most hotels are mid-range resorts, but luxury resorts have risen on many beaches. Several are joint investment ventures between Cuba and Argentina, Canada, Spain or France, and meet high standards. Cuba's own hotels and casual accommodations can leave a lot to be desired, as Cubans are restricted by a lack of facilities and supplies.

ISLAND SIGHTS AND ENTERTAINMENT The world-famous Varadero beach, Havana's East Beaches, Santa Lucia, Guardalavaca and Daiquiri are just some of Cuba's better known seaside resorts. On the offshore cays, such

as Cayo Sabinal and Cayo Coco, facilities are provided for reef snorkeling and diving trips. The most popular cay is Cayo Largo, off Cuba's southern shores, a coral island resort with air links from Varadero, making it an easy day's excursion. Beyond the beaches, Cuba has some of the Caribbean's most historic sites. The Old Town of Havana is 2sq miles (5sq km) of cobbles, colonnades and Spanish colonial palaces. In the south is the "living museum" of 16th-century Trinidad, which has joined Old Havana as a UNESCO World Heritage site. Although gambling is now forbidden in Cuba, there is still a lively entertainment scene, including renowned shows such as Havana's 50-year-old Tropicana.

AFTER THE REVOLUTION
For the average Cuban, life improved after the Revolution. For instance, medical care and education became available to all. At the same time, Castro established a one-party constitution and political dissenters were simply locked up. Castro, usually known as Fidel, was a popular figurehead and to some extent he still is, though most of his population cannot now remember what life was like before the Revolution.

Getting around is relatively easy these days with a good central highway and a 150-year-old railway running down the spine of the country, plus over 18,000 miles (29,000km) of roads. Car rental and chauffeur facilities are good, but expensive. Cubans still drive 1950s American cars—when petrol is available—but ox-carts, horses and bicycles are common alternatives.

Domestic flights link most large towns and the Varadero beach resort, which is also joined by a highway to Matanzas in the south. Flights within Cuba are not expensive and are generally easily booked. Independent travel is possible except in restricted areas, though it can be difficult to find meals outside resorts and hotels can be basic. However, new lodges and camp sites, Cubatur's helpful guides and use of tourist buses and trains have made independent touring a realistic option.

ISLAND LIFE Since 2004 the US dollar has been banned from use in Cuba. Though prices may be quoted in dollars, all transactions must be paid for in convertible pesos or with credit cards backed by non-US banking institutions. Make sure you obtain a receipt for all currency conversions and traveler's checks cashed as you will need to show these in order to reconvert any pesos at the end of your trip. The buying power of ordinary Cubans is meager compared to tourists. Hustlers are appearing in larger numbers, and visitors should be particularly careful with their belongings in Havana and Varadero. Rationing has now reached a point where many people simply do not get enough food. Electricity is restricted and fuel for private vehicles is hard to find. Even the much-vaunted health care and education services are under threat through lack of funds. Real progress is unlikely while the US embargo continues, and, for its part, the Cuban Communist Party has shown little inclination to change. However, the explosion of tourism from Europe and Canada has gone some way to improving matters until the embargo is loosened.

For all their difficulties, the 11 million Cubans are a lively nation, whose Latin Caribbean character shines through in their rhythmic music. It is well worth attending an evening at a *casa de la trova*, where professional musicians play in competition with one another; and in July each year the Cubans drop everything for *Carnaval*, a weekend of dancing through the streets.

MOTORIZED ART
The cars driven by Cubans are a curious leftover from pre-Revolution days, when the island was almost an offshore state of the US. Dating from the 1950s—the last time Cubans were allowed to buy, or could afford, privately owned cars—these magnificent, fin-tailed beasts are adorned with a great expanse of chrome on their bumpers and fittings and are cared for lovingly.

169

TROVA
The trova is a special Cuban ballad which, like many Caribbean songs, has an element of social comment. Trovas are as likely to celebrate a national hero or take a swing at corruption in the Communist Party as they are to sing of love. The name "trova" is derived from the Provençal *trobar* (to compose)—as is the word troubadour, used to describe the medieval romantic poets of Languedoc.

A Cuban country house

*Wrought-iron balconies,
vantage points for view-
ing the streets in Old
Havana (above)
Equally impressive are
the views of Havana
from across the water
(right)*

THROUGH THE KEYHOLE
It is always worth taking
a look inside the
buildings, both public and
private, in Havana, if you
can see or find your way
through the front door.
There may be glimpses of
superb inner courtyards,
with arched colonnades
on each story,
constructed so that the
sunlight and heat did not
penetrate into the rooms.
Others have elaborately
decorated stairways or
beautiful fan-shaped
stained-glass windows.

▶▶ Havana (La Habana)

The modern city of Havana, on the north coast of Cuba
near the western end of the island, has radiated outward
from the earliest colony, which was settled on the western
shore of Havana harbor in 1514 and is now made up of
four distinct districts: Old Havana, Central Havana,
Vedado and Miramar.

Even in its dilapidated state, there is a charmed feel
about **Old Havana▶▶▶**. Its tight alleys and cobbled
squares, colonnades and colonial palaces built in coral
rock are strikingly beautiful compared to the present-day
city's high-rise hotels. Old Havana's finest square is the
Plaza de la Catedral; the 18th-century baroque cathedral
sits on its northern side, flanked by the Museum of
Colonial Art at 61 Calle San Ignacio (tel: 7862 6440. *Open*
Tue–Sat 9.30–6.30. *Admission: inexpensive*) and the
renowned El Patio restaurant. A colorful arts and crafts
market has appeared just off the Plaza de la Catedral.

Hemingway's favorite Bodeguita del Medio restaurant
is nearby, as is the grand Plaza des Armas, which was
originally the parade ground, with its imposing Palace of
the Captain Generals. Also on the Plaza are the City
Museum (*Open* daily 9.30–6.30), and the classical-style El
Templete portico, built to celebrate the first Mass on
Cuban soil. Just off the square, the Castillo de la Fuerza is
Cuba's oldest fortress (1544), whose roof is topped by the
city's symbol, the tiny golden statue of La Giraldilla.
Numerous cannons, which were recently excavated near
the ancient city walls, now surround the fortress.

To the west, Old Havana is bounded by the Paseo de
Martí, an avenue giving easy access to several museums,
including the Memorial Museum, the National Museum

(containing many old masterpieces), the ornate Garcia Lorca Theatre, and the Capitol (a copy of the one in Washington, DC). Overlooking Old Havana is the 17th-century El Morro fortress, part of the Morro-Cabaña Historical and Military Park with the fortress of San Carlos de la Cabaña. It has an extensive collection of antique weapons, and a traditional cannon shot is fired from La Cabaña at 9pm every evening.

Heading north through the open Parque Central, you emerge into the 19th-century Prado, a broad boulevard with a raised promenade where Habaneros sit and pass the time of day. Close by is the old Presidential Palace, an eclectic building of columns and balustrades, which now contains the Revolutionary Museum. This displays photographs, guerrilla maps and stirring revolutionary memorabilia. Outside, military hardware on show includes tanks, planes and Castro's invasion boat.

Along the seafront, the 2-mile (3km) Malecon, a promenade where young Habaneros gather on summer evenings (and where *Carnaval* is staged), leads west to the modern districts of Havana, including Vedado. At the head of La Rampa, a bustling business street, stands the Habana Libre Hotel, built in the 1950s as the Hilton. The Bar Turquino, on the top floor, has a magnificent view of the city. South of here are the stately buildings of the City University and finally the open Plaza de la Revolución, where a statue of national hero José Martí stands beside a huge concrete column constructed in the shape of a communist star. Political rallies are held here and often draw up to as many as 500,000 people.

To the west of the square is the Cementerio Cristobal Colón (the Columbus Cemetery), with an impressive collection of magnificent mausoleums with exquisite stone carving—definitely not to be missed!

Elsewhere, there is a wealth of galleries, museums and palaces. A visit to the Casa de las Americas, which exhibits contemporary Latin American art and craft and has regular recitals and theatrical events, is particularly worthwhile—and Havana's excellent ice cream should be tasted at La Coppelita park on La Rampa.

THE BAY OF PIGS
The Bay of Pigs was catapulted into the headlines in April 1961 when 1,400 Cuban exiles staged an invasion of the island, partially backed by the US, in order to oust Castro and his revolutionaries. It was a military fiasco, and most of the exiles were rounded up within a couple of days. In Cuban revolutionary lore it was written up as the first great defeat of imperialism on Latin American soil. Castro declared Cuba Communist a couple of days later.

HEMINGWAY'S ISLAND
Ernest Hemingway lived in Cuba during the 1940s and 1950s, and he set two of his novels there: *Islands in the Stream* and *The Old Man and the Sea*, whose story supposedly takes place in the village of Cojímar. Two restaurants in Old Havana were particular favorites of his: the riotous Bodeguita del Medio on Calle Empredado and the more formal and stately El Floridita on Calle Obispo, where you can try some of the best lobster in the Caribbean. Hemingway lived in the suburb of San Francisco, in a hillside house called La Vigia, now open to the public. He was a keen deep-sea fisherman—a marina west of Havana bears his name.

171

The epic struggle in Hemingway's The Old Man and the Sea *is recalled in a statue*

An old West Indian legend tells of large Cuban women rolling the world's finest cigars on their thighs. Whether or not this was true, the reality nowadays is rather less picturesque, although it is still intriguing to watch Cuban cigars being rolled by hand, cut with large metal blades and pressed in antique wooden vises.

EARLY SMOKERS

Columbus was the first European to see Indians smoking tobacco, which is indigenous to the Americas. Twisted leaves would be wrapped in dried palm leaves or maize husk and smoked by Mayan Indians during religious ceremonies. The Mayans believed tobacco to be medicinal, and the word "cigar" is derived from their own term for smoking, *sik'ar*. Tobacco quickly gained popularity in Europe, where, in the 17th century, smoking was a sign of great wealth.

CIGAR TYPES

The traditional Cuban cigar is a corona, which measures about 6in (15cm) and has straight sides, with one rounded and one cut end. The corona chica has the same shape, but is about 4in (10cm) in length. Ideales are slender and torpedo-shaped, tapered at the lighting end, as are the smaller bouquets. Panatellas are thin and cut open at both ends; a cheroot is even thinner.

172

Tobacco, a bright green plant with long, oval leaves, grows on many Caribbean islands for use in cigarettes—but only Cuba and the Dominican Republic have cigar industries. The finest Cuban tobacco, reserved for its cigars, grows in the northwestern province of Pinar del Río, where the earth is thick and deep red and the leaves grow with a minimum of starches and sugars. Dotted around the neat tobacco fields are drying houses, with wooden walls and palm-thatch or aluminum roofs, where the leaves are cured for up to three months after picking.

Once dried, the leaves are sorted according to age—older leaves have a stronger flavor but younger leaves are more elastic and better for rolling—and are bundled off to the factories. While one factory worker sits at the head of the room, reading aloud from a newspaper, the others sit at long tables, placing "binder" leaves in their hands, laying tobacco filler (the offcuts of the last rolls) on top and then making the first, skillful roll. Each cigar is then pressed in a vise to give it the correct shape. One half of the strong, evenly colored "wrapper" leaf is then rolled around it, and finally the cigar is trimmed. After the manufacturer's bands have been slipped on, the cigars are packed in boxes, between leaves of aromatic cedar wood, for export.

Some of the most famous cigar manufacturers are based in Cuba, including Monte Cristo, Partagas, Romeo y Julietta, H. Upmann and Davidoff. Within Cuba, cigars are remarkably cheap, and factory tours can be arranged through Intur or Cubatur. Due to sanctions against the Communist regime, Cuban cigars are illegal in the US.

OUTSIDE HAVANA West of Havana is Pinar del Río Province, the home of the finest Cuban tobacco. It takes a good day's drive to see the neatly ranged fields of bright green tobacco plants and thatched drying houses. A worthwhile stop on the way is the lovely **Soroa Orchid Garden▶**, where over 750 species of orchid flourish on a hillside site near the Manantiales waterfall. Around Viñales the landscape is punctuated with strange karst "haystack" hills, known in Cuba as *mogotes*. The town of **Pinar del Río▶** contains an attractive selection of neoclassical houses including Guach Palace and a rum factory renowned for its wild guava-flavored rum, Guayabita de Pinar. Also worth seeing is the cathedral of San Rosendo, the tobacco museum west of town, and one of the local cigar factories that are said to sell the best in Cuba.

UNEASY LEASE
Guantanamo, a remote, easterly province, is a curious anomaly, in that there is a US naval base there, on Cuban sovereign land. It was arranged on a lease in 1902, but since the Revolution the Cubans have refused to accept the nominal annual payment of $5,000.

Cienfuegos traffic

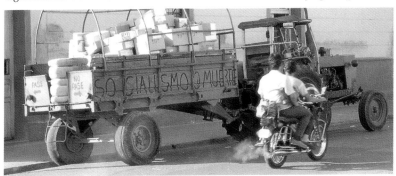

North of Pinar, the charming small town of **Viñales▶** is situated amid the *mogotes* of the Sierra de los Organos, in an area that is a national monument and UNESCO World Heritage Site. Just over a mile (1.5km) west of town, the **Prehistory Wall**, a mural painted by Leovigildo Gonzalez, a disciple of the great Diego Rivera, can be seen; 3–4 miles (5–6.5km) north, look for the Cueva del Indio, a lovely Indian cave that can be toured by foot and by boat. Catch a boat at Palma Rubia to get to Cayo Levisa, part of the Archipelago de los Colorados, with a long, sandy beach with good snorkeling and scuba diving around a reef.

Hemingway aficionados might want to visit **Cojímar▶**, the village where he set his tale *The Old Man and the Sea*. Hemingway himself fished from Cojímar and his International Fishing Tourney originated there, although it now takes place at the Hemingway Marina near Havana.

To the east of Havana is Cuba's best resort town, **Varadero▶**, where hotels and restaurants stand on the Peninsula de Hicacos' 12 miles (19km) of powder-like sand. Windsurfing and parasailing can be arranged here, and there are lively evening bars, including the Cueva del Pirata, a discotheque set in a cave. There is also an art gallery and Veradero Municipal Museum (tel: 4561 3189).

A short drive away at Punta Hicacos, the **Cueva de Ambrosio▶▶** was a ceremonial cave site decorated with dozens of Indian drawings and re-discovered in 1961. Look for the cave between the Marina Chapelin and the Marina Gaviota toward the north end of the peninsula. Varadero has its share of hustlers and prostitutes, who tend to congregate toward the south end of the resort area.

MONCADA GARRISON
The Moncada Garrison in Santiago is honored in revolutionary lore as the place where Castro made his first strike against the Batista regime. On the 26th of July 1953, 130 young rebels assembled to the east of the city, and although some were unarmed, launched an attack. Militarily, it was a dismal failure; most were rounded up as they tried to escape and many were killed. The survivors received long prison sentences. Moncada is recalled on the black and red party flag in the insignia "M-26-7," and the 26th of July has been made a national holiday.

BOTANIC GARDENS

About 10 miles (16km) east of Cienfuegos is the Jardin Botanico de Cienfuegos, set in part of an old sugar plantation. The gardens are devoted to medicinal plants, fruit trees, orchids, bamboos and a great collection of palm trees. It was founded by plantation owner Edwin F. Atkins in 1901.

The international hotels can be found farther north and the very north end of the peninsula has been designated park area and is to be left undeveloped. In general, Varadero offers a fine beach vacation, but it is totally isolated and has more in common with a typical Caribbean beach resort of other islands than with the rest of Cuba.

On the south coast beneath Varadero is the swampy Zapata Peninsula, site of the infamous Bay of Pigs invasion in 1961 and now of the Bay of Pigs Museum and a number of tourist resorts. Farther east, through the sugar flats, is the pretty town of **Cienfuegos▶**, also known as the Pearl of the South. It is one of Cuba's major ports, where interesting buildings include the 1870 neo-Gothic Catedral Purisima Concepción, the **Tomás Terry Theater▶** on the Parque Martí, decorated with an exquisite painted ceiling of muses and Cuban writers, and the Moorish-influenced Valle Palace, an elaborate architectural folly on Punta Gorda. On the west side of Parque Martí, visit the Palacio de Ferrer, dating from 1894, and climb the tower for wonderful views.

The southern slopes of the Sierra Escambray tumble into the sea around the town of **Trinidad▶▶▶**. Founded in 1514 by Diego Velázquez, Trinidad was a successful shipping town in the early 19th century and has been restored to its former grandeur. The cobbled central square, Plaza Martí, one of five main squares, has beautiful colonial Spanish buildings, complemented with bougainvillea blooms, as well as two museums: the **Museo de Arquitectura de Trinidad**, which traces the city's development during the 18th and 19th centuries; and the **Museo Romantico**, displaying furniture and decorative arts. Next door to the Museo Romantico is Trinidad's premier cathedral, the **Iglesia Parroquial de la Santisima Trinidad▶▶▶**

An interior in Trinidad's Museo Romantico

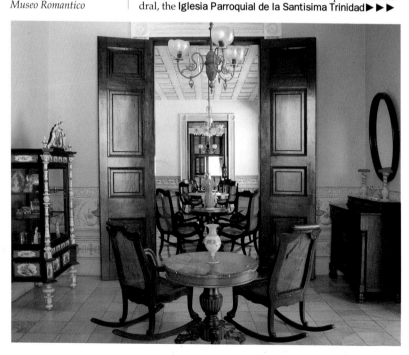

built between 1817 and 1892. The largest church in Cuba, it is famed for its acoustics. Other city museums include the **Museo de Archeológica Arqueologica Guamuhaya▶**, overviewing pre-Columbian to post-conquest times; and the **Museo de Lucha Contra Bandidos▶**, which focuses on the military campaigns waged against counter-revolutionaries in the Escambray Mountains in the 1960s. The Casa de la Cultura on Calle Zerquera showcases cultural events and has a gallery and store; the Casa de la Trova has late-night live music and open-air concerts on Calle Marquez, with singing on Sunday afternoons.

The fishing village of La Boca lies just 5 miles (8km) from Trinidad; you'll pass through en route to the beach at Playa Ancon, which has lovely turquoise water, good diving just offshore, and a couple of resort hotels. To the east, the ruined Torre de Iznaga is an old watch tower built to oversee slaves in the sugar cane fields.

Cuba's second town, **Santiago de Cuba▶ ▶**, commands a stunning position on a vast south-coast harbor, near the east end of the island. In the shadow of the great Sierra Maestra mountains, this city's cathedral is the oldest on the island (1514). Conquistador Diego Velázquez lived in a 1520 mansion on Cespedes Park, which now contains the Cuban Life Museum and its fine furniture collection. In all, the city has 14 museums, of which there are two notable examples: the Bacardi Museum, serving as a reminder of the rum family's origins and displaying pre-Columbian artifacts, art and history exhibits, and the 26 de Julio Museum in the Moncada Barracks, attacked by Castro's revolutionaries on the 26th of July 1953 .

Santiago has a more ethnically mixed population, having been the first Cuban city to receive slaves; French colonists fleeing Haiti's insurrection in the 18th century also arrived at Santiago, as did many migrating Jamaicans. Much of the city is organized around Cespedes Park, most prominently the recently renovated Hotel Casa Granda on the east side and the cathedral **Santa Iglesia Basilica Metropolitana▶** on the south side. Northeast of the center lies the Plaza de la Revolución, dedicated to the 19th-century Cuban revolutionary General Antonio Maceo. The park is dominated by a bronze statue of the general on horseback surrounded by iron machetes, as well as a galvanized steel monument to the revolution.

Santiago's architecture is eclectic, offering everything from neoclassical to art deco. The pastel-hued buildings are in better shape than those in most Cuban towns. The Cementerio Sant Ifigenia, northwest of town, contains José Martí's mausoleum; inside, a statue of Martí—surrounded by six statues of women meant to represent 19th-century Cuba's six provinces—has been positioned to receive a shaft of sun all morning.

If you have a car, take the coastal road along the Sierra Maestra. High points include **El Uvero▶**, about 40 miles (64.5km) west of Santiago, with a museum commemorating an early battle in the revolution; and **Pico Turquino▶**, the highest peak in the Sierra Maestra at almost 6,000ft (2005m). The castle of San Pedro de la Roca, also known as El Moro, has recently been added to the list of UNESCO World Heritage Sites. The road continues to Pilon; in the 1950s, Castro's revolution began in this area, and there are sites devoted to those days.

Casa de Cultura in Cienfuegos

175

EL COBRE
About 6 miles (10km) west of Santiago lies El Sanctuario de Nuestra Senora de la Caridad del Cobre, or "El Cobre," the shrine to Cuba's patron saint, built above a copper mine. There's a legend attached, but more compelling is the idyllic setting in the Sierra Maestra. To get there rent a car from Santiago.

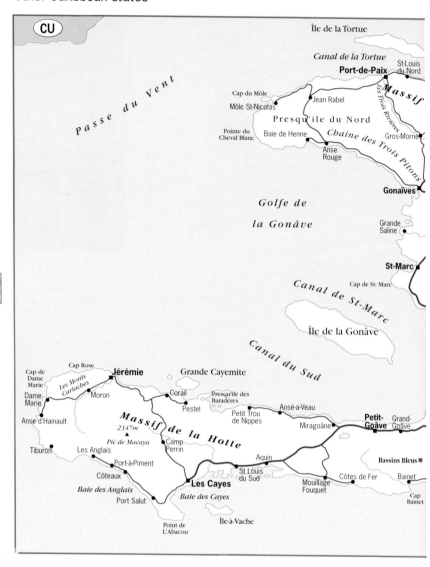

Haiti

Only 30 years ago, Haiti's excellent beaches, sophisticated hotels and proximity to the US made it one of the area's top vacation destinations. Since then, however, the political situation has become tense, with outbreaks of violence. Instability is the norm, and Haiti cannot be recommended as a tourist destination at present. When things calm down again, by all means go. Few countries contain such striking contrasts of devastating poverty and luxurious lifestyles, hardship and hope. Travel there is a bombardment of the senses: the primitivist art, adorning buildings, walls and vehicles; the cramped, brightly painted buses and trucks, called *tap taps* (after the noise

BUCCANEERS
Buccaneers were runaways from many European nations who crept into the remote west of Hispaniola in the early 17th century. Renowned as riflemen, they survived by wandering the plains killing wild cattle. The meat was smoked over a *boucan*, from which their name derives. Later, working from a stronghold on the Ile de la Tortue off the north coast of Haiti, they became pirates, known as the Brethren of the Coast.

Crowds in the streets of Port-au-Prince

made by the original trucks), with their carved wood and religious maxims displayed along the sides and scenes from the Bible on the hoods; the strange world of voodoo; and the ceaseless hubbub of the markets. Love it or hate it, there is nowhere in the world like Haiti.

This is not an easy island for travelers. White visitors are particularly targeted with constant demands for money, from people who are genuinely in dire need. Haiti's currency is the gourde (five gourdes make a *dollar haïtien*), named for the large, hard-shelled fruit of the calabash tree and introduced by the country's despotic leader, Henry Christophe, in the early 19th century.

Most flights from Europe and the US go to Miami for connections to the main airport at the capital, Port-au-Prince. Haiti's capital lies in the southwest, in the deep

A multicolored tap tap

bight of the Golfe de la Gonâve. It is a buzzing city of over one million inhabitants, many of whom live in the shanty towns that cluster around the main town. There are good places to stay in Pétionville, the prosperous suburb above the capital, well priced now in their faded grandeur, not forgetting the beach hotels on the Côte des Arcadins about an hour north of Port-au-Prince. There is also a clutch of good restaurants.

Haiti occupies the western third (10,715sq miles/27,750sq km) of the island of Hispaniola, which it shares with the Dominican Republic. "Haiti," the original Amerindian name for the island, meaning "mountainous land," is an accurate description. Shaped like a crab's claw closing around the Golfe de la Gonâve, it is about 90 miles (145km) north to south and has two long mountainous ranges that stretch west like pincers toward Cuba and Jamaica. The highest peak is the Pic de la Selle (8,795ft/2,680m), in the southeast. The country is fertile and there is a variety of scenery: palm-backed beaches (the closest to Port-au-Prince are Ibo beach and Kyona; Cormier and Labadie are found outside Cap-Haïtien); cactus-covered plains, and rain-forested mountains. However, in a country of around 6 million mainly rural inhabitants, deforestation and soil erosion have now become a serious problem.

Religious and nationalist graffiti, Port-au-Prince

HISTORY Haiti has a history of turmoil. The first 40 European settlers, left there in 1492 by Columbus, all died within a year. In 1697 the French were handed control of western Hispaniola (then called Saint Domingue) by the Spanish and made it a wealthy colony, exporting sugar, coffee and indigo. At the end of the 18th century, after years of torture and starvation at the hands of their colonial masters, the African slaves finally rebelled, led by Toussaint l'Ouverture. In 1804 Haiti declared itself independent—the world's first black republic. Its political life since then has been troubled: Civil war between the north and the south was followed by a succession of tyrannical leaders and US invasion in 1915. The Americans left in 1934, and in 1957 François Duvalier, "Papa Doc," became the ruthless dictator, maintaining his grip on power through the notorious secret police, the *tontons macoute*. His son Jean Claude ("Baby Doc") continued the reign of terror until, in the mid-1980s, a movement of revolt known as Operation Deschoukay drove him out of the country.

Haiti has continued to suffer political instability, which has been characterized by a series of coups d'états, failed elections, and politicans who are unable to maintain a grip on this troubled nation despite American intervention, as in the case of Jean-Bartrand Aristide in the mid-1990s. The February 2006 election has been well received internationally, though the new government has amountain to climb and high expectations to fulfil.

ISLAND LIFE Ordinary islanders, most of whom work on the land, have suffered the consequences of corrupt and repressive government, and Haiti is now the poorest country in the western hemisphere. The majority of its population is descended from Africans; many of the small and powerful "mulatto élite" emigrated during recent troubles. French is the official language and its influence can be heard in the everyday spoken language, Kreyol.

Haiti has an amazingly vibrant artistic and religious life. Its primitive-style art, with primary colors and almost cartoon-like forms, has been copied all over the Caribbean. Many of the traditional themes of Haitian life are portrayed, including agricultural, biblical and voodoo scenes. Voodoo itself is a mix of Catholic and African beliefs, often sensationalized as "black magic," and running deep in the Haitian psyche. Haiti has its own dance rhythm—compas—which fills the streets during Carnival, from the 6th of January to Mardi Gras, before Lent. This is the best time to witness the extraordinary spirit of the Haitians.

THE BLACK JACOBINS

One of the far-reaching effects of the French Revolution was to bring to a head the tensions of Haitian society in the late 18th century. Political rights, granted in theory to the mixed race population by the French National Assembly, were denied within the colony and violence erupted. In 1791 the black population, who had suffered appallingly as slaves to the white colonists, themselves rebeled, and the country was split between those of mixed race living in the south and the northern blacks (where Toussaint l'Ouverture rose to prominence). The story of Toussaint l'Ouverture and the Haitian revolution is told in C.L.R. James's powerful book, *The Black Jacobins*. Published in 1938, this was an influential work at a time when British West Indians were reassessing their history and turning their minds toward independence.

179

Fishing off the north coast town of Cap-Haïtien

Voodoo calls up sinister images: candle-lit cere-monies of dancing, chanting and mesmeric drum rhythms; initiates in trances flailing around, intoning predictions, eating hot coals or making animal sacrifices. There is an ele-ment of truth in these images, but voodoo should not be written off as "black magic." Widely misunderstood outside Haiti, voodoo has a deeply rooted role in everyday island life.

DUPPIES

Duppies, also known as jumbies, are the wander-ing souls of the dead. People who die unhappy or without a proper wake are said to become rest-less spirits, returning to haunt those who knew them in life. Belief in dup-pies is widespread, and even educated people who otherwise disregard obeah (magic) will acknowledge their existence.

Haiti is not the only island where voodoo is practiced. Other forms of the religion exist elsewhere: santería, across the border in Santo Domingo and in Cuba; pocoma-nia in Jamaica; and shango in Trinidad. In these parts of the Caribbean, however, the beliefs are gradually dying out, while in Haiti voodoo continues to touch everyone's life and was particularly prevalent in the days of Papa Doc, who made himself a high priest of voodoo.

Like a number of the Caribbean systems of belief, voodoo has mixed African and European origins. All have a common theme in their appeals to spirits to intervene in life on earth. Spirits, or lwas, are summoned, in drumming and dance, to "mount" a follower, who then falls into a trance, dancing and speaking in tongues or making pre-dictions.

A voodoo ceremony, by Gérard Valcin

ZOMBIES

There is "evidence" in Haiti of people turned into zombies ("undead" souls) while still alive. A poison is believed to reduce their metabolic rate so that they appear dead. After burial, they are supposedly exhumed, revived and then used as slaves.

The worship of spirits was originally brought by slaves from Africa and merged with Caribbean beliefs and Catholic saints. In Haitian voodoo the snake god Damballa, who makes his followers dance in a writhing motion, is equivalent to St. Patrick, often pictured with snakes at his feet; Ogun, the god of war, whose followers appear to be brandishing swords, is associated with St. James, and Erzulie is equated with the Virgin Mary. Like the angels of the Christian pantheon, lwas can be benevo-lent or vengeful. If times are hard it is because the lwa is displeased. *Rada* lwas, such as Erzulie, are known for their wisdom and benevolence; *petro* lwas, like Tijan Petro, for their power.

Voodoo ceremonies are conducted according to a calendar, which includes important Catholic events; for example, devotees celebrate the appearance of the Virgin Mary at the Ville Bonheur waterfall near Mirebalais on the 16th of July each year. Here followers, particularly those with problems of love, come to wash themselves in the *Saut d'eau* (waterfall) in order to receive the blessing of Erzulie and the Virgin Mary. The usual setting for a ceremony is a village temple with a mud floor, a *houmfo*, and the ceremony proceeds under the direction of a *houngan* (priest) or a *mambo* (priestess). After recitations from the Catholic liturgy, the drums strike up with the special rhythms of the lwa to be invoked. An initiate then traces on the ground the lwa's *véver*, a complex pattern of lines laid out with cornmeal. At some point a dancer is mounted by an lwa and exhibits his or her characteristics. The lwa will be presented with its favorite food or drink, and eventually there may be an animal sacrifice. Followers who have been mounted apparently remember nothing after the event.

It is almost impossible for visitors to Haiti to attend a genuine voodoo ceremony, but occasional shows are held with commentaries; contact Le Péristyle de Mariani, on the outskirts of Port-au-Prince.

Obeah Another feature shared by all the Caribbean beliefs is the use of obeah, or magic, known as *myal* in the British Caribbean and *wango* in Haiti. Obeah men (*bocors* in Haiti) act as advisers and intervene in human affairs through the use of incantations and spells. These may be used to heal a sick person, to ensnare a lover or to settle a score; they may also rid a person of a vengeful duppy (ghost). Spells are set with herbal concoctions and other ingredients, such as blood, sweat, eggshells and broken bottles. Obeah was outlawed in Jamaica as early as 1760, but it is still practiced widely, though secretly, in rural areas all over the Caribbean region.

THE DRUMS OF VOODOO
The driving force behind every voodoo ceremony is the drumming, which engenders a trance and summons a particular lwa. There are three drums of different sizes, each one carved of mahogany; and each lwa has its own particular drum rhythms.

OTHER RELIGIONS
Besides the revivalist sects of pocomania and Revival Zion, Jamaica has many spirit-based religions. Kumina is a religion with less European influence than most—probably because it arrived relatively recently, brought by free Africans who came willingly to Jamaica after emancipation in 1838. Kumina appeals to its own zombies, the spirits of ancestors, as well as to the gods of the Congo, its followers' original homeland. Convince is a faith that appeals to the African *bongo* gods and to the spirits of the maroon leaders (see panel, page 147), as does Kromanti. There are similar sects in Trinidad (the Shouters) and in St. Lucia (the Kele).

181

A ritual mask, which is worn by men taken over by female spirits

The Dominican Republic

The country Columbus called "the fairest land under heaven" is home to the oldest European settlement in the western hemisphere, but the Dominican Republic has two modern faces. Its glorious beaches, fascinating colonial heritage and mountain-top "resorts" contrast sharply with the grinding poverty of many of its islanders. With its 3,300-mile (5,300km) shoreline, the Dominican Republic has one of the largest tourist industries in the Caribbean. Most of its hotels are mid-range beach-front resorts, scattered in complexes along the northern and eastern shores, but other options include the luxury Casa de Campo—where polo ponies can be rented—or a hotel in Santo Domingo's historic city center. The island also has quiet, isolated resort towns, such as Cabarete and Las Terrenas, where you can relax in guesthouses under the

Bahía
Escocesa

Cabo Cabrón

Las Terrenas
Las Galeras
Sánchez
Samaná
Babía de Samaná
Sabana de la Mar
Parque Nacional
Los Haitises
Las Cañitas
El Valle
Batey Papgayo
Cordillera Oriental
El Seibo
El Macao
Bayaguana
Hato Mayor
Ramón Santana
Higüey
Cabo Engaño
Los Llanos
Soco
Punta Cana
a Caleta
San Rafael del Yuma
Boca Chica
San Pedro de Macoris
Altos de Chavón
Isla Catalina
La Romana
Bayahibe
Babía de Yuma
Babía La Altagracia
El Algibe
Isla Saona

Canal de la Mona

```
0        20        40      60 km
0             20            40 miles
```

QUISQUEYA
Quisqueya was the name used by the indigenous Taino for their island when Columbus arrived in 1492. It is still used as a poetic name for Hispaniola, but principally survives as the name of a locally brewed beer. (Presidente is a lighter and slightly more bitter but tastier local beer.)

SANTERIA
Just as the Haitians have voodoo (see page 179) and the British Islands have obeah, so the Latin islands observe santería, which is a mix of African animist beliefs and Catholic doctrine. There are the same drum-driven ceremonies, animal sacrifices and posses- sions, as well as witchcraft practitioners, who use local plants and other small objects to make their concoctions.

183

palm trees or windsurf. The Dominican Republic is one of the cheaper and better-value package tour destinations in the Caribbean, and it can be easily reached from the USA, UK and Canada, both by scheduled and charter flights. Cruise ships from the USA stop at Puerto Plata. There are

Carvings set up for sale at a Dominican Republic market stall

Other Caribbean states

LA ISABELLA

Santo Domingo was not the first of the "New World" towns. La Isabella, named for the Spanish queen, was settled by 1,000 willing adventurers in 1493 on Columbus's second voyage. The site is near Luperon on the north coast, but there are only archeological remains now. The colonists moved to Santo Domingo's present site in 1498 because La Isabella, set among malarial swamps, was unhealthy, and riches beckoned after gold was found nearer

charter flights from Europe, although if you are traveling independently you may have to go via Miami or via Spain. Despite the million or so annual visitors to the island, the tourist industry is surprisingly unobtrusive once you have left the fringe of hotels that run along the coast. In contrast to many of the islands in the Caribbean, which are visibly affected by the industry, the Dominican Republic is large enough to allow independent travel and to maintain a lively local Latin culture. In September 1998 Hurricane Georges hammered the southeastern half of the country causing widespread destruction. However, the tourist infrastructure was swiftly repaired, illustrating its vital importance to the local economy.

One of the best places in the Caribbean to immerse yourself in history is the colonial city in Santo Domingo, the oldest city in the Americas, which enjoyed its heyday in the 16th century when conquistadors came here to plan their voyages to the American mainland. Nowadays you can relax in the bars and restaurants of the 12-block Colonial Zone, surrounded by the architectural glories of the Spanish era. This is a Latin American island, full of surprises. Merengue music is heard everywhere; if you get on a bus, you might find the passengers singing along. Islanders gather on the plazas in the late evening to take in the cooler air; and they love to dance, so the clubs are always popular meeting places.

The Dominican Republic occupies the eastern two-thirds of the island of Hispaniola—a contraction of *La Isla Española*, as Columbus called it when he landed in 1492 (Haiti claims the western third of the island, ceded to French rule by the Spaniards in 1697). At 18,765 sq miles (48,115sq km), it is the second largest country in the Caribbean after Cuba; geographically, it is the most extreme. Topping the massive Cordillera Central, Pico Duarte (10,420ft/3,175m) is the tallest mountain in the

Colorful decoration on the wall of a shack

DOMINICAN DISHES
Comida Criolla, or Créole food, as local dishes are known, includes a wide range of meats: beef, farmed by *campesinos* (cowboys) in the south-east, pork, goat (*chivo*) and chicken. These are served in rather heavy but tasty dishes such as stew, *sancocho*, which is made with a variety of meats, and *mondongo*, made with tripe. Seafood and fish are popular, as are many tropical vegetables, including plantains and cassava.

West Indies, and in the southwest, Lago Enriquillo is a lake set in the lowest point of land, 114ft (35m) below sea level. It encircles arid, thorny islands that serve as a protected sanctuary to exotic birds and reptiles, such as the flamingo, the iguana and the indigenous caiman (a kind of crocodile).

In the north there are rampantly fertile mountains with crashing rivers; in the south, on the Barahona peninsula, there is desert. The greater part of the country has seemingly endless stretches of bright green hillsides and cane fields, spiked with magnificent royal palm trees.

ISLAND LIFE The 7.9 million or so Dominicans are of mixed African and European blood dating from the early days of colonial settlement. This is a desperately poor nation; its poverty is particularly evident in the countryside and on the outskirts of the main towns, where many people live in makeshift shanty flats. The limited public services break down on a regular basis (big hotels have their own power plants). Since there is no social safety net, life can be extremely hard for the islanders, some of whom

The freshest of crayfish are barbequed daily

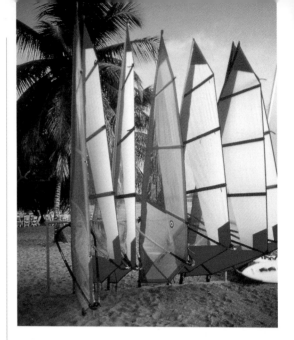

Windsurfers at the luxury resort of Casa de Campo

FRESH FRUIT MILK SHAKES

Dominicans use their fruit to the best advantage in freshly prepared drinks. *Jugo* is plain squeezed fruit juice served with ice, but the best drinks are *bastidas*, squeezed fruits whisked up with milk and ice. Flavors include *piña* (pineapple), *china* (orange), *lechola* (pawpaw), and *guanabana* (soursop).

MERENGUE

The national rhythm of the Dominican Republic is the merengue, a strongly Latin and impossibly quick beat. You will hear it played by local string bands and in the clubs, where dancers exercise their elastic legs, racing across the dance floor in a close embrace. There is a merengue festival in Santo Domingo each year, in the third week of July, when bands and dancers fill the streets.

endeavor to escape to the USA. This journey is a notoriously dangerous one, however, often undertaken in inadequate, leaking boats.

The Dominican Republic throws the contrasts of Caribbean tourism into sharp relief. With so many prosperous tourists passing through, opportunists have come to regard them as walking dispensers of dollars, and outside the tourist complexes you will probably be hassled for money. There is considerable prostitution—"sex tourism" is an established trade in some places—and unsurprisingly there is an increasing incidence of AIDS.

The Dominican Republic has a troubled political tradition, which has hit ordinary Dominicans hard. Throughout the 19th century, control of the island lurched from one ruling power to another, as Spanish, Haitians, Americans and Dominican independence fighters battled for supremacy. Independence finally came in 1844, but the country soon fell into the hands of despots and slid into bankruptcy.

The USA sent troops to administer the country between 1916 and 1924, to a mixed reception from islanders, who longed for stability but resented military rule. In 1930 General Rafael Leonidas Trujillo, the Dominican army's commander, established a ruthless dictatorship. He ruled the country for the next 30 years, treating it as his own personal estate. He was responsible for organizing the "disappearance" of countless opponents and rifling through the treasury.

Trujillo was assassinated in 1961, and there followed a series of coups, civil war and military intervention by the US. Elections were held in 1966, and after a rocky start, the political scene has remained on a fairly stable, pro-US footing for 30 years.

The official language of the country is Spanish, with English spoken in tourist areas.

▶▶▶ Altos de Chavón

Altos de Chavón is near the eastern town of La Romana, attached to the Dominican Republic's premier resort, the huge and luxurious Casa de Campo. The "Heights of Chavón," standing high above the Chavón river, is a pretty replica of a 16th-century Mediterranean village. The village has a slightly unreal feel, for the 30 or so coral-rock houses are so obviously imitations. But many parts of the village are festooned with colorful bougainvillea blooms, there are quaint cobbled streets and artful wrought-iron balconies, which all in all makes this a pleasant and satisfying place to spend an afternoon or evening. It is partly an artists' colony, so shopping here for crafts and art in the galleries and workshops is a treat.

As well as the history and archeology museum, there are good restaurants and bars. The attractive church of St. Stanislaus can be visited, and there is a 5,000-seat amphitheater where concerts are staged. Visiting performers have included Julio Iglesias and Frank Sinatra, who sang for the inaugural concert. There are also fabulous views of the Chavón river valley, particularly when it is lit up at night. Buses connect Altos de Chavón with Casa de Campo.

▶▶ Cordillera Central

The Cordillera Central is the Dominican Republic's highest and most beautiful mountain range, running through the center of the country from the northwest down toward the capital. It contains the highest mountain in the Caribbean, the Pico Duarte (10,420ft/3,175m). To hike to the summit takes three days from the town of La Ciénaga. Make sure you take a guide and all the food you need for the trip. Although the lower mountains are covered in royal palm trees, the pine-clad heights are tall enough to have frost; the steep, fertile valleys (where un-Caribbean fruits such as strawberries and apples prosper) are cut by cold waters from the mountains above. The towns of Constanza and Jarabacoa are cool hillside retreats, popular with visitors from the capital who regard them as an escape from the heat below. Look for the waterfalls of Aguas Blancas, 12 miles (19km) from Constanza, and the 100ft (30m) Jimenoa Falls near Jarabacoa.

NEW COMMUNITIES
As well as the community of German and Austrian Jewish refugees who were granted sanctuary in Sosúa on the north coast in the 1930s (see page 188), Trujillo invited a community of Japanese farmers in the 1950s, offering them land in return for passing on their farming skills. Some of their descendants still live and work around Constanza.

187

Tourist hotels and tropical greenery in the north coast resort of Sosúa

BEACHES
There are fine beaches on the Amber Coast. The resorts are clustered around protected bays, where palm-backed sand shelves gently into the sea. These are the best places to go for watersports. Sosúa gets very crowded, but farther on there are long strips of deserted sand, battered by the Atlantic waves and winds. Cabarete is renowned for windsurfing and also has a fine beach.

AMBER
Amber is the national gem of the Dominican Republic, which has some of the world's largest amber reserves and a large mining area in the Cordillera Septentrional. Strictly speaking, amber is not a stone, but is the sap from trees, which has solidified over millions of years. The youngest is the lightest in color and can be almost translucent; it is graded by color, through rich yellow to red. The most valuable are pieces with prehistoric insects or leaves preserved within them. Be wary of pieces offered to you on the streets: These may be plastic.

▶▶ Puerto Plata and the Amber Coast

The Amber Coast, on the north shore, has the greatest concentration of Dominican tourism. Hotel complexes have mushroomed beside the excellent beaches and these cater to package tourists who fly into the town of Puerto Plata.

Puerto Plata itself has a strong Dominican life. Attractive old Créole houses still stand in the town, and the squares, with shady trees and benches, come alive in the late afternoons with old gents and salesmen selling lottery tickets. There are just a couple of hotels on the rocky seafront, but the town has a number of good restaurants and bars (see pages 282). The **Amber Museum**▶▶ (tel: 586 2848. *Open* Mon–Sat 9–6. *Admission: inexpensive*), in a grand townhouse with classical balustrades and columns, has exhibits explaining the origin and mining process of the gem. A cable car takes passengers 2,425ft (739m) to the top of Mount Isabel de Torres, just south of the town; its running times are unpredictable, but hotels will usually arrange seats for visitors. A statue of Christ dominates the magnificent view of the coast and the Cordillera Septentrional. **Ocean World**▶ (tel: 291 1000. *Open* daily. *Admission: expensive*) is the region's newest attraction. Here you can swim with dolphins, meet sea creatures and enjoy humorous animal shows.

Playa Dorado is a purpose-built resort, a collection of hotels to the east of the town. It is set on a superb beach, where there are watersports and a good beach bar, but this is private and reserved for hotel guests. The resort town of **Sosúa**▶▶ is split into two parts, set on either side of the lively Sosúa beach: Los Charramícos is the westerly, more Dominican half; El Batey has a stronger European influence, a legacy of the Austrian and German Jewish refugees who came here fleeing the Holocaust. Here you will also find some of the best local restaurants and small hotels.

One of the best resorts on the island, **Cabarete**▶▶▶ is a lazy seaside town with palm-thatch garden bars and beachside restaurants; the Windsurfing World Championships are occasionally held here. Beyond Cabarete, the beaches continue, on and off along coast.

Restaurant in Puerto

The Dominican Republic's landscape is graced by thousands of royal palm trees, soaring up to 165ft (50m) from the ground and exploding into bushy palm fronds. Dominicans who travel away from home will often say that they miss the royal palm most of all.

Around 2,600 species of palm trees and shrubs grow in the tropics and subtropics, varying in height from 6in to 200ft (15cm to 60m). Palm trees do not have branches, but their fronds, which can be up to 30ft (9m) in length, emerge in sequence at the top of each stem, pointing vertically at first and gradually leaning to the side as younger fronds push them aside.

The coconut palm As well as being the quintessential Caribbean palm, the coconut is the most useful and versatile. Almost all of its parts can be used: the fronds in thatch and the trunk in building; in the past, the husk of the coconut was used to weave ropes and mats; coconut flesh is eaten and copra (dried coconut flesh) can be used to make oil for washing or burning. Coconut milk has even been used as an intravenous fluid. Throughout the Caribbean islands, vendors will happily

THE PALMCHAT
Native to Hispaniola, the palmchat is the national bird of the Dominican Republic. It has a greenish-brown coat and a white breast with dark streaking and lives and feeds in flocks. Its communal nest has separate compartments for up to 30 pairs and is built on the trunk of the royal palm.

189

slice the top off a coconut to allow you to drink the liquid inside.

The royal palm This most stately and magnificent of palms grows throughout the Caribbean and is Cuba's national tree. It can stand up to 165ft (50m) high, with a smooth trunk as much as 3ft (90cm) thick, and a bushy crown of fronds. The heart of the royal palm is used in salads, and its fruit is used for animal feed.

Other palms The cabbage palm is similar in appearance to the royal palm, although it grows only to about 130ft (40m). Known as the *palma cana* in Spanish, the latania palm, with fan-like fronds, is used for weaving, particularly in St. Barts. The ornamental golden palm is a bright green bush that appears in many Caribbean gardens, and the fishtail palm bears fruit that can be distilled into alcohol.

Picture-postcard views— palms and perfect water in the Dominican Republic

PALM AVENUES
Royal palms and cabbage palms are often planted to form beautiful avenues. Some of the best are the Allée Dumanoir, on Basse-Terre in Guadeloupe, and the driveway that leads to Codrington College in Barbados (see page 220).

Dawn at Las Terrenas,
Samaná peninsula

BEACHES
On the northern side of
the Samaná peninsula
strips of golden sand
stretch on either side of
Las Terrenas, and hotels
rent out watersports
equipment. On Samaná
Bay itself you can
arrange to visit Cayo
Levantado, an offshore
island, or make your way
up to Las Galeras, a small
beach resort in the
northeast.

LARIMAR
The Dominican Republic
is the only country that
produces Larimar, a gem-
stone that resembles
turquoise. This hard,
light-blue stone, sold as
jewelry throughout the
country, is mined in the
Bahoruco mountains on
the southwestern
Barahona peninsula.

▶▶▶ Samaná

In the isolated northeast, the lush Samaná peninsula is
now just on the tourist trail and it is worth making the
effort to get there to spend some time in the town of Las
Terrenas, the island's best resort. Set on the northern
shore of the peninsula across a ridge of mountains, Las
Terrenas has golden sand swept by low-hanging palms.
There is an easy-going feel to the place, with its string of
thatched restaurants, candle-lit at night, and its few
excellent hotels and guesthouses. It makes an ideal backdrop to an afternoon spent listening to a Dominican
string band (guitar, soul-comb, cheese-grater and sit-on
beat-box).

Set on the huge Samaná Bay (named Golfo de las
Flechas, or Gulf of Arrows, by Columbus after the local
Carib Indians showered him with arrows), the town of
Samaná itself is not very attractive, although it has a few
guesthouses and a collection of good restaurants on the
waterfront. You can arrange to see the **whales▶▶▶**
that collect offshore early in the year (from January to
March); try your hand at deep-sea fishing; visit the offshore island of Cayo Levantado, where there is a good
beach and some facilities; and escape to the **Los Haïtises
National Park▶▶**, where among the limestone caves
and mangroves you can see terns, jacanas and ibises. At
Las Galeras, in the northeast, there is a good beach with
a couple of quiet hotels.

▶ Santiago

You may only mean to pass through Santiago, which is
the country's second city, but it makes a good traveler's
stop. It is a working city set on the cliffs above the Yaque
River in the Cibao Valley, one of the country's most fertile regions. It is worth noting that the hustlers are not as
active here as they are in the tourist resorts, so the
chance to "escape" may appeal. At the **Museo Tomás
Morel del Arte Folklorico▶▶** you can see exhibits of
local arts and crafts and also the carnival masks worn at
religious festivals.

Sugar was such a valuable commodity during the 17th and 18th centuries that it became known as "white gold." Empires were built on the sugar trade; whole islands were planted with sugar cane, and navies were sent to capture and defend them. Meanwhile, the planters grew rich and their African slaves lived and labored in miserable subjection.

Sugar cane (*Saccharum officinarum*) is an overgrown grass. It grows to about 12ft (3.5m), can be a green or deep purple color, and takes 18 months to mature, blooming with a tall, white, wispy ear. Cane fields are sometimes burned to rid the canes of their corn-like leaves, creating enormous columns of smoke that are visible for some distance.

Cane-cutting is grueling work. In colonial times, teams of cutters would work in lines, led by singers and drummers and swinging their machetes in time to the music. Once the cane was cut, other gangs carted it off to the mill. The cane-cutting season lasted for about six months, ending in July; the annual Barbados carnival, Cropover, and the zafra in Cuba, are survivors of the end-of-season celebrations.

Technology has advanced from mule-driven mills to wind-driven equipment and finally steam-driven crushing machinery, but sugar production has remained basically unchanged for 350 years. Canes are cut to length and passed repeatedly through metal rollers, so that the juice runs away and the pulp, or bagasse, emerges dry. Bagasse burns well and is used to fire the engines that drive the rollers. The cane juice is clarified in the boiling house in huge copper boiling pans (which are also heated with bagasse). As it cools, the sugar crystallizes into granules. Nowadays the sugar is passed through a centrifuge, separating the crystals from the molasses, which is itself used as animal feed and for distilling rum.

In the mid-19th century, the successful development of sugar beet in Europe as a viable alternative to cane sugar began to threaten the West Indian trade, and now only a few islands cultivate sugar crops in any quantity. The biggest in the Caribbean are Cuba and the Dominican Republic, while Jamaica runs in at a fairly distant third place.

The River Antoine Rum Distillery's sugar mill, Grenada

SUGAR LOAF

Sugar loaf mountains can be found all over the English-speaking world. They take their name from their steep-sided shape, which resembles the "loaf" of early sugar manufacture. Wet processed sugar would be placed in a mould like an inverted pyramid and allowed to drain, so that the brown molasses would seep to the bottom and white sugar crystals would be left at the top. When the mold was broken, a pyramid-shaped "loaf" of sugar was revealed.

Other Caribbean states

192

FRANCIS DRAKE

Francis Drake was something of a scourge around Santo Domingo. He first came to the Caribbean in 1565, on a voyage with Sir John Hawkins, selling African slaves to the Spaniards, and later returned to pursue the more profitable action of attacking and ransoming their settlements. Drake captured Santo Domingo in 1586, setting up his headquarters in the cathedral and ransacking it for any loot he could lay his hands on. After gaining fame in Britain for his defeat of the Spanish Armada in 1588, Drake eventually died of dysentery off Porto Bello in Panama, in 1595.

COLUMBUS'S LIGHTHOUSE

The Faro a Colón has been dogged by bad luck since its construction was first suggested a century ago. It was eventually built to designs submitted to a competition in 1929 by a British architect, J. Gleave. The project was adopted by Trujillo in the 1930s and then abandoned because it was so expensive. In 1987 the lighthouse became the personal project of President Balaguer, who spent vast amounts of his poor country's reserves building it. It is the butt of many sarcastic jokes among Dominicans; when the lighthouse is lit, it drains electricity from the rest of the city. More imposing than attractive, it contains six museums and (it is said) the explorer's remains (tel: 591 1492. *Open* Tue–Sun 9–3.30. *Admission: inexpensive*).

▶▶▶ Santo Domingo

Santo Domingo, the island's capital and largest city, is the oldest surviving European settlement in the Americas. Its heart is the colonial city, on the bank of the Ozama River on the island's southern shore, but La Capital, as it is known, has expanded enormously over the centuries and now has around 2 million inhabitants. It has all the problems of fast-growing cities in poor countries: congestion, inadequate electricity and water supplies, and grinding poverty. But there is also a compelling Latin vibrancy here—best seen on the **Avenida del Puerto▶▶▶**, as crowds gather for their evening promenade.

Hidden by its ancient walls above the Avenida del Puerto, the **colonial city of Santo Domingo▶▶▶**, a UNESCO World Heritage Site, is a calm enclave, with coral-rock alleyways and shady courtyards. Its most impressive building is the **Alcazar de Colón▶▶▶** (tel: 687 5361. *Open* Mon, Wed–Fri 9–5, Sat 9–4, Sun 9–1. *Admission: inexpensive*), just inside the city walls. Built in 1514 for Columbus's son Diego as his vice-regal palace, the solid stone house is fronted by a double row of arches; its interior has been restored in suitable period style. Ranged before it are the viceroy's administrative buildings, the **Atarazana▶▶**. Dating from 1507, these once contained the colonial armory and customs houses; they now house a collection of craft stores and art galleries, restaurants and a couple of bars. The city's oldest building is the Casa del Cordón (1503), which is now a bank, and is across the street from the post office; look for the Franciscan order's cord motif carved above the door.

From the Alcazar the city walls lead to **Calle de las Damas▶▶**, named for colonial ladies who would promenade here. Set in the former colonial offices, the **Museo de las Casas Reales▶▶** (tel: 682 4202. *Open* Tue–Sat 9–6, Sun 10–1. *Admission: inexpensive*) displays exhibits from early Spanish colonial times, including suits of armor and wall maps. The imposing **Panteon Nacional▶** (*Open* Mon–Sat 10–5. *Admission free*), guards an eternal flame that commemorates Duarte, Sánchez and Mella, the national heroes who formed the underground independence

BOCA CHICA
Boca Chica is a lively
tourist town about 20
miles (32km) east of
Santo Domingo. Popular
with Dominicans, it gets
busy at weekends; there
are a number of small
guesthouses and flats
here and many
restaurants and bars
near the beachfront.

EL CONUCO
This lively Santo Domingo
restaurant on Calle
Casimiro de Moya, deco-
rated with palm thatch
and gravel, is based on
the theme of *conuco* (the
country). Ancient farming
tools are hung on the
walls among old wives'
sayings carved on wood.
Meals are local country
fare—mainly tripe and
stews, but there are less
daunting options (such as
Créole-flavored chicken
and plantains in batter),
and the waiters, dressed
up as *campesinos* (cow-
boys), in boots, jeans and
bandanas, have been
known to dart off in the
middle of taking an order
and start dancing.

movement La Trinitaria during the Haitian occupation in
the 1830s, and eventually won independence for the
Republic in 1844. Farther along the street are the cool,
quiet palace courtyard of the **Casa de Bastidas►►** and
the **Fortaleza Ozama►**, a fortress whose cannons have
now been set in peaceful gardens.

The Plaza de Toledo alley leads into the Parque Colón,
Columbus Square, where a statue of the explorer overlooks benches and trees. On the southern side of the
square is the **Catedral Santa María la Menor, Primada de
America►►**, the oldest cathedral in the Americas.
Completed in 1523, the cathedral, with its pointed battlements, was said to be the burial place of Columbus until
his remains were moved to the Faro a Colón in honor of
the quincentennial celebrations in 1992—although there
are rival claims from Cuba and Spain.

From the Parque Colón, El Conde, one of the city's
busiest shopping streets, leads up to the **Parque
Independencia►►**, the chaotic hub of the modern city.
All distances in the country are measured from here.
Behind the old city gates are the imposing memorial and
sunken mausoleum dedicated to Duarte, Mella and
Sánchez. Leading off the square, the Avenida Mella is
another shopping street, where you will find the Mercado
Modelo, the lively market. To the south is the
Malecon►►, the palm-lined seafront boulevard where
Dominicans like to take the evening air.

Inland, the landscaped expanses of the **Plaza de la
Cultura►** house the National Theatre, the National
Library and Modern Art Gallery, and two museums.
Despite its rather dull appearance, it is worth visiting the
Museum of the Dominican Man, where exhibits trace the
history of Caribbean Indians and their customs. Visually
more impressive is the **Palacio Nacional►**, a baroque
palace built by the dictator Trujillo on Calle Dr. Delgado.

On the city's northwestern outskirts, the **Jardín Botánico
Nacional►►** (tel: 687 6211. *Open* Tue–Sun 9–6. *Admission:
inexpensive*) has an orchid house and an aquatic plant
house of flowering lilies. Close by a modern zoological
collection opened in the last decade sits among tropical
parkland. In the eastern suburbs, the **Faro a Colón►►** is
a 100ft (30m) lighthouse built in the shape of a cross as a
monument to Columbus (see opposite).

Alcazar de Colón

Puerto Rico

With good communications and plenty of hotels, you'll find Puerto Rico easy and attractive to explore. San Juan can claim to be the best preserved Spanish colonial city in the Caribbean and has a lively cultural and artistic life; the southwest has the best beaches and quieter accommodations. As a semi-autonomous commonwealth territory of the USA, Puerto Rico is well known to American travelers. It is easy to reach—flights from Miami, New York and several other US cities land at San Juan's Luis Muñoz Marin airport, as do flights from Canada, and European airlines connect at New York. It also has a large and well-organized tourist industry; the beaches around San Juan are as developed as those in Miami, while Old San Juan, seven beautifully restored blocks of 18th-century colonial buildings, has become one of the Caribbean's foremost cruise ship destinations. But there is far more to Puerto Rico than the tourist circuit. As well as a vibrant culture, the island offers endless exploration in its rain forests, caves, mountains,

Billboards are everywhere on the streets of Puerto Rico

PUERTO RICAN EATING
San Juan serves food from all over the world, but do not miss out on the local dishes. Many are based on rice, including *arroz con pollo* (spiced chicken and rice), and *asopao*, like a soupy paella. Seafood is often spiced with traditional flavorings: *sofrito* (onion, garlic and pepper) and *adobo* (lemon, garlic, salt and spices). Side dishes include *mofongo* (mashed fried plantain with garlic) and *yuca frita* (fried cassava).

and hidden beaches, the best of which are on the south-west coast, and the two sleepy offshore islands of Vieques and Culebra. The entire island can be circumnavigated on a highway that touches the coast at several resorts and passes through secondary towns such as Arecibo, Aguadilla, Mayagüezce each of which has an airport. A highway crosses the eastern part of the island from San Juan to Ponce on the south coast, and many secondary roads run into the interior.

The most easterly of the Greater Antilles, Puerto Rico lies 994 miles (1,600km) southeast of Miami and is almost rectangular in shape—110 miles (177km) in length and about 37 miles (60km) from north to south with a range of

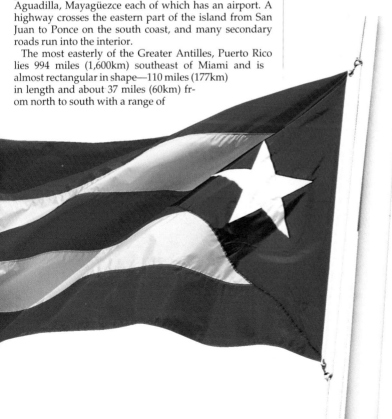

Other Caribbean states

196

TREE FROGS
The call of the coquí, a favorite Puerto Rican variety of tree frog, is almost synonymous with the tropical night. About 1.5in (4cm) long and with overlarge eyes, tree frogs can be heard in every Caribbean island (each species has a slightly different call), and they are particularly noisy at night and just after it has rained.

mountains running through the center of the island from east to west. The range marks a distinct division of climate: On the north side there is rain forest, and the rain in the northwest has created amazing karst cave systems (see page 200); in the south, the land is mainly dry and cactus-covered.

HISTORY Although it was visited by Columbus during his second voyage to the Americas in 1493, Puerto Rico was not settled by Europeans until 1508, when an expedition from Santo Domingo was led by Juan Ponce de Léon, who became the island's first governor. Having first exploited and then defeated the native Taino Indians, Ponce de Léon died in Cuba on a search for the Fountain of Youth. His bones were brought to San Juan and eventually laid in San Juan Cathedral.

For the next 300 years, Puerto Rico's settlers suffered constant invasion—from Caribs, pirates and raiding European armies. After decades of neglect by its mother country, the colony was revived by a Spanish envoy in the 18th century, and trade from its sugar exports began to pick up. A new constitution was granted in 1812 and an independence movement started to emerge, only to be ruthlessly put down by a succession of Spanish military governors. An uprising in 1868, which led to the first

A fire engine and filigree ironwork in the restored Ponce fire station

THE US CONNECTION
Puerto Ricans have formed large communities on the American main-land, particularly in New York, where they are known as Nuyoricans. The island has special Treasury laws, according to which the islanders do not pay Federal taxes and therefore are not represented in Congress.

declaration of a republic, was soon put down by the Spanish, but in 1897 autonomy was finally granted. Before the new government could fulfill its role, the USA, at war with Spain, invaded the island, and seven months later Puerto Rico was ceded to the Americans. US citizenship was granted to islanders in 1917, but senior government appointments remained in American hands. Initially there was a movement toward independence—a 1937 rally ended in 19 deaths after police shot at the protestors. In 1952 the island became a Commonwealth of the USA, and recent political debate has revolved around the question of whether Puerto Rico should become the 51st State of the Union. One of the obvious benefits of the American connection is Puerto Rico's relative prosperity.

The 17th-century Cathedral of Our Lady of Guadeloupe on the main square in Ponce

THE *GUAYABERA*
Predictably, American fashions have come to Puerto Rico in a big way, but the traditional dress for men on the island is the *guayabera*. Shaped rather like a jacket or an extended shirt, this is worn as the outer garment over an under-shirt or T-shirt. Most are made of cotton and are worn during the day, but there is a more formal version for evening wear, made with pineapple fiber. The *guayabera* is usually embellished with patterned embroidery, running in stripes down the chest.

Puerto Rico took a big wallop from Hurricane Georges in September 1998, but the US connection turned the disaster into an economic boom, with $3.5 billion in aid pouring in to repair the 50,000 houses destroyed or severely damaged. In the last decade the tourism base of the island has gone from strength to strength helped by the cruise dock at San Juan.

ISLAND LIFE American and Latin American culture live side by side in Puerto Rico and often meet in an incongru-ous mix. Both English and Spanish are widely used—Spanish is the official language of Parliament; high-rise, air-conditioned office buildings tower over traditional Caribbean markets; cable TV, fast food and American cars are all a way of life, but so are roadside stalls and, away from the larger towns, a simple, rural existence. Like most West Indians, the 3.9 million Puerto Ricans constitute a racial mix and include Africans, Spaniards, Italians and Lebanese. They are strongly Catholic and their most important festivals, the *fiestas patronales* (Saints' Days celebrations), combine a devout faith with the compulsion to dance—particularly to the salsa, a racing beat led by brass and African drums. Held by each individual town, the *fiestas* have costume balls, parades, picnics and fairs; perhaps the most exuberant of them all is the Festival of the Innocents, on the 28th of December, in which the whole town of Hatillo on the north coast becomes a costumed brawl. Music festivals are held throughout the year featuring different styles of island music, such as the *danza*, the *plena* and the *seis*.

Puerto Rico has a strong culinary trad-ition. Many dishes are based on rice, but plantains are also used as a staple in *mofongo* (see panel, page 195) and *piñon* . Daytime snacks can often be bought at the roadside fruit stalls—try *alcapurria* and *bacalao* (crab and codfish batter balls) or *empañadas* and *picadillos* (meat- or cheese-filled sand-wiches). The most popular island pas-times are baseball and cock-fighting (see page 209).

Festival of the Innocents at Hatillo, on the north coast near Arecibo

Hacienda Gripiñas—colonial-style hotel on an old coffee plantation high in the Cordillera Central

ARECIBO OBSERVATORY

The Arecibo Observatory is an impressive sight: a bright white dish, 1,300ft (400m) across, neatly cupped in a karst sinkhole. It listens to waves across the spectrum and bounces them back to the massive recording gear that hangs 650ft (200m) above the dish itself (there is a two-story building up there, too). The information is then relayed to the offices before being sent to Cornell University for analysis (tel: 878 2612. *Open* Wed–Fri noon–4, Sat–Sun and holidays 9–4. *Admission: inexpensive*).

▶ ▶ ▶ Cordillera Central

The Cordillera Central, the major mountain range in Puerto Rico's interior, runs parallel to the coast, splayed east and west on either side of the island's highest peak, Cerro de Punta. Running through them is the *ruta panoramica*▶ ▶ ▶, a scenic road stretching over 120 miles (193km) from coast to coast, taking in forest reserves and waterfalls. It's a long trip (two or three days), particularly if you stop off to explore, but there are mountain hotels en route and good roadside cafés, and the journey reveals a little-known side of Puerto Rico.

The *ruta panoramica* sets off from Maunabo, in the southeast of the island, beyond the tourist resort of Palmas del Mar. From here it rises into the Cayey mountains and the **Carite Forest Reserve**▶, a cool environment with rain forest and dwarf forest inhabited by 50 species of bird, and then Cayey itself, where it crosses the main San Juan to Ponce road. It then continues to Aibonito and Barranquitas, two modern towns in steep-sided valleys. Close by is the **San Cristobal Canyon**▶ ▶, an impressive cleft over 650ft (200m) deep, where there is a 100ft (30m) waterfall. To the south, Coamo is a colonial town, founded in 1579; the medicinal springs to its south were used by the indigenous Indians and later by Ponce de Léon. In the 19th century they became fashionable as baths; restored as a *parador* (government-run hotel; tel 825 2185; www.banosdecoama .com), the hotel retains a period dining room.

Ascending steadily, with magnificent views, the route continues to Doña Juana Recreational Center, where there are 200ft (60m) falls, and on to the Toro Negro Forest Reserve, a magnificent area of undeveloped forest with trails to the island's highest point, Cerro de Punta (4,390 feet/1,338m). Just a few miles from here is one of the island's most delightful retreats, the **Hacienda Gripiñas**▶ ▶ ▶ (tel: 828 1717). This *parador*, set in the wooden estate house of a former coffee plantation, overlooks the valley and represents the best of colonial Puerto Rico.

Although the *ruta panoramica* itself continues westward, it is worth making a detour to the north at the town of Utuado. Beyond another attractive *parador*, lost in greenery on the shores of Lago Caonillas, the **Caguana Indian Ceremonial Park▶▶** (tel: 894 7325. *Open* Wed–Sun 9–4. *Admission free*) is set in a valley surrounded by massive peaks. It has a small museum and about 10 *bateyes*—sport and ceremonial grounds used by the indigenous Amerindians. Surrounded by carved stones, they are believed to date from the 9th century but may be even older.

Just to the north of the park, in karst country (see page 200), is the largest radio telescope in the world, the **Arecibo Observatory▶▶**. This 20-acre (8ha) dish, owned by Cornell University, fills a whole valley and made the first discovery of quasars. Not far off is the **Río Camuy Cave Park▶▶** (tel: 898 3100. *Open* Wed–Sun 8–3.30. *Admission: moderate*), a cave system where an introductory lecture is followed by a trolleybus ride and walks through the caves. Thousands of years of dripping rainwater have created impressive stalactites and stalagmites in caverns 165ft (50m) high. The hillside town of Lares, on the southern boundary of karst country, was the setting for a rebellion against Spanish authorities in 1868, revered in Puerto Rican history as the *Gito de Lares* (the Cry of Lares).

Rejoining the *ruta panoramica* itself at Adjuntas, you go higher for superb views. The road passes through the Guilarte Forest Reserve (there are walking trails) and near the Maricao Forest Reserve, with a fish farm and a viewing tower overlooking the entire west coast. Nearby there is another charming parador, the Hacienda Juanita.

From here, the route descends to sea level, arriving at the coast at Mayagüez, the island's third largest town. The **Mayagüez Zoo▶▶** (tel: 834 8110. *Open* Wed–Sun 9–4. *Admission: moderate*) exhibits animals in open compounds; and a wide range of tropical plants are on view at the **Tropical Agricultural Research Station▶** (tel: 831 3435. *Open* Mon–Fri 7–4. *Admission: moderate*).

Tourist bus logo

Sun and cloud alternate all day in the lush Cordillera Central forest

The Caribbean archipelago runs southeast from the Tropic of Cancer, near the tip of Florida, down to the coast of South America and has an impressive variety of terrain. The islands lie on the join of the Atlantic and Caribbean tectonic plates, where massive ructions have produced a string of volcanoes in the Eastern Caribbean. At the same time, the warm tropical sea has given rise to coral reefs, which have gradually clustered the islands with limestone deposits as they age and die.

CAVE VISITS

All coral-based islands have caves, carved out by rain over the centuries. The best organized cave tours include the Río Camuy Cave Park (see page 199) in Puerto Rico and Harrison's Cave (see page 218) in Barbados. Both tours have introductory explanations and a trip on a trolleybus to view the stalactites and stalagmites. The Cueva del Indio in the Viñales region of Cuba is also worth visiting, as is Anguilla's Fountain Cave, thought to have been an Arawak religious site.

NAMES AND USES

In the British Caribbean old limestone shelves (dead coral reefs) on the seafront are known as "ironshore," and in the Spanish Caribbean as "black teeth." Many early Caribbean buildings were constructed with the bright, pitted coral rock, quarried on the islands.

Over the millennia corals have created whole islands. When a hard coral dies it leaves a limestone skeleton, on which the next generation of corals can fix itself. Eventually a reef is formed and, as the level of the sea rises and falls, the growing reef can be left exposed as land. Wave action breaks down the dead reefs, carving natural bridges, blowholes and coastal caves, as well as creating bright, white sand. The islands that form a line from Anguilla through Antigua to Grande-Terre in Guadeloupe are all coral limestone, as are the Caymans, encrusted around a string of old volcanoes that died off 100 million years ago.

In the Greater Antilles, age-old coral limestone has been pushed up into the mountains by seismic activity. There it has been eroded into areas of cone and tower karst mountains, named for a region of shaggy-topped limestone outcrops in the former Yugoslavia. Karst peaks are distinctive, steep-sided mountains between 330ft and 660ft (100–200m) tall; they once had natural roofs suspended between them, but these were eroded by heavy rain and collapsed long ago. From above they look like shaggy egg cartons; beneath them, the rocky earth is laced with sinkholes, caverns and underground rivers. In Jamaica they are known as "cockpits" (steep-banked pits for cock fights). Karst peaks can also be seen around Viñales in Cuba (where they are called *mogotes*), in the Dominican Republic's Los Haïtises National Park, and in the northwest of Puerto Rico.

▶▶▶ Ponce and surrounds

Isolated from San Juan by the central mountain range, Ponce has a radically different feel from the island's capital; the area is hotter and has less rain, so its pace of life is more leisurely. The 200,000 Ponceños are renowned for their independence and for their pride in a heritage that dates from the 17th century, when Ponce de Léon's great-grandson founded the city.

Ponce's tree-lined central plaza and a number of streets surrounding it have been restored. Most striking is the striped red and black fire station, the **Parque de Bombas**▶▶ (tel: 284 4141. *Open* Wed–Mon 9.30–6. *Admission free*), built in 1882. Constructed to a Spanish-influenced Puerto Rican design, the Cathedral of Our Lady of Guadeloupe dates from 1670, and the Casa Armstrong Poventud, an early 20th-century townhouse, has been well restored with period furniture and now houses a tourist office. The **Ponce Museum of Art**▶▶ (tel: 848 0505. *Open* daily 10–5. *Admission: inexpensive*) has an excellent collection of European and Latin American art.

One of the best views of the city is from El Vigia, the enormous cross on the hill, where an earlier version guided ships to land. Also on the hill, **Castillo Serallés**▶▶ (tel: 259 1774. *Open* Tue–Thu 9–5, Fri–Sun 9.30–5.30. *Admission: inexpensive*) is the extravagant former home of the distillers of local rum, Don Q. Weekend ferries leave the Playa de Ponce for the small , popular offshore island Caja de Muertos (named for the coffin it resembles), which has excellent beaches and coral reefs.

The **Tibes Indian Ceremonial Center**▶▶ (tel: 840 2255. *Open* Tue–Sun 9–4. *Admission: inexpensive*) is set in forested parkland behind the town. On an Amerindian village site, thatched houses and *bateyes* have been re-created and a museum displays finds from the area. On Route 10, in the hills above the town, is the **Hacienda Buena Vista**▶▶ (tel: 722 5882. *Open* Public tours Fri–Sun 8.30, 10.30, 1.30, 3.30. Group tours Wed–Thu booked in advance). *Admission: inexpensive*), a restored late 19th-century coffee estate. There is a small museum and original water-driven machinery. You will also see the bags that were used to export the product a century ago.

ARAWAK CEREMONIES
It takes a stretch of the imagination to re-create in your mind the excitement surrounding the games and dancing of the ceremonial parks when Arawak Indians were celebrating. Games were played with shuttlecocks and heavy balls, which had to be kept aloft using a huge belt around the waist. Festivals would continue for two or three days, and the participants would spend a lot of time under the influence of a hallucinogenic drug. Having purged himself by vomiting, the chief would make predictions. As well as the Tibes Indian Ceremonial Center, the park at Caguana, near Utuado, set in a lovely forested valley, deserves a visit.

201

Red and black stripes on the Parque de Bombas

In his book The Old Man and the Sea, *Ernest Hemingway tells of a poor fisherman in Cuba and his fight to hook an enormous blue marlin. In another of his novels,* Islands in the Stream, *a boy and a marlin are engaged in a desperate struggle. Big-game fishing suited Hemingway's macho image, and he was one of the sport's most passionate practitioners, relishing the rich sealife of the Caribbean waters.*

BIG AND BEAUTIFUL

One of the most beautiful fish in these waters is the sleek sailfish, with a silver belly, a blue back and a large, blue dorsal fin that looks like a sail. It can grow to about 10ft (3m) in length and weigh 200 lb (90kg). Other smaller fish include wahoo, a gray-blue fish with a crescent tail, which grows to nearly 7ft (2m) and can weigh up to 120 lb (54kg) and, about the same size, the tarpon, slim with silvery scales. The dorado (so-called because of its golden color) or mahi-mahi has red fins and grows to about 3ft (90cm) long.

Barracuda

Big-game fishing was made possible by the invention of the motorized boat at the end of the 19th century, and fishermen soon gathered along the coasts of the Gulf Stream (Cuba, the Florida Keys and Bimini in the Bahamas), where the biggest fish live. Today it is possible to fish off most of the Caribbean islands, and the sport is particularly popular off Cuba, Jamaica, the Dominican Republic and the Cayman Islands.

Deep-sea fishing boats have tall upper decks, or tuna towers, from which their pilots can look out and trail a number of lines from different rods. This is a strenuous, physical sport, and once a fish has been hooked, the fisherman will strap himself into a "fighting chair." Some species are immensely strong, weighing over 1,000 lb (450kg), and the fight can last for several hours: Line is played out in order to prevent it from snapping. The unfortunate catch is then slowly hauled in; most fish are killed in the process (though catch-and-release fishing is increasingly popular).

The Caribbean's principal big-game fish are the blue and the white marlin. Both have spears extending from their noses and long dorsal fins. The blue marlin can grow up to 1,500 lb (680kg). Other fish include tuna: yellowfin, albacore and skipjack (the most important commercial fish, which is trawled and processed in Puerto Rico), and the blue-fin tuna, which can grow to 14ft (4m) and weigh 1,700 lb (770kg).

▶▶ San Germán and the Southwest

Puerto Ricans take their vacations in the southwest of the island. Here, the country is hotter than elsewhere, and there are good beaches in the area; consequently, a number of small local tourist towns have collected along the coast and come alive in the summer.

The main road from Ponce to Mayagüez cuts inland and passes the town of **San Germán**▶▶▶, the second on the island to be founded by the Spaniards (in 1573). It remained prominent until the 19th century, despite threats from pirates, and now has a university and attractive old townhouses. Dating from 1606, the **Porta Coeli Church**▶▶ (tel: 892 5845. *Open* Wed–Sun 9–4.15. *Admission free*) has been restored and contains a museum of religious art and colonial paintings from 18th and 19th centuries.

A golden sunset over the hot southwest coast of Puerto Rico, where locals go to relax

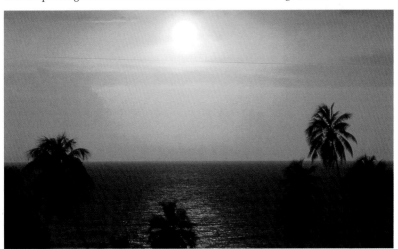

On the coast directly south of San Germán is the town of **Parguera**▶▶, which has a more hedonistic, seaside feel. Local seafood restaurants, cabins on stilts and small villas overlook the mangroves on the coast, and the beach (not one of the best) is some way out of town. A more worthwhile local attraction is the nearby phosphorescent lake (see panel, page 210).

Perhaps the best town in the area is **Boquerón**▶▶, a small seafront resort on the southwest coast. Backed with huge palm trees, its beach is one of the island's best and gets very lively at weekends. Watersports equipment is for rent, and there are several cafés. Other, more isolated beaches can be enjoyed on the island's southwestern tip near the lighthouse and the old lagoons where the islanders used to harvest salt. There is also a small forest reserve here with mangroves.

To the north along the coastline are more resort towns, with *paradores* and restaurants lining the seafront at Playa Joyuda and Playa Laguna. This west-facing coast is excellent for sunset-watching, and offshore there are a number of small islands that are rarely visited, including Desecheo and Mona, a deserted nature reserve with soaring cliffs, which can only be reached by taking a charter plane or fishing boat.

PUERTO RICAN PARADORES
The *paradores* of Puerto Rico are hotels dotted around the island, which are judged to be of a certain standard and style by the tourist board (from whom a list can be requested). They are usually small, and while they are neither fancy nor chic, they often have great local character and are generally in superb settings. Puerto Ricans themselves use *paradores*, so you are highly likely to meet islanders there. The *mesons gastronomicos* are restaurants chosen according to similar criterion specializing in local cuisine.

*Outdoor cafés in
Old San Juan*

*The battlements of the
Castillo de San Felipe
del Morro*

▶▶▶ San Juan (Old City)

Approached from the sea, Old San Juan looks like a massive fortress. The city is enclosed by over 6 miles (9km) of walls, 50ft (15m) high and 20ft (6m) thick, and a ring of stone sentry boxes, or *garitas*. It needed to be this formidable during the turbulent days when there was continual threat of invasion; both Francis Drake and Jack Hawkins led attacks on the city in the 16th century.

Parts of San Juan date from its foundation in 1520, but most of the colonial city has been restored to its 18th-century appearance. The streets are laid with blue cobblestones shipped from Spain as ballast, and the wrought-iron streetlamps, balconies and shuttered windows all add to the rather self-conscious sense of history. Admittedly this is a tourist showpiece and it can be overrun by visitors from the cruise ships, but Old San Juan is also a city with genuine character and life.

As well as walking around the city, there is a wealth of museums and galleries to explore, including the Museo Pablo Casals on Calle San Sebastián, where the cellist's instruments are on display; the Museo de San Juan, Calle Norzagaray, which showcases Puerto Rican art, music and festivals; and the Casa del Libro, in an 18th-century house at the southern end of Calle del Cristo, with displays about printing and a library of antiquarian books. A few steps away, the Centro Nacional de Artes Populares y Artesanías is a great place to pick up souvenirs from a varied and colorful selection of locally produced arts and crafts. At this end of town, Calle Fortaleza and Calle San Francisco are the twin poles of the main shopping district, and late in the evening Calle de San Sebastián comes alive with promenaders taking the air.

OLD SAN JUAN

Walk

Old San Juan

Start at La Casita, a colonial building housing the tourist office on the inner harbor. Walk uphill, following the city wall to Calle San José. The Plaza de Armas is the city's main square and site of the Alcaldía (City Hall). Calle Fortaleza leads to **La Fortaleza**▶▶ (hourly tours Mon–Fri 9–3.30. *Admission free*), used as the Governor's Mansion since its construction in 1520 and renovated in 1846.

At the foot of Calle del Cristo, lined with stores and restaurants, is the tiny **Capilla del Santo Cristo**▶, a chapel marking the spot where a horseman plunged over the walls during a race around the city. Heading north, you reach the Catedral de San Juan, built

in 1540 and altered in the 19th century; Ponce de Léon's bones are entombed there. A stepped alley leads downhill to one of the city gates, and beyond the walls, parkland leads to the vast **Castillo de San Felipe del Morro**▶▶▶, San Juan's main defense. Started in 1540, it took more than 240 years to complete; its walls rise 138ft (42m), and it has six levels of tunnels and dungeons (*Open daily 9–5. Admission: inexpensive*).

The route back to town brings you to the **Casa Blanca**▶▶. Built in 1521, this was the ancestral home of the Ponce de Léon family and now contains a museum of colonial life. On nearby **Plaza de San José**▶▶ was the family chapel. From the **Convento Dominicano**▶, with its charming inner courtyard, and the Plaza del Quinto Centenario, follow the cobbled streets to **Fuerte San Cristóbal**▶▶ (*Open Dec–May 9–6; Jun–Nov 9–5. Admission: inexpensive*), a 17th-century labyrinth of tunnels. Take Calle Fortaleza to return to the dock.

One of the most seductive aspects of the Caribbean landscape is its luxuriant greenery. Some islands are so fertile, it is said that you could plant a pencil and expect it to take root. Hundreds of plants grow here, including flowering trees, tropical fruit trees, curious crops and creepers, and the infinite variety of flowers that adorns West Indian gardens.

BOTANICAL GARDENS
The Caribbean has many excellent botanical gardens: Hope Gardens, Kingston, and Castleton in the Blue Mountains in Jamaica; the Jardin Botanico Nacional in Santo Domingo, capital of the Dominican Republic; the Rio Piedras Gardens in the south of San Juan, Puerto Rico; the Jardin de Balata in Martinique; the Botanical Gardens of St. Vincent; the Flower Forest and Andromeda Gardens on Barbados; the Queen Elizabeth Botanic Park on Grand Cayman; the Emperor Valley Gardens in Port of Spain, Trinidad; and the J. R. O'Neal Botanic Gardens in Road Town, Tortola, BVI.

The multihued

206

Beaches and swamps Palm trees on the seashore, overhanging the sandy beaches, are a travel brochure cliché nowadays, but they are not the only coastal trees by far—manchineel (see panel opposite), sea grape (with bunches of edible, bitter grapes) and sea almond trees (bearing inedible fruit) all grow near the sea. Around the swamps and coastal lagoons are the mangroves, hardy trees that have adapted to salt water and muddy ground, where they drop a tangle of buttress and aerial roots in order to support themselves. Flowering lilies can often be seen on fresh inland water.

Dry land The drier Caribbean islands, which include low-lying areas such as the Caymans, the Dutch Leewards and the outer chain of the former British Leewards, are generally covered in green scrub, which turns to yellow as it is bleached by the sun. On Aruba and Curaçao, where this scrubland is known as *cunucu*, the cactus-like aloe vera produces oil that is used extensively in cosmetics, and the century plant throws out a 30ft (10m) flowering stem about once every 10 years. In this poor soil the divi-divi tree grows stunted, with branches that bend over in the winds, looking like a head of wind-blown hair. Numerous cacti cover the arid land and are cultivated to make living fences in many settlements.

Grasses and flowers On the more fertile islands, grassland known as savannah is grazed by cattle, and gardens situated close to sea level grow an enormous variety of flowers. The best known are bougainvillea, which bloom in spiny fingers of purple, pink and orange, and hibiscus, with around 200 different delicate and brightly colored blooms, each of which lasts only one day. Other species to look for include white flowering frangipani, many different-colored ixora, allamanda, and plumbago, which has purple blooms; and the more exotic garden flowers including helico-nia (known as "lobster claw" because of its strange shape), red hot cat tail, a fluffy, dangling bright red bloom, and the bird of paradise (*strelitzia*), with a bird-like form. The ubiquitous anthurium, with its plastic-looking leaf and furry stigma, is used to adorn dinner tables in houses all over the Caribbean islands.

Flowering trees The Caribbean's many dazzling flowering trees include the yellow and pink pouis, African tulip trees and the immortelle, which is planted to give shade to cocoa beans and makes whole valleys flame in January. The flamboyant, or poinciana, blooms red in June and July, and the ackee produces red pods, whose yellow flesh can be eaten.

Other food-bearing trees include the breadfruit and the spiky breadnut; fruit trees are a valuable source of income for many islands (see page 143). The calabash fruit cannot be eaten, but its hard shell was used as a container in years gone by; and the cannon ball tree, despite its delicate flowers, grows fruit like lumps of wood. *Lignum vitae*, or the tree of life, has wood so hard and heavy that it sinks in water; mahogany tree pods release sycamore-like whirling seeds. Beware of the sharp spines on the trunk of the sandbox, so-called because its pods were used to hold sand for ink blotters. The Traveler's Tree (see panel) is so called because rain collects in the cupped spaces

THE TRAVELER'S TREE
The Traveler's Tree, also known as the compass tree because it grows pointing east and west, is sometimes (and incorrectly) called a palm tree. Its leaves grow like a fan, splaying sideways as each new leaf is superseded by another in the middle. Occasionally, a spiky, inedible fruit pokes out and reveals its strange, blue, wax-like material.

207

Roadside flora in Dominica

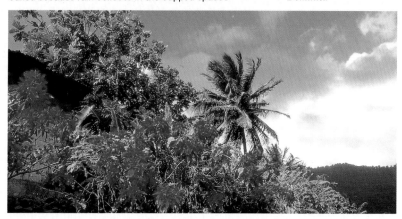

between the leaves, giving travelers a ready supply of drinking water.

Higher up the slopes of the larger islands, there is a change in the vegetation and the forests begin. Countless varieties of ferns swirl into an impenetrable, tangled mass; vines clamber up the trunks and drop their lianas into the soil; and "air-plants," orchids and bromeliads thrive on the upper branches and telephone wires. At the highest altitudes, you will find small and stunted "dwarf forest."

FORBIDDEN FRUIT
The manchineel is a bushy evergreen whose small fruits are extremely poisonous; one of Columbus's sailors tried his luck and the fruit quickly became known as the "apple of death."

Skyscraper hotels tower above the beach at Isla Verde, San Juan

SAN JUAN SNACKS
Like other Caribbean islanders, the Puerto Ricans adore roadside snacks, and there is a grand variety of tasty fillers at *kioskos* in San Juan and around the countryside. *Chicharron* is popular, although perhaps an acquired taste—spiced fried pork rind. *Bacalao* is frittered codfish and *alcapurrias* are also fritters, either meat or local fish, fried and served on a banana leaf. *Empañadas* are strangely flattened sandwiches and *picadillas* are meat patties.

▶ San Juan (New City)

Beyond the historic walls of colonial San Juan there is a real working city with a population of over one million, and urban development has sprawled along the coast and around the lagoons. Hotels and apartment houses crowd the coastline, while farther inland there is a mixture of swanky commercial buildings and poor shanties that highlight the contrasts of Puerto Rican life.

To the east of Columbus Square, which marks the edge of the colonial city, is **El Capitolio▶▶**, the seat of the Puerto Rican Senate and House of Representatives. Built in the 1920s, it imitates that of the White House in Washington; in the rotunda, visitors can see a copy of the Puerto Rican constitution, which was originally drawn up in 1954.

Farther along the coast is **Condado▶▶**, one of the town's main tourist strips. Huge hotels, interspersed with stores and conference centers, stand right on the seafront, and behind them are streets full of restaurants and bars. This line of tall buildings extends along the coast solidly for the 6 or so miles (10km) to **Isla Verde▶▶**, the other main tourist area, which is crammed with yet more luxury hotels and an interesting variety of restaurants and bars overlooking a large, popular beach.

Inland are the working areas of the capital. Hato Rey is the commercial heart of San Juan, which is one of the biggest financial markets in the Caribbean. A more traditional Caribbean market operates in Río Piedras, with tropical fruits and vegetables for sale. To the south, the **Río Piedras Botanical Gardens▶** (tel: 763 4408. *Open daily 9–4.30. Admission free*) provide a green and welcome retreat from the hustle of the city and its endless traffic. A ferry ride across the bay from Old San Juan takes you to Catano, where the **Bacardí Rum Distillery and Museum▶▶** provides tours for visitors (tel: 788 1500. *Open* Mon–Sat 8.30–5.30, Sun 10–5. *Admission free*).

As tourists have flooded into their resorts and towns, many Caribbean islands have gained reputations for their gambling centers. But beyond the roulette tables, there is a popular tradition of West Indian gambling and bar games, from domino contests to local wrestling matches or even cock fights.

Caribbean casinos have all the usual games that an avid gambler may expect to find: *vingt et un*, roulette, craps and slot machines. If casino gambling is an important factor in your vacation choice, the following islands should be on your list: Aruba, which has a choice of glitzy gaming rooms with cabaret shows; Aruba's diminutive neighbor, Bonaire, will be able to offer a little low-key gambling; the Dominican Republic has casinos in all the main resorts; Guadeloupe and Martinique; Puerto Rico, with a host of casinos in Condado and Isla Verde and at hotels around the island; Antigua and St. Kitts in the Leeward Islands; St. Croix, in the USVI, is a relative newcomer, and the Dutch side of Sint Maarten, where gamblers will find a strip of casinos in Philipsburg.

GAMBLING TRAVELERS
Cuba was one of the biggest gambling islands, attracting thousands of US visitors to its gaming houses, until 1959, when casinos and all other trappings of capitalism were outlawed by the Cuban revolutionaries. Since then Puerto Rico (and the Bahamas, which are also close to the States) have taken over as the favorite gambling destinations for American visitors.

209

Enjoying a game of dominoes outside a local bar

Cock-fighting On the French- and Spanish-speaking Caribbean islands, cock-fighting is a major spectator sport. It is a brutal event—the cocks are occasionally killed—staged in a cockpit with steeply banked seats. Cocks are prepared for weeks in advance for a fight, with special diets and grooming. On the day of the fight owners bring their birds into the ring, showing them off to the crowd and brandishing them at one another as the bets are placed. As the fight begins, two cocks lunge at each other, pecking and slashing with their claws. while the watching audience erupts into screams and shouts of encouragement. In the past raising fighting cocks was a traditional Caribbean method of becoming rich.

In the French Caribbean, a variation on the bloodsport theme is occasionally introduced, when snakes are pitted against one another in a contest to the death.

DOMINOES
Played in just about every bar throughout the Caribbean, dominoes are even enjoyed by Fidel Castro, the president of Cuba. The pieces are usually laid on the playing board with a grand flourish and a loud slap; in Barbados they are referred to as "cards," and are even "shuffled" in preparation for the game.

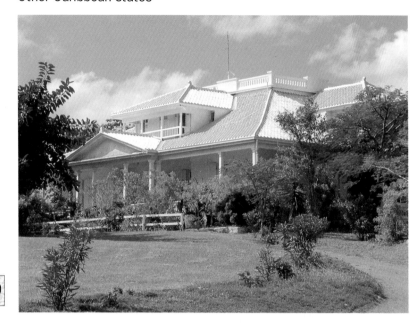

Casa del Frances, Vieques, built as a plantation house

LUMINOUS LAKE
The phosphorescent lake at Mosquito Bay, Vieques, has an eerie beauty. At night it glows where paddles cut the water; fish leave streaks as they dart away, and in a storm the whole surface is set alight. The cause is bioluminescence; tiny creatures emitting light when agitated.

Puerto Rican license plate

▶▶ Vieques and Culebra

If you look east from Fajardo, on Puerto Rico's east coast, you will see that the sea is sprinkled with islands and cays as far as the horizon, culminating in the Virgin Islands. About 6 miles (9km) from the mainland, Vieques is the largest of the Puerto Rican islands; not far beyond it is Culebra, surrounded by a collection of little satellites. These islands are dry and low, with rolling hills and some of the best beaches in Puerto Rico. The wildlife is different from that on the mainland—you might see red-billed tropicbirds and turtles—and Culebra is partly given over to a wildlife refuge.

Vieques A 45-minute ferry ride from the mainland brings you to Vieques' northern shore and its main town, Isabel Segunda, where the majority of the island's 8,000 inhabitants live. The central square is quiet and pleasant, and has an information office. A restored 19th-century **fort▶** stands on the hill above the town. In **Esperanza▶▶**, on the southern coast, bars and restaurants are strung along the shorefront, a stone's throw from the island's best beaches. During World War II, Vieques was the fall-back base for the British Navy should Britain fall to a German invasion. Postwar much of the island belong to the US Navy for use in naval exercises but though there is still a naval presence, 14,573 acres (5,829ha) of land was transferred to the Department of the Interior in 2003 for use as a wildlife refuge.

Culebra This tranquil island sits among a small crowd of tiny coral outcrops, 25 miles (40km) east of the mainland. Only 1,600 islanders live on Culebra, many in the only town of Dewey, better known as Pueblo, where there is a small information office. Parts of the island were designated a National Wildlife Refuge by President Theodore Roosevelt in 1909. Culebra's beaches and coral reefs are superb, and the snorkeling is wonderful.

▶▶▶ El Yunque Caribbean National Forest

The most accessible area of Puerto Rico from the capital is the northeast, with its rich variety of mountains, mangroves and beaches. Perhaps the most popular tour is to El Yunque, an area of rain forest which, because of its position in the far northeast of the island, enjoys the best of the water-laden Atlantic winds (which bring about 120 billion gallons or 450 billion liters of rain every year).

El Yunque is approached by Route 3 from town or by following the coast road out of Isla Verde and then heading into the mountains, rampant with tropical foliage, on Route 191. In this 27,000-acre (11,000ha) national park, 240 species of tree grow in three different varieties of forest (rain forest, montane forest, and stunted dwarf forest, near the 3,000ft/900m peaks). Trails have been cut into the forest, with explanatory signposts and lookout platforms. The **El Portal Rain Forest Center▶▶** (tel: 888 1810 or 888 5335. *Open* daily 9–5. *Admission: inexpensive*) dispenses information about the plants, animals and about 60 or so bird species, including the endangered Puerto Rican parrot. **Guided Forest Adventure Tours▶▶** (*Open* Thu–Mon 10–3. *Admission: moderate*) can be arranged through hotel travel desks and are accessed from the Palo Colorado Interpretive Site (km11.7 on route 191, tel: 888 1810. *Open* daily 10.30–3.30. Tours filled on a first come first served basis). As this is rain forest, there are frequent showers.

On the far northeastern tip of the island there is another nature reserve at **Las Cabezas de San Juan▶▶** (tel: 722 5882 or 860 2560. *Open* Fri–Sun for tours at 9.30, 10.30 and 1.30 by appointment. *Admission: moderate*), where boardwalks lead through the mangroves past the shore and swamp birdlife. A visitor center is housed in the restored 19th-century El Faro (or lighthouse), from which there are superb views out toward the Virgin Islands. The route back to town on the north coast road passes Luquillo, site of one of the island's most popular public beaches and a string of excellent roadside snack outlets. At Piñones, just before the road comes into Isla Verde, is another area of protected mangrove swamps, which is the habitat of birds such as snowy egrets, pelicans and herons.

MANGROVE BIRDLIFE
Mangrove swamps harbor lots of crustaceans, providing food for herons, terns, sandpipers and stilts. The easiest to visit from San Juan are Piñones (from Boca de Cangrejos marina) and Las Cabezas de San Juan. Guanica, in the southwest, is designated a World Biosphere site by UNESCO.

Bar at Esperanza

Barbados

Probably the most British of the Caribbean islands, Barbados has a gentle, undulating interior, ringed by safe and attractive beaches. It is relatively prosperous, relaxed and welcoming, and has absorbed the tourist industry gradually, without allowing it to overwhelm the life and character of the island. Popular attractions include its famous rum, its lively south coast nightlife and its passion for cricket. Away from the low-key sophistication and luxury hotels of the west coast, Barbados's (and one of the Caribbean's) premier tourist areas, are the high-rise hotels, guesthouses and flats of the south. In contrast, the east coast is quiet and mostly undeveloped. Because the island has so many hotels and is easily reached on regular

SETTLING BY FORCE

Three centuries ago, to be "Barbadosed" was to be sent forcibly to the West Indies. Settlers were needed on the islands and the courts deported common thieves and prisoners of war there. They were set to work alongside indentured laborers, who sold their labor for five or seven years in return for their passage to the islands, on the understanding that they would be given land to plant at the end of their term. In the late 17th century, African slaves provided a large-scale labor force for the sugar plantations.

British naval hero, Lord Nelson, commemorated in Bridgetown

flights from Europe and the USA, good package deals are available to Barbados through numerous tour operators and travel agents.

Barbados is one of the best Caribbean islands for beach activities. By day, watersports are easy to arrange, and there are plenty of beach bars to retire to. Divers come to enjoy the marine life of the coral reefs, and several companies offer equipment rental and scuba diving instruction. Snorkeling is an easier alternative, and non-divers have access to underwater views from the dry comfort of the **Atlantis Submarine**▶▶ (tel: 436 8929 for reservations). Barbados has more exploring potential than other islands. The interior, although nowhere near as dramatic or lush as Jamaica or St. Lucia, has pleasant scenery, with mahogany woodlands, cattle and black-bellied sheep grazing on rough meadows, traditional wooden chattel houses and forests of sugar cane. There are also magnificent plantation houses—some open to the public, some still the homes of "high white" families of the old plantocracy, some the hub of working plantations, and one or two available for rent to visitors. By night there is a wide choice of nightclubs and many good restaurants, serving local as well as international food. Although not very cheap, several of them include magnificent coastal settings in the price.

Shaped like a pear set at a slightly tipsy angle, Barbados is made entirely of coral limestone. It measures 21 miles by 14 miles (33km by 23km) and lies 100 miles (160km) east of the Windward Island of St. Vincent. From the sheltered western beaches, gently lapped by small waves, the land rises steadily through the cane fields and cultivated land of the central plains, culminating in the 985ft (300m)

LITTLE ENGLAND
In colonial days, the leading Barbadians were proud of their association with Britain and of being the only British Caribbean island never to be conquered by another power. They called their island, which was a highly successful colony, Little England, and having been nicknamed "Bims" by their slaves, styled themselves as inhabitants of "Bimshire," as though Barbados were a county of Britain.

214

King's Beach, on the west coast

LITTLE BRISTOL
In the 17th century, during the early days of colonization, Bristol was the major port on the west coast of England, and many settlers on Barbados came originally from the West Country (southwest England). Speightstown's West Country residents earned it the nickname Little Bristol, and their accent can still be heard in the drawled Bajan vowels.

RUM AND EXERCISE
The Sunday walk with the Barbados National Trust (a preservation body) and the Bajan rum shop are both equally hallowed institutions. On the former, a guide leads walkers through a chosen area of historic interest (perhaps a section of old railway, or an abandoned fort) for a couple of hours on Sunday mornings (tel: 426 2421; a small fee is charged). In the rum shops, customers may offer informal instruction in such essential pursuits as dominoes and talking politics.

215

escarpment of Hackleton's Cliff in the east. North of here is the hilly Scotland district, where the island reaches its highest point, Mount Hillaby, at 1,115ft (340m). Powerful Atlantic waves (nicknamed "white horses") crash constantly against the dramatic eastern shoreline, carving out bizarre rock formations and steadily eroding the coast.

ISLAND LIFE The island's population of 279,000 is one of the densest in the world, a fact that is clearly visible in the urban sprawl radiating from Bridgetown along the western and, increasingly, the southern coasts. Solitude may be hard to find on Barbados, but the island is made special by its people. Bajans, mostly of African descent, are some of the friendliest West Indians; whether at the weekly Sunday **National Trust walk**▶▶ (see panel) or in a local rum shop for a game of dominoes, the Bajans will give you an amiable welcome and are always ready to fill you in on all the latest island gossip.

The Barbados economy is one of the healthiest in the region, and the island is busy and businesslike, with extensive investment in its tourism infrastructure. Bajans treat tourism as an important industry, and they are particularly gracious to visitors, making this an excellent island for those who wish to visit the Caribbean for the first time.

Much is made of Barbados's Englishness, the result of a long-standing colonial connection with Britain. For a time the island was even known as Little England (see panel opposite). While it is true that Barbados has visibly kept more British traits than other islands, the American influence can also clearly be seen today. Since independence in 1966, the people have started to take pride in their Afro-Caribbean heritage, and more recently have developed their indigenous Bajan culture.

Other Caribbean states

THE CAREENAGE

The Careenage takes its name from the system of tilting, or careening, the hull of a ship. (A number of waterfronts in the Windwards and nearby French islands share the same name.) A weight was attached to the ship's mast in shallow water and the ship would be tilted so that its hull and bottom were exposed, so it could be scrubbed free of barnacles and weeds.

*The Careenage,
Bridgetown*

▶▶ Bridgetown

The capital of Barbados lies on a broad, protected bay in the southwestern corner of the island. Old colonial buildings and modern offices stand side by side in the center of Bridgetown, but over the years the city, which has around 100,000 inhabitants, has spread steadily north and southeast along the coasts.

Bridgetown is the center of island life, where the offices of government and big business stand above lively West Indian street markets. Its traditional heart is the Careenage, a sea inlet where, in the days of seaborne travel, lighters would bring ashore passengers from the ocean-going ships. There is not much nautical activity any more (passengers now arriving by sea will usually dock at the deep-water harbor), but yachts and fishing boats still use the inlet, and a selection of waterfront bars and cafés cater to landlubbers.

NELSON

Lord Nelson, "Preserver of the West Indies," arrived in pursuit of the French Admiral Villeneuve during the Napoleonic Wars and removed the threat of French invasion. His statue was erected on the former Trafalger Square (now renamed National Heroes Square) in 1813, but as a legacy of the colonial era, he was considered a somewhat contentious figure and has been relocated after years of deliberation and pressure from proud Bajans. "Put up a Bajan man," sang the Mighty Gabby, a famous calypso star and consciousness-raiser.

On the north side of the Careenage is National Heroes Square, the hub of the city center, flanked by two distinctive colonial public buildings, built from local coral rock in the 1870s. Crenellated and with pointed arches, they have red tin roofs and green louvered windows, which keep out the sun but allow ventilation when there is a breeze. The House of Assembly, the seat of the Barbados Parliament, which was founded in 1639, is open to visitors. British monarchs from James I to Victoria are commemorated in stained-glass windows in the Parliament chamber.

At the center of National Heroes Square is a small fountain, its bowls supported on the tails of brightly painted dolphins, which was erected in 1865 to mark the arrival of piped water—obviously a significant event in a hot town. From the square leads one of the town's most important commercial streets, Broad Street, where Bridgetown's major stores, department stores and duty free emporiums are housed in old colonial buildings. North of here is Swan Street, a typically Caribbean (weekday) street market, where vendors stand by their colorful stalls selling anything from oranges to fluorescent shoe laces or mirror shades.

217

BAJAN DISHES
Whatever it has taken from the British in other respects, Barbados owes little to them in the way of food. Bajan fare depends more on local ingredients, including fish and vegetables such as yam, plantain and sweet potato, cooked according to Amerindian and African techniques. The most famous Bajan seafood is flying fish, so named because they seem to fly up from the water. Legend has it that those who sample flying fish will return to Barbados again and again. Mauby, a bitter-sweet concoction made by boiling local roots and spices, is sold on street corners in plastic jugs. Bajans swear by its rejuvenating powers.

St. Michael's Cathedral, a few blocks east of the square, was built in 1789 and provides a haven from the town's hubbub. The restored Synagogue, originally built in the 17th century, is off Magazine Lane near the law courts; in the yard is a gravestone dedicated to Benjamin Messiah, who was renowned as a circumciser, apparently performing with "Great Applause and Dexterity."

Cheapside Market, at the northwest end of Lower Broad Street, is in a traditional tin market building and sells mainly local food and vegetables. In the Rasta Mall goods include rastafarian herbal concoctions and leather pendants from Africa. Pelican Village sells arts and crafts.

In the northeastern area of the city, you will find the **Tyrol Cot Heritage Village▶▶** (tel: 424 2074; www.barbados.org). *Open Mon–Fri 9–5. Admission: moderate*) in the grounds of the former home of the Bajan political family, the Adams. The 1850s house is open for tours, and there are artisan workshops set in traditional Bajan "chattel houses."

A few miles to the south of the Careenage is the Garrison Savannah, the military district of the colonial era. The old Georgian barrack buildings are still visible, some restored, others in decay, but the 300-acre (120ha) Savannah itself is now used mainly for sports events, including horse-racing and local cricket matches. The **Barbados Museum▶▶** (tel: 427 0201; www.barbmuse .org.bb. *Open Mon–Sat 9–5. Sun 2–6. Admission: moderate*), at the corner of the Savannah, is situated in the island's former prison. The museum displays aspects of life in Barbados during Amerindian and colonial times, including the ill-fated Barbados Railway (see panel). Rooms here have been fitted using period furniture, and a gallery of maps and prints is set in the old cells.

THE BARBADOS RAILWAY
During the 19th century the British built railways throughout their empire, and despite its small size, even Barbados had one built in the 1880s. The line ran east from Bridgetown through the central sugar cane lands before descending to the Atlantic coast at Bathsheba and continuing to Belleplaine. It was used by workers coming into town in the week and was usually packed for church outings at the weekends. Having suffered financial problems from the start, it finally folded in 1937.

Relaxing on one of the Caribbean's famous beaches

▶▶▶ Caribbean (West) Coast

The beach that stretches up the west coast of Barbados is one of the finest in the Caribbean. Nicknamed the Platinum Coast, its golden sand is washed by calm seas, and behind a fringe of coconut palms and casuarina trees are superb hotels such as the Sandy Lane and the Coral Reef Club, long-renowned and now-renovated havens of luxury, which have given Barbados its name for tropical refinement. Interspersed among them are private villas, restaurants and cheaper hotels.

The roads north out of Bridgetown lead to the Spring Garden Highway, which comes alive each year on the first Monday in August with colorful dancing parades during the **Crop Over Festival▶▶▶**. North of the town center is the Kensington Oval, the Barbados cricket stadium—the Bajans' fervor for the game makes attending a cricket match a rousing experience. On the coast nearby are the **Mountgay Visitor Centre▶▶** (tel: 425 8757. *Open* Mon–Fri 9.30–3.30) and the **Malibu Visitor Centre▶▶** (tel: 425 9393), where tours include a look at the vats and the distilling process and a taste of the rum. The history of sugar-refining is traced at the **Sir Frank Hutson Sugar Museum▶** (tel: 432 0100; www.barbados.org. *Open* Mon–Sat 9–5. *Admission* museum and factory *moderate*; museum *inexpensive*) where the Portvale Sugar Factory still processes a crop beween February and May.

Holetown was the site of the first European settlement on Barbados in 1627, colonized after it was claimed for the British by Captain John Powell in 1625. The small but stately St. James Parish Church is notable for its English style of architecture, but Holetown today mainly consists of open spaces and excellent restaurants and bars. The **Folkestone Marine Park▶** has a small marine museum and a snorkeling trail through the offshore corals.

Back on the coast, **Speightstown▶**, 7 miles (11km) north of the capital, seems a sleepy town but has some good bars; beyond it, the countryside opens out to cane fields, small settlements and deserted beaches. At the island's northern tip you can visit Animal Flower Cave (*Open* Mon–Sat 9–5), named for the sea anemones that live there.

WEST COAST BEACHES

Calm and west-facing, the Platinum Coast is an almost continuous strip of beautiful sands, ideal for early morning walks or for sunset-watching. Though the beaches are never really crowded, you cannot expect to be alone here because there are so many hotels set along the coast. There are few divisions between the beaches, and in some places you can wade through the shallows to the next beach. All beaches are public and provide a right of way, and hotels have watersports facilities—nonresidents can usually negotiate their use. Paynes Bay, with its easy access and choice of watersports deals, is a good option.

Sports are a unifying feature of an area made diverse by its geography. Within the former British Caribbean islands, cricket is something of an obsession: Islanders will drop everything to listen to the commentary of an international match in which the West Indies team is playing. In the Spanish Caribbean the most popular sport is baseball, and life comes to a halt if an important game is being played.

Cricket The West Indies have had a world-class cricket team for years—a remarkable achievement for an area with so small a pool of players to choose from. Players for the team are drawn from all the British Caribbean islands, but the main centers are the islands where there are international-class (Test Match) grounds: Jamaica, Antigua, Barbados, Trinidad and Guyana. Barbados has an impressive record, having won the inter-island competition (now called the Busta Cup) more often than any other team.

Cricket is played on the beaches and in back streets, with a tennis ball and sticks for stumps; tourists are often asked to join in. Success at cricket is a route to fame and wealth, so it is fiercely contested: The best players attain national hero status. Famous names include Viv Richards (Antigua), Clive Lloyd (Guyana), Gary Sobers (Barbados) and Brian Lara (Trinidad).

OTHER SPORT
By means of cable TV, the Caribbean is steadily being influenced by sports from America. Basketball is very popular, as is soccer, although the latter is restricted to the small screen and is not played on the islands. The major participant sport in the French Caribbean is American football, but the most popular spectator sport is cock-fighting (see page 209), also followed on the Spanish islands, but virtually unknown in the British Caribbean.

219

Baseball This is the national sport in Cuba, the Dominican Republic and Puerto Rico, and has been played on the US Virgin Islands since the Americans arrived. Just as many West Indian cricketers go to the UK to play, so the Dominicans and Puerto Ricans, as well as several Cuban defectors, have graduated to the American pro leagues, and some have achieved considerable fame and fortune. In the streets the children play a toned-down version of baseball, not unlike New York's stickball, in which they are not allowed to run.

The diamond at Charlotte Amalie, St. Thomas

GUN HILL SIGNAL STATION

Now restored, Gun Hill Signal Station (tel: 429 1358. *Open* Mon–Sat 9–5. *Admission: expensive*) stands in the center of the island with impressive views all around. It is one of a string of old military signal posts that could send messages (by mirror-flash or by colored lantern) across the island in minutes, warning the barracks of approaching ships and the merchants of trading vessels. Set far away from the malarial swamps on the coast and bathed in fresh winds, the station was used as a hospital in the later colonial era.

The fishing village of Bathsheba on the wild and weather-beaten Atlantic coast

▶▶ Central Barbados

Inland from the capital, the land rises steadily through the Bridgetown suburbs into open country and cane fields, toward the cliffs that tower above the Atlantic coast. **Francia Plantation**▶▶ (tel: 429 0474. *Open* Mon–Fri 10–4. *Admission: inexpensive*) gives a vivid idea of the privileged lifestyle of the old Barbados planters. Standing on high ground in attractive gardens, Francia is furnished with antique furniture and decorated with maps and prints of old Barbados. Another plantation house worth visiting is **Sunbury Plantation House**▶▶ (tel: 423 6270. *Open* daily 9–5, last tour 4.30. *Admission: inexpensive*), which has been restored. In the gardens, there are cannon and a collection of old horse-drawn carriages. It is worth taking a quick look at **Codrington College**▶, an imposing, early 18th-century religious seminary and school (buildings not open to visitors), approached along an avenue of splendid royal palm trees. **Harrison's Cave**▶▶ (tel: 438 6640. *Open* daily 9–6, last tour 4pm. *Admission: expensive*) is an extensive series of pale-gold limestone caverns off Highway 2, complete with exquisitely formed stalactites and stalagmites, subterranean streams and a 40ft (12m) waterfall.

The steep, somewhat remote east coast of Barbados is an unexpected find. From the top of Hackleton's Cliff, the site of **St. John's Parish Church**▶, there is a marvelous view over small country villages and down to the east coast, where Atlantic waves roll in against huge sculpted rocks. The sea here is rough and unpredictable—signs on the beaches warn of dangerous currents and advise people not to swim.

THE ATLANTIS HOTEL

In its dramatic setting atop the cliff in Bathsheba, the Atlantis Hotel (tel: 433 9445) has a fine view of the Atlantic waves. The hotel is past its best, but its Sunday brunch (a traditional West Indian buffet) has become legendary. Advanced reservations are advised.

Andromeda Gardens▶▶ (tel: 433 9261. *Open* daily 9–5. *Admission: moderate*), near Bathsheba, are set out on the hillside, made beautiful by fiery blooms and flowering trees from the tropical world, including frangipani, orchids and the Traveler's Tree (see panel, page 207). Bathsheba and Cattlewash are now fishing villages, but attractive seafront villas remain from when colonials came here to escape from the Bridgetown heat. The Round House (tel: 433 9678; www.roundhousebarbados.com) makes a good lunch stop, with terrific views over the Soup Bowl, which is a favorite surfing spot.

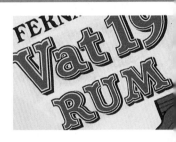

An old rhyme describes the rum punch drunk by planters in colonial days: "One of sour, two of sweet, three of strong, and four of weak." The sour is lime, the sweet is cane juice, the strong is rum, and the weak is water (more likely to be fruit juice nowadays). Mix these ingredients, sprinkle with grated nutmeg, and you have a genuine Caribbean rum punch.

Practically every Caribbean island distills its own rum, but the main producers are Cuba and Puerto Rico, where rums are traditionally light in color, and Barbados and Jamaica, where they are darker and fuller in flavor. On the French islands some of the finer rums are aged to be drunk like a brandy after dinner. Most islands also produce a white rum for local consumption. St. Croix produces both light and dark Cruzan rum.

Rum is a by-product of sugar, distilled from the fermented juice of sugar cane, or a mix of cane juice and molasses. Visits can often be arranged to rum distilleries, full of gurgling vats and stills and the heady, sweet smell of fermentation. All distillations of rum result in a clear liquid; darker rums gain their color from the addition of caramel during the ageing process, and from the oak barrels in which the rum is stored. Barrels of rum were used as currency in colonial times, when rum first became an important export.

Perhaps the most famous rum manufacturer is Bacardí, which was based in Cuba before its revolution but now works mainly from Puerto Rico, where there is a huge factory outside San Juan. In Jamaica the biggest name is Appleton, producing gold rums of different ages and a strong white rum known as John Crow Batty (crow's backside). The Appleton factory can be reached from Montego Bay. From Barbados come Mountgay and Cockspur, as well as white rums such as Alleynes, and from Haiti the renowned Barbaucourt. The French islands have a long tradition of high-quality "rhum agricole" that includes Rhum St. James and Trois Rivières of Martinique (both of which can be visited). Caribbean rum is used as filling in expensive chocolates, and as the basis of a number of liqueurs such as Malibu.

RUM HISTORY
Rum first appeared in Barbados in about 1650, when it was known as "kill-devil" and "rumbullion." Pirates would drink an explosive mixture of rum and gunpowder. British sailors were entitled to a daily measure of rum from the 18th century until 1970.

221

Exotic liqueurs are produced all around the islands: Camerhogne is Grenada's mixture of rum, spices and fruit

The Morgan Lewis Mill: one of the last of over 500 windmills that once turned on the island

SCOTTISH ORIGINS

As Barbados was once known as Little England, it is somehow fitting that there should be a hilly district to the north called Scotland. The parish is even named for St. Andrew. Many Scotsmen were banished to the east of the island, including Scotland, during an early episode of racial and religious segregation in the mid-17th century, and a few of their descendants still live there, in poor white communities. These settlers became known as Redlegs, supposedly because they did not tan under their kilts.

EUROPEAN INFLUENCES

Privately owned St. Nicholas Abbey was built to European designs and included fireplaces; the settlers had not yet realized that even on winter nights they did not need a fire for warmth. Its curved gables help to date it to about 1650 (following the maxim "curly early, straighter later"). Competing in age with St. Nicholas Abbey is Drax Hall, a privately owned 1650s stone building off Highway 4, with a wood-paneled interior and mastic-wood staircase (open only once a year).

▶▶ Scotland

Scotland is a hilly district in northeast Barbados; a series of peaks, including Mount Hillaby, the island's highest, overlook the Atlantic coast. This remote district makes an interesting half-day drive, through isolated settlements.

The Flower Forest▶▶ (tel: 433 8152. *Open* daily 9–5. *Admission: moderate*), just off Highway 2, has marked paths lined with trees such as mango and breadfruit, with their green cannonball-sized fruits, and a fine show of tropical blooms such as hibiscus and poinsettia. **Turner's Hall Woods▶** are the last remaining area of the natural woodland that covered Barbados until it was cleared for sugar plantations. Here you can see trees native to the island—fustic, West Indian locust and sand-box trees—as well as birds such as the Lesser Antillean bullfinch and the black Carib grackle.

In the days when it was carpeted with sugar cane, Barbados had about 500 windmills, whose sails turned constantly in the trade winds, driving the millstones that crushed the sugar cane to release its juice. The **Morgan Lewis Mill▶** (tel: 422 7429. *Open* Mon–Fri 9–5. *Admission: inexpensive*) is the last surviving example, and although it does not actually turn, the old crushing gear is on view. The **Grenade Hall Signal Station▶▶** (tel: 429 1358. *Open* Mon–Sat 9–5. *Admission: inexpensive*) is a restored link in the military communications chain. Close by, the **Barbados Wildlife Reserve▶▶** (tel: 422 8826. *Open* daily 10–5. *Admission: expensive*) is a free-range reserve with paths laid out in a mahogany wood and where agouti (see page 24), spectacled cayman (which looks like an alligator) and iguana roam.

Close by is Farley Hill, declared a National Park by Queen Elizabeth II in 1966, the year that Barbados achieved independence. Set in a fine natural tropical forest of mahogany with views down to the ocean the plantation house (c.1818) now lies in ruins after a fire. The grounds are used for festivals several times a year.

▶ South Coast

The south coast of Barbados has a completely different feel from the better known, more sedate west coast. It attracts a younger, livelier crowd and lays a greater emphasis on activity outside the hotels, which are smaller and less expensive (package tourists often end up in this area and there are also guesthouses here). Visitors tend to spend their days sunning themselves and windsurfing; in the evenings they pour into the restaurants and bars, moving on to the clubs in St. Lawrence Gap and Bridgetown, where dancing and live music continue until the early hours. There are places to explore in the southeast, where coves include Foul Bay, Harrismith Beach and Bottom Bay, but most life centers around the "gaps," the small roads that lead down to the coast off Highway 7.

Highway 7 leads from Bridgetown past the Garrison Savannah and through the seemingly never-ending urbanized sprawl of Hastings, St. Lawrence and Worthing. Farther east, The Crane hotel sits on a hilltop overlooking the Atlantic. **St. Lawrence Gap▶▶** is a popular and busy area, with watersports facilities on the beaches around the small bay, and the main center for nightlife nearby with plenty of restaurants and bars where local bands play to packed crowds. There is usually a friendly atmosphere, but tourists have occasionally been robbed here, and you should be careful.

Beyond Maxwell, known for its windsurfing, is Barbados's fourth town, Oistins, a fishing community where the daily catch is sold on the waterfront. The fish market has gained a reputation as a lively place to eat out for simple dishes (especially fish) in the early evenings—worth a detour to join in. Continue east and there is another windsurfing center at Silver Sands Beach.

At the **Heritage Park and Four Square Rum Distillery▶** (tel: 420 1977. *Open* Mon–Fri 9–5, Sat 1–6, Sun 11–5. *Admission: moderate*), visitors can observe sugar and rum manufacturing, as well as contemporary Bajan artists at work in the foundry, and pick up crafts and local produce in the stores.

223

Watching the world from a rum shop in Bridgetown

BIRDWATCHING

With fruit-filled feeders just a few feet away, the veranda at the Asa Wright Nature Centre, one of the largest and finest in the whole Caribbean, provides people who are not normally birdwatchers with an excellent view of Trinidad's spectacular birdlife. It is said that you can see 25 species before breakfast: honey creepers, hummingbirds, *cro pendulas* and toucans, among others (tel: 667 4655).

Trinidad and Tobago

This two-island nation presents a vivid contrast between bustling, cosmopolitan Trinidad and peaceful, rural Tobago. Trinidad is loud, lively and full of ethnic and cultural diversity; Tobago tends to be less developed and much more traditionally Caribbean, with its delightful beaches and rolling countryside. Trinidad's Port of Spain attracts hundreds of thousands of spectators each year to its spectacular and exhilarating carnival, while Tobago is a better option for those looking for a quieter dose of sand and sun.

This southernmost nation of the Caribbean lies off the coast of South America. Trinidad was still joined to the continent 10,000 years ago, and in some places its mountains (the Southern, Northern and Central ranges), fertile plains and mangrove swamps are separated from Venezuela by only 7 miles (16km) of water. Its spectacular flora and fauna are similar to the mainland's; there are hundreds of species of butterflies and birds (more than can be found on any other

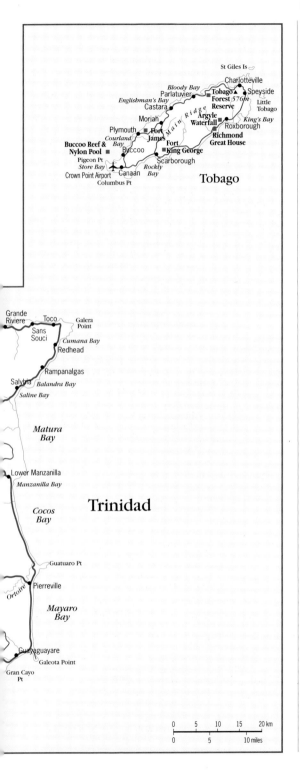

St Giles Is
Charlotteville
Bloody Bay
Parlatuvier
Tobago ▲ Speyside
Englishman's Bay
Castara
Forest 576m
Reserve
Little
Tobago
Moriah
Main Ridge
Argyle
Waterfall
King's Bay
Plymouth
Courland
Bay
Fort
James
Roxborough
Buccoo Reef &
Nylon Pool
Fort
King George
Richmond
Great House
Buccoo
Pigeon Pt
Store Bay
Rockly
Bay
Scarborough
Crown Point Airport
Canaan
Columbus Pt

Tobago

Grande
Riviere
Toco
Galera
Point
Sans
Souci
Cumana Bay
Redhead
Rampanalgas
Salybia
Balandra Bay
Saline Bay

*Matura
Bay*

Lower Manzanilla
Manzanilla Bay

*Cocos
Bay*

Trinidad

Ortoire

Guatuaro Pt
Pierreville

*Mayaro
Bay*

Guayaguayare
Galeota Point
Gran Cayo
Pt

225

FESTIVALS

Divali is celebrated in Trinidad during October or November and honors Lakshmi, the Hindu goddess of light. During the festival, followers go from one open house to the next, drinking and feasting, and hundreds of coconut oil lamps are lit in small clay pots, illuminating whole valleys. Phagwa is celebrated in the streets in March with huge paper floats and red food dye, which is thrown over spectators, and the Muslim festival of Hosay (dates vary) commemorates the martyrdom of Hussein and features a parade of his tomb, accompanied by dancers and drummers. At the end of the year, you will hear traditional Christmas "parang" songs.

| 0 | 5 | 10 | 15 | 20 km |

| 0 | 5 | 10 miles |

Caribbean island), including 17 varieties of humming-bird and the scarlet ibis—the national bird—which can be seen flying in to roost in the Caroni Swamp (situated just south of Port of Spain) during the evening.

Tobago broke off from the continent in an earlier geological age and lies some 22 miles (34km) northeast of Trinidad. Its spine of volcanic mountains, the Main Ridge, is mantled with rain forest, which descends to a plain in the southwest. Much of the coastline is gouged with steep-sided bays and the underwater slopes are clad with corals, but in the gentler western end of the island there are some fine white sand beaches that are well worth seeking out.

HISTORY Christopher Columbus landed on Trinidad in 1498, during his third voyage to the Americas, and named it in honor of the Holy Trinity. During the 16th century, the island was used as a Spanish staging post in the search for the elusive El Dorado, the Golden One, whose kingdom was thought to be on the mainland near here. Tobago was probably not seen by Columbus, but after Europeans had settled there in the mid-17th century, fierce battles followed for its posses-sion, and the island changed hands more times than any other island in the Caribbean before it was eventually taken into British ownership in 1814.

Trinidad and Tobago were politically linked in 1888 and remained a British colony until 1962, so they retain similarities to other English-speaking islands in the area—but theirs is a far more complex heritage. Spanish placenames are com-mon in Trinidad, and there are strong traces of French Créole, a legacy of the Royalist settlers who fled from the French colonies in the wake of the 1789 Revolution. The islanders joke that when the British took over Trinidad, it became a Caribbean island with a French population, governed by the British according to laws laid down by Spain.

ISLAND LIFE The British added new strains to Trinidad's already potent mix of peoples, shipping in African slaves to work the sugar plantations and, later, after emancipation, turning to East Indian, Chinese and Mideastern immigrants, who worked as indentured laborers. The result is that Trinidad has a cosmopolitan population, of which nearly half is made up of descendants of Indian immigrants. Hindi, some French and French Créole are spoken as well as English; parish churches stand side by side with Hindu temples and Islamic minarets; Indian and Chinese restaurants operate alongside tropical fruit stalls; and Hindu and Muslim festivals such as Divali and Hosay are celebrated as well as the Caribbean Carnival.

Tobago was also a plantation island and most of its population is of African descent, but for the traveler and the tourist, the two islands offer radically different experiences. Trinidad has a vibrant cultural life—theaters, a concert hall and festivals—while Tobago is altogether quieter (Trinidadians tend to go there for a rest), with secluded sandy coves. It has been developed somewhat in recent years, with new hotels and guesthouses springing up along the northwest coast.

Trinidad is the place to experience hectic Caribbean bustle. Port of Spain is a lively and busy city, and music, heard everywhere, is an essential part of life. A visit to a calypso evening, or a "tent" at Carnival time, is an essential Trinidadian experience (even though the language and repartee are hard to follow); the songs, which deal with island gossip and current affairs, are performed with great gusto by popular calypsonians, especially in the days leading up to the ultimate Trinidadian experience—Carnival▶▶▶ (see pages 234–235). After a week of steel bands (which were invented here) and calypso shows, Carnival culminates on Mardi Gras with a two-day pageant around the streets of Port of Spain, with hundreds of thousands of costumed revelers and onlookers dancing in the streets.

The simple life in Buccoo, Tobago

BAMBOO CANNON
Loud explosions resounding through a Trinidadian valley (or elsewhere in the Caribbean) may indicate that someone has been given a bamboo cannon, a popular child's toy that is still used at Caribbean festivities. The cannon is made by hollowing out a length of bamboo, leaving only the bottom section untouched. A small hole is then cut about 6in (15cm) from the end, and kerosene is poured inside and warmed so that it turns into gas, which is lit with touch-paper, causing a heart-stopping bang.

Trinidad

Miguel Street is fictitious, created by Trinidadian writer V. S. Naipaul in his novel of the same name; but it does have all the characters and life of a typical West Indian town. It could be almost anywhere in the Caribbean, but Naipaul, perhaps the Caribbean's best-known writer, was born in Trinidad and set his story in the island's capital.

Port of Spain is a large, active, modern city of about 300,000 people, lying on the Gulf of Paria in the northwest. In style it's a typical Caribbean mix, with modern high-rises and traditional Créole wooden houses overlooking the bustling streets, where vendors sell wares from their carefully arranged stalls.

The heart of the town is Brian Lara Promenade, a wide avenue a couple of blocks in from the waterfront. At right angles to the square is one of the city's main shopping areas, Frederick Street. A walk up this street brings you to Woodford Square, named for Governor Woodford, who had the town rebuilt in 1813 following its destruction by fire five years earlier. On the square's western side is the **Red House ▶▶**, Trinidad's parliament building, a massive Victorian pile whose two chambers can be visited, and diagonally opposite is the Anglican Cathedral of the Holy Trinity. The center of the square, tree-shaded and surrounded by iron railings, is a local gathering place. This was the spot where Dr. Eric Williams, the leader of Trinidad for many years before and after independence, held his political rallies.

Farther along Frederick Street is the **National Museum and Art Gallery ▶▶** (tel: 623 5941. *Open* Tue–Sat 10–6, Sun 2–6. *Admission free*), where displays of Trinidad historical and cultural life include the latest Carnival costumes and archive photographs dating back to the 1960s. There is also an exhibition of the paintings by the 19th-century Trinidadian artist Michel Cazabon.

TRINIDADIAN DISHES
Trinidad's food is as varied as its racial heritage and includes Indian, Chinese and French as well as Caribbean cuisine. Probably the finest local fare can be bought at Veni Mange (tel: 624 4597), at 67A Ariapita Avenue, where two sisters prepare meals for lunch only. The breakfast sheds on the waterfront in downtown Port of Spain sell rice and peas or callaloo soup at good prices, and street stalls sell snacks such as *rotis* (chapati envelopes filled with chicken, beef, shrimp or potato stew) or doubles (unleavened bread doubled over with a filling of split peas). Phulouri are batter balls served with a mango sauce.

King George III's cypher on a cannon that once protected Trinidad from rival European powers

Carib Beer, a Caribbean-wide Trinidadian export

Just north of Frederick Street, Port of Spain's vast central park, the 200-acre (80ha) **Savannah▶▶**, officially called Queen's Park Savannah, is where Trinidadians go to walk, jog, play cricket, hockey and soccer, and buy their chilled coconuts and evening snacks. Look out for the spectacularly extravagant houses known as the "Magnificent Seven" on the park's western side.

North of the Savannah is the **Botanic Gardens▶▶** (*Open* daily 6–6) Among the plants on display are the red blossoms of the Trinidad national flower, the chaconia, a wild poinsettia that takes its name from the last Spanish governor. If you are lucky you might see some toucans flying home to roost in the evening. Local animals such as the jaguar-like, buff-brown ocelot are kept in the **Emperor Valley Zoo▶▶** (tel: 622 3530; www.trinizoo.com. *Open* daily 9.30–5.30. *Admission: inexpensive*), next door to the Presidential House.

OUTSIDE PORT OF SPAIN Beyond **Fort George▶**, an old defensive bastion with a line of cannons covering the approaches to Port of Spain, the Western Main Road passes through some of the city's most prosperous suburbs and continues to the northwestern Chaguaramas peninsula. At the head of the Diego Martin ValleyRiver Estate, a historic sugar and cocoa plantation that still displays the original mill waterwheel.

During World War II the Chaguaramas peninsula was an US base, and in the 1950s it was hoped that it would house the parliament building for the ill-fated Federation of the West Indies, in which the islands of the British Caribbean would come together in one political unit. A golf course is laid out nearby, and the Anchorage is a popular bathing area.

For the intrepid explorer, there are caves and colonial military ruins on Gaspard Grande Island, in the channel, and at the end of the peninsula is the Dragons' Mouths, the short channel that separates Trinidad from the Venezuelan coast.

VIEWS OF THE PAST
C. L. R. James and Eric Williams were two Trinidadian historians who between them overturned the conventional colonial view of British Caribbean history. James, who lived in London until his death in 1989, was a Marxist historian, best known for his account of the Haitian Revolution, *The Black Jacobins*, whose works include *From Columbus to Castro* and *A History of the Peoples of Trinidad and Tobago*, was prime minister of Trinidad for many years until his death in 1981.

When Europeans first arrived in the Caribbean, turtles provided a reliable source of food because they could be kept alive on their backs on board ship. Today, numbers have dwindled drastically, and some species of turtle are endangered. Their eggs (highly prized by some as an aphrodisiac) are often stolen, and the turtles themselves are particularly vulnerable since they lay their eggs on the beach.

HELPING HAND

St. Croix in the USVI is one of the few places turtle numbers are improving. Numbers of leatherback turtles seen at Sandy Point and Green Cay are on the increase. On nightly patrols from July through to October, biologists from the Buck Island Reef Hawksbill Turtle Research Program are out under the stars recording and analyzing the nesting patterns of hawksbill, green and leatherback turtles. Their efforts have contributed significantly to the understanding and survival of the species.

HE OR SHE?

The sex of a turtle, like that of alligators and crocodiles, is determined by the temperature of the nest; the warmer the weather, the more females are hatched. The earlier hatchlings tend to be male (at the beginning of the year) and the later ones females, when the temperatures warm up.

230

Sea-turtles are marine reptiles with hard shells and flippers, which have remained basically unchanged for 250 million years. Five species of turtle live in the Caribbean: the loggerhead, the hawksbill, the ridley, the green turtle (once the most common, but now endangered) and, largest of all, the leatherback (also endangered), which can dive to 5,000ft (1,500m), weigh up to 1,550 lb (700kg) and live to 150 years old. Caribbean leatherbacks have been known to cross the Atlantic and swim as far north as Newfoundland.

The most fascinating part of a turtle's life-cycle is the way the young are hatched. The female leatherback

nests between April and June, arriving at night (often returning to the beach from which she originally came) and crawling laboriously up onto the sand to a point above the high water mark. For two hours she digs a hole with her hind flippers and lays up to 200 eggs, each the size of a billiard ball. Then she covers them with sand and crawls back into the sea. The process is repeated perhaps 10 times during the season.

Over the next eight weeks the eggs incubate, and eventually the 4in (10cm) hatchlings dig their way to the surface and set off for the sea, running the gauntlet of predators; apart from humans, herons and crabs lie in wait, and mongooses dig them out of their nests. There is safety only in numbers. Several Caribbean hotels can arrange special trips to watch turtles nesting, and at the turtle farm on Grand Cayman, in the Cayman Islands, visitors can see turtles at different stages of development.

The beaches nearest to Port of Spain are on the north coast, over the mountains of the Northern Range, which tower above the city. The best route, and the most spectacular drive, is through the Maraval Valley. Popular **Maracas Bay ▶ ▶**, one mile (1.5km) wide, is flanked by massive headlands, thrown off by El Tucuche, Trinidad's highest peak. It's a traditional Trinidadian day out—part of the experience is to sample a "shark and bake," a battered fish sandwich from one of the stalls. Here, the water is occasionally rough; it is calmer at Las Cuevas, a few miles beyond, where there are also beach facilities. From the north coast fishing village of Blanchisseuse, a road heads southward across the Northern Range, another long, twisting and visually stunning drive.

The Eastern Main Road leads from just behind the waterfront in downtown Port of Spain toward St. Joseph, the original Spanish capital. It then passes between the Northern Range and the northern edge of the **Caroni Lagoon National Park ▶ ▶ ▶** (tel: 645 1305. *Admission free*), which harbors about half of the island's bird species, including the scarlet ibis, which flies in during the evening. It is said that up to 10,000 ibises can be roosting here at a time, and tours (with a guide) start at around 4.30pm. Angostura Bitters is produced in a factory in St. Joseph, which is open to visitors (see panel), and high above the town is the **Mount St. Benedict Monastery ▶**, a peaceful spot with a fine view over the central plain.

A little farther on up the Arouca River, the **Lopinot Complex ▶ ▶** (*Open* daily 6–6) is an old cocoa estate cut into the huge valley early in the 19th century by the Comte de Lopinot, a refugee from turbulent Saint Domingue (Haiti). The cottage-like original estate house survives, and Trinidadians picnic under the giant Saaman trees at weekends. Early in the year the immortelle trees that were planted to shade the cocoa plants burst into a blaze of orange blooms. Native American descendants live in this area, where many locals speak French patois.

Whitehall, one of the "Magnificent Seven" houses that overlook the Savannah

ANGOSTURA BITTERS
Trinidad is the home of the world-famous aromatic Angostura Bitters, used in cooking and cocktails. The business was started by the Venezuelan Siegert family in the 19th century, and the recipe is a secret, but involves a mixture of roots, barks, dried leaves and spices with alcohol, boiled to give the dark bitters. The Angostura factory (tel: 623 1841), on the main road to St. Joseph, is open to visitors.

In the Arima Valley is another delightful retreat, the **Asa Wright Nature Centre**▶▶▶ (tel: 667 4655. *Open* daily 9–5, guided walks available. *Admission: moderate*), a balconied estate house (with rooms for rent; see page 277) looking out onto a vast, green valley. Here you can hear the strange "boing, boing" call of bellbirds and see the colorful flash of a toucan or an *oro pendula* in flight. Another excellent birdwatching spot is the Hollis Reservoir just north of Valencia (for more details contact one of the birdwatching organizations listed in **Travel Facts**).

Beyond Valencia, southeast of the nature center, the strip of urban development gives way to forested and cultivated land. The road forks here and heads south toward the Atlantic coast at Manzanilla or north via Balandra to Toco, where there are good beaches.

To reach the south of the country from Port of Spain, turn right on the Uriah Butler Highway, which skirts the Caroni Lagoon National Park and then heads out into the cane fields. The first major town is Chaguanas; V. S. Naipaul lived here, and the house described in *A House for Mr. Biswas* stands on Main Street. The road continues to San Fernando, Trinidad's second city, where it passes the shell of the Pointe-à-Pierre oil refinery. A wetland bird sanctuary managed by the Pointe-à-Pierre Wildlife Trust thrives in the shadow of the industrial giant.

Trinidadians refer to the wilder country beyond San Fernando as the Deep South. At the town of La Brea, about 10 miles (16km) along the coast, is the **Pitch Lake**▶▶, a 100-acre (40ha) cauldron of natural asphalt, fed by tar from beneath and forever turning; occasionally branches, ancient artifacts and even bones are pushed up to the surface. It is worked as a mine and the pitch has been used in roads all over the world.

V. S. NAIPAUL
Vidiadhar Surajprasad Naipaul was born of a Brahmin family in Trinidad in 1932 and educated at Queen's Royal College, Port of Spain, and University College, Oxford. Many of his novels express pessimistic and critical views of his native culture. *A House for Mr. Biswas* (1961), whose hero is based on Naipaul's father, describes the collapse of the Caribbean way of life, and his earliest books, *The Mystic Masseur* (1957), *The Suffrage of Elvira* (1958) and *Miguel Street* (1959) all satirize life and politics in Trinidad.

Maracas Bay, Trinidad

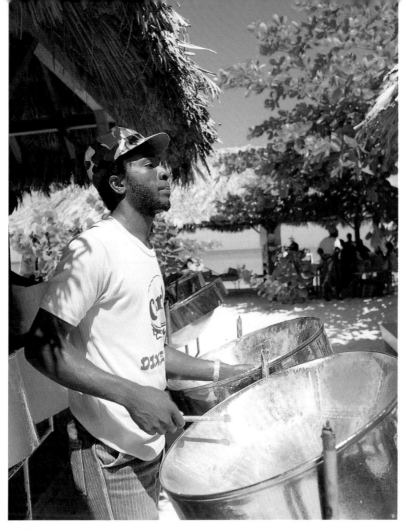

Tobago

A steel band performer making music on Tobago

With few large hotels and no crowds, this little island (only 20 miles by 6 miles/32km by 9km) still has a tranquil charm. Tourism has developed around the southwestern tip of the island, where the best beaches are to be found, but elsewhere there are deserted coves set in the sinuous coastline, and quiet West Indian villages.

Most people arrive on Tobago at Crown Point Airport, on the far southwestern tip of the island. From here it is a short walk to most of the guesthouses and small hotels and to **Store Bay**▶▶, one of the island's liveliest beaches, where breakfast sheds have been set up selling such local dishes as "bakes" (like Johnny Cakes), served with salt fish buljol. Just north of Store Bay is the most popular beach, **Pigeon Point**▶▶, where there are palm-thatched bars and watersports. An entry charge can be avoided by walking in below the high-water mark (where the sand is not private).

Continued on page 236.

SENSITIVE SOUVENIRS
Vendors at Caribbean beaches sell all sorts of trinkets and jewelry made from local materials. There is some good work made with calabash shells in Trinidad and Tobago and from other local beads. Beware of buying jewelry made from turtle shell or coral, because they may well have been obtained illegally.

Trinidad's annual carnival is the Caribbean's largest, liveliest and most flamboyant party. For two days before Lent, hundreds of thousands of revelers flood onto the streets of Port of Spain, clad in bright Lycra, sequins and feathered headdresses, and dance in "bands" of a thousand or more, all shuffling and strutting in rhythm. Mas, as it is familiarly known, has been adopted by other islands all over the Caribbean, but the Trinidadians still claim to do it better than anyone else.

234

Mas has its roots in Catholic pre-Lenten festivities of two centuries ago, in which the Trinidadian French Créoles would visit one another's houses for masked balls. After emancipation in the 1830s, ex-slaves adopted the masquerade, turning it into a drum-driven street party. Suppressed by the authorities many times, it has grown since World War II into a massive and exuberant celebration.

Carnival begins to warm up soon after Christmas, when the calypsonians (see page 238) release their songs and the steel band preliminaries are held. "Mas Camps" are busily sewing the costumes, which can be designed up to a year in advance and depict themes as varied as birdlife and pirates.

The real action begins during the weekend before the beginning of Lent. On the Friday night, a competition is held to select the winning King and Queen of the Bands— magnificent centerpiece figures that can be up to 35ft (11m) tall and are lavishly constructed.

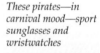

These pirates—in carnival mood—sport sunglasses and wristwatches

On Saturday the children take their turn in Kiddies Carnival, and in the evening Panorama, the finals of the steel band competition (see pages 80–81), features the last eight steel bands, many 60-players strong, competing for the year's top title.

The Calypso Competition finals are held on Sunday night, with calypsonians vying for the year's most prestigious singing title, the Calypso Monarch. During the evening the winners of the King and Queen of the Band competitions put in an appearance.

On Monday the dancing begins and the revelers are out on the streets by 3am for jouvert (from the French Créole *jour ouvert*, but pronounced "jouvay"), with music provided exclusively by steel bands. Leading the parade are impish "djab-djabs" (from the French *diable*) and "moko-jumbies" who walk on stilts. Many dancers cover themselves in axle grease and mud (snazzily dressed onlookers are liable to be hugged). Jouvert comes to an end at about 9am and is followed at midday by more formal music and dancing by the Carnival Bands.

Tuesday, Mardi Gras, is the day of the main procession, or road march, and judging day for the Carnival Bands. They assemble early in the morning and begin their strut around the streets, passing the four main judging areas— Brian Lara Promenade, Adam Smith Square in Woodbrook, Park Street and the Queen's Park Savannah. Each band, which may have as many as 3,000 players, is divided into sections, with players dressed in different costumes. At the rear of each band are the King and Queen. Music is provided by trucks interspersed among the sections and the noise is deafening. In the full heat of the Trinidadian sun, dancing is exhausting work, and the players usually employ someone to wheel a portable bar around. By dusk the procession is finished, with dancing until the official finish at midnight.

Although many Caribbean carnivals are held on Mardi Gras and run along similar lines, some islands stage them at New Year or in the summer, to celebrate the end of the cane-cutting season. In Barbados, Cropover is on the first Monday in August, and in Cuba, the Zafra celebrations are at the end of July. Perhaps the most enjoyable feature of Caribbean carnivals is that, unlike those of Rio or New Orleans, anyone can join in and dance.

CARNIVAL DANCES
Dances go in and out of vogue year by year, but the traditional step is the "chip," in which players drag their feet and swing their knees and hips, occasionally throwing their arms up in the air. Winding and grinding are dances in which players move their hips with their legs wide apart, sometimes alone, sometimes pushing up against another dancer (or in a conga). Groins and backsides feature prominently in the dance, and partners perform in all imaginable combinations (back to back, back to front, etc.).

235

PELICAN PERILS
Pelicans can often be seen throughout the Caribbean islands sitting on a rock or a convenient offshore post, diving for fish—hurtling arrow-like down at the water but barely entering it. In time, this battering damages their eyes and many of them gradually go blind. Unable to fish well, eventually they die.

Continued from page 233.

Offshore are two Tobagonian landmarks: **Buccoo Reef▶▶**, although sadly overrun, still impresses with colorful coral and fish, which visitors can observe through a glass-bottomed boat, and the **Nylon Pool▶▶**, a waist-deep area of warm water with a silky, sand bottom. On the other side of the bay is the village of **Buccoo▶▶**, where fishing boats with brightly painted diamond patterns lie on the sands. The Hendrix Bar is the scene of a weekly celebration known as **Sunday School▶▶**.

Past Mount Irvine Bay, the site of Tobago's 18-hole golf course, and Stonehaven Bay (both good beaches), is Courland Bay. The name Courland has a strange origin: It comes from a peninsula in what is now Latvia, from which a number of settlements of Tobago were attempted in the 17th century. There is a monument to their memory in **Plymouth▶**, Tobago's second town, where there are just a couple of streets, and Fort James, on the point overlooking the bay. **Back Bay▶▶**, on the other side of Plymouth, is an attractive stretch of sand.

Drinks-shack and vegetable stall, Tobago

Beaching the boat in Tobago after fishing on the high seas

Beyond Plymouth, the road winds its way into Tobago's countryside, through hillside villages such as Les Coteaux and Moriah, before descending to the coast and a series of sandy, palm-backed bays: **Castara▶▶**, **Englishman's Bay▶▶▶** and **Parlatuvier▶▶**. From Bloody Bay the main road leads up into the **Tobago Forest Reserve▶▶**, a rain forest with walking trails, before descending to the island's south coast at Roxborough.

Scarborough▶ is the capital of Tobago, a quiet and undistinguished town set over the hills above Rockly Bay on the south coast. At the top of the hill is the town's old defense, **Fort King George▶**, which is well preserved with its cannon covering the approaches to the town. Next door is the **Tobago Museum▶▶** (tel: 639 3970. *Open* Mon–Fri 9–5. *Admission: inexpensive*), with displays of island history and Ameridian and colonial artifacts; and on the other side of town are the **Botanical Gardens▶** (tel: 639 3970. *Open* Mon–Fri 9–5.30. *Admission: inexpensive*).

The road to the eastern end of the island winds its way along the palm-backed south coast, in and out of huge bays and through small Tobagonian settlements. A 15-minute walk from Roxborough, near the junction of the inland and coastal roads, is the **Argyle Waterfall▶▶**, a three-stepped cascade where you can take a swim after the walk. There is another waterfall at **King's Bay▶**, to the east of Roxborough.

After climbing an impossibly steep hill the road reaches Speyside and then Charlotteville (lying at the island's eastern tip), two quiet Tobagonian towns in the island's best scuba diving area. On the Atlantic coast, Speyside overlooks the island seabird sanctuary of **Little Tobago▶▶**, and boat trips leave from the dock.

THE FRIGATEBIRD
The magnificent frigatebird, or Man-o'-War bird, nests on Tobago's northeastern cliffs. With its dark plumage, scissorshaped tail and a wingspan of over 3ft (90cm), this is an impressive but aggressive bird, which attacks other species for their food. It swoops from above or behind, shaking the victim until it disgorges its meal. Tours of Tobago's wildlife are arranged by David Rooks (tel: 756 8954 or 660 6168; www.rookstobago.com).

Calypso is a flamboyant and witty singing tradition that originated in Trinidad. Styles range from rap to serenade, and lyrics touch on life, the universe, politics and more. Some have a socially conscious edge; some are comical and gossipy, others are just plain "slack" (raunchy). But all calypsos entertain, and they jam the airwaves as Carnival approaches.

CALYPSO STARS

Most calypsonians adopt singing names as colorful as their lyrics and dress. It's all part of the theater that defines calypso. The most popular prefixes are "The Mighty" and "Lord." The two biggest names in the world of calypso are The Mighty Sparrow (alias Slinger Francisco), who first won the Calypso Monarch title in 1956 and has been crowned a total of eight times, and fellow Trinidadian, Lord Kitchener (Aldwyn Roberts), known for composing steel band songs and who won the Roadmarch title 11 times before his death in 2000. Singing Sandra, the 1999 and 2003 Calypso Monarch, is one of only two women to win the title. Other names include Atilla the Hun, Lord Executor, Lord Invader, Watchman (a policeman) and The Mighty Chalkdust (a schoolteacher).

Calypso is a legacy of Trinidad's dual African and French heritage. The first known calypsonian or "shantwell" was Gros Jean, who sang for a French planter 200 years ago. Since the beginning of this century calypsos have been sung in English, the language of Trinidad, and as their popularity has increased, other English-speaking Caribbean islands have adopted the tradition.

Calypsos are the major musical force behind Carnival, at the beginning of Lent each year (see pages 234–235). There are three main calypso competitions. The Roadmarch competition judges the year's best dancing tune in the parties (fêtes) and in the Carnival parade. The title is won by the calypsonian whose song is played most as the Carnival bands cross the judging stages.

In Ex-tempo, two calypsonians compete in quickfire singing, alternating verse by verse. A topic written on a piece of paper is handed to the singers, who are given 30 seconds to prepare a calypso. Teasing the opponent is more important than rhyme or meter, and the winner is usually the person who gets the biggest laugh.

The most coveted and fiercely contested title is the Calypso Monarch (changed from Calypso King when women entered the field). Calypsonians release their songs in January. Then they perform in calypso "tents," acting the songs out in an attempt to be selected for the next round. Calypso Monarch finals are held on the Sunday before Lent—a cross between a variety show and a comedy evening. They perform to huge audiences, making digs at the other singers and adding topical comments to their songs to provoke a response from the crowd.

238

Travel Facts

Arriving and departing

By air: The best way of reaching the Caribbean is to put yourself in the hands of an experienced tour operator, which usually commands the best rates from airlines. US tour operators include Apple Vacations (www. applevacations.com) and Travel Impressions (www.travelimpressions .com). Other specialized tour operators include Caribbean Concepts (tel: 800/777 0907).

Airlines with regularly scheduled flights from the US include Air Jamaica (tel: 800/523-5585), American (tel: 800/433-7300), BWIA (tel: 800/538-2942), Continental (tel: 800/231-0856), Delta (tel: 800/221-1212) and US Airways (tel: 800/943 5436). There are also numerous charter flights to the more popular destinations, mainly during the winter season (Dec–Apr).

For top of the range companies in the UK contact: Caribtours (tel: 020 7751 0660), Elegant Resorts (tel: 01244 897777) and Harlequin Worldwide (tel: 01708 850300). Slightly less expensive are: BA Holidays (tel: 0845 606 0747), Kuoni (tel: 01306 747002) and Thomas Cook (tel: 0870 750 5711). Less expensive still are Airtours (tel: 0870 238 7788), Thomson Holidays (tel: 0870 165 0079) and Virgin Holidays (tel: 0870 220 2788). Airlines with regular scheduled services from Europe to the Caribbean, some via the US, include Continental Airlines, US Airways, Air Jamaica, BWIA, Delta, American Airlines and Air France. British Airways (tel: 0870 850 9850) also act as sales agents for LIAT, one of the major airlines linking the Caribbean islands. LIAT (tel: 1 268 480 5601; www.liatairline.com) offers the Super-Explorer allowing unlimited travel for 30 days on the ILAT network; the Mini-Explorer with four stopovers during 21 days of validity; and the LIAT Airpass, allowing European travelers three to six stopovers for a set price. The Airpass must be booked at the same time as a flight to the Caribbean from Europe, it cannot be booked after arrival in the Caribbean.

BWIA (tel: UK 0870 499 2942; www.bwee.com) offers a four-stop pass for US$350 or an unlimited stop

pass for US$450. All travel must be completed within 30 days and passes don't incl.ude routes to Havana, Dominican Republic or Costa Rica.

Air Jamaica offers a Caribbean Hopper air pass that requires a minimum three additional stopovers when purchased with a flight from North America to any of its ten island destinations, plus Panama; it's good for 30 days, but backtracking is not allowed. There are some tiny inter-island airlinks (see listings).

Departure tax is payable from most islands; this varies and there may be exemptions for children. Some islands include this in the ticket price but others take it on departure, so don't forget to have enough currency to cover this.

For general information, contact the

BARBADUS

July–November

March–October

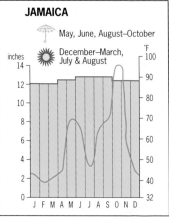

JAMAICA

May, June, August–October

December–March, July & August

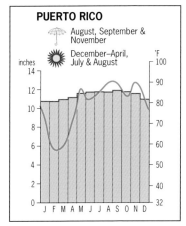

PUERTO RICO

August, September & November

December–April, July & August

Caribbean Tourism Organisation 80 Broad Street, 32nd Floor, New York NY 10004 (tel: 212/635-9530);30 Bloor Street West, Suite 301, Toronto, Ontario M5S 1N5 (tel: 416/935-0767) 22 The Quadrant, Richmond, Surrey, TW0 1BP (tel: 0208 948 0057).

By boat: Lines offering trips and cruises include: Carnival; Celebrity; Costa; Cunard; Holland America; Norwegian; Premier; Princess; Seabourn; and Windstar. The Disney Corporation has also entered the marketplace, along with low-cost airline EasyJet with its Easycruise ships.

Camping and student/youth travel

In general camping is discouraged in private and national park campsites, particularly on beaches. Few islands have designated campsites and there are few youth hostels with the exception of St. John in the US Virgin Islands where the well-organized campsites are booked up quickly. Some landowners allow tent-camping in the French Antilles. In Barbados, the Girl Guides (Girl Scouts), Boy Scouts and Cadet Corps conduct organized camping for their counterparts. There are inexpensive guesthouses and diving lodges on many islands, which usually do not appear in brochures. Most tourist offices have lists.

Climate

Temperatures generally average 78°F–85°F (25°C–29°C) but are lower the greater the altitude. October and

November are the wettest months (June in Trinidad and Tobago); Dec–May is the driest season and the hurricane season is Jul–Oct.

Crime

Attacks and robberies are rare; the most hassle you are likely to encounter is from persistent souvenir salespersons, but be careful in large towns and cities. There is much poverty, which brings with it the temptation to petty theft. Keep doors locked, take care of your valuables, and watch where you walk after dark. Don't take too much money out with you and don't display wealth. Most hotels have safes. Report lost property first to the apartment or hotel manager, and then to the police.

Dialing codes

Numbers given below should be prefaced with the international dialing code if you are calling from abroad or from an island with a different national code. You do not need to use the international dialing code when calling the islands from the US (instead, dial 1 before the island code), except when dialing the Dutch and French islands, which require the international prefix (011). International calls from within the islands require the 011 prefix (but 00 when calling from the Dutch or French Antilles).
264 Anguilla
268 Antigua and Barbuda
297 Aruba
246 Barbados
284 British Virgin Islands
345 Cayman Islands
53 Cuba
767 Dominica
809 Dominican Republic
599 Dutch Antilles (followed by: Curaçao 9
590 Guadaloupe
473 Grenada
509 Haiti
876 Jamaica
596 Martinique
664 Montserrat
869 Nevis and St. Kitts
787 Puerto Rico
596 St. Barts
758 St. Lucia
784 St. Vincent and Grenadines

241

596 Saint-Martin
868 Trinidad and Tobago
340 US Virgin Islands

Emergency telephone numbers
These telephone numbers are being
standardized. Check them on arrival.
Anguilla Police and ambulance: 911
Antigua and Barbuda Police and
ambulance 999 or 911
Aruba Police: 100; ambulance: 115
Barbados Police: 211; ambulance: 511
Bonaire Police and ambulance: 191
Curaçao Police: 911; ambulance: 912
Cayman Islands Police: 911;
ambulance: 555 or 911
Dominica Police and ambulance: 999
Dominican Republic Police and
ambulance: 911
Grenada Police: 911; ambulance: 434
Guadeloupe Police: 17; medical assis-
tance 15
Jamaica Police: 119; ambulance: 110
Martinique Police: 17; ambulance: 15
Montserrat Accident and Emergency
491 2802
Puerto Rico Police and ambulance: 911
Saba Police: 416 3222; ambulance 911;
Saba hospital 416 3288
St. Barts Police: 17; ambulance: 18
St. Eustatius Police: 911;
ambulance: 912
St. Kitts and Nevis Police and
ambulance: 911
St. Lucia Police and ambulance: 911
Saint-Martin Police: 17; ambulance: 18
Sint Maarten Police: 111;
ambulance: 130
St. Vincent and the Grenadines Police
and ambulance: 999
Trinidad and Tobago Police: 999;
ambulance: 990
Virgin Islands (British) Police and
ambulance: 999 or 911
Virgin Islands (US) Police and
ambulance: 911

Health
Immunization against yellow fever
may be required if you arrive from an
infected area. Otherwise immunization is not generally required, but
typhoid, polio and tetanus shots are
often recommended, as well as hep-
atitis A for those staying outside
tourist areas. Malaria is a problem in
remote areas of Haiti and the
Dominican Republic. The risks of HIV
are well known and apply in the

Caribbean as anywhere else. Consult
your doctor before leaving. Obtain
health insurance prior to travel; if on
regular medication take supplies with
you in case they are not available. Tap
water is not always safe to drink.

Money
On islands where the official currency
is the Eastern Caribbean dollar (EC$),
the exchange rate is fixed to the US
dollar and US currency is widely
accepted: **Anguilla; Antigua; Dominica;
Grenada; Montserrat; Nevis; St. Kitts;
St. Lucia; St. Vincent; the Grenadines.**
Other currencies: **Aruba** Aruban
florin (Af); **Barbados** Barbados dollar
(BDS$); **Bonaire** Netherlands Antilles
florin/guilder (NAf); **Cayman Islands**
Caymanian dollar (CI$); **Cuba**
Convertible Peso; **Curaçao**
Netherlands Antilles florin/guilder
(NAf); **Dominican Republic**
Dominican peso (RD$); **Guadeloupe**
euro; **Jamaica** Jamaican dollar (J$);
Martinique euro; **Puerto Rico** US dol-
lar; **Saba** Netherlands Antilles
florin/guilder (NAf); **St. Barts** euro;
St. Eustatius Netherlands Antilles
florin/guilder (NAf); **Saint-Martin**
euro; **Sint Maarten** Netherlands
Antilles guilder/florin (NAf);
Trinidad and Tobago Trinidad and
Tobago dollar (TT$); **Virgin Islands
(British and US)** US dollar. U.S. dol-
lars are also accepted on all islands
except the Dominican Republic and
Trinidad and Tobago.

Public amenities
Some islands have basic beach facilities (not great), usually attached to a
rustic bar. It will probably be better to
stick to hotels and restaurants.

Travel insurance
This should cover accident, health,
baggage and possessions, cancel-
lation, etc. If you are taken ill or have
an accident, you will nearly always
be expected to pay, and health care is
not cheap. Medicaments, if not
already on the island, are usually
flown in from the US, and there are
plenty of pharmacies for over-the-
counter items.

Travelers with disabilities
San Juan and Condado in Puerto Rico

242

are well-equipped for wheelchair access; Luquillo Beach offers a ramp for access to the water. Puerto Rico and the US Virgins comply with the Americans with Disabilities Act. The Jamaica Tourist Board lists hotels with facilities, as does Trinidad and Tobago, but check before booking. Individual island tourist boards can give details about specific properties.

THE WINDWARD ISLANDS

Dominica (area code 767)

Car rental and driving
A local driving license is required, obtainable from airports, the Vehicle Licensing Office, High Street, Roseau and some rental companies (Mon–Fri). You must be 25–65 and have a valid driving license and at least two years' driving experience.

Rental companies include **Best Deal Rent-a-Car** (tel: 449-9204), **Garraway Rent-a-Car** (tel: 448 2891), **Island Car Rental** (tel: 255 6844), **Valley Rent-a-Car** (Roseau 448 3233; Portsmouth 445 5252).

Driving is on the left. The main roads are good; others are hazardous, with potholes and hairpin bends and few road signs. The speed limit is 20mph (32kph) in populated areas. Fuel is paid for in cash. Seatbelts are recommended. Drunk-driving laws are enforced.

Getting around
By air: There are no direct flights to Dominica from the US or Europe; the main international gateways are Antigua, Barbados, St. Lucia and Sint-Maarten, and the neighboring Guadeloupe and Martinique. Dominica has two airports: the most convenient for the south of the island is Canefield, just outside Roseau; the other, Melville Hall, is in the north 38 miles/61km (an hour's journey time) from the capital. Local carrier **LIAT** serves both; **American Eagle** from Puerto Rico flies into Melville Hall, as does **American Airlines** from Antigua and **Air Caraïbes**
By boat: High-speed catamarans operated by **Express des Iles** link Dominica with Guadeloupe, Martinique and St. Lucia. For infor-

mation and reservations, contact **Whitchurch Travel Agency** (tel: 488 2181). Dominica also has cruise ship berths on the Roseau waterfront and in Cabrits National Park, Portsmouth.
By road: Taxis, minibuses and rental vehicles have license plates with H as the last letter. Taxi rates are fixed and quoted in EC$ and US$: make sure you know which is being quoted. They are displayed at the airport and tourist office. In Roseau, try **Mally's Taxi Service** (tel: 448 3114) and **Linton's Taxi and Tow Services** (tel: 448 2558). Few taxis work after 6pm, except by prior arrangement.

Buses are cheaper; flag them down on the road by the airport.

Sightseeing and activities
Tours, including hiking and photo safaris, are offered by: **Antours Dominica** (tel: 448 6460), **Dominica Tours** (tel: 448 2638), **Ken's Hinterland Adventure Tours** (tel: 448 4850), **Mally's Tour & Taxi Service** (tel: 448 3114), **Nature Island Destinations** (tel: 449 6233), **Paradise Tours** (tel: 448 5999), **Rainbow Rover Tours** (tel: 448 8650), **Whitchurch Travel Agency** (tel: 448 2181). You need an experienced guide for tours in the Morne Trois Pitons National Park. Dominica is excellent for scuba diving. Arrange trips to view corals and whale watching (Oct–May) through **Dive Dominica** (tel: 448 2188), the **Anchorage Dive Centre** (tel: 448 2638), and **Dive Castaways** (tel: 449 6245). Book sailing at dive shops.

Tourist information
The Dominica Division of Tourism, National Development Corporation, PO Box 293, Roseau, Commonwealth of Dominica (tel: 448 2045; www.ndc-dominica.com) has information books at the airport. In the UK, contact the Office of the High Commission, 1 Collingham Gardens, London SW5 0HW (tel: 020 7370 5194).

Grenada (area code 473)

Car rental and driving
A local driving permit can be bought from most rental companies or the Police Station on the Carenage; show

243

your national or international driver's license. Rental companies include: **Adams Auto Rentals** (tel: 405 0582); **Avis** (tel: 440 3936); **David's Car Rentals** (tel: 444 3399); **Jerry's Auto Service** (tel: 440 1730); **Thomas & Son** (tel: 444 4384); **Thrift Rent-a-Car** (tel: 444 4984); **Y&R Car Rentals** (tel: 444 4448). Carriacou: **Franklin Rentals** (tel: 443 8496). Driving is on the left. Seatbelts are not mandatory but recommended. Fuel is paid for in cash.

Getting around
By air: Point Salines International Airport receives daily **American Eagle** flights from Puerto Rico, regular **BWIA** international services from New York, Miami and Toronto, and London via Trinidad. **BA** and **Thomas Cook** offer twice-weekly flights from the UK. Local inter-island carriers include **LIAT** and **Caribbean Star** (www.flycaribbeanstar.com).
By boat: Ferries operate daily from St. George's to Carriacou and then to Petite Martinique daily except Saturday. See list of local tour operators for yacht charter companies.
By road: Rental vehicles have a license plate with the letter H. Taxi rates are set by the government and quoted in US dollars, but you can pay in either currency. Buses leave from Market Square, St. George's and can be flagged down elsewhere. Minibuses ply shorter routes. From Carriacou, buses link Hillsborough with Windwardside and Tyrrel Bay. Motorcycles and bicycles can often be rented from hotels or car-rental firms.

Sightseeing and activities
Taxis can be rented as sightseeing guides. Contact local tour operators for excursions around Grenada, trips to Carriacou, Petite Martinique and the Grenadines, hiking tours, boat trips, car rental and taxi service. St. George's: **Adventure Jeep Tour** (tel: 444 5337); **Fun Tours** (tel: 444 3167); **Sunsation Tours** (tel: 444 1594); **Henry's Safari Tours** (tel: 444 5313); **Carib Tours** (tel: 444 4363); **Sunshine Tours** (tel: 444 2831). Sports and watersports operators include: **(scuba) Dive Grenada** (tel: 444 1092) and **Eco Dive & Trek** (tel: 444 7777); horseback riding: **The Horseman** (tel:

440 5368); hiking: **Henry's Safari Tours** (tel: 444 5313) and **Telfor Hiking Tours** (tel: 442 6200); dolphin and whale-watching excursions (Dec–Apr) can be arranged with **Starwind Enterprise** (tel: 440 3678); deep sea fishing: **Caribbean Horizons** (tel: 444 1555) and **Evans Chartering Service** (tel: 444 4422); yacht charter companies: **Footloose Yacht Charters** (tel: 440 7949); **The Moorings** (tel: 444 4439); **Starwind Enterprises** (tel: 440 3678). Carriacou: tours can be arranged through **Martin Bullen Tours** (tel: 443 7221); scuba diving through **Carriacou Silver Diving** (tel: 443 7882) and **Aquanauts Grenada** (tel: 444 1126).

Tourist information
Grenada Board of Tourism (www.grenadagrenadines.com), the cruise ship dock, St. George's (tel: 440 2001); on Carriacou (tel: 443 7948). In the US: PO Box 16668, Lake Worth, FL 33460 (tel: 588-8176/800/927-9553). In the UK: 11 Blades Court, 121 Deodar Road, London SW15 2NU (tel: 020 8877 4516). Grenada Hotel Association PO Box 40, St. George's.

St. Lucia (area code 758)

Car rental and driving
A St. Lucia temporary driver's license must be purchased at the airport, the police station in Castries or the car rental office. Take your current driver's license. Companies include **Avis** (tel: 452 2202), **Budget** (tel: 452 9887), **Cool Breeze Jeep/Car Rental** (tel: 459 7729), **St. Lucia Yacht Car Rental** (tel: 452 5057). Some companies insist on a minimum number of years' driving experience.
Driving is on the left and the speed limit is 30mph (48kph). There are penalties for drinking and driving and illegal parking. The preferred form of payment for fuel is cash.

Getting around
By air: St. Lucia has two airports: Hewanorra International Airport in the far south of the island (road transfers to the hotels in the north take at least 90 minutes); and George Charles Airport (better known as Vigie) in the capital, Castries. Hewanorra is served by **Air Jamaica**

and **BWIA** from the US; **Air Canada, British Airways, Virgin Atlantic** and **BWIA** from the UK; as well as several charter operators from North America and Europe. **American Eagle** flights from Puerto Rico fly in and out of Castries and inter-island travelers will find local carriers **LIAT, BWIA** and **Helenair,** who also fly into the capital, offer options for exploring the region.
By boat: A hydrofoil ferry service, **Caribbean Express,** operates between St. Lucia and Martinique, Guadeloupe and Dominica. A few hotels have their own boats; for day sails contact **Brig Unicorn** (tel: 452 6811) through your hotel, or **Endless Summer** (tel: 450 8651). Yacht charter companies include: **Destination St. Lucia,** RodneyBay Marina (tel: 452 8531); **The Moorings,** Marigot Bay (tel: 451 4357).
By road: The north is well served by buses and private minibuses, until about 10pm (later on Fri). The last bus from Soufrière to Castries leaves at noon. Taxis or minibuses are easily available and can organize tours: **Vigie Taxi** (tel: 452 1599), **Ben's Taxi Service** (tel: 459 5457), **Courtesy Taxi Co-operative Society** (tel: 452 1773).

Sightseeing and activities
Tours are usually organized through the hotel or tour company rep. Local tour operators include: **Barefoot Holidays** (tel: 452 0865); **Barnards Travel** (tel: 458 0865); **Carib Travel Agency** (tel: 452 3176); **Cox & Co.** (tel: 456 5000); **Pitons Travel Agency** (tel: 450 1486); **Spice Travel** (tel: 452 0865); **St. Lucia International Travel** (tel: 452 1293); **Sunlink Tours** (tel: 456 9100); for local cultural tours: **St. Lucia Heritage Tourism** (tel: 451 6220). For deep sea fishing: **Captain Mike's** (tel: 452 7044). Dive operators include: **Buddies Scuba,** Rodney Bay (tel: 452 5228) and **Scuba St. Lucia,** Anse Chastenet (tel: 459 7755).
Windsurfing: contact **Club Mistral** (tel: 454 3327); **Island Windsurfing,** Vieux Fort (tel: 454 7400). For horse riding: **Trim's Riding Stables** (tel: 452 8273) and **Morne Coubaril Estate,** Soufrière (tel: 459 7340).

Tourist information
St. Lucia Tourist Board, PO Box 221,

Top Floor, Sure Line Building, Vide Bouteille, Castries (tel: 452 4094; www.stlucia.org). Offices in Jeremie Street, Castries, Soufrière, and in both the airports. In the US: 9th Floor, 800 2nd Avenue, New York, NY 10017 (tel: 212/867-2950, 800/456-3984). In the UK: St Lucia Tourist Board, 1 Collingwood Gardens, London SW5 0HW (tel: 0870 900 7697).

St. Vincent and the Grenadines (area code 784)

Car rental and driving
Take your normal or international license to the airport, the police station in Bay Street or the Licensing Authority in Halifax Street to purchase a local license. The minimum age is 17, but some companies may impose a higher bottom limit. Rental companies on St. Vincent include: **Avis** (tel: 456 4389); **Ben's Auto Rental** (tel: 456 2907); **David's Auto Clinic** (tel: 456 4026); **Kim's Rentals** (tel: 456 1884); **Rent and Drive** (tel: 457 5601). Drive on the left. Seatbelt laws exist and speed limits are 20mph (32kph), 15mph (24kph) for buses and trucks. Pay for fuel with cash.

Getting around
By air: St. Vincent and the Grenadines are not served by direct flights from either the UK or US. The islands can be reached by air via six main gateways—Barbados, Grenada, Martinique, St. Lucia, Puerto Rico and Trinidad—with connections to St. Vincent, Bequia, Canouan, Mustique and Union Island. International services to the gateway destinations are provided by **Air Canada, Air France, Air Jamaica, American Airlines, British Airways** and **BWIA,** while inter-island operators include **Air Martinique, American Eagle, Caribbean Star Airlines, Mustique Airways** and **St. Vincent Grenadines Air.**
By boat: Ferries leave St. Vincent every day to Bequia and three times a week to the Grenadines (Canouan, Mayreau and Union): they depart from Grenadines dock in Kingstown harbor and arrive at Port Elizabeth in Bequia 70–90 minutes later. **M.V. Admiral I** and **II** (tel: 458 3348) and

the *Gem Star* (tel: 458 3472) all serve
Bequia. The **MV** *Barracuda* (tel:
456 5180) mail boat travels south on
Mon and Thu at 10.30am, stopping at
Bequia, Canouan, Mayreau and
Union Island, returning Tue and Fri.
Yacht charter companies include on
St. Vincent: **Barefoot Yacht Charters**,
Blue Lagoon (tel: 456 9526); **Sunsail
Worldwide Sailing Ltd.** (tel: 458 4308).
Bequia: **Frangipani Yacht Service**
(tel: 458 3244). Union: **Anchorage
Yacht Club** (tel: 458 8221). Day sails
and boat trips to inaccessible beaches
can be arranged by **Baleine Tours**
(tel: 457 4089); **Fantasea Tours**
(tel: 457 4477); and **Union Island
Seckie Tours** (tel: 530 5913). Based in
Bequia, the traditional schooner
Friendship Rose (tel: 495 0886) takes
day trips to the southern Grenadines.
Union Island, contact **Captain Yannis**
(tel: 458 8513) or the **Anchorage Yacht
Club** (tel: 458 8221). Scuba diving:
Dive St. Vincent (tel: 457 4928); **Dive
Bequia** (tel: 458 3504); **Dive Fantasea**
(tel: 457 5560); **Grenadines Dive Union**
(tel: 458 8138).
By road: The roads of St. Vincent and
Bequia are rough and windy, but
most areas are accessible by bus
and taxi. Rates are fixed and a list of
these is available at the Department
of Tourism offices or at the airport.
If you wish to pre-arrange a taxi tour,
ask in your hotel or contact the **Curtis
Taxi** (tel: 448 3811) or **Sam Taxi Tours
and Yacht Agency** (tel: 456 4338;
Bequia: 458 3686).

Minibuses depart from Market
Square in Kingstown. They can be
hailed anywhere along the route,
which is indicated on the windshield.
Smaller islands have taxi-vans and
pick-up trucks with benches. Water
taxis are available from docks.

Bicycles can be rented from **Sailor's
Tours**, Kingston, St. Vincent (tel:
457 1712) and from **Handy Andy's
Kingston** (tel: 458 3722).

Sightseeing

Tours and trips can be organized
through **Archipelago Tours**, Kingston
(tel: 456 1686); **Barefoot Holidays**,
Blue Lagoon (tel: 450 0661); **Corea &
Co**, Halifax Street, Kingstown (tel:
456 1201); **Emerald Travel & Tours**,
Halifax Street (tel: 457 1996). Visitors

with a particular interest in eco tours
should contact **HazECO Tours** (tel: 457
8634). On Bequia: **Sun Tours**, Port
Elizabeth (tel: 458 3782). On Union:
Wind and Sea, Clifton (tel: 458 8678).

Tourist information

St. Vincent and the Grenadines
Department of Tourism, PO Box 834,
St. Vincent (tel: 457 1502). A tourist
information office is situated in Bay
Street, Kingstown; also at E. T. Joshua
Airport. Bequia's Tourism Bureau is
on the main dock, Port Elizabeth (tel:
458 3286); Union Island Tourist
Information (tel: 458 8350). In the
US contact 801 2nd Avenue, 21st
Floor, NY 10017 (tel: 212/687-4981,
800/729-1726). In the UK: St Vincent
and the Grenadines Tourist Office, 10
Kensington Court, London W8 5DL
(tel: 020 7937 6570).

THE LEEWARD ISLANDS

Anguilla (area code 264)

Car rental and driving

You need a valid driver's license for a
temporary license, on sale at rental
companies or at the police station in
The Valley. The minimum age for car
rental can be 18, 21 or 25. Rental
companies include **Carib Rent a Car**
(tel: 497 6020) and **Island Car Rentals**
(tel: 497 2723). Drive on the left. The
speed limit is 30mph (48kph).
Seatbelts are recommended. Smaller
gas stations prefer cash.

Getting around

By air: The nearest international airport gateways to Anguilla are Sint
Maarten, Antigua, St. Kitts, St.
Thomas (USVI) and San Juan, Puerto
Rico. Wallblake Airport is served by
local couriers including **Winair**, **Air
Anguilla**, **LIAT** and **American Eagle**.
By boat: Ferries between Blowing
Point and Marigot, Saint Martin,
leave every 30 minutes from 7.30; also
day trips to St. Barts. Ferry information (tel: 497 6665). Book boat trips
with **Island Yacht Charter Co. Ltd.**
(tel: 497 3743), who offer a choice of
full- or half-day charters, excursions
to St. Barts, snorkeling and fishing
trips. Scuba diving: **Shoal Bay Scuba
and Watersports** (tel: 497 4371) and

246

Anguillian Divers (tel: 497 4750).
By road: Use taxis (rates are set by the government) or rental cars. For larger groups, rental and taxi companies have minibuses. Bicycles can be rented through travel agents (see below) or **Exotic Plus** (tel: 497 8528).

Sightseeing
Tours are organized through your hotel, villa manager or travel agent. Taxi drivers will also arrange tours (fees are negotiable). Local tour operators include: **Malliouhana Travel & Tours**, Box 237, The Valley (tel: 497 2431 or 497 2348).

Tourist information
Anguilla Tourist Office, PO Box 1388, The Valley (tel: 497 2759; www.anguilla-vacation.com). In the US: 246 Central Avenue, White Plains, NY 10606 (tel: 914/287-2400). In the UK: Anguilla Tourist Office, 7a Crealock Street, London SW18 2BS (tel: 020 8871 0012).

Antigua and Barbuda
(area code 268)

Car rental and driving
You need to purchase a provisional license, issued on presentation of a valid driver's license. You have to be 18 to drive and some companies set a minimum age for renting a car (21 or 25), and include "extras" in their quotes. Companies include **Budget** (tel: 462 3009), **National** (tel: 462 2113), **Capital** (tel: 462 0863), **Dollar** (tel: 462 0362) and **Avis** (tel: 462 2847).

It is virtually impossible to rent a car during Carnival, so if you're going to need one then, book ahead. To rent a car in Barbuda, arrange it before leaving Antigua. Driving is on the left; the speed limit 40mph (64kph). Seatbelts are recommended and there are no drunk-driving laws. Fuel usually has to be paid for in cash.

Getting around
By air: Services from North America (via San Juan and other cities) are operated by **American Airlines**, **Air Canada** and **BWIA**; **British Airways** and **Virgin Atlantic** fly direct from the UK, as do various charter companies. Antigua is a hub for local island transport: **LIAT** has the greatest number of services. Other operators include **Caribbean Star**, **Air Caraïbe** and **Air St. Kitts-Nevis**. Small charter planes are available through **Carib Aviation**. **LIAT** has several flights a day to Barbuda.
By boat: Barbuda Express (tel: 560 7989) runs up to four passenger (no vehicles) services a day between St. Johns and Barbuda. The journey takes 90 minutes. They also offer day tours. Or visit on a day-sail excursion with swimming and snorkeling. Try **Kokomo Cat** (tel: 462 7245), **Horizon Yacht Charter** (tel: 562 4725), *The Jolly Roger* "pirate" ship (tel: 462 2064) or **Obsession Deep Sea Fishing Charters** (tel: 462 2824). Watersports operators include: **Kelly's Watersports Antigua** (tel: 462 8693) and **Sea Sports** (tel: 462 3355); for windsurfing, **Antigua Paddles** (tel: 463 1944) and scuba diving, **Dive Antigua** (tel: 462 3483) and, in English Harbour, **Dockyard Divers** (tel: 460 1178). To charter a yacht, contact **Nicholson Yacht Charters** (tel: 460 1530), **Sunsail** (tel: 463 6224) or **Sun Yacht Charters** (tel: 460 2615).
By road: Taxi rates are displayed at the airport and drivers should carry a rate card. Check whether they are quoting the fare in US or EC dollars. All taxi drivers double as guides and hotels may have a team who also take tours. Alternatively contact **Capital Car Rental** (tel: 462 0863). A private bus system runs in the south and east, with no timetables and few stops; this is the cheapest way around (ask in your hotel for the nearest stop). There are no buses in Dickenson Bay or Barbuda: it is best to rent a jeep.

Bicycles can be rented from **Sun Cycles** in Antigua (tel: 461 0324).

Sightseeing
Local tour operators will also fix island and inter-island excursions. Try **Antours** (tel: 462 4788), **Alexander Parrish** (tel: 462 0187) and **Kiskidee** (tel: 462 4801).

Tourist information
The Antigua and Barbuda Department of Tourism, PO Box 363, Government Complex, Queen Elizabeth Highway, St. John's (tel: 462

0480; www.antigua-barbuda.org).
Also at the airport. Try also Antigua
Hotel and Tourist Association, Island
New Gates Street, St. John's (tel: 462
0374). In the US: 25 SE 2nd Avenue,
Suite 300, Miami, FL 3313 (tel:
305/381-6762). In the UK: Antigua
and Barbuda Tourist Office, Antigua
House, 15 Thayer Street, London
W1M 5LD (tel: 020 7486 7073
www.nevisisland.com).

Montserrat (area code 664)
Because of the volcanic activity, most
car rental companies, watersports
operators and travel agents have
ceased trading for the time being.
Montserrat tourist information
(www.visitmontserrat.com)

Car rental and driving
There are no rental companies at the
airport, but it is normally possible to
arrange delivery to meet your flight.
Present a valid driver's license to purchase a temporary Montserrat driving
permit from Police Headquarters in
Salem (tel: 491 2555). Car rental
companies: **Be-Peep's** (tel: 491 3787);
Grant Enterprises R Trading (tel:
491 9654); **Neville Bradshaw Agencies**
(tel: 491 5270). Drive on the left; the
speed limit is 30mph (48kph).

Getting around
By air: A new international airport
opened at Geralds in July 2005. The
transcontinental gateway to
Montserrat is through Antigua or St.
Maarten and Carib Aviation provide
onward travel to the island, In addi-
tion there are regular helicopter
services to the island (daily except
Wed and Sun; see panel on page 79).
Caribbean Helicopters, Jolly Harbour,
Antigua (tel: 460 5900) offer
Montserrat volcano viewing tours.
By boat: For ferry services from
Antigua, see panel on page 79. On the
island, boat trips and sport fishing
excursions can be arranged through
Bruce Farara (tel: 491 8802) and **Danny
Sweeney** (tel: 491 5645).
By road: There are just a few minibuses, so rental cars and private taxis
are preferable. Taxi fares between
principal destinations are set by the
government; check whether the fare
quoted is in US or EC dollars.

Nevis (area code 869)

Car rental and driving
Driving is on the left. Watch out for
potholes and livestock on the roads.
A local temporary driving license
must be bought from the traffic
department, at the police station in
Charlestown. Rental companies will
pick you up from the airport or your
hotel and help with arrangements.
Most insist on a minimum age of 25.
Companies include: **Hertz** (tel: 469
7476); **Nevis Car Rental** (tel: 469 9837);
Noel's Car Rental (tel: 469 5199);
Stanley's Services (tel: 469 2597);
Striker's Car Rental (tel: 469 2654);
and **TDC Rentals** (tel: 469 494 5430).

Getting around
By air: International visitors can make
connections for Nevis from the
airport gateways of St. Kitts, Antigua,
Sint Maarten and San Juan, Puerto
Rico. Newcastle Airport is well
served by local carriers including
LIAT, **Winair American Eagle** and
Carib Aviation.
By boat: Several companies offer
inter-island ferry services between
Nevis and St. Kitts. There are up to
eight sailings in each direction daily
with a crossing time of 40–60 minutes.
For schedules see the latest edition of
the free *St. Kitts & Nevis Visitor* magazine. To charter a sea taxi from Oualie
Beach to Turtle Beach on St. Kitts contact **Nevis Watersports** (tel: 469 9690).
For a day's catamaran tour, with
snorkeling, contact **Leeward Island
Charters** (tel: 469 8494).
By road: Private minibuses operate a
round-island bus service in both
directions from Charlestown, leaving
from the main square. Taxis have set
rates, which are usually in EC dollars.
Payment, however, can be made in
either currency. You will need to add
25 percent between 11pm and 6am.
Taxi numbers include **Charlestown
Taxi** (tel: 469 5631).

Sightseeing and activities
Taxis provide half-day island tours,
or contact **All Seasons Streamline
Tours** (tel: 469 1138). For walking
tours to the rain forest contact **Top to
Bottom** (tel: 469 9080), and for a
walking tour of the plantations try

248

Eco-Rambles (tel: 469 2091). Horse-riding is available through **Hermitage Inn** (tel: 469 3477). **The Four Seasons Resort** has a golf course (tel: 469 1111). Watersports are available on Pinney's Beach and at Oualie Beach. Contact **Nevis Watersports** (tel: 469 9060), **Windsurfing Nevis** (tel: 469 9682) or **Scuba Safaris** (tel: 469 9518).

Tourist information
Local information is available from the Nevis Office of Tourism, Main Street, Charlestown (tel: 869 469 7550; www.nevisisland.com), near the waterfront ferry dock, and at the airport. In the UK: Nevis Island Estates, Elm House, Park Lane, Lower Froyle, Alton, Hampshire, GU34 4LT (tel: 01420 520810).

St. Kitts (area code 869)

Car rental and driving
Purchase local driving licenses from the traffic department at the fire station in Basseterre (tel: 465 2241). Regulations and prices as for Nevis. Rental companies: **Avis** (tel: 465 6507); **Caines Rent-a-Car** (tel: 465 2366); **Courtesy Rent a Car** (tel: 465 7804); **Delisle Walwyn** (tel: 465 8449); **TDCThrifty Rentals Ltd.** (tel: 465 2991).

Getting around
By air: Robert Llewelyn Bradshaw Airport in St. Kitts is accessible via charter flights from Europe and North America. For scheduled airline services change in Antigua or Sint Maarten, or link with **American Eagle** from San Juan, Puerto Rico. St. Kitts is well served by local carriers (see Nevis opposite).
By boat: There are daily ferry services between St. Kitts and Nevis (see the latest edition of *St. Kitts and Nevis Visitor* magazine) and you can also charter a sea taxi from Turtle Beach on the south peninsula for the 10-minute crossing to Nevis. **Leeward Island Charters** (tel: 465 7474) offer day sail cruises to Nevis aboard sleek 65ft (20m) catamarans with time for snorkeling and lunch, as well as deep-sea fishing expeditions. Day sails are also available from **Blue Water**

Safaris (tel: 466 4933).
By road: On St. Kitts privately run minibuses make regular unscheduled trips along the main coastal roads, starting at the ferry terminal on the waterfront in Basseterre. Taxis have set rates. Add 25 percent between 11pm and 6am. Try **St. Kitts Taxi Association** (tel: 465 4253) and the **Circus Taxi Stand** (tel: 465 3006).

Sightseeing and activities
Island tours can be arranged through taxi drivers and tour companies: **Kantours** (tel: 465 2098); **TDC Flamboyant Tours** (tel: 465 6170); and **Tropical Tours** (tel: 465 4167). An island tour takes 3–4 hours. For half- or full-day walking tours to the rain forest, contact **Greg's Safaris** (tel: 465 4121); for walks into the crater of Mount Liamuiga, **Kriss Tours** (tel: 465 4042). Horse-riding is available through **Trinity Stables** in Frigate Bay (tel: 465 3226). For golf **The St. Kitt's Royal Golf Club** (tel: 466 2700) was refurbished and expanded in 2004. For windsurfing, jet skis and snorkeling, contact **Mr X Watersports** (tel: 465 0673), which you will find next to the Monkey Bar on Frigate Bay. Scuba operators include **Pro Divers** (tel: 466 3483) at Turtle Beach and **Dive St. Kitts** (tel: 465 1189) at Bird Rock.

Tourist information
The St. Kitts Tourism Authority office is in the Pelican Mall (PO Box 132), Bay Road, Basseterre (tel: 465 4040; www.stkitts-tourism.com). Tourist information can also be found at the airport. In the US: Suite 5, 414 East 75th Street, New York, NY 10021 (tel: 212/535-1234) In the UK: 10 Kensington Court, London W8 5DL (tel: 020 7376 0881).

THE VIRGIN ISLANDS

British Virgin Islands (area code 284)

Car rental and driving
A temporary BVI license must be purchased, issued on presentation of a current foreign license (obtained from rental companies). The driver's minimum age is 25. Cars can be rented in Tortola, from: **Alphonso Car**

249

Rentals (tel: 494 8746); **Avis** (tel: 494 3322); **Dollar** (tel: 494 6093); **Hertz** in Road Town (tel: 494 6228); **National** (tel: 494 3194). In Virgin Gorda, **L & S Jeep Rental** (tel: 495 5297). Driving is on the left and the speed limit is 40mph (64kph) but 20mph (32kph) in residential areas. Most cars are left-hand drive. Filling stations take credit cards. Seatbelts are compulsory. You can usually share someone else's taxi in Virgin Gorda.

Getting around

By air: There are airports on Tortola and Virgin Gorda, and connections from Europe are via Antigua or San Juan, from the US via San Juan or St. Thomas (and then by ferry). Tortola is linked to the USVI by **American Eagle**, **LIAT** and **Winair** among others, and all three also fly down to the Eastern Caribbean. **Clair Aero Services** (tel: 495 2271) fly from Tortola to Anegada four days a week. A small plane can also be chartered through **Fly BVI** (tel: 495 1747).

By boat: There are daily passenger launches between Tortola, Virgin Gorda, Jost Van Dyke, St. Thomas and St. John. Ferries from Tortola to St. Thomas and St. John are operated by **Native Son** (tel: 495 4617), **Smith's Ferry Services** (tel: 495 4495), **Inter Island Boat Services** (tel: 495 4166). From Tortola to Peter Island: **Peter Island Ferry** (tel: 495 2000); from Tortola to Virgin Gorda: **Speedy's** (tel: 495 5240), **Smith's Ferry Services** (see above) and **North Sound Express** (tel: 495 2138). From Virgin Gorda to St. Thomas, **Speedy's** (see above) and **Native Son** (see above). From Tortola to Jost Van Dyke: **New Horizon Ferry Service** (tel: 495 9278). Bareboats can be rented for cruises; local boats for special tours. Contact: **The Moorings**, Road Town (tel: 494 2332), **Sunsail**, West End (tel: 495 4740). Day sails can be arranged through **White Squall II** (tel: 494 2564), **Kuralu** (tel: 495 4381) and **Pentesilea II** (tel: 496 8048). In Virgin Gorda contact **Spice Charters** (tel: 496 6633) or **Spirit of Anegada Day Sails** (tel: 496 6825).

Sightseeing and activities

Guided tours: **BVI Taxi Association** (tel: 494 2322) and **Travel Plan Tours** (tel: 494 2872). On Virgin Gorda contact **Mahogany Taxi Service** (tel: 495 5469), which organizes tours for a minimum of two people. Scuba diving companies include **UBS Dive Center** (tel: 494 0024) and in Jost Van Dyke, **Jost Van Dyke Watersports** (tel: 495 0271). In Virgin Gorda try **Dive BVI** (tel: 495 5513). For windsurfing off Tortola contact **Boardsailing BVI** (tel: 495 2447).

Tourist information

BVI Tourist Board (www.bvitourism.com), 2nd floor, Akara Building, DeCastro Street, Road Town, Tortola (tel: 494 3134) and in Virgin Gorda Yacht Harbour (tel: 495 5181). In the US: 1270 Broadway, Suite 705, New York, NY 10001 (tel: 212/696-0400, 800/835-8530). In the UK: BVI Tourist Board, 15 Upper Grosvenor Street, London W1K 7JP (tel: 020 7355 9585).

US Virgin Islands
(area code 340)

St. Croix

Car rental and driving

The minimum age is 18; 25 with some companies. A full driver's license will suffice. Companies include: **Budget** (tel: 778 9636),**Avis Car Rental Henry Rolson Airport** (tel: 778 9355); **Hertz** (tel: 778 1402), **Judy of Croix** (tel: 773 1232); **Thrifty** (tel: 773 7200). Drive on the left. The speed limit is 55mph (88kph). Drunk driving and seatbelt laws are strictly enforced. Fuel is inexpensive; credit cards accepted.

Getting around

By air: International carriers serving the USVI are **American, Continental, Delta, United** and **US Air**. Local carriers include **Air Sunshine, American Eagle, Cape Air**, and **LIAT**. **Seabourne Aviation** (tel: 773 6442) operate a daily seaplane service linking Christiansted with St. Thomas. The first flight is 6.50am from St. Croix (Sun 8.15am) and the last is at 5.40pm.

By boat: For day sails and tours of Buck Island, contact **Bilinda Charters** (tel: 773 1641); **Diva** (tel: 778 4675); **Teroro II** (tel: 773 3161). For windsurfing tuition and rentals, wave runners, sea kayaking and parasailing contact **St. Croix Watersports** (tel: 773 7060). For scuba diving in Christiansted try **Scubawest** (tel: 800 352 0107) and **VI Divers** (tel: 773 6045) in Frederiksted.

By road: Taxi vans can be called from your hotel or found at the airport and, when cruise ships are in, at the pier in Frederiksted. The **St. Croix Taxi Association** (tel: 778 1088) runs taxi vans on the main roads from Christiansted to Frederiksted; try also **Cruzan Taxi Association** (tel: 773 6388) and **Caribbean Taxi and Tours** (tel: 773 9799).

Sightseeing and activities
Island bus tours are offered by **St. Croix Transit Tours** (tel: 772 3333) and **St. Croix Safari Tours** (tel: 773 6700). Horseback tours are run by **Paul and Jill's Equestrian Stable** (tel: 772 2880). For guided hikes in the scenic East End or Annaly Bay, contact **Caribbean Adventure Tours** (tel: 778 1522). For bicycling contact **Endurance Sports** (tel: 719 1990) in Sunny Isle Shopping Center. For springtime whale-watching excursions (Feb–Mar), contact the **Environmental Association of St. Thomas-St. John** (tel: 774 8816).

Tourist information
The US Virgin Islands Division of Tourism (www.usvitourism.vi) has an office at 41a Queen Cross Street (Box 4538), Christiansted, St. Croix 00822 (tel: 773 0495). St. Croix Hotel and Tourism Association, PO Box 24238 (tel: 773 7117 or 800/542 2026). In the US: 1270 Avenue of the Americas, Suite 2108, New York, NY 10020 (tel: 800/372-USVI). In the UK: Molasses House, Clove Hitch Quay, Plantation Wharf, London SW11 3TN (tel: 020 7978 5262).

St. Thomas and St. John

Car rental and driving
You need a valid driver's license; the minimum age for drivers is 18 but in general rental companies prefer you to be at least 25. On St. Thomas: **Avis** at Cyril E. King Airport (tel: 774 1468); **Budget** (tel: 776 5774); **E-Z Car** (tel: 775 6255); **Dependable** (tel: 774 2253);

Discount (tel: 715 0029); **Tri-Island** (tel: 776 2879). On St. John: **C & C Rental** (tel: 693 8164); **Hertz** (tel: 693 7580); **St. John Car Rental** (tel: 776 6103). Driving is on the left. Wearing a seatbelt is compulsory and the drunk-driving laws are enforced. The speed limit is 35mph (56kph). Credit cards are accepted; pay before filling up.

Getting around
By air: Services from the US include **American Airlines**, **Delta**, **United** and many charter airlines. Some of these also make the link to St. Croix, as does **American Eagle** or the seaplane service (tel: 773 6442). From Europe best connections are made via Antigua or San Juan, Puerto Rico. Links to the rest of the Caribbean are made by **Air Sunshine**, **Cape Air** and **LIAT**, or try **Air Centre Helicopters** (tel: 775 7335).

251

By boat: There are two ferry routes between the islands: Charlotte Amalie to Cruz Bay (six a day) and Red Hook to Cruz Bay (daily, every hour: 6.30am, 7.30am, 8am–midnight). For more details, contact **Transportation Services** (tel: 776 6282).

Ferries link St. Thomas and the British Virgin Islands (Tortola, Virgin Gorda, and Jost Van Dyke); proof of citizenship is required to embark here. Ferries from Red Hook (St. Thomas) to Jost Van Dyke, stopping en route at Cruz Bay (St. John), take an hour (contact **Inter Island Boat Services** tel: 776 6597). Ferries from Charlotte Amalie (St. Thomas) to Tortola take 45 minutes to the West End or an hour and a half to Road Town; contact **Native Son** (tel: 774 8685) or **Smith's Ferry** (tel: 775 7292). There are ferries from Red Hook (St. Thomas) to West End (Tortola), 30 minutes (contact Native Son or Smith's Ferry); and from Cruz Bay (St. John) to West End (Tortola), 30 minutes (contact Inter Island). Ferries also leave from Charlotte Amalie and Red Hook for Virgin Gorda. For direct Red Hook–Virgin Gorda services, contact Inter Island or Transportation Services; for Charlotte Amalie–Tortola–Virgin Gorda, contact Smith's Ferry.

Yachts can be chartered with or without a crew, usually through a broker. Check that the vessel is a member of the VI Charter Yacht League (tel: 774 3944), the local professional association of crewed charter boats. A full list of brokers is available from the tourist office.

Powerboats with or without captains can be rented from numerous companies. Contact **Nauti Nymph** (tel: 775 5066) or **See and Ski** (tel: 775 6265). You can also book day sails, submarine rides or short fishing excursions with **Fantasy** (tel: 775 5652), **Jester** (tel: 775 2044)) or **Island Girl** (tel: 775 5055). **Atlantis Submarine** (tel: 776 5650) is based in Havensight Mall. Scuba operators include **Aqua Action Dive Center** (tel: 775 6285) and **Chris Sawyer** (tel: 777 7804). For scuba diving contact **Watersports Low Key** (tel: 693 8999).
By road: On St. Thomas, taxis are usually found at the ferry, airport, shopping and resort areas, opposite Emancipation Park, and along the waterfront in Charlotte Amalie. In St. John they tend to cluster around Cruz Bay Dock, but can be hailed anywhere. Taxi fares are fixed and prices are published at the airport and hotels. St. Thomas taxis are usually estates or minivans taking five or six passengers; on St. John open safari buses serve as taxis. Public buses on St. Thomas are irregular, although there is a country bus service between Red Hook and Charlotte Amalie. An hourly bus service begins at 5.30am from town and the last one leaves Red Hook around 8.30pm. Open-air safari buses operated by the VI Taxi Commission run between Charlotte Amalie and Red Hook, and Charlotte Amalie and Havensight Mall. The service is available Mon–Fri 12.15–5.15pm (every 15 min).

Sightseeing
St. Thomas: tours are mainly conducted in minivans or safari buses. The **Virgin Islands Taxi Association City-Island Tour** (tel: 774 4550) offers a variety of island tours; **Tropic Tours** (tel: 774 1855) runs half-day tours, which includes shopping and sightseeing, by bus.

St. John: the **St. John National Park Visitor Centre**, Cruz Bay (tel: 776 6201) does guided tours on and

offshore; a **St. John Taxi Services Inc** (tel: 693 7530) island tour covers Cruz Bay, Annaberg Plantation and the north coast beaches.

Tourist information
The USVI Division of Tourism can be contacted at PO Box 6400, Charlotte Amalie (tel: 774 8784) and at P.O. Box 200, Cruz Bay, St. John (tel: 776 6450). Visitor centers in Charlotte Amalie are opposite Emancipation Park and at Havensight Mall. The National Park Service has visitor centers at the ferry areas on St. Thomas (Red Hook) and St. John (Cruz Bay). In the US: 1270 Avenue of the Americas, Suite 2108, New York, NY 10020 (tel: 800/372-USVI). In the UK: Molasses House, Clove Hitch Quay, Plantation Wharf, London SW11 3TN (tel: 020 7978 5262).

FRENCH ANTILLES

Guadeloupe (area code 590)

Car rental and driving
Normal driver's licenses are valid for up to 20 days, after which an international one is needed. The minimum driving age is usually 18. Cars can be rented at the airport from: **Avis** (tel: 0590 21 13 54), **Budget** (tel: 0590 21 13 48); **Hertz** (tel: 0590 21 13 46); **Jumbo Car** Pôles Caraïbes Airport (tel: 0590 2113 50); **Europcar** Pointe à Pitre (tel: 0590 21 13 52), **Karukéra Car** (tel: 0590 21 13 79); **Citer** (tel: 83 22 88); **Pop's Car** (tel: 0590 21 13 56); **Pro Rent** (tel: 0590 26 73 44);and **Soltour** (tel: 0590 21 13 77). Car rental companies have desks at the airport, hotels and in Pointe-à-Pitre and Basse-Terre. Drive on the right; seatbelt and drunk-driving laws are enforced. Most filling stations take credit cards.

Getting around
By air: Pôle Caraïbes international airport outside Pointe-à-Pitre is the main airport gateway to Guadeloupe. It is served by **American Airlines**, **Air Canada**, **Air France** and **Air Caraïbes** from North America, and by **Air France**, **Corsair** and **Air Caraïbes** from Europe. Numerous local airlines provide inter-island services including **Air Caraïbes** and **Air Antilles** for

the other French islands and a few other stops, plus the Caribbean-wide services of **LIAT, Winair and BWIA**. Helicopter tours are offered by **Azur Aéro Services** (tel: 0590 94 86 77) and sightseeing flights are by **Alpha Aviation** (tel: 0590 88 70 10).

By boat: A number of operators serve the offshore islands. For daily services to Marie-Galante (Grand Bourg) from Pointe-à-Pitre, contact **Brudey Frères** (tel: 0590 90 04 48) or take the fast catamaran service provided by **Express des Iles** (tel: 0825 42 04 05). Exprss des Iles also runs a ferry service to Marie Galante's second town St. Louis.. For Les Saintes, both **Brudey Frères** and **Express des Iles** provide a daily service to Terre-de-Haut from Pointe-à-Pitre; while **CTM Deher** (tel: 0590 23 81 71) makes daily crossings to Terre-de-Haut from Trois-Rivières on the east coast of Basse-Terre.

As well as trips to the out islands, **Express des Iles** also link Pointe-à-Pitre with Martinique, Dominica and St. Lucia. All times and prices are subject to change, so it is wise to check before traveling. There are, however, no ferries to St. Barts or Saint-Martin. Safe anchorages and marinas, for ferries and yachts in Grande-Terre, are at Marina du Bas-du-Fort, Gosier and Marina de St-François (in the heart of town); or Marina de Rivière Sens, Basse-Terre.

Numerous companies around the Bas-du-Fort marina rent out bareboat or crewed yachts and motorboats, including **Star Voyages Antilles** (tel: UK 0142 561526), **Sun Sail** (tel: 90 82 80) and **Tropical Yacht Services** (tel: 90 84 52).

By road: Taxi fares are set by the government and prices are posted at the airport, taxi stands and major hotels. Taxi stands in Pointe-à-Pitre are on boulevard Faidherbe et Chanzy, rue Achille René Boisneuf, rue Alexandre Isaac, in front of the tourist office or contact Taxi Caraïbes Services (tel: 0690 42 30 98 mobile). In Basse-Terre the taxi stand on Cours Nolivos (tel: 0590 81 79 70) offers tours at set fares; the tourist office or your hotel can arrange for an English-speaking driver.

A public bus service operates

253

CONVERSION CHARTS

FROM	TO	MULTIPLY BY
Inches	Centimeters	2.54
Centimeters	Inches	0.3937
Feet	Meters	0.3048
Meters	Feet	3.2810
Yards	Meters	0.9144
Meters	Yards	1.0940
Miles	Kilometers	1.6090
Kilometers	Miles	0.6214
Acres	Hectares	0.4047
Hectares	Acres	2.4710
Gallons	Liters	4.5460
Liters	Gallons	0.2200
Ounces	Grams	28.35
Grams	Ounces	0.0353
Pounds	Grams	453.6
Grams	Pounds	0.0022
Pounds	Kilograms	0.4536
Kilograms	Pounds	2.205
Tons	Tonnes	1.0160
Tonnes	Tons	0.9842

MEN'S SUITS							
UK	36	38	40	42	44	46	48
Rest of Europe	46	48	50	52	54	56	58
US	36	38	40	42	44	46	48

DRESS SIZES						
UK	8	10	12	14	16	18
France	36	38	40	42	44	46
Italy	38	40	42	44	46	48
Rest of Europe	34	36	38	40	42	44
US	6	8	10	12	14	16

MEN'S SHIRTS						
UK	14	14.5	15	15.5	16	16.5	17
Rest of Europe	36	37	38 39/40 41	42	43
US	14	14.5	15	15.5	16	16.5	17

MEN'S SHOES						
UK	7	7.5	8.5	9.5	10.5	11
Rest of Europe	41	42	43	44	45	46
US	8	8.5	9.5	10.5	11.5	12

WOMEN'S SHOES						
UK	4.5	5	5.5	6	6.5	7
Rest of Europe	38	38	39	39	40	41
US	6	6.5	7	7.5	8	8.5

around the island, 5am–6pm, stopping at *arrêtbus* signs, or wherever you hail it. Pay when you get off. The bus stations in Pointe-à-Pitre, La Darse, Mortenol, and Bergevin, serve different parts of the island. Fares are posted at the station.

Scooter rentals are widely available in the main towns and coastal resorts. Bicycles are also popular and several companies offer mountain bicycle tours (see below) as well as rentals. Just remember that Grande-Terre is rather flat, while Basse-Terre is mountainous.

Sightseeing and activities
Ask the tourist offices for English-speaking guides when booking a tour. Pick-ups are usually from the hotels; lunch and guide services are usually included in the price. Local tour operators include **Selectour Navitour** (tel: 0590 38 34 74) and **Nouvelles Frontières** (tel: 0590 90 36 36). Sea excursions, particularly to the mangrove reserve, can be organized by companies around Bas-du-Fort Marina, or contact the **King Papyrus** bateau-mouche (tel: 0590 90 92 98), which departs from the Marina Pointe-à-Pitre for trips to the Réserve Naturelle du Grand Cul de Sac Marin marine preserve. Day sails can be arranged through **Les Heures Saines** (tel: 0590 98 86 63), who also offer whale-watching excursions aboard their catamaran based at Rocher de Malendure, Pigeon-Bouillante on the west coast of Basse-Terre. This is in the Réserve Cousteau, a must for divers, and **Heures Saines**' dives (tel: 98 86 63) organizes both day and night dives. Other dive operators include **Aux Aquanautes Antillais** (tel: 0590 98 87 30), **CIP Bouillante** (tel: 98 81 72) and **Archipel Plongée Bouillante** (tel: 0590 98 93 93).

Hiking in the national park and up the Soufrière volcano can be arranged through **Vert Intense** (tel: 0590 55 40 47). There are various adventure tour operators offering mountain bicycling, hiking, sea kayaking and canyoning experiences: these include **Parfum d'Aventure** (tel: 0590 88 47 62), **Point Bleu Soleil** (Gourbeyre (tel: 0590 81 42 79) and Petit-Canal (tel- 0590 83 66 24); or **Vert**

Intense (see above). Watersports are equally well catered for with (among others) jet ski excursions arranged by **Aventures des Iles** (tel: 0590 85 02 77), windsurfing with the **Arawak Surf Club** (tel: 0590 23 27 91), and waterskiing with **AGSN** (tel: 0590 26 17 47).

Tourist information
www.lesilesdeguadeloupe.com
Office Départemental du Tourisme de la Guadeloupe, 5 square de la Banque, 97110 Pointe-à-Pitre Cédex (Guadeloupe) (tel: 0590 82 09 30).
Office du Tourisme de Basse-Terre, Hoel de Ville, Place de la Mairie, 97100 Basse-Terre (tel: 0590 80 56 48);
Office du Tourisme de St-François, Hotel de Ville, Place de la Mairie, 97118 St-François (tel: 0590 88 53 18) and in Bouillante (tel: 0590 98 73 48).
French Government Tourist Office US: 444 Madison Avenue, New York, NY 10022 (tel: 212/838-7800).
UK: 178 Piccadilly, London W1V 0AL (tel: 09068 224 123). There is a tourist information booth at the airport.

Martinique (area code 596)

Car rental and driving
Drivers must be at least 21 and hold a full license; after 20 days you'll need an International Driver's Permit. Companies include: **Avis** (airport tel: 0596 66 04 38); **Budget** (Fort-de-France tel: 0596 70 22 75, airport tel: 0596 42 16 79); **Europcar** (airport tel: 0596 42 42 42); **Hertz** (tel: airport 0596 65 10 10); **Jumbo/Thrifty** (Pointe du Bout tel: 0596 66 11 55, Ste-Anne tel: 0596 76 80 82, airport tel: 0596 42 16 99); **National/Citer/Alamo** (tel: 0596 42 16 82); **Pop's Car** airport (tel: 0596 42 16 84); and **Euradom** (airport tel: 0596 60 10 93).
The speed limits are 62mph (100kph) on the highway and 31mph (50kph) in town. Seatbelts are mandatory; drunk-driving is strictly penalized.

Getting around
By air: From Europe, **Air France** and **Air Caraïbes** and **Corsair** fly transatlantic from France into Lamentin Airport outside Fort-de-France. From the US, **Air France** fly several times a week from Miami, and there are more frequent connections from San Juan,

254

Puerto Rico. Local carriers include **American Eagle** (out of Puerto Rico offering numerous connections with flights to and from the US mainland), **Air Caraïbes**, **Take Airlines** and **LIAT**. Sightseeing flights are offered by **Alizés Air Services**, Ste-Anne (tel: 0596 25 26 98).

By boat: A fast catamaran links Martinique with Guadeloupe and the Windward Islands of Dominica and St. Lucia. It is operated by **Express des Iles**, Terminal Inter-Iles, quai Ouest, Fort-de-France (tel: 0596 63 32 75). Reservations through local travel agents. Though inexpensive, the crossings can be pretty rough. Local ferries ply Fort-de-France bay, taking passengers from quai Desnambuc on the central waterfront across to the beaches of Pointe de Bout, Anse Mitan and Anse à l'Ane.

By road: Taxis can be found mainly at the airport, at taxi ranks in Fort-de-France and at major hotels. For **Coopérative Martinique Taxis** call 0596 63 63 62. Fares are regulated by the government (a list is available at the airport) and are expensive, especially at night when a 40 percent surcharge is added. Private taxis can be found at the Savane, along boulevard General de Gaulle and place Clemenceau in Fort-de-France. You can also travel by bus or shared taxi: the main terminal to catch either is at Pointe-Simon, on the seafront in Fort-de-France, otherwise try around boulevard General de Gaulle. Buses are run privately, from 5am to 8pm, and leave when they're full. Shout *arrêt* to stop one. There is also an inter-urban bus network. Shared taxis (*taxi collectif* or *taxicos*) start early and run until 6pm with fixed routes. Most start at Pointe-Simon and serve all the *communes*.

Motorscooters and bicycles can be rented from agencies in all the main tourist resorts. **Locobikes** (tel: 0596 63 33 05), offers 18-speed mountain bicycles (*vélo tout terrain*), as do **Centrale du Cycle Lamentin** (tel: 0596 50 28 54) and excursion specialists **Sud Loisirs** (tel: 0596 76 81 82). The **Parc Naturel Regional de la Martinique** (tel: 0596 73 19 30) has designated bicycle routes off the beaten track and organizes bicycle and walking tours.

Sightseeing and activities

The following local agents will find you guided tours by car or bus, trips on sailing boats and cruise ships, excursions in glass-bottom boats and trips to Dominica, St. Lucia and the Grenadines: **Caribtours** (tel: 0596 50 93 52); **Madinina Tours** (tel: 0596 70 65 25). **Azimut** (tel: 0596 70 07 00) offers a guided tour of Fort-de-France. For hiking, contact the **Bureau de la Randonnée** (tel: 0596 78 30 77) or **Aventures Tropicales** (tel: 0596 64 58 49), who also organize adventurous pursuits from jeep safaris and mountain bicycling to canyoning. Scuba operators include: **Planète Bleue**, Pointe du Bout (tel: 0596 66 08 79) and **Sub Diamond Rock** (tel: 0596 76 21 70). Windsurfing equipment can be rented from the east coast centers of **Club Nautique du Vauclin** (tel: 74 50 83) and the **Club Nautique du Marin** (tel: 74 92 48). More general watersports operators include **Alizé Fun** in Ste-Anne (tel: 74 71 58). Charter sailing boats can be rented through **The Moorings** (tel: 74 75 39) and **Star Voyage** (tel: 66 00 72).

Tourist information

Comité Martinique du Tourism, Imm. Le Beaupre Pointe de Jaham, 97276 Schoeler CEDEX (tel: 0596 61 61 77; www.martinique.org). There are information offices on the waterfront and at the airport. In the US contact: The French Government Tourist Office, 444 Madison Avenue, 16th Floor, New York, NY 10022 (tel: 212/838-7800). In the UK: French Government Office, 178 Piccadilly, London W1V 0AL (tel: 020 7399 3500/09068 244 123).

St. Barthélemy (area code 590)

Car rental and driving

Cars can be rented at the airport: in peak season there may be a three-day minimum. Some hotels have their own car fleets and many offer 24-hour emergency road service. **Avis** (tel: 0590 27 71 43), **Budget** (tel: 0590 27 66 30), and **Europcar** Quartier du Roy (tel: 059027 79 16). There are two filling stations, one near the airport (credit card-operated self-service pumps, open 24 hours, closed Sun),

255

the other in Lorient (closed Thu, Sat afternoon and Sun).

Getting around

By air: St. Barts' tiny airport at St. Jean can only handle small planes, so the main international gateway to the island is Juliana Airport on neighboring Sint Maarten. **Air Caraïbes** shuttles back and forth between St. Barts and Sint Maarten and, together with **Saint-Barth Commuter**, offers services to French Saint-Martin. **Winair** makes a twice-weekly flight to Anguilla, and **Air St. Thomas** links the island to St. Thomas, USVI. Helicopter tours can be arranged with **Caribbean Helicopters Ltd.**, Antigua (tel: 268/460-5900).

By boat: St. Barts is linked to the neighboring island of Sint Maarten/Saint-Martin by regular high-speed ferry services. For information contact **The Edge** (tel: 599/544 2640), which plies the route between Philipsburg and Gustavia; while **Voyager** (tel: 27 54 10) serves Baie Nettlé and Philipsburg from Gustavia. **HC Katia** (tel 0590 27 89 00) operates a 35-minute service from Pointe Blanche Sint Maarten. **Marine Service** (tel: 0590 27 70 34) run day trips around St. Barts and cruises to Saint-Martin, Anguilla, Saba and the Virgin Islands on their four-cabin catamaran; also rent out powerboats; **Océan Must** (tel: 0590 27 62 25) operates day sails around St. Barts and to other neighboring islands.

By road: There are taxi stands at the airport and in Gustavia on rue de la République. Cabs are unmetered, so you may be charged more if you stop on the way. Minibuses and taxis do island tours. Radio cabs can be called on 0590 27 66 31 or 0590 27 75 81. Fares are 50 percent higher after 8pm. Motorcycles can be rented near the airport and in Gustavia (helmet compulsory). Try **Beranger Rental** (tel: 0590 27 89 00) and **Denis Dufau** (tel: 0590 27 54 83).

Sightseeing and activities

Arrang tours through your hotel, the tourist office or taxi operators, including **JC Taxi** (tel: 0590 49 02 97) and **Florian Laplace** (tel: 0590 27 63 58). Local operators include **St. Barth**

Tours and Travel (tel: 0590 27 60 33). Scuba diving: **Ouanalao Dive Grand Cul de Sac** (tel: 0590 63 74 34) and **Plongée Caraïbe** (tel: 0590 27 55 94). **Windwave Power** (tel: 0590 27 82 57) offers watersport equipment rentals on Grand Cul de Sac beach.

Tourist information

The Office du Tourisme de Saint Barthélemy, quai du Général de Gaulle, Gustavia (tel: 27 87 27). For the US and UK see Guadeloupe.

Saint-Martin/Sint Maarten
(area code French side, 0590 plus six digits; Dutch side, 599 plus seven digits)

Car rental and driving

Your own driver's license is sufficient to rent a car on both sides: you must be at least 25. Cars can be rented at Juliana Airport. Companies include: **Avis** (tel: 0590 87 50 60 or 545 2316); **Budget** (tel: 0590 87 21 91 or 545 4030); **Continental** (tel: 0590 87 77 64); **Esperance** (tel: 0590 87 51 09); **Jumbo Sandy Ground** (tel: 0590 87 88 25); **National/Europcar** Anse Marigot (tel: 0590 27 32 80 or Airport 0590 554 2066); **Sandy G Car Rental** (tel: 0590 87 88 25). Motorcycles and scooters are also widely available.

Driving is on the right and road signs are international. Speed limits are 50mph (80kph) outside the towns, 19mph (30kph) in towns; drunk-driving carries fines, as do illegal parking, speeding and running traffic lights; seatbelts should be worn and fuel is paid for in cash.

Getting around

By air: Sint Maarten/Saint-Martin is is well served by international and local carriers. Juliana Airport on the Dutch side receives international air traffic including **American Airlines**, **Continental Airlines** and **Corsair** flights from North America, and **Air France** and **KLM** flights from Europe. **Air Antilles** and **Air Caraïbes** fly into Grand Case Airport on the French side as well as Juliana; **Winair** operates out of Juliana. Other local carriers include **BWIA** and **LIAT**. **Heli-Inter Caraïbes** (tel: 0590 87 35 88) run sightseeing excursions and act as taxis or as emergency services.

By boat: There are anchorages around the island and a flourishing yachting scene. For trips to the neighboring French island of St. Barts or Saba, contact **The Edge**, Philipsburg (tel: 0590 544 2640) or **Voyager** (Baie Nettlé tel: 0590 87 10 68, Philipsburg tel: 542 4096). You will need a form of identification with a photograph and there is a departure tax.

Companies chartering boats, with or without a skipper, include: **The Moorings** (tel: 0590 87 49 47) in Oyster Pond, and **Sunsail** (tel: 0590 29 50 50). Day trips by sail or motorboat to nearby islands or coves, including Anguilla, are organized from the Dutch side aboard *Blue Beard* (tel: 557 5935), **Celine** (tel: 545 3961) and *Sualiga* (tel: 542 2167). From the French side, sailing excursions are organized through **Saint Martin Evasion** (tel: 0590 87 13 60), **Rising Sun Tours** (tel: 0590 87 14 22), **Any Way Marine** (tel: 0590 87 91 41) and **Scoobidoo** (tel: 0590 52 02 53). General watersports operators offering equipment rentals include **Aquamania Adventures** (tel: 544 2640), **Kakao Watersports** in Baie Orientale (tel: 0590 27 07 48) and nearby **Kontiki Watersports** (tel: 0590 87 46 89). Scuba diving: **Ocean Explorers** (tel: 544 52 52) and **Scuba Fun** in Anse Marcel (tel: 0590 87 36 13).

By road: Taxi rates across the island are fixed and standardized—you can get a list from the tourist offices and rates are posted at the airport. Call: 0590 87 56 54 (Marigot); 545 4317 (Juliana Airport); and 542 2359 (Philipsburg). Authorized taxis display stickers of the Sint Maarten Taxi Association. Buses run between 7am and 7pm from Philipsburg through Cole Bay to Marigot.

Sightseeing
For sightseeing, contact **Island Reps Tours** (tel: 545 2392), **Rising Sun Tours** (tel: 544 2855 or 87 14 22), **St. Maarten Sightseeing** (tel: 545 3921) and **Dutch Tours** (tel: 542 3316).

Tourist information
Dutch side: Sint Maarten Tourist Bureau, W. G. Buncamper Road 33, Philipsburg, Sint Maarten (tel:

542 2337). French side: Office du Tourisme de Saint-Martin, Route de Sandy Ground, 97150 Saint-Martin (tel: 0590 87 57 21; www.st-martin .org), on the waterfront in Marigot. In the US: St. Martin Tourist Office, 675 Third Avenue, Suite 1807, New York, NY 10017 (tel: 646/227-9440) In the UK: the Maison de la France, 178 Piccadilly, London W1V 0AL (tel: 020 7399 3500).

NETHERLANDS ANTILLES

Aruba (area code 297)

Car rental and driving
You need either a valid national or international license; age range policies may vary with different companies. All companies include unlimited mileage, but not insurance. Try **Avis** (tel: Oranjestad 582 7202; airport 582 5496), **Budget** (tel: 582 8600; airport 582 5423), **Dollar** (tel: airport 588 7570; Gasparito 586 0505), **Hertz** (tel: 582 1845; airport 588 7570), **Thrifty** (tel: 585 5300), **Toyota Rent-a-Car** (tel: 583 4832; airport 583 4902). Main roads are in good condition, but most attractions are down dirt roads: four-wheel-drive vehicles are recommended. Drive on the right. Road signs are international. Speed limit in towns is 25mph (40kph), 37mph (60kph) out of town.

Getting around
By air: Aruba is well-served by North American carriers. Those offering direct flights from US destinations include **American Airlines**, **Delta Continental**, **United** and **US Airways**; **Air Canada** also flies direct; and there are a number of charter flights. There are numerous air services to destinations throughout South America with airlines including Varig, Avianca and KLM. From Europe, **KLM** provides a service from Amsterdam.

By boat: Based in Oranjestad's Seaport Village Marina, **Atlantis Submarine** (tel: 588 6881) transfer passengers by catamaran out to the Barcadera Reef and their mini-submarine. The sub dives to a depth of 150ft (45m) and the excursion lasts for around 50 minutes. They also operate the semi-submersible

Seaworld Explorer, which visits a reef area and the site of a World War II German shipwreck.

Sailing cruises around the island, or moonlight, catamaran or dinner cruises, with stops for swimming and snorkeling, can be arranged through **Aruba Watersports Center** (tel: 586 6613), **De Palm Tours** (tel: 582 4400), **Red Sail Sports** (tel: 586 1603), **Pelican Watersports** (tel: 587 2302) and **Wave Dancers** (tel: 582 5520).

The tourist office has a list of boats available for day or half-day charter for deep-sea fishing.

By road: Taxi rates are fixed—make sure you agree on the price before setting off; prices go up in the evening and overnight. Taxis can be flagged down, or call 822116 (main dispatch office, Oranjestad). Taxi drivers should all have Tourism Guide Certificates and speak English.

Buses run between Oranjestad and the southeast of the island and to the beach hotels, and between Oranjestad and the airport. Oranjestad bus station is on Zoutmanstraat. There are also jitney cars that operate like shared taxis. A jitney or bus from Oranjestad to San Nicolas will drop you off at the airport. Buses stick to their timetables—which are available from the tourist offices—and run one or two an hour.

To rent motorcycles, scooters and mopeds, contact **Donata Car & Cycle** (tel: 587 8300); **Ron's Motorcycle Rental** (tel: 586 2090); **George's** (tel: 582 5975); **Semver Cycle Rental** (tel: 586 6851).

Sightseeing and activities

The major local operator, **De Palm Tours** (tel: 582 4400), has offices in most hotels offering a three-hour tour of Aruba's highlights and a day-tour to Curaçao and to Caracas, Venezuela. For a two-and-a-half-hour guided adventure tour of the North Coast and Arikok National Park, contact **Rancho Diamari** (tel: 586 6284).

Other operators include: **ECO Destination Management** (tel: 587 2921); **Kremer Touristic Services** (tel: 587 9057); **Watapana Tours** (tel: 583 5191). The rugged North Coast region and Arikok National Park make for a great horseback safari; stables offer-

ing rides include **Rancho Diamari** (tel: 586 6284) and **Rancho Notorious** (tel: 586 0508). There is excellent windsurfing off Aruba; check out **Roger's Windsurf Place** (tel: 586 1918) or **Sailboard Vacations** (tel: 586 2527), among others. Scuba diving operators include **Aruba Watersports Center** (tel: 586 6613), **Dive Aruba** (tel: 582 7337), **Pro–Dive** (tel: 582 2520).

Tourist information

Aruba Tourism Authority, L.G. Smith Boulevard 172, Box 1019, Eagle, Aruba (tel: 582 3777) is a useful place to collect brochures and guides. There are also tourist offices at the harbor in Oranjestad and at the airport. In the US: Tourist Authority Office, 1200 Harbor Boulevard, Weehawken, NJ 07007 (tel: 201/330-8757).
In the UK: Saltmarsh Partnership, The Copperfields, 25 Copperfield Street, London SE1 OEN (tel: 020 7928 1600).

Bonaire (area code 599)

Car rental and driving

A national or international license is required and most of the 10 or so companies stipulate a minimum age. Try **A B Car Rental** (tel: 717 8980), **Avis** (tel: 717 5795), **Budget** (tel: 717 4700), **Flamingo Car Rentals** (tel: 717 5588), **Everts Car Rental** (tel: 717 8719), **Total** (tel: 717 8313), **Island Car Rental** (tel: 717 2100).

Drive on the right. The speed limit in built-up areas is 20mph (32kph) and outside towns 37mph (60kph) unless otherwise specified. There are no traffic lights and the main roads are good, but there are 20 miles (32km) of unpaved roads that get very muddy during the rainy season. There are very few watering holes: on island trips take food and drink supplies.

There are filling stations in Rincon, Kralendijk and Antrejol, Mon–Sat 7am–9pm; Kralendijk is open Sunday.

Getting around

By air: There are few direct flights from outside the Caribbean. **Continental** offers a once-a-week route from Houston and **KLM** links

Bonaire with Amsterdam twice a day. Most visitors arrive from Puerto Rico, Jamaica, Curaçao or Aruba on direct flights provided by **American Eagle**, **Dutch Antilles Arlines** and **Air Jamaica**. Local airline **Divi Divi** connects regularly with Curaçao.

By boat: More people come to Bonaire to dive than to sail or putter around in boats (ask hotels about their diving packages). Klein Bonaire is reached by diving boats: hitch a lift if you don't plan to dive and don't miss the return. Snorkeling, picnicking and sunset cruises are offered by the Siamese junk *Samur* (tel: 717 5592), the *Woodwind* (tel: 786 7055) and the *Sea Witch* (tel: 717 5433).

By road: Taxis are not metered, but prices are fixed and should be agreed with the driver beforehand. Taxis can be ordered through hotels or from a central dispatch office (tel: 717 8100); they do not drive around looking for fares. Any taxi will take you on an island tour. Motorcycle and scooter rentals are widely available.

Sightseeing and activities

Ask in the tourist office about visits to the two flamingo nesting sites. **Bonaire Tours** (tel: 717 8778) and **Tropical Travel** (tel: 567 0239 mobile) offer bus tours of the island. For a more active biking or snorkeling tour, contact **Discover Bonaire** (tel: 717 7558). Scuba diving operators are in the hotels: **Captain Don's Habitat** (tel: 717 8290) and **Sea and Discover** (tel: 717 5322). For windsurfing and kayaking: **Jibe City** (tel: 717 5233).

Tourist information

Bonaire Tourism Corporation, Kaya Grandi #2, Kralendijk (tel: 717 8322 or 717 8649; www.infobonaire.com). Visitors from Europe can contact Bonaire Tourist Office Europe, PO Box 472, NL-2000 AL Haarlem, The Netherlands (tel: 00 31 23 54 30 704).
Curaçao (area code 599)

Car rental and driving

Your own driver's license must be presented. Many of the car rental companies have airport offices, allowing you to compare prices: **Budget** (tel: 868 3420); **Hertz** (tel: 888 0088); **National/Alamo** (tel: 869 4433). The north coast is worth seeing by car but much of it is down dusty lanes.

Driving is on the right and international signs are used. The speed limit in built-up areas is 25mph (40kph) and out of town 37mph (60kph) unless specified. Traffic from the right has right of way.

Getting around

By air: Curaçao is linked to Europe by daily flights with **KLM** through the hub at Amsterdam. There are also direct flights to the US with **American Airlines** and to Venezuela and Colombia. Within the Caribbean **American Eagle** offers flights from Puerto Rico that link to other islands. **Air Jamaica** and **Divi Divi** offer similar services. **Bonaire Express** links Curaçao with nearby Dutch Bonaire.

By boat: There are three dive trips a week aboard the **Sailing Ship** *Bounty* (tel: 560 1887), a lovely gaff-rigged schooner, while **Mermaid Boat Trips** (tel: 560 1530) offer three trips a week to Klein Curaçao for a buffet lunch, snorkeling or quiet relaxation. Contact **Miss Ann** (tel: 767 1579) for details of excursions, boat and surfboard rentals, and water-skiing. For deep-sea fishing trips, try **Ed's Fishing** (tel: 526 7312), or **Let's Fish** (tel: 747 4489).

By road: Taxis have TX on their licenses. Fares are fixed and should be agreed upon first. There are taxi stands at the airport and hotels and Plaza Jojo Correa, downtown Willemstad. Fares go up by 25 percent after 11pm and there may be a charge for excess baggage. For the central taxi office call 869 0747. Tipping is not obligatory.

Yellow public buses (known locally as convoys) or private vans or cars with BUS on their license plates, take 6–14 passengers and are an inexpensive way of getting around. There are regular bus routes between major sights, leaving from Punda Bus Terminal (market place) or Otrabanda Bus Terminal, Rif Fort.

Sightseeing and activities

For tours beyond Willemstad, try: **ABC Fiesta Tours** (tel: 767 2141); **Casper Tours** (tel: 465 3010); **Taber Tours** (tel: 737 6637); Wild Curaçao (tel: 562 0027) offers caving and walking tours, while hourly tours of the Hato Caves are given by local guides; for information call 868 0379. Christoffelpark (tel: 864 0363) offers birdwatching and guided jeep trips—take the Westpunt bus from Otrobanda bus terminal, every two hours from 7am. The big hotels have scuba diving operators, or you can try **Hooks Diving** (tel: 461 0515), **Sunset Divers** (tel: 864 1708) and **Toucan Diving** (tel: 456 3790).

Tourist information

The Curaçao Tourism Development Board has a booth at the airport (tel: 868 6789) and the head office on Pietermaai 19, PO Box 3266, Willemstad (tel: 434 8200; www.curacao-tourism.com). There are also various visitor information kiosks, one at the Cruise Terminal in Otrabanda, and another at Wilhelminaplein in Punda. In the US: 3361 SW Third Avenue, Suite 102, Miami, FL 33145 (tel: 800/CURACAO) In the UK: Curaçao Tourist Board, 421a Finchley Road, London NW3 6HT (tel: 020 7431 4045).

Saba (area code 599)

Car rental and driving

Cars can be rented (produce your own driver's license), including a full tank of fuel and unlimited mileage, from **Caja's Car Rental** (tel: 416 2388); **Johnson's Car Rental** (tel: 416 2269) or **Scout's Place** (tel: 416 2205).

Driving is on the right, along the island's only road, The Road. In the event of a breakdown, call the only filling station (Fort Bay) on 416 3272.

Getting around

By air: All access to Saba is via Sint-Maarten/Saint Martin. Local carrier **Winair** makes the short flight several times a day from Sint Maarten's Juliana International Airport.
By boat: Sea crossings (1hr) to Saba are offered by **The Edge** from Pelican Marina, Sint Maarten (Wed–Sun), **Voyager** from Bobby's Marina, Sint Maarten (Thu), and **Marigot**, Saint-Martin (Tue). For scuba diving, contact **Saba Deep** (tel: 416 3347),

Saba Divers (tel: 416 2740) and **Sea Saba** (tel: 416 2246), all of whom have boats which are available for round-island trips, deep-sea fishing and trips to nearby islands or other parts of Saba.
By road: There are about 10 taxi drivers on Saba and they all do guided tours. They can also arrange diving or nature walks; some can even offer you a place to stay in a guesthouse. There are no buses. Hiking: Saba has 18 nature trails through the rain forest and up Mount Scenery. For a botanical tour, try **James Johnson** (tel: 416 2630).

Tourist information

Saba Tourist Office, PO Box 5271, Windwardside (tel: 416 2231; www.sabatourism.com).

St. Eustatius (area code 599)

Car rental and driving

You will need a valid driver's license from your own country, or an international driver's license. Local rental agencies include: **ARC Rental** (tel: 318 2595); **Browns Car Rental** (tel: 318 2266); and **Walter's Car Rental** (tel: 318 2719). Cars are reliable, but the roads are not: watch out for potholes. Some roads are very narrow and liable to be frequented by cows, goats and sheep, so it is worth keeping your speed down. Driving is on the right and road signs are in Dutch and English.

Getting around

By air: Winair is the primary airline serving Statia with flights from Sint Maarten several times a day, Saba (10 minutes), and to St. Kitts. Caribbean Sun airlines also links the island with Sint Maarten daily.
By road: Taxi drivers will give any tourist a tour of the island, which takes about an hour. Taxi drivers include Darlington (Bobby) Berkel (tel: 318 2419) and Taxi Wendy (tel: 318 4545). More information can be found from the Historical Foundation Museum, Simon Doncker House, Oranjestad (tel: 318 2639).

Motorized transportation may not be necessary as most places are within walking distance: The Historical

Foundation has a brochure detailing a 90-minute walking tour of the Upper and Lower Towns.

Hiking: There are 12 nature trails—leaflets available from the tourist office. Or take a two-hour guided trek into tropical rain forest on the Quill volcano, organized through the tourist office. Scuba diving can be arranged through **Dive Statia** (tel: 318 2435) and **Scubaqua** (tel: 318 2160).

Tourist information
There are tourist offices at the airport (tel: 318 2620) and the main office (tel: 318 2433; www.statiatourism.com) at the entrance to Fort Oranje, 3 Fort Oranjestraat, Oranjestad, St. Eustatius, Netherlands Antilles .

OTHER CARIBBEAN STATES

Jamaica (area code 876)

Car rental and driving
Most major international companies are represented and there are many local ones; a list of the Jamaica U-Drive Association members is obtainable from Jamaica Tourist Board (see page 262). A valid driver's license is required and you must be at least 24. A sales tax of 15 percent is added on top; accident and health insurance and collision damage waiver optional. Some filling stations are closed on Sundays, and fuel is paid in cash. The speed limit is 30mph (48kph) in towns and 50mph (80kph) on highways. Drive on the left.

Ocho Rios: **Caribbean Car Rentals** (tel: 974 2123). Port Antonio: **Eastern Rentals** (tel: 993 3624). Kingston: **Island Car Rentals** (tel: 926 8861); **Galaxy Car Rentals** (tel: 925 4176).

Car rental: **Avis** (tel: 800/331-1212). Kingston: Apex Car Rental (tel: 952 75870. Port Antonio: Derron's (tel: 993 7111). Montego Bay: Avia (tel: 952 0762), Budget (tel: 952 3838), Dollar (tel: 952 9100.

Getting around
By air: Jamaica is a major Caribbean gateway with an abundance of scheduled flights and charter services from destinations throughout North America, as well as South America

and Europe. The majority of services land in Montego Bay, and some continue to Kingston. From North America, **Air Jamaica** offers regular flights from New York, Atlanta, Philadelphia, Baltimore, Chicago and three Florida airports, as well as Nassau, Bahamas. **American Airlines**, **Continental**, **Northwest**, **US Airways** and **Air Canada** also provide scheduled services. Air Jamaica and **British Airways** fly transatlantic direct. Local carriers offer inter-island services: Jamaica is linked to the Eastern Caribbean by **BWIA** and **Air Jamaica**; Grand Cayman by **Cayman Airways**; Havana, Cuba by **Cubana**.

Helitours (tel: 974 2265) run sightseeing trips, with pick-ups at most local airports. Helicopters can be chartered.

By boat: Ask at your hotel or nearest tourist information center about private charters for deep-sea fishing, scuba diving and sailing.
By road: Buses are by far the cheapest way of getting around. They run all over the island and can be flagged down at bus stops and in between. Bicycles and motorcycles can be rented at most resorts. Taxis are in all resort areas but are not often metered; prices between destinations are fixed, so ask the price beforehand or be prepared to bargain with the driver. Look out for red Public Passenger Vehicle (PPV) plates.

Sightseeing and activities
The Tourist Board visitor guide, *One Love*, lists main excursions and attractions. Your hotel will be able to organize any tour, which may be in a taxi with driver-guide or minibus: the cost will include the admission prices.

Local tour operators will organize your own island tour and inter-island travel: In Montego Bay: **Blue Danube** (tel: 953 8255); **Caribic Vacations** (tel: 953 9878); **Forsythe's Jamaica** (tel: 952 0394); **Glamour Tours** (tel: 940 3277); **Jamaica Tours** (tel: 953 2107); **Juta Tours** (tel: 952 0813); **Tropical Tours** (tel: 953 9100). . In Port Antonio: **Valley Hikes** (tel: 993 3085) for walks and eco-tours. In Ocho Rios: **Blue Mountain Tours** (tel: 974 7075) for guided downhill bicycle tours with visits to coffee farms and a waterfall swim; **Tourwise** (tel: 952 4943); **Holiday Services** (tel: 974 2948). Scuba operators are based in all main towns. In Montego Bay, try **Poseidon Divers** (tel: 952 3624); in Negril, **Sun Divers** (tel: 957 4503) and **Negril Scuba Center** (tel: 957 9641); in Ocho Rios, try **Reef Divers** (tel: 973 4400); in Port Antonio, **Lady G'diver** (tel: 993 8988).

Tourist information

Jamaica Tourist Board, PO Box 360, 64 Knutsford Boulevard, Kingston (tel: 929 9200; www.visitjamaica.com); and Montego Bay; Negril; Ocho Rios; Port Antonio. In teh US: 5021 Blue Lagoon Drive, Suite 670, Miami FL 33126 (tel: 305/665-0557). In the UK: Jamaica Tourist Board, 1–2 Prince Consort Road, London SW7 2BZ (tel: 020 7225 9090).

Cayman Islands (area code 345)

Car rental and driving

A valid driver's license and a Cayman driving permit must be shown. Different companies specify different minimum ages for renting cars. The main companies are: **Ace/Hertz** (tel: 949 2280); **Andy's Rent-a-Car** (tel: 949 8111); **Budget** (tel: 949 5605); **CICO-Avis** (tel: 949 2468); **Coconut Car Rentals** (tel: 949 4377); **Economy Car Rental** (tel: 949 9550); **Thrifty** (tel: 949 6640). Fuel is sold in imperial (160oz) gallons. Rental firms can be contacted on their US toll free numbers: **Ace/Hertz** (tel: 800/654-3131) and **Coconut** (tel: 800/941-4562).

Driving is on the left; some rental vehicles have left-hand drive; drunk-driving laws are strictly observed; seatbelts are recommended.

Getting around

By air: Grand Cayman's Owen Roberts International Airport is the main port of entry to the islands. From North America, **American Airlines, Continental, Delta, Northwest** and **US Air** all offer direct services from a variety of departure points, and there are frequent daily services from Miami to Grand Cayman with American Airlines and **Cayman Airways**. Cayman Airways also serves several other US and

Caribbean destinations, and there are a number of charter flights from the US and Canada. **British Airways** flies twice-weekly from the UK via Nassau, Bahamas. The local carrier **Island Air** flies between Grand Cayman and the sister islands of Cayman Brac and Little Cayman four times a day (journey time about 45 mins). There are Cayman Airways flights to Cayman Brac also.

By boat: On Grand Cayman boat excursions can be arranged through **Red Sail Sports** (tel: 945 5965) and **Soto's Cruises Ltd** (tel: 945 4576). Diving can be organized through: **Fisheye** (tel: 945 4209); **Dive 'n' Stuff** (tel: 947 2822); **Sunset Divers** (tel: 949 7111); **Divers Down** (tel: 945 1611), and **Ocean Frontiers** (tel: 947 7500). Cayman Brac: **Dive Tiara** (tel: 948 1553). Little Cayman: **Paradise Divers** (tel: 948 0001).

By road: There is a limited public bus system in operation on Grand Cayman but there are plenty of cars, scooters, bicycles and taxis to rent. Taxi rates are determined by the government and published in CI$, so always ask the driver how much the trip will cost before you start. Private bus services run between West Bay and George Town at irregular intervals. Buses can be flagged down along the route. On Cayman Brac, jeeps, cars, scooters and bicycles can be rented from **B&S Motor Ventures, Cycle & Car Rentals** (tel: 948 1646).

Sightseeing and activities

There are numerous local travel agents (see below) that offer land and water-based excursions and tours; all such activities can be booked on arrival in Grand Cayman.

Local tour operators are mostly in Grand Cayman: **EVCO Tours** (tel: 947 8418); **Majestic Tours** (tel: 949 7773); **Reid/Royal Tours** (tel: 945 8124); **Tropicana Tours** (tel: 949 0944); **Cayman Kayaks** (tel: 926 4467). On the smaller islands, go through the hotels.

Tourist information

Department of Tourism, The Pavilion, Cricket Square, George Town (tel: 949 0623). In the US: 3 Park Avenue, 39th Floor, New York, NY 10016 (tel: 212/889-9009). In the UK: Cayman

Islands Department of Tourism, 6 Arlington Street, London SW1A 1RE (tel: 020 7491 7771).

Cuba (area code 537)

Getting there

Contrary to popular opinion, Americans can legally visit Cuba— they just can't spend American dollars there, which is meant to make traveling impossible. Exceptions are made for former Cubans with relatives in need, government officials, journalists and professional researchers, all of whom must obtain an official license to go. The licenses are issued by the Treasury Department (tel: 202/622-2480). A second option for US citizens is to sidestep the embargo by going through a third country: Canada, Mexico and Jamaica offer regular flights in and out of Havana, Varadero or Santiago de Cuba. Many of the other Caribbean and Latin American nations offer flights as well. The Cubans know the drill— they issue Americans a tourist card instead of stamping passports, so it is rather easy to "get away with it." The tourist cards are generally provided by the airlines at check-in, and by travel agencies in these "third countries" which specialize in arranging American tours of Cuba. Law-abiding American citizens, be forewarned: under the terms of the current embargo, these trips are not legal.

Car rental and driving

Renting a car is definitely the best way of seeing Cuba, but it is expensive. Your own national driving license is sufficient to rent a car; you must also present your passport. Car rentals are available from Cuba's two main rental operators in Havana: **Cubacar** (tel: 33 2277 or 33 7233) and **Havanautos** (tel: 833 3484). Other Havana-based local agencies include **Rent a Car Transtur** (tel: 24 5532 or 24 7644), **Via Rent a Car** (tel: 204 4445), **Micar** (tel: 55 3535) and **Rex** (tel: 33 9160), which also offers a limousine service. Cuba is subject to intermittent fuel shortages, so if you see an open fuel station, fill your tank. Although almost anyone with a car will pick up tourists and take them to

their destination, increased crime involving tourists means you should only use official taxis. Roads connecting all the country's major regions and towns are in decent condition.

Getting around

Getting around is relatively easy by plane or train, although trains are crowded and seats should be reserved well in advance. Contact your tour company for further information.
By air: Air Cubana (tel: 266 4644) flies from Havana to most of Cuba's major cities and resorts. Tickets are relatively inexpensive.
By road: Roads connecting all the country's major regions and towns are in decent condition.

Within the cities, buses (*guaguas*) run on fixed routes; exact change needed. These are crowded and unreliable, but run through the night. Destinations are sometimes on the windshield.

There are two kinds of taxis: Peso taxis (black and white checks on their front doors) are not supposed to take tourists but they will. Hail them even if they appear to be taken: The driver will split the fare (negotiate as you get in). The Peso taxi base is by the bus terminal in Havana. In the main resort areas of Havana, Varadero and Santiago, dollar or turistaxis operate.

In Havana, companies include **Taxis OK** (tel: 204 9518) and **Taxis Transtur** (tel: 208 6666) or book through a hotel. Newer taxis should set their meters at No. 1 in the day and No. 2 at night; older taxis have no meters and have fixed rates in or around Havana; agree the rate first.

Around the island: *guaguas* run between towns within a province: They are crowded but unbeatable for a taste of local life. However, in the present difficulties they are almost impossible to catch. Long-distance buses run all over the island (Havana to Baracoa in the east) and are usually large, quite comfortable coaches. Book a day in advance for buses and trains.

Shared taxis (*colectivos*) supplement the local buses, leaving the inter-municipal bus station once they are

263

full; you just have to find one going where you want to go. They are roughly twice the bus fare.

Sightseeing and activities

Organized bus tours: day trips to Trinidad or Pinar del Río can be booked through Cubatur offices in hotels. Or, negotiate to share a *colectivo*. **Cubatur** has information desks in tourist hotels, with tickets for organized excursions (head office: Calle F, No. 157, e/9na y Calzada, Vedado, La Habana 4; tel: 836 9555). They can also help with booking hotels and advise on transportation. **Havanatur**, Edificio Sierra Maestra, Av. 1ra, e/Calle O y 2, Miramar, Havana (tel: 204 8409) also in hotels, has some English-speaking guides.

Cubatur offers day trips from Havana to Soroa, Viñales, Trinidad, Varadero, Cienfuegos and Guama; also a *Vuelta a Cuba*, seven-day trip around the island by bus and air and excursions to Cayo Largo. Departure can depend on a minimum number of people signing up for a tour. Check whether the trip is on and what the departure time will be. Another outlet worth trying is **Cubamar**, Vedado (tel: 833 2523) offering specialized nature-based tourism. **Cuban Adventures of Canada** (tel: 604 524 2251) and **Tropical Tours** in Jamaica (tel: 876/953 9100) also provide tours.

Tourist information

www.cubatavel.cu
Cubatur (see above) is the government agency that organizes most travel within Cuba. You might also try Havanatur (above). In Canada contact the Cuban Tourist Office, 1200 Bay Street, Suite 305, Toronto, Ontario M5R 2A5 (tel: 416/362-0700). In the UK: The Cuban Tourist Office, 154 Shaftsbury Avenue, London WC2H 8JT (tel: 020 7240 6655).

Dominican Republic (area code 809)

Car rental and driving

Your own driver's license or an international license allows you to drive here for 90 days. The minimum age for renting a car is 25.

The following companies all have offices in Santo Domingo: **Avis** (tel: 535 7191); **Budget** (tel: 549 0351); **Dollar** (tel: 221 7368); **Nelly** (tel: 687 7997); **Hertz** (tel: 221 5333); **Kobi Rent** (tel: 571 4169); **National** (tel: 562 1444). Car rental is expensive because of high tariffs on vehicles; credit cards are accepted and a large deposit taken, usually twice the weekly rental.

Driving is on the right, but local drivers can be erratic; watch out also for motorcyclists in towns. Tolls of a few cents are levied on all principal roads out of the capital. Speed limits are 50mph (80kph) on highways, 37mph (60kph) in suburban areas; 25mph (40kph) in cities unless otherwise specified. Filling stations are few and far between in country areas and generally close at about 6pm. Avoid night driving as narrow mountain roads are dark and treacherous. Cars driven by tourists are often stopped by police at the entrance to and exit from towns—this is nothing to worry about.

Getting around

By air: There are several international airport gateways into the Dominican Republic. The busiest is Las Américas International Airport outside Santo Domingo, but vacationers heading for the north coast resorts of Cabarete, Playa Dorada, Puerto Plata and Sosúa will find plenty of flights making directly for Gregorio Luperón International Airport. There are also airports at Barahona, Punta Cana, Santiago and the new Romana International at Casa de Campo. More than 60 charter flight operators from the US and Europe serve the Dominican Republic. Scheduled flights from North America are offered by **American Airlines**, **Continental** and **US Airways**. There are also good inter-island connections to major regional transportation hubs such as **American Eagle's** frequent daily services to San Juan, Puerto Rico; while **Air Caraïbes** flies to Sint-Maarten and Curaçao. There are no direct scheduled flights from the UK although services are provided by Air France and Iberia via Paris and Madrid respectively. There are, however, numerous charter flights. For domestic flights, contact **Air Santo**

Domingo (tel: 683 8006).

By boat: Leisure craft take you on trips to offshore islands, such as Cayo Levantado, from the dock at Samana and from Los Cacaos.

By road: Taxis are unmetered. Although fares are government-regulated, they are negotiable assuming you and the driver speak the same language. Fares to destinations outside the city are posted in major hotels and at the airport.

Telephone taxi services are another option: this is a 24-hour service with rates agreed over the telephone, depending on distances covered.

Publicos, blue-and-white or blue-and-red cars that run regular routes stopping to let passengers on and off, are much cheaper; rates are fixed between cities. However, the cars are often crowded and uncomfortable.

Private buses—*conchos* or *colectivos*—are the colorful way to get around. Most leave from around Parque Independencia in Santo Domingo; exact fare required.

Private air-conditioned buses make regular trips from Santo Domingo to a number of regions. To reserve a seat call **Metro Buses** (tel: 566 7126 in Santo Domingo, 586 6062 in Puerto Plata, 587 4711 in Santiago) or **Caribe Tours** (tel: 221 4422), whose prices tend to be cheaper.

Motoconchos (motorcycle taxis) are found on the streets of Puerto Plata, Sosúa and Jarabacoa: flag them down on the road and negotiate the fare.

Motorcycles can be rented around Puerto Plata and Playa Dorada; you must ensure that you use the lock, as there is no insurance on theft. Bicycles can be rented from many of the hotels on the north coast. Ask at reception.

Sightseeing and activities

Prieto Tours (tel: 685 0102) offers half-day bus tours of Santo Domingo, beach tours, tours to Cibao Valley and the Amber Coast, and others. **Turinter** (tel: 686 4020) does a full-day tour of Samana and specialty tours (museums, shopping, fishing). **Apolo Tours** (tel: 586 6610) offers a full-day tour covering Playa Grande, Santiago and Sosúa. **Colonial Tours and Travel** (tel: 688 5285) offer a combination of tours, jeep safaris and activities from rafting

to horse-riding. The safaris head up into the hills to visit coffee plantations and flower farms. Try **Iguana Mama** (tel: 571 0908) for mountain bicycling excursions and hiking. Sosúa is a good scuba diving center. Dive trips and equipment rentals can be arranged through dive shops in main resorts.

Tourist information

The main office of the Ministry of Tourism is at the corner of Avenida México and Avenida 30 de Marzo, PO Box 497, Santo Domingo (tel: 221 4660; www.dominicanrepublic.com). There is also an office in the Zona Colonial, at main airports and regional tourist areas such as Cabarete, Pueto Plata and Sosúa. In the US; 136 E 57th Street, Suite 803, New York, NY 10022 (tel: 212/588-1012). In the UK: 18–20 Hand Court, High Holborn, London WC1V 6RZ (tel: 020 7242 7778).

Puerto Rico (area code 787)

Car rental and driving

Your national driver's license is preferred by companies to an international license. There are several rental agencies including **Avis** (tel: 253 5926), **Hertz** (tel: 791 0840), **National** (tel: 791 1805) and **Budget** (tel: 791 0600).

Driving is on the right, with a maximum speed on the expressway 55mph (88kph). Take a phrasebook if you are going off the beaten track.

Getting around

By air: Puerto Rico is a major Caribbean transportation hub served by direct flights from all over North America; carriers include **Air Canada**, **American Airlines**, **Continental**, **TWA**, **United** and **US Airways**. There are no direct scheduled flights from the UK. Most flights with **BA**, **American Airlines** and **Virgin Atlantic** have stops in the US and are completed by code share airlines. Puerto Rico-based **American Eagle** serves 21 Caribbean destinations from the neighboring USVI right down to Tobago. Other local operators include **Seabourne Aviation** providing regular services to the British and US Virgin Islands. There are also domestic flights to main towns such as Arecibo,

Mayagüez and Ponce, and the offshore islands of Culebra and Vieques are accessible by small plane from San Juan and Fajardo.

By boat: Regular ferry services cross San Juan Bay from Old San Juan to the suburb of Cataño.

For the islands off the east coast, passenger ferries run by the **Fajardo Port Authority** (tel: 863 0705) shuttle between Fajardo Beach and Vieques three times a day (45 minutes). From Fajardo to Culebra there are three ferries daily. Tickets on both routes are inexpensive. For information about ferries from Mayagüez, on the west coast, to the Dominican Republic (tel: 832 4800).

Sportfishing charters can be arranged through **Captain Mike's Sport Fishing Center** (tel: 721 7335) and **Grand Illusion Charter** (tel: 796 4645), both in San Juan Bay Marina, or **Tropical Fishing Charters**, El Conquistador Marina, Fajardo (tel: 266 4524).

By road: All taxis are metered but can be rented unmetered for sightseeing. In San Juan, white taxis *turísticos* with a logo on the door serve the main tourist areas, and offer fixed-rate fares between the airport or cruise-ship piers and tourist destinations such as Old San Juan, Condado, Isla Verde and Miramar. There are additional charges for more than two pieces of luggage, waiting times and night journeys between 10pm–6am.

Another option is the **Gray Line** (tel: 766 0789) shared shuttle van service from the airport to hotels in Condado, Isla Verde and Old San Juan.

Metropolitan Bus Authority services are an inexpensive and easy way to get from Isla Verde and Condado into Old San Juan. Buses A5 and B21 run every 20 minutes or so. Bus stops can be identified by Parada. Open-air trolleys also rattle around Old San Juan covering a central route up to Plaza de Armas and a northern route to El Morro. The service is free and passengers can get on and off at any stop.

Another option are the shared taxis (*publicos*), which have yellow license plates with P or PD at the end and operate all over the island,

stopping in each town's main plaza. These can take up to 17 passengers and their routes and fares are fixed by the Public Service Commission. The main terminals are at the airport and Plaza Colón in Old San Juan.

Sightseeing and activities

For scuba diving contact **Caribbean School of Aquatics** (tel: 728 6606) and **Caribe Aquatic Adventures** (tel: 281 8858). In the southwest, contact **Parguera Divers** (tel: 899 4015). Tours of San Juan, the Bacardi Rum plant, the beaches and the rain forest can be arranged via: **Rico SunTours** (tel: 722 2080); **United Tour Guides** (tel: 723 5578). Some eco-based tour operators include **Tropix Wellness Outings** (tel: 268 2173) and **Encantos Ecotours** (tel: 272 0005).

Tourist information

Puerto Rico Tourism Company, PO Box 902 3906, San Juan 00902 3906 (tel: 721 2400 or 800/866-7827; www.gotopuertorico.com) offers a wealth of assistance in the form of maps, contact lists and brochures including the comprehensive *Qué Pasa* visitors guide. There are tourist information offices at the airport (tel: 791 1014), at La Casita, near Pier 1, Old San Juan (tel: 722 1709) and also in Ponce at 2911 Los Cabos Avenue (tel: 843 0465). Town halls throughout the country will have information desks. In the US: 666 Fifth Avenue, 15th floor, New York, NY 10103 (tel: 880/866-78270.

Barbados (area code 246)

Car rental and driving

A visitor's driver's license must be purchased from car rental companies; drivers must have held a full license for at least two years and be over 24. Car rental companies are in every district (the tourist board has the complete list), including: **Calypso Rentals** (422 6405); **Chelsea Motors** (tel: 422 6405); **Corbins Car Rentals** (tel: 427 9531); **Coconut Car Rentals** (tel: 437 0297); **Sixt** (tel: 435 7979); **Stoutes Car Rentals** (tel: 416 4456).

Motorscooters and bicycles are also a good way to get around.

Driving is on the left. Speed limits are 30mph (48kph) in towns and 50mph (80kph) on the highway. Seatbelts are not mandatory and there are no drunk-driving laws as such. Fuel generally has to be paid for in cash.

Getting around

By air: Barbados is a major regional transportation hub with excellent connections to the UK and North America. **Air Canada**, **Air Jamaica**, **American Airlines** and **BWIA** all fly direct from North America, while **American Eagle** provides frequent onward connecting services from Puerto Rico. From the UK, there are scheduled flights with **British Airways** and **Virgin Atlantic**, plus a wide range of charter flights. The neighboring Windward Islands and the Grenadines are easily accessed through local operators including **Air Caraïbes**, **Caribbean Star**, **LIAT** and **Mustique Airways**.

Helicopter tours are offered by **Bajan Helicopters** (tel: 431 0069). **By road:** Bright yellow minibuses with blue stripes, run by the Barbados Transport Board, provide a regular service around the island, with destinations usually displayed at the bottom left-hand corner of the windshield. There are two terminals in Bridgetown, plus Speightstown Terminal in the north providing a service to Bridgetown along the west coast, to eastern areas and a bypass service from Speightstown to the south coast. A number of privately owned maxi-taxis (minibuses) and route taxis also operate (not color-coded). These can be picked up at normal bus stops. Taxi fares between principal destinations are set in BDS. dollars—check first.

Sightseeing and activities

Tours can be organized through hotels or through companies such as **Boyce's Tours** (tel: 425 5366). For a four-wheel-drive tour to remote areas, contact **Adventureland 4x4 Tours** (tel: 429 3687) or **Island Safari** (tel: 429 5337). **VIP Tour Services** (tel: 432 2901) runs private air-conditioned cars with driver/guides. **Barbados National Trust** (tel: 426 2421) organizes guided Sunday walks. For visits to the

Grenadines, St. Lucia, Grenada, Tobago and Angel Falls by sea and air: **St. James Travel & Tours** (tel: 432 0774) or **Chantours** (tel: 432 5591).

Scuba diving operators include: **Blue Reef Watersports** (tel: 422 3133), **Hightide Watersports** (tel: 432 0931) or **Safari Adventures Barbados** (tel: 429 5337). For windsurfing contact **Club Mistral** (tel: 428 7277) on the south coast. Boat trip options include the *Jolly Roger* party boat (tel: 436 2622); catamaran cruises with **Cool Runnings** (tel: 436 0911) and **Tiami** (tel: 430 0900); or ocean kayaking with **Ocean Adventures** (tel: 436 2088).

Tourist information

Barbados Tourism Authority, PO Box 242, Harbour Road, Bridgetown (tel: 427 2623, www.visitbarbados.org). In the US: 800 2nd Avenue, New York, NY 10017 (tel: 212/986-6516); also in Los Angeles and Miami. In the UK: 263 Tottenham Court Road, London W1T 7LA (tel: 020 7636 9448).

Trinidad and Tobago
(area code 868)

Car rental and driving

To rent a car you must have a valid driver's license and be at least 21. For a comprehensive list of car rental companies in Port of Spain, Piarco Airport, San Fernando and the south of Trinidad and Tobago, ask for the *Discover Trinidad and Tobago* booklet from the tourist office. Companies include: **Budget** (tel: 669 1635); **Thrifty** (tel: 669 0602); **Econo Car Rentals Ltd** (tel: 622 8074); and **Johnney's Car Rental** (tel: 674 0463).

On Tobago it is more economical to rent a jeep than take a taxi, although there are some great taxi drivers who double as guides. Tobago car rental: **Auto Rentals** (tel: 639 0644); **Rattan's Car Rental** (tel: 639 8271); **Budget** (tel: 631 8456); **Tobago Travel** (tel: 639 8778).

Driving is on the left. There is a front-seatbelt law and the drinking and driving laws are strictly enforced (by fining or detention). Speed limits are 50mph (80kph) on the highways, 25–37mph (40–60kph) on minor roads, and 18mph (30kph) in residential areas.

Getting around

By air: The national airline, **BWIA**, flies direct from New York and Miami to Trinidad's Piarco Airport outside Port of Spain, and to Tobago's Crown Point Airport. **American Airlines** has a Trinidad flight out of Miami, and **American Eagle** provides connections from Puerto Rico to Port of Spain. There are also good connections to Europe: **BWIA** also flies direct to Trinidad from the UK; **British Airways** flies to Tobago and there are regular charter services. **Air Caribbean** and **LIAT** make the 15-minute hop between Trinidad and Tobago up to 10 times a day; LIAT's inter-island services link the islands to the rest of the Eastern Caribbean and Puerto Rico. Charter aircraft in Trinidad through **Trinidad & Tobago Sightseeing Tours** (tel: 628 1051).

By boat: A car ferry service from Port of Spain to Tobago (Scarborough) leaves daily, taking somewhere between 5 and 6 hours, with food and drink on board; you can return by plane. A cabin can be rented for an evening sail. Reservations can be made through the tourist board (see below); buy tickets at ferry offices in Port of Spain (tel: 625 3055) and Scarborough (tel: 639 2417).

For scuba diving and snorkeling: try **Tobago Dive Experience** (tel: 660 2222); **Aquamarine Dive Ltd,** Speyside (tel: 639 4416); **Adventure Eco Divers** (tel: 239 8729). For trips to Buccoo Reef, day sails and general watersports, contact the hotels or **Kalina Cats** (tel: 639 6306) and **Play Hard Fishing Charters** (tel: 639 7108).

By road: There are two types of taxi: rental and route, identifiable by their H license plates. Rental taxis are private and do not have meters and although their rates are theoretically fixed, they tend to be negotiable (especially during Carnival). Drivers also do tours. Less expensive are route taxis, which operate like buses on certain routes, picking up as many passengers as they can fit in their vehicles. They tend to start and finish their journey around Brian Lara Promenade, Port of Spain and come in two forms: cars taking four or five passengers and maxi-taxis. These are color-coded minibuses that seat 11 or 25 and ply particular routes according to their color. Yellow taxis operate around Port of Spain, red in eastern Trinidad, green for south Trinidad, black for Princes Town, brown for San Fernando, and blue in Tobago. Both sound their horns as they go to let you know if they still have some room on board.

Public buses run by the Public Transport Service Corporation (PTSC) are either very old (blue) or new and air-conditioned (red, white and black). They follow special bus lanes from Port of Spain to San Fernando, to Arima and to Chaguanas.

Sightseeing and activities

In Trinidad, tours of the Caroni Bird Sanctuary are run by naturalists **Winston Nanan** (tel: 645 1305) and **David Ramsahai** (tel: 663 4767). General tour companies in Port of Spain include: **Bacchus Taxi and Car Rentals** (tel: 622 5588); **Legacy Tours** (tel: 623 0150); **St. Christopher Taxi Service** (tel: 627 2257); **The Travel Centre** (tel: 622 0112); **Trinidad & Tobago Tours** (tel: 628 1051); **Southeast Eco-Tours** (tel: 644 1012); **Pax Nature Tours** (tel: 662 4084); **Naipaul's Tours & Travel** (tel: 623 5516). For operators outside Port of Spain, consult the *Discover Trinidad & Tobago* booklet from tourist offices.

In Tobago, David Rooks of **Nature Tours** (tel: 639 4276) offers guided walks and trips to offshore bird colonies.

Tourist information

Tourism Development Company Ltd (TDC), Level 1, Maritime Centre, 29 Tenth Avenue, Barataria, Trinidad (tel: 675 7034). TDC is also at Piarco Airport (tel: 669 5196) and Crown Point Airport (tel: 639 0509). Trinidad and Tobago Hotel and Tourism Association, Unit B, 36 Scott Bushe Road, Port of Spain (tel: 624 3928). In the US: Marketing Challenges International Inc., 10 East 21st Street, New York, NY 10010 (tel: 212/529 8484). In the UK: International Hotel Management Ltd, Albany House, Albany Crescent, Claygate, Surrey, KT10 0PF (tel: 01372 469818).

Accommodations & Restaurants

ACCOMMODATIONS

Styles and standards of Caribbean accommodations vary enormously. There are sophisticated beach clubs where individual cottages have ocean views, but most hotel rooms are in large resort complexes. In every recommendation except the most inexpensive, rooms have their own bathrooms. A number of villas and short-term apartments are mentioned below. For independent travelers there are a few guesthouses and local business hotels on each island. Most hotels are set on the beach. Most also have swimming pools.

There is no standardized system of classification in the Caribbean, but all hotels booked through tour operators and travel agents will be registered with the tourist board on the island and checked by the operators.

Prices, highest from December to April, are reduced by 20–25 percent during the rest of the year. Each island has a different system, with supplementary room taxes. A service charge of 10–15 percent is often levied.

Accommodations are divided into four price categories, based on the rate for a double room in high season:

Inexpensive ($): (a double room for less than US$125)
Moderate ($$): (a double room for between US$125 and $250)
Expensive ($$$): (a double room for between US$250 and US$450)
Very expensive ($$$$): (expect to pay more than US$450)

Dialing codes Most Caribbean islands have a three-digit code. However, if you are calling from Europe, this may be prefixed by 1, the country code for the US. Check before dialing.

THE WINDWARD ISLANDS

Dominica (767)
Hotels on Dominica levy 5 percent goverment tax on all bills .

Evergreen Hotel ($)
Castle Comfort tel: 448 3288
Pool and pleasant waterfront setting; dive packages. Small and welcoming.
The Garraway Hotel ($$)
Roseau tel: 449 8800;
www.garrawayhotel.com
Modern high-rise building well positioned on the waterfront in town. Very comfortable rooms with a good restaurant and good service.
Papillote Wilderness Retreat ($)
tel: 448 2287; www.papillote.com
Ten rooms set in a grand tropical garden fed by the Trafalgar Falls. Good walking.
Picard Beach Cottage Resort ($$)
Portsmouth tel: 445 5131
Eight beach cabins, comfortable Caribbean style, right on a good black sand beach.

Grenada (473)
Hotels on Grenada and Carriacou levy an 8 percent government tax on all bills.

Coyaba ($$$)
Grand Anse tel: 444 4129; www.coyaba.com
This friendly beach resort has been updated and extended with comfortable rooms set in tropical gardens. Entertainment in the bar and thatch-roof restaurant; good sports facilities.
La Sagesse Nature Center ($$)
tel: 444 6458; www.lasagesse.com
Romantic hideaway in a 1920s beachfront estate house with nine simple but stylish rooms, plus two veranda cottages (one offering real Robinson Crusoe budget rooms).
Spice Island Inn ($$$$)
tel: 444 4258
High luxury on Grand Anse beach. The 66 rooms are large and air-conditioned, and some Whirlpool Suites stand directly behind the palms and sand. Entertainment in the beachfront restaurant and bar.
Twelve Degrees North ($$$)
St. George's tel: 444 4580; www.twelvedegreesnorth.com
A small eight-unit retreat at L'Anse aux Épines where you'll have the benefit of your own cook/housekeeper to cater to your every whim. No children under 15.

The Grenadines (784)
Hotels charge 7 percent government tax.

Cotton House Hotel ($$$$)
Mustique tel: 456 4777;
www.cottonhouse.net
Set in the ancient stone estate building of a former cotton plantation; sumptuous beds and furnishings. Pool and fantastic views to go with superb food.
Frangipani ($–$$)
Bequia tel: 458 3255;
www.frangipaniabequia.com
Set in and around an old family vacation villa on the Port Elizabeth waterfront. Antique gentility and personable West Indian style.
Friendship Bay Hotel ($$–$$$)
Friendship Bay tel: 458 3222;
www.friendshipbayhotel.com
Appealing complex on the south side of the island. Passable beach; excellent beach bar; some watersports.
Spring on Bequia ($–$$)
tel: 458 3414; www.springonbequia.com
Small, family-run hotel set on a 28-acre (11ha) working pantation. The rooms are stone built with views of the surrounding hills. There's a bar and reastaurant.

St. Lucia (758)
All hotels on St. Lucia levy an 8 percent government room charge.

Anse Chastanet ($$$–$$$$)
Soufrière tel: 459
7000;www.ansechastanet.com
Forty-eight rooms and villas scattered on the

hillside and on the gray sands of secluded Chastanet bay; good diving and seclusion.

Ladera Resort ($$$$)
tel: 459 7323; www.ladera.com
A magnificent setting on the shoulder of one of the Pitons. Antique furniture, rooms open to the view and the noise of tree frogs.

Marigot Beach Club and Dive Resort ($$–$$$$)
Marigot Bay tel: 451 4974; www.marigotdiveresort.com
In the wonderful setting of a narrow, steep-sided inlet festooned with palms. Villas and cottages; charming and laid-back.

Royal ($$$$)
Reduit Beach tel: 452 9999; www.rexresorts.com
A grand and luxurious hotel, with central atrium and wings, commanding the beach. Every modern convenience in the huge rooms.

St. Vincent (784)

All hotels on St. Vincent levy a 7 percent government room tax.

Petit Byahaut Eco-Resort ($$$)
tel: 457 7008; www.petitbyahaut.com
Just five units (one a room-size tent) above the secluded beach of Petit Byahaut bay, which can be reached only by boat. Stylishly rustic, but has hot running water.

Sunset Shores Beach Hotel ($–$$)
Villa tel: 458 4411; www.sunsetshores.com
An excellent choice at the budget end of the market with 32 low-rise rooms, pool, restaurant and bar.

Young Island ($$$$)
tel: 458 4826; www.youngisland.com
A Caribbean gem—cottages scattered around the tropical garden of Young Island, just off St. Vincent's southern coast. Facilities include pool, bar, restaurant and sports.

THE LEEWARD ISLANDS

Anguilla (264)

Hotels on Anguilla add a government tax of 10 percent.

Cap Juluca ($$$$)
Maunday's Bay tel: 497 6666; www.capjaluca.com
A line of bright, white Moorish domes rising out of the Anguillian scrub along the superb sandy stretch of this peerless coastline. High luxury: baths and richly colored oriental rugs.

Malliouhana ($$$$)
Mead's Bay tel: 497 6111; www.malliouhana.com
On a cliff overlooking the sweeping beach below, Malliouhana has a mix of styles; terracotta tiles, slender columns and arches, touched with colorful Haitian prints. Smoothly run hotel, with a very elegant dining room.

The Pavillion Hotel ($)
Blowing Hole tel: 497 8284; www.pavillionhotel.com
A spotlessly clean, efficient, if basic, hotel

with family rooms. This is for those doing the Caribbean on a budget.

La Sirena ($$)
Mead's Bay tel: 497 6827; www.la-sirena.com
A small and friendly hotel perched above the beach. Affordable rates on an island of heavyweights. Some entertainment.

Antigua (268)

Hotels on Antigua add a government tax of 8.5 percent; 7 percent for restaurants.

Admiral's Inn ($$)
English Harbour tel: 460 1027; www.admiralsinnantigua.com
Within the historic walls of Nelson's Dockyard; rooms quite simple. A lively crowd of sailors collects at the bar.

Catamaran Hotel ($–$$)
tel: 460 1036; www.catamaran-antigua.com
Well-priced hotel with kitchenettes not far from the activity of English Harbour in the south.

Copper and Lumber Store ($$–$$$)
English Harbour tel: 460 1058; www.copperandlumberantigua.com
A small hotel set in the grounds of Nelson's Dockyard; functional brick walls beautified with tropical plants and urgent naval air transformed into a retreat of historic laziness. All units have kitchenettes.

Curtain Bluff ($$$$)
Morris Bay tel: 462 8400; www.curtainbluff.com
Once again the height of Antiguan elegance since its renovation. Main house on the bluff, between two excellent beaches. Lavish in the dining room and wine cellar.

Hawksbill Beach Resort ($$$)
Five Islands tel: 462 0301; www.rexresorts.com
Very comfortable all-inclusive beach-front resort south of St. Johns. Cottages ranged above a series of bays; plenty of watersports.

Montserrat (664)

Hotels on Montserrat add a government tax of 10 percent.

Erindell Villa Guesthouse ($)
Woodlands tel: 491 3655
Comfy, well-equipped rooms with private entrances, set in tropical gardens. Food service available, a large pool and laundry.

Vue Point Hotel ($)
tel: 491 5210; www.vuepointe.com
Twelve refurbished self-catering cottages overlooking Old Road Bay. Pool, tennis and popular beach bar down below.

Nevis (869)

Hotels on Nevis add a government tax of 9 percent.

Four Seasons ($$$$)
Pinney's Beach tel: 469 1111; www.fourseasons.com

Accommodations and Restaurants

A reliable beach vacation spot. Elegantly decorated and luxurious rooms. "Olde Worlde" decor and tropical profusion in the garden.

Hermitage ($$$)
Fig Tree Parish tel: 469 3477;
www.hermitagenevis.com
A gem of the Caribbean, set in one of its most ancient wooden houses. Romantic, pretty rooms in cottages embellished with gingerbread pointing around a lawned garden with palms, each with a hammock and view.

Oualie Beach Hotel ($$$)
Oualie Beach tel: 469 9735;
www.oualiebeach.com
West Indian gingerbread cottages providing 32 rooms in the north of the island, overlooking St. Kitts. Low-key but fun.

St. Kitts (869)

Hotels on St. Kitts add a government tax of 9 percent.

Rawlins Plantation ($$$$)
Mount Pleasant tel: 465 6221;
www.rawlinsplantation.com
The closest you can come to the lavish grandeur of plantation life. Ten luxurious rooms scattered around the estate grounds; fine West Indian cuisine and rum punch with a view from the impressive 18th-century great house.

Timothy Beach Resort ($–$$)
South of Basseterre tel: 465 8597;
www.timothybeach.com
Good-value suites on the fine strip of sand in Frigate Bay. Beach hotel, but pretty quiet.

THE VIRGIN ISLANDS

British Virgin Islands (284)

Hotels in the BVI add a government tax of 7 percent to all bills.

Anegada, Cooper Island and Jost van Dyke

Anegada Reef Hotel ($$$)
Anegada tel: 495 8002;
www.anegadareef.com
Just 20 simple, stylish beachfront and garden rooms (full-board). Excellent diving and fishing.

Cooper Island Beach Club ($$)
tel: 495 9084; www.cooper-island.com
Comfortable rooms in pretty cottages on the friendly, active Cooper Island.

Sandcastle ($$–$$$)
Jost van Dyke tel: 495 9888;
www.sandcastle-bvi.com
Four beach cottages and two rooms, gardens, and bar a stone's throw from White Bay.

Tortola

Cane Garden Bay Beach Hotel ($–$$)
tel: 495 4639
A lively hangout on Tortola's busiest beach. Rooms air-conditioned and simple, but plenty of activity all around.

Long Bay Beach Resort ($$$–$$$$)
tel: 495 4252; www.longbay.com
Delightful rooms and villas, some on stilts above the beach, others nestled in tropical gardens. Quiet but classy.

Virgin Gorda

Bitter End Yacht Club ($$$$)
North Sound tel: 494 2746;www.beyc.com
Lively resort for watersports fans—sailing school, windsurfing, short hops to nearby beach bars. Some entertainment, but also hideaway hillside cabins of high luxury.

Little Dix Bay ($$$$)
tel: 495 5555; www.rosewoodhotels.com
Low-key high luxury. Cottages in spacious, neatly tended grounds, looking onto an excellent strip of sand.

Mango Bay Resort ($$$–$$$$)
tel: 495 5672; www.mangobayresort.com
A series of studios, and two- and three-bedroom villas, some set on the water's edge, others surrounded by tropical foliage.

US Virgin Islands (340)

St. Croix

Hotels in the USVI add a government tax of 8 percent but many hotels also add a fuel surcharge of up to 8 percent on the room rate.

Buccaneer Hotel ($$$–$$$$)
tel: 712 2100; www.thebucaneer.com
Luxurious beach and golf resort ranged across grassy slopes leading down to the sea. Spacious and attractive rooms with private balconies or terraces, plus fine dining.

Cormorant Beach Club ($$$)
tel: 778 8920; www.cormorantbeachclub.com
Low-key beach hotel—attractive rooms with terraces or balconies overlooking the palms and sea. Refined, with an excellent restaurant.

St. John

Caneel Bay ($$$$)
tel: 776 6111; www.caneelbay.com
Elegant resort where rooms are set in beautifully tended gardens around a great house. fWatersports on the resort's seven beaches, otherwise reliable relaxation.

Gallows Point Resort ($$$$)
tel: 776 6434; www.gallowspointresort.com
Elegant suites with all modern comforts. Just a short walk from downtown Cruz Bay.

Maho Bay Camps ($$)
tel: 715 0501; www.maho.org
An eco-conscious place with simple tented units on a wooded hillside above the bay and more luxurious showcase eco-friendly studios.

St. Thomas

Bolongo Bay Beach Club ($$$)
tel: 775 1800; www.bolongobay.com
Lively resort—watersports, scuba, tennis—on a sandy bay on the south of the island.

Hotel 1829 ($–$$)
Charlotte Amalie tel: 776 1829;
www.hotel1829.com
A lovely townhouse hotel with a quiet, sophisticated air. Dinner is usually served to a piano accompaniment.
Ritz-Carlton ($$$$)
Great Bay tel: 775 3333; www.ritz-carlton.com
The most luxurious in St. Thomas: a large suite-hotel set around a bay on the east coast. Watersports (excellent windsurfing) and gourmet dining.
Sapphire Beach Resort and Marina
($$$–$$$$)
Sapphire Beach tel: 775 6100
Renovated and expanded resort hotel right on the beach with good snorkeling and watersports. All comforts are available; there is a lively beach party each Sunday.

THE FRENCH ANTILLES

Guadeloupe (590)
Some hotels on Guadeloupe add a room tax of a few dollars.

Auberge de la Vieille Tour ($$–$$$)
Gosier tel: 0590 84 23 23; www.sofitel.com
Large but genteel resort; rooms ranged on the hillside around an old windmill tower. Dining room above the private hotel beach.
Auberge des Petits Saints
aux Anacardiers ($–$$)
Terre de Haut, Les Saintes
tel: 0590 99 50 99; www.petitssaints.com
A charming art- and antique-filled Créole home in town. Fine French cuisine.
Le Rayon Vert ($)
Deshaiesy tel: 0590 28 43 23;
www.hotel.lerayonvert.free.fr
Beautiful small hotel set in the verdant hills of Basse-Terre with views of the ocean below and a good deal of style for the price range. Closed in June.

Martinique (596)
Some hotels on Martinique add a room tax of a few dollars.

Auberge de l'Anse Mitan ($–$$)
Anse Mitan tel: 0596 66 01 12
A friendly hotel, still with some old West Indian charm; tucked away at the end of the beach, but not far from the action of the town.
La Bonne Auberge ($)
Trois-Ilets tel: 0596 66 01 55
Small and friendly hotel, with simple rooms set in modern buildings in the heart of the tourist town of Trois-Ilets. Nice tropical dining room.
Habitation Lagrange ($$$)
Le Marigot tel: 0596 53 60 60;
www.habitationlagrange.com
Set in a superb restored plantation house in the banana groves in the northeast. No beach but elegant relaxation and fine cuisine.
Hotel Diamant les Bains ($$)
Diamant tel: 0596 76 40 14

Quiet and very friendly hotel; 24 rooms overlooking a pretty garden; views of Diamond Rock. An ideal retreat.

Saint-Barthélemy (590)
Some hotels on St. Barts add a room tax of a few dollars.

Hôtel la Banane ($$$)
Lorient tel: 0590 52 03 00;
www.labanane.com
Amusing crowd in the bar; rooms decorated with traditional Caribbean flourishes. Building lost in a tropical garden that overhangs a pool. Minimum stay of 10 nights Dec–Jan.
Les Ilets Fleuris ($$)
Hauts de Lorient tel: 0590 27 64 22
One-bedroom cottages with kitchens and views perched on one of St. Barts' numerous hilltops. The affordable rates include car rental, and the beach is 5 minutes away.
Hotel Manapany ($$$–$$$$)
Anse des Cayes tel: 0590 27 66 55;
www.lemanapany.com
The finest luxury; 52 rooms in sumptuous suites and cottages, near a good beach.

Saint-Martin (590)
Some hotels on Saint-Martin add a room tax to your bill.

Esmeralda Resort ($$$–$$$$)
Baie Orientale tel: 0590 87 36 36
Right on the beach, this resort has adopted traditional gingerbread style and added to its luxurious cottages, each of which has its own pool. Sports and restaurants.
Hévéa Hotel ($)
Grand Case tel: 0590 87 56 85;
www.hotel-hevea.com
In the center of town, this small Créole hotel-restaurant has an easy charm.
La Samanna ($$$$)
Baie Longue tel: 0590 87 64 00;
www.lasammana.com
Very chic and stylish, standing above the excellent sand of Long Beach. Built in a curious mix of styles, with vast rooms, fine views, extreme luxury and extreme prices.

THE NETHERLANDS ANTILLES

Aruba (297)
Hotels on Aruba add a government tax of 5 percent to all bills.

Amsterdam Manor Beach Hotel ($$–$$$)
Eagle Beach tel: 527 1100;
www.amsterdammanor.com
Attractive Dutch-style complex with 72 self-catering units ranging from studios to two-bedroom apartments set around quiet courtyards. Restaurant and mini-mart.
Divi Aruba Beach Resort ($$$)
tel: 525 5200; www.diviaruba.com
A low-rise hotel in the land of high-rises with an excellent beachfront setting. There are also attractive gardens.

273

Accommodations and Restaurants

Bonaire (599)

Hotels on Bonaire add a government tax of $5.50–$6.50 to all bills.

Captain Don's Habitat ($$)
Kralendijk tel: 717 8290;
www.habitatdiveresorts.com
Has grown from a small diving resort to a very comfortable and laid-back hotel, now with cottages and villas as well as rooms.
Carib Inn ($–$$)
Kralendijk tel: 717 8819; www.caribinn.com
Excellent choice for relative comfort and price. Nine simple rooms, good diving. No restaurant, but kitchenettes.
Harbour Village Beach Club ($$$–$$$$)
Playa Lechi tel: 717 7500;
www.harbourvillage.com
The most comfortable hotel on Bonaire, with plush and brightly painted suites in villas dotted around a sandy garden and pool.

Curaçao (599)

Hotels on Curaçao add a government tax of 7 percent to all bills.

Avila Beach Hotel ($$$–$$$$)
Willemstad tel: 461 4377;
www.avilahotel.com
The most elegant and traditional of Curaçao's hotels, which has now been modernized. It is set on the edge of town with a small beach and a dining room open to the breezes.

Saba (599)

Hotels on Saba add a government tax of 5 percent to all bills.

Juliana's ($–$$)
Windwardside tel: 416 2269;
www.julianashotel.com
Small, cozy and informal, Juliana's is a favorite with the dive crowd. This is helped by being just outside the inexpensive price bracket. The property has both rooms and self-catering apartments, plus a pool and a restaurant.
Queen's Gardens ($$$–$$$$)
Troy Hill tel: 416 2494; www.jqueensaba.com
The most upscale of Saba's properties, this resort, 360 feet (1200m) up, is surrounded by verdant peaks and has views down to the sea.

St. Eustatius (599)

Hotels on St. Eustatius add a government tax of 7 percent to all bills.

Kings Well Resort ($)
Bay Road, Oranjebaai tel: 318 2538;
www.kingswellstatia.com
Simple but spacious rooms are offered, plus a few with kitchenettes. If you don't wish to cook there is a small yet lively restaurant.
Old Gin House ($$–$$$)
Lower Town tel: 318 2319;
www.oldginhouse.com
Fully refurbished, this historic hotel has period rooms and part-Mediterranean, part-Caribbean styling.

Sint Maarten (599)

Hotels on Sint Maarten add a government tax of 5 percent to all bills.

The Horny Toad Guesthouse ($$)
tel: 545 4323;
www.thehornytoadguesthouse.com
Excellent setting on Simpson Bay; attentive service and friendly; fully equipped rooms.
Passangrahan Royal Inn ($$)
Philipsburg tel: 542 3588;
www.pasanhotel.com
Old colonial air in the louvered lobby and a welcome oasis of peace and quiet in the shopping turmoil of Front Street. Thirty rooms; restaurant and bar.

OTHER CARIBBEAN STATES

Jamaica (876)

Hotels in Jamaica add a general consumption tax of 8.25 percent to all bills, and service.

Blue Mountains

Strawberry Hill ($$$)
Irishtown tel: 944 8400;
www.islandoutpost.com
A sybaritic mountain retreat, one of numerous Caribbean properties owned by Chris Blackwell of Island Records. Handsome villa accommodations with views, discrete yet charming service, a spa and superb food, plus utter peace and quiet and deliciously (comfortably) cool evenings.

Kingston

Terra Nova Hotel ($$)
New Kingston tel: 926 9334
Elegant grand old upscale house in lawned gardens; 32 attractive rooms, pool, and a good dining room.

Mandeville

Astra Country Inn ($)
tel: 962 3265
Forty rooms are set in a modern building just outside town: family-run and friendly. Tours can be arranged to the surrounding countryside.

Montego Bay

Cobaya Beach Resort and Club ($$$)
Mahoe Bay tel: 953 9150;
cobayaresortjamaica.com
A plantation-style inn on the beachfront just east of the city. Although there are 50 rooms, the property has a more intimate character and offers a warm welcome to families. Facilities include restaurants, bars, tennis, dive shop and other watersports.
Half Moon Club ($$$–$$$$)
tel: 953 2211' www.halfmoon-resort.com
Simply the classiest in Jamaican high luxury,

on a fine beach. Elegant rooms decorated in black and white; 19 pools, tennis, golf, riding, health club and very fine dining.

Richmond Hill Inn ($–$$)
tel: 952 3859; www.richmond-hill-inn.com
On the hilltop above the Montego Bay, an elegant townhouse with additional rooms and suites (20 in all) in rather quaint style. Restaurant, pool, and free beach/town shuttle.

Negril

Charela Inn ($$)
tel: 957 4277; www.charela.com
Despite its 49 rooms, this beach hotel has an intimate feel. Watersports are on offer and there is a fine French restaurant.

Grand Lido ($$$$)
tel: 925 0925; www.grandlido.com
On the fine sand of Bloody Bay, this is a top all-inclusive hotel—the champagne is on demand.

Sunset at the Palms ($$$–$$$$)
tel: 957 5350; sunsetatthepalms.com
Renovated and upgraded, this all-inclusive resort offers award-winning Caribbean/Asian-inspired design with 65 tree-house rooms set in a verdant tropical hideaway.

Ocho Rios

Beaches Boscobel Resort and Golf Glub ($$$–$$$$)
tel: 975 7330; www.beaches.com
All-inclusive resort on a fine beach, designed especially for families with children. Finger-painting instruction through to disco lessons will occupy them while you indulge in water-sports and sunning.

Hibiscus Lodge Hotel ($–$$)
tel: 974 2676
Simple rooms on the clifftops, near the action of town, but also only a short walk to the beach. Good food can be found in the restaurants and facilities include a garden and watersports.

Jamaica Inn ($$$$)
tel: 974 2514; www.jamaicainn.com
Sir Winston Churchill was a fan of this venerable establishment, and would probably still feel quite at home in the slightly formal surroundings (jackets for dinner). Well-proportioned rooms combine colonial decor with modern comforts and wonderful private verandas. Dining, pool, croquet plus a secluded beach.

Port Antonio

Mocking Bird Hill ($$$)
tel: 993 7267; www.hotelmockingbirdhill.com
Small and charming hotel with just 10 rooms and an eco-friendly ethos that prefers ceiling fans to aircon and heats water by solar power. Restaurant, bar and pool, plus eco-tours.

The Cayman Islands (345)

Hotels on the Cayman Islands add 6 percent government tax to all bills.

Brac Reef Beach Resort ($$)
Cayman Brac tel: 948 1323; www.bracref.com
Good base for a diving vacation with a dive shop on site, an attractive beachfront position, relaxed atmosphere and 40 rooms with patio or balcony. New spa and fitness center.

The Discovery Point Club ($$$–$$$$)
tel: 945 4724; www.discoverypointclub.com
All-suite two-bedroom units with kitchen on the coast at Seven Mile Beach. Each unit is individually styled with a balcony or terrace.

Hyatt Regency Grand Cayman Beach Suites ($$$$)
Grand Cayman tel: 949 1234; www.hyatt.com
One of the most luxurious hotels in Cayman, just across the road from Seven Mile Beach. Modern building, but with attractive old-colonial flourishes. Restaurants, golf course, watersports on the beach.

Sunset House ($$)
Grand Cayman tel: 949 7111; www.sunsethouse.com
This unpretentious waterfront dive resort has simple rooms and a laid-back atmosphere. It is a short distance south of George Town and only five minutes from a sandy beach.

Cuba (53)

Havana

Habana Libre Tryp ($$$)
tel: 07/834 6100; www.solmelia.com
Tall building at the head of La Rampa, built as the Havana Hilton back in the 1950s and renamed the Habana Libre by the young revolutionaries.

Inglaterra ($–$$)
tel: 07/62 7075
On the Parque Central, at the edge of the colonial city, the Inglaterra is a short walk away from the sights. There is a pleasant bar in the elaborate lobby and the rooms are comfortable.

Plaza ($–$$)
tel: 07/33 8583; www.hotelplazacuba.com
A fine, colonnaded building on the Parque Central; grand breezy interior with palms and pillars. Comfortable rooms.

Outside Havana

Hotel Casa Granda Santiago ($$–$$$)
tel: 0226/686600
Built in 1914, the elegant Casa Granda has 58 fully equipped rooms right in the heart of atmospheric Santiago.

Iberostar Varadero ($$)
tel: Spain (922 07 03 00; www.iberostar.com
Large, modern luxury, all-inclusive complex directly on the beach. There's a spa and gym plus four pools.

Paradisus Varadero Beach Resort ($$$)
Varadero tel: 535/66 8267
Luxury rooms in beach villas; good Caribbean beach location with non-motorized watersports, bars and clubs.

Pelícano ($$–$$$)
Cayo Largo tel: 45/4833; www.solmelia.com
The island of Key Largo offers great beaches and the best diving in Cuba. The 300 beach-front rooms come with an all-inclusive package. Amenities include a pool, restaurants, multiple bars and plentiful water-sports.

Sol Cayo Santa Maria ($$)
tel: 42/351500; www.solmelia.com
Large, all-inclusive resort of low-rise buildings, the Sol Cayo Santa Maria has a range of eater-ies and a good variety of on-site activities.

The Dominican Republic (809)

Hotels in the Dominican Republic add a government tax of 10 percent.

Altos de Chavón and the Southeast, Cordillera Central

Barceló Bávaro Beach ($$$)
Punto Cana Higuey tel: 686 5797; www.barcelo.com
Behind the superb palm-fringed beach lie a clutch of popular resort hotels, of which this is one. Simple air-conditioned rooms, plenty of restaurants and bars, plus watersports, golf and tennis.

Casa de Campo ($$$–$$$$)
La Romana tel: 523 3333; www.casadecampo.com
A top resort complex with some of the Caribbean's most chic villas and hotel rooms—polo, golf, beach sports, a choice of restaurants—all set in beautifully landscaped grounds.

Puerto Plata and the Amber Coast

Natura Cabanas ($$)
Cabarete tel: 571 1507; www.naturacabana.com
Guests stay in thatched garden bungalows at this soothing beachfront spa offering aromatherapy, massage, mud baths, and more, plus activities from biking to jeep safaris.

Piergiorgio Palace Hotel ($$)
Sosúa tel: 571 2626; www.piergiorgiohotel.com
Victorian seaside inn gets an Italian makeover in this elaborate homage to Sosúa's heyday, set in landscaped gardens with pools and cliff-side restaurant.

Samaná

Hotel Tropic Banana ($)
Las Terrenas tel: 240 6110
One of the best travelers' haunts in the Caribbean, where a lively crowd gathers for music at the poolside; 30 rooms in a spacious palm garden near the beach.

Occidental Gran Bahía ($$$)
tel: 538 3111; www.occidentalhotels.com
Supremely elegant gingerbread-style buildings opposite the beaches of Cajo Levantado, this all-inclusive property has an old Caribbean air of comfort, with high standards of service.

Santo Domingo

Hotetur Dominican Bay Resort ($$)
tel: 412 2001; www.hotetur.com
The closest beach resort to the capital—about 30 minutes away. The Boca Chica offers an all-inclusive plan with a sophisticated ambi-ence and elegant rooms.

Hotel Sofitel Frances ($$)
Calle Las Mercedes tel: 685 9331; www.sofitel.com
Small and charming hotel in an historic building arranged around a fountain courtyard, which invites you to linger with a book. Nineteen stylishly uncluttered rooms and a French restaurant.

Renaissance Jaragua ($$)
Avenida Washington tel: 221 2222; www.marriott.com
Luxury is available in this large and glitzy hotel on the Malecon. Choose from its four restaurants, a club with entertainers and a casino. Tours can also be arranged.

Puerto Rico (787)

Hotels in Puerto Rico add a government tax of 9 percent (11 percent in hotels with a casino).

Cordillera Central

Hacienda Gripiñas ($)
Jayuya tel: 828 1717
A *parador* set in a charming timber-framed coffee estate house. It is not elaborate, but has a wonderful old-time Caribbean feel.

Horned Dorset Primavera ($$$)
Rincón tel: 823 4030
Luxurious rooms that overlook the hotel garden or the sunset out to sea. Elegant central area with a library for afternoon tea and cocktails. Very fine cuisine.

Ponce

Hotel Melia ($)
Calle Cristina 75 tel: 842 0260
The Melia is just off the central square in Ponce. The well-priced rooms are modern and air-conditioned.

San German and the South West

Parador Boquemar ($)
Boqueron tel: 851 2158
This modern building near the beach can offer the traveler comfortable rooms, a pool and a restaurant.

Villa Parguera ($$)
Lajas tel: 899 7777
Low rates for a welcoming resort hotel on the waterfront, set in a tropical garden. Pool and good local restaurant on the bay.

San Juan: New City

Coqui Inn ($$)
Calle Uno 14 tel: 762 8662
These simple—yet air-conditioned—rooms
are near Isla Verde beach. The Inn also has
a restaurant.
**Intercontinental San Juan Resort &
Casino** ($$$–$$$$)
tel: 7791 6100; www.ichotelsgroup.com
Huge resort hotel by this leading quality chain
sits directly on the beach, though the free-form
pool is enticing. There's also a full-service spa.
Radisson Ambassador Plaza ($$–$$$)
1369 Ashford Avenue tel: 721 7300
Right on the Condado strip near to the beach,
close to stores and 10 minutes from Old San
Juan. Rooms and suites; rooftop pool,
children's activity programs, casino.

San Juan: Old City

The Gallery Inn ($$–$$$)
tel: 722 1808; www.galleryinn.com
Restored townhouse with circular staircases,
courtyards and terraces: bohemian feel as it
incorporates an art gallery.
Hotel El Convento ($$$)
*Calle Cristo 100 tel: 723 9020;
www.elconvento.com*
A magnificent old building in the colonial city—
black and white tiles, stained paneling and
tapestries hung on the walls. Once a convent,
it retains a calm and cloistered air.

Vieques

Hix Island House ($$$)
tel: 741 2302; www.hixislandhouse.com
On of the most celebrated of the new hotels in
the Caribbean, with a couple of environmental
design awards. Thirteen loft-style rooms set
within modern-styled buildings surrounded by
island vegetation. Pool on site.

Barbados (246)
Hotels on Barbados add a 7.5 percent
government tax to all bills.

South Coast

Bougainvillea Beach Resort ($$–$$$$)
Maxwell tel: 418 0990
Studios and suites in an attractive resort with
pools, restaurants, watersports and tennis. All
rooms have terrace or balcony and kitchenette.
The Crane ($$–$$$$)
St. Philip tel: 423 6220
Recently refurbished to offer upscale accom-
modations and facilities, The Crane has a
superb setting on the cliffs above a pretty
cove.
Peach and Quiet ($)
tel: Inch Marlow tel: 428 2467
A classy property for the price range, this small
family-owned hotel sits on the water's edge in
4 acres (1.6ha) of gardens. There is a restau-
rant and pool on site.

West Coast

Cobbler's Cove ($$$$)
tel: 422 2291
South of Speightstown, Cobbler's Cove has 39
beautifully decorated suites set above a fine
strip of sand.
Sandridge Beach Hotel ($–$$)
St. Peter tel: 422 2361
This is an oasis of beachfront affordability
on the upper reaches of the Platinum Coast.
The 58 units range from rooms to studios
and self-catering suites, all with access
to a number of pools, restaurants and
watersports.
Sandy Lane Hotel ($$$$)
St. James tel: 432 1311
A legend in Caribbean elegance and
hospitality, Sandy Lane has undergone a complete remodeling.

Trinidad and Tobago (868)
All hotels in Trinidad and Tobago add tax of
15 percent to published prices.

Trinidad

Asa Wright Nature Centre ($$)
Arima tel: 667 4655
An old colonial estate house with an enormous
screened veranda: it is set in the secluded
forests of the northern range. This nature
center makes an ideal base for birdwatching
and general relaxation.
Hilton ($$)
Port of Spain tel: 624 3211
This is a busy center for those passing
through the capital, but it is also quite well
organized for tourists. It has superb views
over the Savannah.
Hotel Normandie ($)
St. Ann's tel: 624 1181
Quiet hotel tucked away in a valley that has
now been swallowed up by Port of Spain. Fine
French fare.

Tobago

Arnos Vale ($$–$$$)
tel: 639 2881
In its own steep-sided valley festooned with
tropical blooms, the Arnos Vale has 38 rooms
and suites in a complex and in a central estate
house. There is a beach bar, a pool and a bou-
tique.
Half Moon Blue ($$)
tel: 639 3551
On a hillside just outside Scarborough, with
very comfortable rooms clustering around a
pool. A wonderful choice if you are looking for
privacy and seclusion, and is attached to an
excellent restaurant.
Plantation Beach Villas ($$$–$$$$)
tel: 639 0455
Very attractive, old colonial-style villas above
the beach at Stonehaven Bay. Kitchen; swim-
ming pool and bar down below; cooking can
be arranged.

RESTAURANTS

Good food is found in many Caribbean hotels as well as the establishments listed below. The price categories relate to average local prices on each island.

Inexpensive: ($)
Moderate: ($$)
Expensive: ($$$)

THE WINDWARD ISLANDS

Dominica

Garraway Hotel ($$$)
tel: 449 8800
Excellent fare in the hotel's Balisier Restaurant overlooking the waterfront in Roseau itself.
Guiyave ($$)
Roseau tel: 448 2930
Pretty balcony setting above the street for a hearty local lunch (no dinner).
La Robe Creole ($$–$$$)
Roseau tel: 448 2896
Cozy historic building down near Fort Young and good Créole food featuring local specialties stylishly presented.

Grenada and Carriacou

Aquarium ($–$$)
Pointe Salines tel: 444 1410
A full menu of Caribbean favorites and American staples means that there's something for everyone, here right on the beach.
La Belle Créole ($$$)
Grande Anse tel: 444 4316
The terrace dining room of the Blue Horizons hotel: *nouvelle cuisine* with a West Indian lilt.
Callaloo by the Sea ($)
Hillsborough, Carriacou tel: 443 8004
Great lunch spot with a waterfront terrace at the south end of Main Street.
Red Crab ($$)
L'Anse Aux Epines tel: 444 4424
International food and fresh seafood form the staples at this popular island meeting place.

The Grenadines

On the small Grenadine islands you will be dependent on your hotel.

Basil's Bar ($$)
Mustique tel: 488 8350
In a charmed setting on stilts on a magnificent bay; the favorite haunt of island visitors and passing yachtsmen. Entertainment.
Dennis' Hideaway ($$)
Mayreau tel: 458 8594
Bar and dining room on a terrace on the hillside with good local fare.
Mac's Pizzeria ($$)
Bequia tel: 458 3474
Wooden deck above a tropical garden; excellent pizzas, plus seafood and Créole dishes.

St. Lucia

Bang Between the Pitons ($)
tel: 459 7864
Courtyard surrounded by old wooden Créole houses between the comical pitons. Local and international fare with flair.
Bon Appetit ($$)
Castries tel: 452 2757
Tiny place where the food is freshly prepared—signature dish is crayfish. Great views.
Dasheene ($$$)
tel: 459 7323
The location—between the Pitons and high above the sea—will take your breath away, as will the top-notch cuisine and the fine wine list. A must for gourmets.
Jammer's ($$–$$$)
Windjammer Landing tel: 452 0913
Grat place throughout the day from breakfast to dinner with classic carte options and a choice of Caribbean dishes. Good wine list.

St. Vincent

Basil's Bar ($$)
Kingstown tel: 457 2713
Downstairs from the Cobblestone Inn, set in an old stone trading warehouse; international and local fare.
French Veranda Restaurant ($$$)
tel: 457 4000
In the Mariner's Hotel overlooking Villa Beach, this is a great place for a relaxed lunch or romantic dinner overlooking the water. The menu is a French and Caribbean mix.
Rooftop ($–$$)
Kingstown tel: 457 2845
Excellent Creole dishes and seafood at ths popular bar with terrace views of Kingstown.

THE LEEWARD ISLANDS

Anguilla

Blanchard's ($$$)
Mead's Bay tel: 497 6100
Top-quality international fare and notable wine list offered in a charming and elegant house.
Mango's ($$$)
Barnes Bay tel: 497 6479/3490
Above the beach on a breezy veranda; reserve a table for well-prepared new American cuisine.
Ripples ($$)
Sandy Ground tel: 497 3380
Busy beach bar-restaurant with both indoor and outdoor seating and menu featuring salads, grilled fish and pasta dishes.

Antigua

Admiral's Inn ($$–$$$)
Nelson's Dockyard tel: 460 1027
Housed in a lovely Georgian building dating from 1788, the inn offers fresh seafood, home-made soups and other fare in a lively nautical atmosphere. The secluded dining terrace overlooks English Harbour.

Julian's Alfresco ($$$)
Runaway Bay tel: 563 1545
Respected Caribbean restaurateur Julian
Waterer mixes island cuisine with European
and Asian influences. Reservations needed.
Shirley Heights Lookout ($$)
tel: 460 1785
High above English Harbour, a veranda with a
view. Burgers, salads or local dishes; best
known for riotous Sunday afternoon assembly.

Montserrat
In the present situation, the hotels are a good
option: try **Tropical Mansions**, Sweeneys (tel:
491 8767) or the **Vue Pointe** (tel: 491 5210).
For a good dinner reserve ahead at **Ziggy's**,
Mahogany Loop (tel: 491 8282).

Nevis

Hermitage Plantation ($$$)
Fig Tree Parish tel: 469 3477
Elegant, candlelit veranda in the main house of
the hotel; adventurous and delightful West
Indian cuisine. Reservations advised.
Nisbet Plantation ($$$)
Newcastle tel: 469 9325
In the charming old colonial setting of an
18th-century great house. Victorian decor and
tempting menu of Continental and Caribbean
dishes. Reservations advised.
Sunshine Beach Bar & Grill ($)
Pinney's Beach tel: 469 5817
Proprietor Sunshine mixes a mean rum-based
Killer Bee to wash down freshly grilled shrimp,
fish, chicken and slightly more pricey lobster.

St. Kitts

Golden Lemon ($$$)
Dieppe Bay tel: 465 7260
Exquisite local and Continental fare in the
delightfully restored historic surroundings. Fine
lunchtime stop, but even better at dinner.
Rawlins Plantation ($$$)
Mount Pleasant tel: 465 6221
Some of the best local food in the islands,
served in the charming setting of a plantation
house: a good choice for lunch.
StoneWalls ($–$$)
Princes Street, Basseterre tel: 465 5248
Great bar in a tropical garden setting serving
a hearty line in jerk pork and pasta dishes.

THE VIRGIN ISLANDS

The British Virgin Islands

Cooper Island Beach Club ($$)
tel: 494 3721
The only bar on Cooper Island, a bright patio
right above the sand where you can enjoy a
grill and a salad with a passing sailing crowd.
Peter Island ($$$)
tel: 476 9988
Worth the short ride from Roadtown to Peter
Island for top Caribbean and international
cuisine after a day out on the island.

Tortola

Brandywine Bay ($$$)
East End tel: 495 2301
Enjoy the fine Italian cuisine with a magnificent
view of the Channel from the breezy terrace.
Mrs Scatliffe ($$)
Carrot Bay tel: 495 4556
Delectable local fare, pumpkin soup and curry
goat followed by tropical fruit ice creams.
Pusser's Store and Pub ($$)
Road Town tel: 494 3897
Lively haunt, near the ferry terminal; warmly
decorated with burnished brass and paneled
walls. Hearty pub grub.
Sugar Mill Restaurant ($$$)
Apple Bay tel: 495 4355
Excellent West Indian cuisine in a candlelit
stone building from old colonial times..

Virgin Gorda

Chez Bamboo ($$)
The Valley tel: 495 5752
Brightly painted dining room in town serving
Créole and Caribbean fare.
The Rock ($–$$)
Tower Road tel: 495 5482
Bar-restaurant with a great boulder-strewn
setting close to The Baths. An Italian-
Caribbean-American menu; live music;
cold beers and cocktails.

The US Virgin Islands

St. Croix

Blue Moon ($$–$$$)
Frederiksted tel: 772 2222
Deep and dark setting under the arches in an
old Front Street trading building. Jazz and cajun
fare: Be warned—it does get busy.
Top Hat ($$$)
Company Street, Christiansted tel: 773 2346
Very pleasant restaurant upstairs in an old
townhouse. The menu is international and
particularly notable for its Danish dishes.

St. John

Morgan's Mango ($$)
Cruz Bay tel: 693 8141
Great veranda setting opposite the National
Park dock with new Caribbean and some
Argentinian fare. Live music sometimes.
Paradiso Restaurant ($$$)
Mongoose Junction, Cruz Bay tel: 693 8899
The decor here is worthy of a Manhattan
nightclub, and the cocktail bar and quiet music
add to the atmosphere. The Italian dishes are
the best.

St. Thomas

Craig and Sally's ($$$)
Frenchtown tel: 777 9949
A varied and interesting Mediterranean-Asian
menu with an excellent wine list.

279

Hotels and Restaurants

Cuzzins's Caribbean Restaurant ($$)
7 Back Street, Charlotte Amalie tel: 777 4711
Deliciously prepared local food from conch,
Créole and curries to stuffed lobster, served by
friendly staff in an historic (and conveniently
central) building.
Off the Hook ($$)
Red Hook tel: 775 6350
Seafood and fish on a deck above the lagoon at
the ferry dock; lively and fun.

THE FRENCH ANTILLES

Guadeloupe

Château de Feuilles ($$$)
Anse Bertrand tel: 0590 22 30 30
Worth a trip to the northern tip of Grande-Terre,
where you dine on a terrace in a profuse
garden. Excellent French and local fare.
Côté Jardin ($$$)
Point-à-Pitre tel: 0590 90 91 28
Elegant, air-conditioned dining with a good
wine list in the lively yacht-filled marina.
Les Oiseaux ($$)
Saint François tel: 0590 88 56 92
Pleasant, veranda setting for an eclectic
combination of French and Créole food.
Le Vieux Port ($$)
St. François tel: 0590 88 46 60
On the waterfront, this lively and rustic setting
specializes in fresh fish and lobster.

Martinique

La Belle Epoque ($$$)
Didier, Fort de France tel: 0590 64 41 19
Award-winning gastronomic restaurant set
high above town. This is an excellent fine
dining option for those willing to spend a
little more.
Le Colibri ($$)
Morne des Esses tel: 0590 69 91 95
A veranda with a fantastic view and some of
the most adventurous French Créole food on
the island, all prepared by Clothilde Palladino.
'Ti Plage ($–$$)
Anse d'Arlets tel: 0590 29 59 89
Informal eatery overlooking the fishing port.
The menu includes tasty French/Caribbean
dishes—it's a great place for a drink too.

Saint-Barthélemy

Maya's ($$$)
Public tel: 0590 27 75 73
Popular waterfront restaurant under the palms
in public. Fish and Créole are specialties.
Le Sapotillier ($$$)
Gustavia tel: 0590 27 60 28
Set in the capital of St. Barts, this is a
charming and elegant restaurant with excel-
lent classical French cuisine.
Wall House ($$)
La Point, Gustavia tel: 0590 27 71 83
This small restaurant has an excellent fixed-
price lunch menu of Caribbean fusion cuisine.
The service is well renowned.

Saint-Martin

Bar de la Mer
Marigot tel: 0590 87 81 79
Cocktail bar-restaurant just off the waterfront.
Bistrot Nu ($$)
Marigot tel: 059087 97 09
Brasserie-style French dishes.
Fish Pot ($$$)
Grand Case tel: 0590 87 50 88
Elegant surroundings and superb French-
Caribbean cuisine, plus a balcony over the bay.
Il Nettuno ($$$)
Grand Case tel: 0590 87 77 38
Set on the beach, this restaurant serves Italian
staples such as fresh pasta, including signa-
ture fettucini, and exceptional seafood.
Le Tastevin ($$$)
Grand Case tel: 0590 87 55 45
On a tropical terrace above the waves. Classic
French cuisine and service.

THE NETHERLANDS ANTILLES

Aruba

Charlie's Bar ($)
Zeppenferdstraat 56 tel: 584 5086
Bar and restaurant in the east of Aruba, hung
with memorabiliia; famous for jumbo shrimp.
Gasparito ($$)
Gasparito 3 tel: 586 7044
Delicious Dutch Antillean food in a traditional
old Aruban country house, behind Palm Beach.
Papiamento ($$$)
Washington 61 tel: 586 4544
The best cuisine in the best setting, a country
house where tables are inside or by the pool: a
delightful experience, but make reservations.

Bonaire

Rendez-vous ($–$$)
Kralendijk tel: 717 8454
Charming restaurant set in a modern
townhouse. You dine on the veranda or inside.
The Rib's Factory ($–$$)
Harbourside Mall tel: 717 4600
Excellent ribs are not surprisingly the signature
item here. However the menu has a good range
of Mexican dishes, salads and fresh seafood.
The Swiss Chalet ($$)
Kralendijk tel: 717 3366
A really eclectic mixture of Caribbean and
European dishes, but most people come for the
excellent Swiss dishes of fondue and rösti.

Curaçao

Fort Nassau ($$$)
Seru Fort Nassau tel: 461 3450
Excellent views over the island from this
restaurant set within the walls of Fort Nassau.
Fine Continental menu and good wine list.
Indis Spice Bar ($)
Otrobanda tel: 462 868
Some of the most authentic Indian food on the
island at this unpretentious restaurant.

Landuis Daniel ($$)
Banda Abou tel: 864 8400
In a c.1700 plantation house, serving break-
fast, lunch and dinner. Dutch specialties.
Larry's ($$)
*Oude Caracasbaaiweg Naast 93
tel: 461 0856*
Settle down to a beer and prime beef in various
forms. Tempting salads and Tex-Mex too.

Saba

In Two Deep ($)
Fort Bay tel: 416 3438
Café for sandwiches and salads and a drink
after scuba diving.
Saba Chinese Restaurant ($$)
Windwardside tel: 416 2268/2353
Modern house high on the hill with a long list of
Cantonese dishes to eat in or take out.
Scout's Place ($$)
Windwardside tel: 416 2740/2205
Drinks and hearty portions of wholesome
Caribbean food; some entertainment.

St. Eustatius

Kings Well Bar & Restaurant ($$)
Bay Road (by Smoke Alley) tel: 318 2538
Grand position on Oranjebaai with views of the
Lower Town. The menu is an eclectic German-
Continental-American hybrid featuring prime
US beef and schnitzels.
Stone Oven ($)
Faeschweg, Oranjested tel: 318 2809
Good Caribbean food in a small townhouse set
with neat wooden tables.

Sint Maarten

Kangaroo Court Café ($–$$)
tel: 542 4278
Great baked goods and fine coffee make this
pleasant courtyard café the best breakfast
spot in Philipsburg. On a side street not far
from the cruise ship dock.
Lee's Roadside Grill ($)
Simpson Bay tel: 544 4233
Rustic roadside place offering fried and grilled
fish, chicken and seafood fresh from the boat
Turtle Pier Restaurant ($$)
Simpson Bay tel: 545 2560
Great waterfront family venue with a huge
menu of American European and Caribbean
dishes with lobster a specialty.

OTHER CARIBBEAN STATES

Jamaica
Restaurants add a General Consumption tax of
10 percent to all bills.

Blue Mountains

Blue Mountain Inn ($$$)
Gordon Town tel: 927 1900
Old plantation house setting; very fine fare of
Créole dishes as well as international classics.

The Gap Café ($)
tel: 923 7078
Stupendous view over Kingston; good stop for
lunch or tea.

Kingston

Chelsea Jerk Centre ($)
Chelsea Avenue tel: 926 6322
Very local; pork and chicken jerked meat;
watch the hot pepper sauce.
Guilt Trip ($$)
Barbican Road tel: 977 5130
Hip gathering point, with cakes by day and
international and new Jamaican cuisine
by night.
Palm Court ($$–$$$)
Hilton New Kingston tel: 926 5430
Elegant restaurant in a swish high-rise Hilton
popular with business visitors. The mezzanine
level dining room offers a very good and
stylishly presented Continental menu.

Montego Bay

Houseboat Grill ($$–$$$)
Freeport tel: 979 8845
Montego Bay's floating houseboat restaurant
on the mangrove swamps serves an ever-
changing menu of international dishes.
Marguerite's ($$)
Gloucester Avenue tel: 952 4777
Terrace on the sea and under the stars, for
cocktails and light meals. Margueritaville, next
door, offers international fare in a rowdy,
sports-bar atmosphere.
Pork Pit ($)
Gloucester Avenue tel: 952 1046
Take-away or sit at the garden benches to eat
pork, chicken, fish and spare ribs with coconut
milk or beer.

Negril

Cosmo's Seafood Restaurant ($$–$$$)
Manley Boulevard tel: 957 4330
Al fresco beachfront bistro with shady tables
under spreading seagrape trees. Meaty conch
chowder is a specialty, check out the catch
of the day, or splash out on delicious plain
grilled lobster.
Rick's Café ($$)
West End Road tel: 957 0380
Rick's is a local institution and bastion of
Negril culture from its nightly sunset cocktail
session to cliff-diving performances. The so-so
pub food is eclipsed by the atmosphere.

Ocho Rios

Almond Tree ($$$)
Hibiscus Lodge Hotel tel: 974 2813
Fine setting on the cliffs with floodlit greenery;
good for local cuisine.
Double V Jerk Centre ($)
Main Street heading east tel: 974 0174
A wooden cabin in a tropical garden; good
stopover for jerk.

281

Plantation Inn ($$$)
Main Street tel: 974 5601
The Plantation Inn has been open for 40 years
and still serves Jamaican and international
dishes in genteel surroundings.
The Ruins at the Falls ($$)
DaCosta Drive tel: 974 2442
Set at the base of a cascade, this restaurant
serves a mixture of oriental, Caribbean and
vegetarian dishes.

Port Antonio
Restaurant Mille Fleurs ($$$)
Hotel Mocking Bird Hill tel: 993 7134
With magnificent views overlooking the coast ,
Mille Fleurs offers nouvelle Caribbean cuisine.
San Tropez ($$)
tel: 993 7399
Genuine Italian dishes include hand-made
pizzas. Quaffable Italian wines.
Trident Hotel ($$$)
tel: 993 2602
Renovated after 2005 hurricane damage, the
complex including the restaurant is smart and
elegant. Long-standing culinary reputation.

The Cayman Islands

Apollo 11 ($)
North Sound, Grand Cayman tel: 947 9568
Cool waterfront bar in an old shed. Live music.
Cracked Conch by the Sea ($$)
West Bay, Grand Cayman tel: 945 5217
Lively bar and restaurant. Conch is served
cracked (beaten tender), along with other fish.
Grand Old House ($$$)
South Church Street, Grand Cayman
tel: 949 9333
In a charming old colonial house; excellent
Continental dishes as well as a few local ones.
Make a reservation.
Pirates Point Resort ($$)
Preston Bay, Little Cayman tel: 948 1010
Reservations are also required to sample
Gladys Howard's delicious and stylish brand of
cooking.
Ristorante Pappagallo ($$$)
Spanish Cove, Grand Cayman tel: 949 1119
Huge palm-thatched, air-conditioned *cabana*
set on an isolated lagoon. Northern Italian
menu. Reserve a table.

Cuba

Havana

D'Giovanni ($$)
Calle Tacon, Zana Colonial tel: 7 860 5979
Italian dishes in an old colonial house.
El Floridita ($$$)
Calle Montserrate 557 tel: 7 867 1301
A favorite of Hemingway's, famed for its
daiquiris (worth going just for them). Elegant if
ritzy dining room; fine cuisine.
El Patio ($$)
Plaza de la Catedral tel: 7 861 8504
Charming setting in the Zona Colonial. Café
downstairs on the cobbles, meals upstairs.

Papa's ($$)
Hemingway Marina tel: 7 209 7920
Waterfront setting and seafood specialties in
the lively marina complex, which is popular
with visitors for its atmosphere and disco.

Outside Havana

Casa del Queso Cubano ($$)
Varadero tel: 45 67747
Charming bodega-style eatery with a great
selection of Cuban cheeses.
El Mesón de Quijote ($$)
Varadero tel: 45 67747
Set in open grounds far down the peninsula;
Spanish menu.
El Retiro ($$)
Varadero tel: 45 667228
International fair in a '30s-style house.

The Dominican Republic

Altos de Chavon

Casa del Río ($$$)
Altos de Chavón tel: 523 3333
Fantastic setting above floodlit river with a mix
of Caribbean and international dishes.
La Casita ($$)
La Romana tel: 523 8788
Good Italian joint serving plenty of seafood
dishes as well as pastas and risottos.

Puerto Plata and the Amber Coast

Barco's ($–$$)
Malcón 6, Puerto Plata tel: 320 0389
Great people-watching from the sidewalk
terrace and a mixed menu of pizzas, steaks,
seafood and more.
Casa del Pescador ($$$)
Carretera 5, Cabarete tel: 571 0760
Top choice for a romantic evening out.
Excellent seafood is the hallmark of this
candlelit dining room on the beach.
Hemingways's Café ($–$$)
Playa Dorado tel: 320 2230
A modern-day shrine to Papa Hemingway with
old photos and strangely named dishes such as
the For Whom the Bell Tolls fajitas. Late-night
live music draws a young crowd.
On the Waterfront ($–$$)
Calle Dr. Rosen, El Batay, Sosúa
tel: 571 2670
Great seafood restaurant with oceanfront deck;
also provides breakfast and a welcoming bar.

Samaná

Camilo ($$)
Malcón, Samaná tel: 538 2498
Head to the waterfront for tasty local food in an
attractive setting. The creamy *pollo asopao*
(chicken with rice) is a good bet.
L'Hacienda
tel: 538 2383
Grilled food on a breezy veranda to Latin music
and hot salsa.

Santo Domingo

El Chef ($$)
Calle Gustavo Lara tel: 562 4657
Award-winning restaurant serving excellent local Dominican cuisine that has a loyal local clientele.
El Conuco ($$)
Calle Casimiro de Moya tel: 686 0129
Riotous restaurant with decorations from the *conuco* (country); with singing waiters.
Vesuvio ($$–$$$)
on the Malecon tel: 221 1954
Big, very popular restaurant. Top Italian and Dominican fare.

Puerto Rico

San German and the Southwest

El Bohio ($$)
Playa Joyuda tel: 851 2755
On a breezy deck above the waves. Unpretentious but the best of local fish.
Vista Bahía ($$)
Cabo Rojo tel: 851 4140
Right on Playa Joyuda; steaks and seafood.

Ponce

El Ancla ($$$)
Avenida Hostos 9 tel: 840 2450
Out of the city center, an air-conditioned lounge on Ponce beach; menu consists mainly of seafood with copious local vegetables.

San Juan

Amadeus ($$)
Calle San Sebastian 106 tel: 722 8635
Stylish restaurant serving nouvelle Puerto Rican cuisine.
La Casita Blanca ($$)
Calle Tapia 351, Santurce tel: 726 5501
Small but very lively restaurant specializing in Puerto Rican food, and lots of it. Charming setting, amusing waiters.
La Mallorquina ($$$)
Calle San Justo 207 tel: 722 3261
Set in a century-old house, still with its antique furnishings. Good local food.

Barbados

Atlantis ($$)
Bathsheba tel: 433 9445
The hotel itself is clearly past its prime, but the setting on the clifftops and the food, a West Indian buffet, is still superb.
The Cliff ($$$)
St. James tel: 432 1922
Top-notch international cuisine in an extremely elegant and dramatic setting.
Josef's ($$$)
St. Lawrence Gap tel: 435 8245
Private home turned into elegant oceanfront restaurant; the cooking is international and the quality is excellent.

Pisces ($$)
St. Lawrence Gap tel: 435 6564
Charming setting on a trellis-lined veranda above St. Lawrence Bay. Mainly seafood and fish but with some other dishes.
Il Tempio ($$)
Fitts, St. James tel: 417 0057
Italian family-owned restaurant that serves genuine Latin fare including pizza, fresh pasta and delicious seafood.
Weiser's on the Beach ($–$$)
St. Michael tel: 425 6450
Great beach bar with Caribbean gingerbread-decorated deck. Live music and karaoke evenings back up the American-, seafood- and fusion-influenced menu.

Trinidad and Tobago

Trinidad

Jenny's on the Boulevard ($–$$$)
Cipriani Boulevard tel: 625 1807
The new place to be in the capital, Jenny's is a mixture of pub, Chinese and American restaurant, all set in a restored town house.
Moon Over Bourbon Street ($$)
West Mall, Port of Spain tel: 637 3448
A delightful cocktail bar and rooftop restaurant out of town, decked out like a transatlantic liner. Some entertainment.
Plantation House Restaurant ($$$)
Ariapita Avenue, Port of Spain tel: 628 5551
Set in a charming gingerbread town house the menu here offers fresh seafood and game. Quality service.
Rafters ($$)
Warner Street, Port of Spain tel: 628 9258
Hip video bar and restaurant in an old warehouse.
Tiki Village ($$)
Kapok Hotel, Port of Spain tel: 622 5765
Popular top floor restaurant with views over the city; Polynesian and Chinese menu.
Veni Mange ($$)
Ariapita Avenue, Port of Spain tel: 624 4597
Popular lunchtime (only) haunt, serving delicious West Indian cuisine—it comes highly recommended.

Tobago

La Belle Creole ($$$)
Just out of Scarborough tel: 639 3551
Charming floodlit garden and pretty house; good local and international fare.
Black Rock Café ($$$)
Black Rock tel: 639 7625
Veranda painted pink with white louvers. Créole dishes with salads and steaks.
Kariwak Village ($$)
Crown Point tel: 639- 8442
Styled as an Amerindian meeting hut, this serves great dishes using local ingredients.
Rouselle's ($$)
Scarborough tel: 639 4738
Upstairs lounge bar with tables where you can eat good local food.

Index

Index

285

Index / Acknowledgments

Picture credits

The Automobile Association would like to thank the following photographers, companies and picture libraries for their assistance in the preparation of this book:

Abbreviations for the picture credits are as follows – (t) top; (b) bottom; (l) left; (r) right: (AA) AA World Travel Library.

BRIDGEMAN ART LIBRARY 180-1 Voodoo Dance by Jean Pierre; 180 Voodoo ceremony around a tree by Valcin; S CAMPBELL 162 Sunrise at Brac Reef; 163 Totem pole; 164 Swimming with stingrays; 165 Straw-weaver. MARY EVANS PICTURE LIBRARY 25b Raiding cattle ranches; 26-7t Corn Dance; 26c Gathering grass seed; 28–9t Columbus's fleet 1492; 30–1 Drake attacks Spanish; 30 Pirates; 31 Buccaneer; 32–3 Slaves working; 32 Slaves dancing; 33 Slave in chains; 34–5 Treadmill; 35 Sugar mill; 36–7 Emancipation parade; 36 Emancipation; 37 Burke in House of Commons; 43b Spaniards and Caribs; 101 Spaniards loading ship. J HENDERSON 9l Barbados; 10t St. Vincent; 12–13 Children; 15b Oranjestad, Aruba; 16–17 Church, Trinidad; 18–9 Poster; 27 Arawak carvings; 40 Calabas Hotel; 49 St. Georges; 50t Market, St. Georges; 52 Maurice Bishop, St. Georges; 53 Admiralty Harbour; 68 Man; 70 Boat; 76 Barbuda; 83 Nevis; 83 Old windmill; 91b Bombas, Tortola; 96 Jost van Dyke; 98 Frederiksted, St. Croix; 103 Legislature, Charlotte Amalie; 112l Guadaloupe cemetery; 113t Boats; 113b Deshaires; 120 Islands; 121t Airport, St. Barts; 121b Club La Banane; 124l Aruba; 124b Bolatabla, Curaçao; 125–6 Sailing ship; 125 Saba; 126 Craft stall; 128–9 Oranjestad, Aruba; 129t Windmill; 129b Jet ski; 130, 131 Salt stacks, Bonaire; 134–5 Handelsgade, Willemstad; 134l, c Floating market; 135 Fisherman; 136 House; 137b Windwardside, Saba; 137tr Flags; 138t Sint Eustatius; 139t Sign; 139b Children; 140 Car; 141t St. Georges; 143b Breadfruit; 166 Car; 167 Main Square, Trinidad, Cuba; 168 Poster; 169t Santa Clara; 169b House, Cuba; 173 Cien Fuegos; 176 Tap-tap; 177 Fishermen; 183 Carvings; 186 Windsurfers; 187 Hotel Sousa; 189 Palm fronds; 190 Boats; 191 Sugar mill; 192 Children; 193t Columbus lighthouse; 193b Columbus Palace; 197b Festival of the Innocents; 198 Hacienda Gripinas; 210 Fire station, Ponce; 203 Sunset, Puerto Rico; 206 Croton; 210t Casa del Frances, Vieques; 211 Limers Bar, Esperanza; 215t Bridgetown Harbour; 215b Sombaero; 219b Baseball; 228 Canon, Trinidad; 234b Carnival, St. Lucia; 236 Shack; 238b Calypso singer. IMAGES COLOUR LIBRARY 181 Mask. IMAGES DES ANTILLES 109 Course de Yoles. INTERNATIONAL PHOTOBANK 20t Ocho Rios market; 24 drinks; 45b Dunn's River Falls; 47, 50b St. George's Saturday Market; 58b Woman and bananas; 80–1 Steel band; 155 Straw market, Montego Bay; 159 Beach, Ocho Rios; 160 Port Antonio; 206–7 Royal Poinciana tree; 233 Tobago steel band. NATURE PHOTOGRAPHERS LTD 116t Scarlet Ibis (P R Sterry); 230t Green turtle (D A Smith); 230b Loggerhead turtle (J Sutherland). PARIA PUBLISHING CO LTD 61t The Soucouyant; 61l Mama Dio; 61r Pappa Bois. PHOTODISC 74-5t Scuba diver. REX FEATURES LTD 152t Shabba Ranks; 152b Shaggy; 156t, b Bob Marley. ROYAL GEOGRAPHICAL SOCIETY 25t Map SPECTRUM COLOUR LIBRARY 111 Rainforest; 131 Kralendick Town, Bonaire; 133 Curaçao; 162 Drinks; Havana; 188 Restaurant, Puerto Plata; 189 Palm-fringed beach; 234–5 Carnival; 238t Nightlife. WORLD PICTURES 209b Dominoes.

Acknowledgments

The Automobile Association would also like to thank the Sandridge Beach Hotel, Barbados, and the Ocean View Hotel, Barbados for their assistance in the making of this book

Contributors

Original copy editor: Nia Williams

Revision verifier: Lindsay Bennett. Revision management: Bookwork Creative Associates Ltd.